CORPORATE
CITIZEN

CORPORATE CITIZEN

CITIZEN

New Perspectives on the Globalized Rule of Law

Edited by Oonagh E. Fitzgerald

Centre for International
Governance Innovation

ISBN 978-1-928096-93-1 (hardcover)
ISBN 978-1-928096-92-4 (softcover)
ISBN 978-1-928096-94-8 (HTML)
ISBN 978-1-928096-95-5 (PDF)

Library and Archives Canada Cataloguing in Publication

Title: Corporate citizen : new perspectives on the globalized rule of law / edited by Oonagh E. Fitzgerald.

Other titles: Corporate citizen (Centre for International Governance Innovation)

Names: Fitzgerald, Oonagh E., editor.

Identifiers: Canadiana (print) 20200235729 | Canadiana (ebook) 20200235826 | ISBN 9781928096931 (hardcover) | ISBN 9781928096924 (softcover) | ISBN 9781928096948 (HTML) | ISBN 9781928096955 (PDF)

Subjects: LCSH: International business enterprises—Law and legislation. | LCSH: Commercial law. | LCSH: Tort liability of corporations.

Classification: LCC K1322 .C67 2020 | DDC 346.07—dc23

The opinions expressed in this publication are those of the authors and do not necessarily reflect the views of the Centre for International Governance Innovation or its Board of Directors.

Printed and bound in Canada on 100 percent post-consumer recycled paper.

Cover design by Abhilasha Dewan.

Page design by Melodie Wakefield.

Centre for International Governance Innovation and CIGI are registered trademarks.

**Centre for International
Governance Innovation**

Centre for International Governance Innovation
67 Erb Street West
Waterloo, ON Canada N2L 6C2

www.cigionline.org

CONTENTS

ACRONYMS AND ABBREVIATIONS

AI	artificial intelligence
ALI	American Law Institute
BITs	bilateral investment treaties
CBCA	Canada Business Corporations Act
CCGG	Canadian Coalition for Good Governance
CEO	chief executive officer
CETA	Comprehensive Economic and Trade Agreement
CIGI	Centre for International Governance Innovation
CoE	comply or explain
COMESA	Common Market for Eastern and Southern Africa

CORE	Canadian Ombudsperson for Responsible Enterprise
CPPIB	Canada Pension Plan Investment Board
CPTPP	Comprehensive and Progressive Agreement for Trans-Pacific Partnership
CSA	Canadian Securities Administrators
CSR	corporate social responsibility
CUSMA	Canada–United States–Mexico Agreement
DoB	denial of benefits
ECGI	European Corporate Governance Institute
ECT	Energy Charter Treaty
ERISA	Employee Retirement Income Security Act
ESCR-Net	International Network for Economic, Social and Cultural Rights
FCN	friendship, commerce and navigation
FDI	foreign direct investment
FET	fair and equitable treatment
FSAP	Financial Sector Assessment Program
FSF	Financial Stability Forum
FTSE	Financial Times Stock Exchange
G20	Group of Twenty
G77	Group of 77
GBA+	Gender-Based Analysis Plus
IACHR	Inter-American Commission on Human Rights
IAIB	institutional approaches to international business
ICAR	International Corporate Accountability Roundtable
ICJ	International Court of Justice
ICSID	International Centre for Settlement of Investment Disputes
IEA	International Energy Agency
IIAs	international investment agreements
IISD	International Institute for Sustainable Development
ILC	International Law Commission
ILO	International Labour Organization

IMF	International Monetary Fund
IOSCO	International Organization of Securities Commissions
IoT	Internet of Things
IPCC	Intergovernmental Panel on Climate Change
ISA	investor-state arbitration
ISDS	investor-state dispute settlement
ISS	Institutional Shareholder Services
MAI	Multilateral Agreement on Investment
MBA	master of business administration
MNEs	multinational enterprises
MMIWG	National Inquiry into Missing and Murdered Indigenous Women and Girls
MNCs	multinational corporations
MSR	Minera San Rafael S.A.
MST	minimum standard of treatment
NGOs	non-governmental organizations
NHRI	national human rights institution
OECD	Organisation for Economic Co-operation and Development
OEIGWG	Open-ended Intergovernmental Working Group on Transnational Corporations and Other Business Enterprises with Respect to Human Rights
OHCHR	Office of the United Nations High Commissioner for Human Rights
OSC	Ontario Securities Commission
PAIC	Pan-African Investment Code
PCIJ	Permanent Court of International Justice
QCCA	Quebec Court of Appeal
SADC	Southern African Development Community
SCC	Supreme Court of Canada
SDGs	Sustainable Development Goals
SEC	Securities and Exchange Commission
STEM	science, technology, engineering and math
TCFD	Task Force on Climate-related Financial Disclosures

TI   Transparency International Canada

TNCs   transnational corporations

TPA   Trade Promotion Agreement

TSX   Toronto Stock Exchange

TSX-V   TSX-Venture

UKSC   UK Supreme Court

UNCITRAL   United Nations Commission on International Trade Law

UNCTAD   United Nations Conference on Trade and Development

UNDRIP   United Nations Declaration on the Rights of Indigenous Peoples

UNGPs   United Nations Guiding Principles on Business and Human Rights

UNHRC   UN Human Rights Commission

WEF   World Economic Forum

WEP   Women's Empowerment Principles

WGBHR   Working Group on Business and Human Rights

WHO   World Health Organization

INTRODUCTION

Oonagh E. Fitzgerald

After the serial devastation and destruction of two world wars, when the international community was trying to establish the conditions for world peace, security and justice, the Charter of the United Nations was adopted.[1] In that charter, nations expressed their determination "to save succeeding generations from the scourge of war," "to reaffirm faith in fundamental human rights," "to establish conditions under which justice and respect for" international law obligations can be maintained, "and to promote social progress and better standards of life in larger freedom." They pledged, *inter alia*, "[t]o achieve international co-operation in solving international problems of an economic, social, cultural, or humanitarian character, and in promoting and encouraging respect for human rights." There was no specific pledge by nations to empower the transnational corporation, but the last 75 years have seen the corporation's rise and runaway success as a vehicle of economic growth, job creation, technology innovation, wealth accumulation and political influence.

---

1   The *Charter of the United Nations* (Can TS 1945 No 7) [*UN Charter*] was signed on June 26, 1945, in San Francisco, at the conclusion of the United Nations Conference on International Organization, and came into force on October 24, 1945.

The modern global economy is dominated by great corporations. We are consumers of their products and services; we are their employees, advisers or suppliers; and we are their investors, through government or private pension funds. National governments, caught in a global regulatory arbitrage, continuously adjust the domestic regulatory and taxation landscape to try to make their country as hospitable as possible for corporations to invest for the long term, so these enterprises do not uproot themselves and relocate to more welcoming jurisdictions. Our understanding of and perspectives on the world and culture are substantially influenced by these corporations, as they provide us with the digital platforms on which we watch news, find entertainment and engage in social and political discourse. In some respects, "we the people" are the corporation, and by many threads our prosperity and well-being are tied to the corporation's success.

Corporate law has become ubiquitous to facilitate the path of globalization. The transnational corporation can consider itself a global citizen, able to establish itself almost anywhere on reasonably predictable terms. It can expect its decision to enter new markets and expand its global reach will be assessed rationally by politicians and government regulators, in accordance with international trade rules and the web of interconnecting international investment agreements (IIAs). To smooth any risk of difficulties with an overseas investment, or with exporting its products and services, the corporation can obtain diplomatic, financial and legal assistance, and risk insurance. In the case of an alleged breach of a state's obligations to investors, the corporation may have legal recourse to investor-state arbitration (ISA) under an applicable IIA, and there is even the possibility that a national government will take up its cause for state-to-state dispute settlement before the World Trade Organization.

Klaus Schwab, creator of the World Economic Forum (WEF), can be credited with socializing the notion of "global corporate citizenship" and legitimizing the idea that transnational corporations are "key stakeholders," with a central role to play in global governance. He describes the citizenship concept as a business strategy quite distinct from soft corporate social responsibility (CSR):

> [F]or global corporate citizenship to be meaningful, effective, and sustainable, it must align with a company's specific capabilities and with its business model and profit motive. This also requires the active involvement of CEOs and should reflect their vision of what is good for the corporation and society...

> [G]lobal corporate citizenship should never be undertaken from a defensive or apologetic position. The ultimate role of business in society remains to do business. Global corporate citizenship should not develop from a bad conscience or a feeling that one must give back to society; it should be a feature of this globalizing world that stretches traditional boundaries....It is a form of corporate engagement that can reinforce the positive role of business in society and enhance profitability in the long term. Indeed, global corporate citizenship integrates both the rights and the responsibilities that corporations have as global citizens. And in relying on a multi-

stakeholder approach to tackling global problems, it can point out the way to new models of effective global governance that integrate business as a key stakeholder.[2]

With this language, Schwab elevates the transnational corporation to a new status that no human enjoys — that of global citizen and key stakeholder — and appropriates for this global corporate citizen a seat at the international tables where decisions are made. These tables, Schwab asserts, must be multi-stakeholder in order to include corporations. With this concept, it is no longer only for states to determine what laws should govern the global community and its stewardship over human beings and the environment. For Schwab, the multinational corporation must be consulted and involved.

Schwab may have articulated this vision with the benign motive of making corporations do more good for society. The language may also have served to soothe powerful corporate interests, solicit corporate sponsorship for the WEF,[3] and gradually engineer a corporate power grab from the United Nations Organization and its member states, especially smaller and developing states. One might well wonder, in the rarified atmosphere of a Davos WEF meeting, whether the language of the UN Charter, with its focus on developing "friendly relations among nations based on respect for the principle of equal rights and self-determination of peoples,"[4] has much resonance.

The idea of corporate global citizenship sounds like it could provide the basis for establishing enforceable corporate responsibility at home and around the world, in the same way that citizenship in a nation implies both rights and duties. But this is not how the concept has played out in practice. It has empowered corporate interests to lobby national governments and international meetings in order to delay, weaken or block measures that might increase corporate accountability.

Corporate thinking has influenced governments increasingly in recent decades, with public administration unfavourably compared to private business, and with both mundane services and key strategic functions being outsourced to corporate providers and international consulting firms. Despite concerted efforts to reduce the influence of corporate money in democratic governance, corporate influence continues unabated. Corporately owned digital media platforms have become today's agora, holding politicians and civil society in their thrall as they set the rules of discourse while enjoying broad legal immunities.[5] As mere humans living in the shadow of this corporate world, what do we have to say about the corporation in international, transnational and domestic law and governance?

---

2   Klaus Schwab, "Global Corporate Citizenship: Working with Governments and Civil Society", *Foreign Affairs* (January/February 2008), online: <www.foreignaffairs.com/articles/2008-01-01/global-corporate-citizenship>; see also Klaus Schwab, "Global Corporate Citizenship" (Remarks delivered to the Foreign Policy Association, 17 April 2008), online (video): *Youtube* <www.youtube.com/watch?v=tmK0-3rrrIY>.

3   World Economic Forum, *Annual Report 2018–2019* (Geneva: World Economic Forum), online: <www3.weforum.org/docs/WEF_Annual_Report_18-19.pdf>.

4   *UN Charter, supra* note 1, ch 1, art 2.

5   See e.g. Matt Laslo, "The Fight Over Section 230—and the Internet as We Know It", *Wired* (13 August 2019), online: <www.wired.com/story/fight-over-section-230-internet-as-we-know-it/>; Pierre François Docquir, "The Social Media Council: Bringing Human Rights Standards to Content Moderation on Social Media" CIGI, 28 October 2019, online: <www.cigionline.org/articles/social-media-council-bringing-human-rights-standards-content-moderation-social-media>; Christian Fuchs, "Social Media and the Public Sphere" (2014) 12:1 J Global Sustainable Information Society.

Background to the Project

For several years I taught an international business law course at the University of Ottawa Faculty of Law (Common Law) and a graduate international business challenges course at the Telfer School of Business on topics related to international corporate governance and social responsibility. To prepare for both courses I relied heavily on *Corporate Social Responsibility: A Legal Analysis*, by Michael Kerr, Richard Janda and Chip Pitts.[6] This groundbreaking book provides a careful legal analysis of the many initiatives and ideas about CSR that have developed over the years of rapid globalization. Toward the end of the book, the authors state: "So-called voluntary standards and initiatives expanding rapidly today in fact have significant legal content and effect, complementing existing hard law to form a meta-regulatory system of 'enforced self-regulation in the shadow of the law.'"[7] They conclude by saying: "our goal was to show that a legal analysis of CSR is now possible."[8] In teaching these courses I also relied heavily on chapters in a book I co-edited, *The Globalized Rule of Law: Relationships between International and Domestic Law*,[9] in which international law academics and practitioners explained how international law becomes part of Canadian law, and how Canadian courts should deal with international law issues that come before them. There was no book that specifically offered guidance on how transnational business was or ought to be governed by international or domestic law but, thanks to the work of the United Nations Global Compact, Business and Human Rights, Human Rights Watch, Amnesty International and many academic writers, there was a growing body of compelling business case studies to help elucidate the ethical challenges and governance gaps arising from globalization.[10]

This book project was launched in the fall of 2018, when many legal academics, practitioners and civil society activists were organizing conferences and workshops to discuss aspects of international corporate governance and social responsibility, in light of attempts by Indigenous peoples in Ecuador to enforce, in Canada, an Ecuadorean Supreme Court judgment against Chevron for environmental damage, and by Eritrean labourers to seek remedies in Canada from parent company Nevsun Resources for alleged forced labour and torture at a copper mine in Eritrea. There was a sense that the existing domestic law on corporate liability and corporate group responsibility was straining to find justice for victims of environmental and human rights harms that implicated transnational corporations in faraway lands.

Seeing that it might be counterproductive to hold an additional conference when so much was already on offer, the Centre for International Governance Innovation (CIGI) partnered with the University of Calgary for a conference in Banff to produce an online essay series, *Environmental*

---

6 Michael Kerr, Richard Janda & Chip Pitts, *Corporate Social Responsibility: A Legal Analysis* (Toronto: LexisNexis Canada, 2009).

7 *Ibid* at 609.

8 *Ibid* at 612.

9 Oonagh E Fitzgerald, chief ed; editorial board members Elisabeth Eid, Don Fleming, Anne Warner La Forest, Armand de Mestral & Lorraine Pelot, *The Globalized Rule of Law: Relationships between International and Domestic Law* (Toronto: Irwin Law, 2006); *Règle de droit et mondialisation : Rapports entre le droit international et le droit interne* (Cowansville, QC: Éditions Yvon Blais, 2006).

10 See e.g. Ralph Hamann, Stu Woolman & Courtenay Sprague, eds, *The Business of Sustainable Development in Africa: Human Rights, Partnerships, Alternative Business Models* (Pretoria: Unisa Press, 2008); *Embedding Human Rights in Business Practice II* (New York: UN Global Compact, 2007).

Challenges on Indigenous Lands,[11] and invited known experts to contribute chapters to a book on the corporation in international, transnational and domestic law and governance. A one-day writers' workshop was held in March 2019 to give all contributors a chance to understand what others were planning to write about, and then the authors dispersed to write their chapters.

Overview of *Corporate Citizen: New Perspectives on the Globalized Rule of Law*

Through 17 chapters organized in five parts ("Legal Frameworks Straining Boundaries"; "Accountability Frameworks Taking Shape"; "Corporate Conduct Reflecting Values"; "Investor Obligations Drawing Focus"; and "Institutions Articulating Transnational Justice"), *Corporate Citizen* examines the modern multinational corporation from many different angles and in a diversity of voices.

Written by Canadian experts in international economic law, corporate law, investment law, Indigenous law and human rights law, the chapters of this book explore how domestic and international law frames the rights and obligations of the corporation in a way that allows multinational corporations to travel the world as global corporate citizens, exercising power and influence in national and international policy discussions and simultaneously evading responsibilities and liabilities toward the citizens of the countries in which they operate.

The international law and governance issues relating to the modern transnational corporation are complex, and we see the contributing authors struggle to identify and isolate the challenges of globalization, disagree about whether corporate law needs to reform, and diverge on what would be suitable solutions. Through these writings, however, the enormity of the problem becomes clearer and possible solutions start to emerge.

Part I: Legal Frameworks Straining Boundaries

In their chapter entitled "Foreign Wrongs, Corporate Rights and the Arc of Transnational Law," Jason MacLean and Chris Tollefson explore how corporations' "non-status" under international law has allowed them to benefit from rights without being burdened by corresponding duties. They observe that over the course of the recent decades of globalization, large transnational corporations have effectively set the standards and laws for international business, empowering these corporations against states and their citizens, but largely absolving the corporations of any concomitant accountability. Revisiting an earlier study by Steven Ratner on human rights accountability of transnational corporations, the authors note that the profound governance gap persists, two decades since Ratner's landmark work. They ponder how to inspire and activate reform when political economy considerations make national governments reticent to take strong measures — such as enacting domestic laws or entering into an international treaty — to regulate the conduct of transnational corporations. The authors see a role for international lawyers and domestic courts in envisioning and articulating accountability mechanisms for

---

11   With grateful acknowledgement to my co-editors, Kathleen Mahoney and Robert Hamilton, see *Environmental Challenges on Indigenous Lands*, CIGI, Essay Series, online: <www.cigionline.org/environmental-challenges-indigenous-lands>.

transnational corporations, and they take some solace from recent judicial statements suggesting civil liability rules could evolve to help achieve justice in some cases of human rights violations by transnational corporations.

Christopher C. Nicholls, in his chapter entitled "The Corporation and Modern Capitalism: Folk, Broke and Woke," dismantles hopeful exhortations that modern capitalism should return to its roots in order to be more socially responsible. He questions the assumption that modern capitalism is broken and in need of radical reform, and that the pro-social business corporation has reliable historical precedents. He critically scrutinizes corporate reform proposals that he considers would dramatically shift the basic wealth-increasing function of the corporation. Noting there have been well-intentioned efforts to reconcile the goals of shareholder primacy and CSR, Nicholls opposes rejection of straightforward shareholder primacy as implying a broader rejection of the value of free markets and a tendency to demonize the business corporation's purpose of wealth production. He suggests that the proliferation of pro-social initiatives aimed at moving from "broke" capitalism to "woke" capitalism are misguided, and that there is little evidence that notions of good or responsible corporate citizenship have substantive content or normative force. He contends that a more realistic view is that business corporations benefit society simply by operating in competitive markets and internalizing negative external effects of their operations, without pursuing non-financial or philanthropic goals.

Anita Indira Anand examines the implications of the growth of a sophisticated shareholder base in public corporations in her chapter. She notes the growing prevalence of sophisticated, activist institutional shareholders (pension or hedge fund) is impacting capital markets around the world as they seek both governance changes and a return on investment, and are not willing to observe passively on the sidelines while corporate managers and boards determine the direction for the corporation. She considers that they carry out an important monitoring function in corporate governance and can form activist groups, known as "wolf packs," to coordinate governance and other reforms. With the decline in individual investors, there has been a paradigm shift from passive to active ownership in public corporations. Anand suggests that regulators should leverage existing disclosure regimes that apply to blockholders to address their coordinated activity and actively facilitate shareholder engagement with corporate affairs by fostering a "stewardship culture" from which all market participants would benefit. Anand assesses the current legal mechanisms in place, identifies existing gaps, highlights legal and policy initiatives under way to address challenges, and offers some policy proposals. She asks whether, in the absence of law, the market itself will allow the beneficial aspects of shareholder activism to develop on their own.

In the last chapter to Part I, Edward Iacobucci assesses the pros and cons of domestic enforcement of competition policy in a globalized world. He notes that commerce in many goods is global, whereas competition policy is domestic, creating inevitable tensions. Iacobucci points out that most jurisdictions may pursue local remedies to address local competition concerns, but leave the basic decision to allow or disallow intrinsically global mergers to the European Union and the United States. However, he predicts that this convenient status quo may not last because political considerations are gaining prominence in public discourse around antitrust, especially in relation to technology platforms, and China is emerging as a significant antitrust jurisdiction. He notes there are growing calls for antitrust action and other regulation to deal with globally powerful technology platforms, but suggests the concern is less about market power than about how their size and access to data make them politically powerful. Iacobucci observes that as the economic consensus over basic antitrust objectives recedes in importance, it is unlikely that a consensus over political goals will emerge quickly.

Part II: Accountability Frameworks Taking Shape

Rebecca Johnson and Bonnie Leonard take up the invitation to share Canadian perspectives on the corporation in international, transnational and domestic law and governance by recounting and discussing "Coyote and the Cannibal Boy," a *Secwépemc* story, as a reflection on how we understand the corporation as a legal person, with agency, interests and ways of being responsible to others. Their exploration is motivated by a conviction that Indigenous legal orders continue to operate in the world, that contemporary state-based legal orders are embedded in colonization's denial of Indigenous law and sovereignty, and that Indigenous and non-Indigenous people alike can overcome this history by engaging with Indigenous law, legal theorizing and legal resources. The story explores the logic of consumption without limits and the persistent human desire for a slave to do the work of the community. It invites us to ask, if there is a structural hunger at the heart of the corporation, what is the place of directors in working with and managing that hunger, and what are the relationships between the shareholders and other stakeholders whom the corporation is expected to serve, as well as the broader community living in proximity to this hunger? The story allows reflection on important questions about the legal and governance regime needed to manage the hunger of the transnational corporation in its globalized search for wealth.

In their chapter entitled "Climate Change: A New Bellwether of Corporate Accountability for Systemic Risks," Edward J. Waitzer and Douglas Sarro explore how corporate law and practice could adapt to respond to the challenges of climate change. The scale of the reductions in greenhouse gas emissions contemplated by the Intergovernmental Panel on Climate Change in seeking to hold global warming to 1.5°C above pre-industrial levels means incurring significant and politically controversial costs in the short term, which political institutions seem unwilling to do. Climate change is a tragedy of the horizon, in that current generations are insufficiently motivated to fix a problem that will most severely impact future generations, and a tragedy of the commons, in that instead of taking decisive and responsible action, we tend to free-ride on the efforts of others and only deal with climate issues when they hit home directly. The authors suggest that in situations where political processes and institutions are not motivated to protect the public interest, private actors such as corporations should fill the gap, especially as their future growth and success depends on the continued availability of natural resources and stable political and civil institutions. Waitzer and Sarro consider judicial activism as a means for imposing and elaborating corporate responsibilities, using norms of "reasonableness." They discuss how legal duties and remedies are evolving in corporate and securities law to hold corporate directors and officers to account for monitoring and responding to climate risk. They highlight how various legal avenues might be pursued to accelerate corporate climate action by developing a modernized corporate accountability framework, grounded in norms of reasonableness.

In their chapter entitled "*Made in Everywhere:* Transformative Technologies and the (Re)codification of CSR in Global Supply Chains," Lucas Mathieu and Richard Janda discuss how new information and communication technologies, in particular the Internet of Things, blockchain and artificial intelligence can be used to strengthen the capacity of transnational corporations to monitor their CSR performance in global supply chains. Whereas these global supply chains are a key locus for addressing CSR, it is difficult for national governments, consumers and even the transnational corporations themselves to track compliance with legal and CSR standards throughout the chains. New information and communications technologies offer promising avenues to address the challenges inherent in measuring CSR, by allowing for the assembly of data from complex systems relating to an array of environmental, economic and social impacts, and for better traceability and accountability among actors along the supply chains. The authors acknowledge that implementation of these new technologies will raise additional CSR issues and risks, including questions about data and technology governance (for example, data privacy and cyber security) and whether the right elements of production are being measured. They suggest that technology-enabled real-time traceability of social and environmental impacts can lead to a transformation of law, generating a new normative architecture.

Darcy Lindberg examines *nêhiyaw* (Plains Cree) environmental principles as told in the story of "The Creation of Buffalo Lake," and how they could apply to redress environmental harms on Indigenous lands caused by multinational corporations. He explains that *acimowina* (stories) provide nêhiyaw peoples with a rigorous and pliable frame to analyze relationships of *wâhkôtowin* (kinship) and answer questions about legal obligations to peoples and non-human beings and things, within and between nations, and on new lands and jurisdictions. He applies wâhkôtowin and related laws to propose an adaptation to the principle of corporate separateness used to protect domestic corporations from the liabilities of subsidiaries that have committed ecological harms and human rights violations in other jurisdictions. He suggests that rather than allowing corporations to avoid humane obligations to others and thereby deny meaningful retribution, restoration and reparation for interjurisdictional harms, corporate obligations should be seen as equally important as corporate rights. Lindberg suggests that Indigenous legal principles could enrich Canadian state law's ability to take into account relationships to the ecological world, but that coloniality has interrupted that transmission. Nonetheless, he sees opportunities in both the "tangle-rooted" nature of Canadian constitutionalism and domestic implementation of the United Nations Declaration on the Rights of Indigenous Peoples to reimagine and revitalize law by including the practice of kinship with the ecological world and with our unmet human relations.

Part III: Corporate Conduct Reflecting Values

Malcolm Rogge considers the meaning of corporate responsibility in a transnational context in a chapter entitled "Vesting Transnational Corporate Responsibility in *Natural Persons v Legal Persons:* What Matters Today?" Reflecting on respect for human rights as a corporate responsibility (according to the UN Guiding Principles on Business and Human Rights), Rogge considers that because today's transnational legal order does not adequately capture human rights in legal terms, the human rights victim faces an accountability void. He views this global governance gap as no oversight, but a constitutive element of the globalized legal order. He asks, in a world of multinational enterprises, where the nominally autonomous corporation takes its place within complex corporate group structures that transcend national boundaries, what entity or what person ought to be regarded as responsible for human rights violations that the multinational enterprise has caused? He finds the answer depends on one's position in relation to the matter at hand, illustrated by a stylized value-maximizing economist, a corporate counsel and a human rights victim. Rogge suggests that the relative ease with which legal liability and governance responsibility can be shifted from one corporate entity to another is a fact of global corporate law, but may seem like an aggravating factor to victims of corporate human rights violations, who view the corporate leaders at head office as the persons ultimately responsible for the abuses on the ground. He concludes that corporate responsibility is best regarded as transnational ethical responsibility that runs all the way from the lowest-level subsidiary to the very apex of the multinational corporate group, and includes shareholders and the ultimate investors.

In her chapter entitled "Corporate Capture and Institutional Work: Lessons for the Canadian Ombudsperson for Responsible Enterprise," Daniela Chimisso dos Santos notes that despite the global conversation about business and human rights, corporate capture of public institutions is widespread, affecting human rights institutions and causing them to lose their institutional independence, accountability and legitimacy. As home and host states create and reform institutions to manage, monitor and administer the tool kit of the business and human rights agenda, the concern about corporate capture is significant. Through her analysis of corporate capture and institutional approaches to international business, whereby the relationship between institutions and corporations and the creation, maintenance and disruption of institutions by corporations is termed "institutional work," Chimisso dos Santos highlights the vulnerabilities of the new role of the Canadian Ombudsperson for Responsible Enterprise (CORE). She notes that institutional work occurs in countries at all levels of development, enabled by institutional ambiguity and uncertainty. Although the CORE is intended to act as a home-state grievance and redress mechanism that fosters corporate accountability in the extractives and textiles industries, Chimisso dos Santos finds institutional ambiguity in the lack of clarity about investigative powers, enforcement, relationships with the corporations being investigated, and interactions with other Canadian institutions. She urges the Canadian government to pay special attention to these risks in implementing the CORE.

Keith MacMaster and Sara Seck discuss the issue of inclusion of women on corporate boards and senior management within the context of achieving the 2030 Sustainable Development Goal of gender equality and the UN Global Compact's Women's Empowerment Principles, in their chapter entitled "Mining for Equality: Soft Targets and Hard Floors for Boards of Directors?" They suggest that this movement should be of particular importance to the Canadian mining sector, which is male-dominated, has low representation of women in corporate leadership and has been implicated in violations of the human rights of women and girls, especially Indigenous women and girls, both at home and in international operations. They review the 2018 amendments to the Canada Business Corporations Act, which mandate corporate disclosure on the number and percentage of designated persons, including women, on boards, whether there is a written policy in respect of diversity, and whether there are targets for representation. MacMaster and Seck consider international initiatives promoting corporate board diversity, examine existing data and literature on women in corporate leadership, and propose more inclusive notions of firm performance that acknowledge business responsibilities to respect human rights at home and abroad. They conclude that more needs to be done to take seriously Canada's international law obligations to prevent and remedy violations of the human rights of women and girls arising from resource extraction and that women's empowerment through board and management diversity initiatives may be a crucial piece of the solution.

In Part III's final chapter, "Voluntary Codes of Corporate Governance: Evolution and Implications," Cally Jordan discusses the growth and internationalization of voluntary codes of corporate governance. The United Kingdom's Cadbury Report of 1992 informed development of the Organisation for Economic Co-operation and Development (OECD) Principles of Corporate Governance, a set of international standards that first appeared in 1999. The OECD Principles popularized and disseminated "comply or explain" voluntary codes of corporate governance around the world. A complex dynamic of domestic initiatives developed, rooted in local circumstances and international standards. Jordan asks whether proliferation indicates success or whether the expectation of compliance has faded and comply-or-explain has become simply "explain," as seen in the US disclosure-based regulatory regimes. She contends that the growing politicization of the OECD Principles disconnected them from commercial or economic realities and undermined their coherence and credibility. For example, the OECD's glossing over of the important current corporate governance issue of board diversity, due to the disproportionate influence of the United States, is causing other major economies, especially in Europe, to disengage. While proponents still laud the flexibility and ease of adjustment of the voluntary codes approach, critics contend that frequent revisions to the UK Code of Corporate Governance indicate a failure to address issues decisively through legislation. Jordan concludes that, despite the ubiquity of the OECD Principles, there are signs that the discourse on corporate governance has advanced beyond such comply-or-explain voluntary codes.

Part IV: Investor Obligations Drawing Focus

In "Remedies in the Context of Investor Responsibilities," Hugo Perezcano Díaz and Ksenia Polonskaya consider the potential for reforming IIAs and ISA to address aspects of CSR. They note that a structural difficulty in giving effect to these ideas is that existing IIAs grant foreign investors a right to bring a claim and seek a remedy against a state party but generally do not impose obligations on investors or provide for other aggrieved parties to bring claims against foreign investors. They note that some recently negotiated agreements, such as the Comprehensive Economic and Trade Agreement (between Canada and the European Union) and the Comprehensive and Progressive Agreement for Trans-Pacific Partnership, have begun to incorporate soft references to investors' CSR responsibilities. Recent ISA reform proposals include redesigning IIAs not only to avoid harmful investment, but also to maximize investors' positive contribution to the host state, ensuring foreign investment activities are consistent with international and national environmental, human rights and labour standards, and enhancing host-state access to arbitration against foreign investors. With the growing interest in coupling foreign investor rights with responsibilities, the authors ask, what would be the meaningful legal consequences of including investor responsibilities in IIAs? They argue that remedies should be a central piece of the discourse on investor responsibilities and ISA reform, suggesting that the UN "Protect, Respect and Remedy" Framework on Business and Human Rights might provide some guidance on this complex issue.

Charles-Emmanuel Côté focuses on denial of benefits (DoB) clauses in his chapter entitled "Piercing the Corporate Veil in International Investment Law: Problems with the Denial of Benefits Clause." A DoB clause excludes from an investment treaty's protections nationals of third states who, through corporate structuring, seek to benefit from investor rights that the treaty parties did not intend to apply to them. Côté explains that the corporation's separateness from its shareholders was affirmed by the International Court of Justice in the *Barcelona Traction* case, when the court asserted that the state of incorporation determines the nationality of a corporation, regardless of whether it is owned or controlled by third-country shareholders. While international law permits treaty shopping through corporate restructuring, DoB clauses in IIAs are designed to counter this corporate strategy. DoB clauses remain relatively rare, but the United Nations Conference on Trade and Development encourages states, especially developing countries, to include them in investment agreements to support their sustainable development. Côté notes these clauses rebalance interests of the host state and the state of incorporation, prevent third-country investors from free-riding on bilateral investment agreements, allow states to preserve reciprocity in their obligations and negotiate future agreements with third countries, and prevent host-state nationals from using an IIA to bypass domestic courts. Noting that DoB clauses have become a progressive feature of all recent mega-regional agreements with investment chapters, Côté observes that this development may lead to foreign investors treaty shopping for older agreements or trying to take advantage of asymmetrical ISA rules within multilateral agreements, such as those found in the Canada-United States-Mexico Agreement and in the Comprehensive and Progressive Agreement for Trans-Pacific Partnership, to avoid a possible denial of their benefits.

In his chapter entitled "Reconceptualizing International Investment Governance: The Challenges of Establishing Foreign Investor Obligations," Enrique Boone Barrera refers to the damning report to the United Nations from independent expert Alfred-Maurice de Zayas on how the international regime of foreign investment protection threatens "a democratic and equitable international order," and needs systematic reforms to bring it into conformity with the UN Charter and international human rights law. Citing Joseph Stiglitz for the proposition that transnational corporations have become a threat to international governance, Boone Barrera observes that the effects of this imbalance may be felt differently, depending on the country and its state of development. In a developed country, it may be felt as regulatory chill or undermining of the domestic judicial system. In a developing country with deficient institutions and weak rule of law, international investment by a wealthy multinational corporation can create incentives for corruption or alliance with a despotic regime, undermining democratic institutions and exposing vulnerable populations such as Indigenous peoples to potential harm. He notes that one of the arguments in favour of IIAs was that they would act as an external constraint to improve domestic governance of host states, but this has proved to be one-sided, in that existing IIAs lack provisions to hold foreign investors accountable. Boone Barrera considers it to be progress that states are finally rejecting the old conception of the regime of foreign investment protection as an isolated economic law framework, but concludes that what is needed is a full reconceptualization of the purpose and ethos of the regime, with a comprehensive global governance approach to regulate the conduct of transnational corporations.

In the final chapter to Part IV, entitled "Using International Investment Agreements to Address Access to Justice for Victims of Human Rights Violations Associated with Transnational

Resource Extraction," Penelope Simons and J. Anthony VanDuzer consider how to address the difficulties faced by individuals and communities when they seek access to justice for human rights and environmental harms caused by transnational resource extraction projects. The authors argue that international investment law is implicated in both transnational corporate impunity and the problem of access to justice. IIAs provide an additional layer of protection for foreign investors because they contain broad protections against host-state action. Typically, investors have the right to seek compensation from host states through ISDS for new public interest measures that violate treaty standards. The potential for such claims to be brought has a chilling effect on states' willingness and capacity to address investors' human rights abuses and environmental harms. IIAs provide no recourse to the host state (or individuals and communities in the host state) for harms caused by the investor. Investors may even be able to use international arbitration to nullify attempts by victims to access justice in the host state's courts. The authors suggest that revisions to IIAs could address some of these impediments as part of a broader response to filling the governance gap that currently affords such impunity to transnational corporations. For example, IIAs could impose human rights obligations on investors that could then be implemented by the treaty parties. IIAs could require that both the host state and home state create domestic civil liability regimes that provide effective access to justice for victims of human rights and environmental harms caused by transnational corporate investors. State parties could agree that their courts will take jurisdiction over claims from host-state victims and not permit investors to challenge jurisdiction on grounds of *forum non conveniens*, act of state or international comity.

Part V: Institutions Articulating Transnational Justice

In a concluding chapter, I review some of the challenges identified by the various authors and the slow progress in finding global governance solutions that justly reconcile economic, social and environmental interests. I look to the developing Canadian jurisprudence, most importantly, the recent decision of the Supreme Court of Canada in *Nevsun Resources Ltd v Araya*, as possibly providing the beginnings of a way forward for achieving transnational justice, by courts and governments coordinating their efforts to align corporate responsibilities with the UN Charter and the Sustainable Development Goals.

Through the diverse perspectives of the contributors to this book, we see the question of the international law and governance of the "global corporate citizen" from many angles and in different lights. Today's global corporate citizen is the apotheosis of the international economic order created after World War II — a dynamic and sophisticated engine of economic development, employment, wealth creation and hegemonic power. This runaway success notwithstanding, it seems improbable that world leaders surveying the devastation of that war and trying to shape a more peaceful, secure and just future world order expected that in three-quarters of a century their own leadership role in global governance would have been, in large measure, ceded to the global corporate citizens.

The media are replete with tales of corporate malevolence, benevolence and negligence, but often ignore the quotidian, average multinational corporation simply motivated to meet the needs of its customers, retain good employees and leaders, lower costs, build customer loyalty, and increase profits, market share and shareholder value. The issues relating to the modern transnational corporation are complex, and seeing these contributing authors struggling to identify and isolate the challenges of globalization, and disagreeing about the need for or contours of reform, hints at the delicacy required to embark on a review and reset of the international, transnational and domestic law and governance pertaining to the global corporate citizen.

Having provided a clearer sense of the complexity and enormity of the challenge and the possibility of solutions, this book leaves much to do for policy makers, diplomats, judges, arbitrators, civil society advocates, corporate lawyers, professors and the next generation of international law students in working out the details of international law and governance reform. It will take imagination, tenacity and cooperation to piece together solutions that better align our human need for economic security with our need for peace, justice, human rights, health, and a clean and safe natural environment.

I.
LEGAL FRAMEWORKS STRAINING BOUNDARIES

1

FOREIGN WRONGS, CORPORATE RIGHTS AND THE ARC OF TRANSNATIONAL LAW

Jason MacLean and Chris Tollefson

An international lawyer has got to dream...it comes with the territory.

— Robert Howse[1]

Introduction

This chapter reflects on the challenge — and the *aspiration* — of bringing transnational corporations (TNCs) more fully and coherently under the rule of international law. An extensive literature ruminates upon the disjunction between the extant norms of our international legal order — many of which continue to cling to antiquated Westphalian-era suppositions — and the massive changes that have attended the ascendance of TNCs in the post-World War II era

---

1   Robert Howse, "Response to Ratner: 'An international lawyer has got to dream...it comes with the territory'" (4 June 2015) EJIL (blog), online: *Talk!* <www.ejiltalk.org/response-to-ratner-an-international-lawyer-has-got-to-dreamit-comes-with-the-territory/>.

and the associated privatization of global authority and governance.[2] The place of corporations in international law remains at once unclear and hotly contested as a matter of theory, doctrine and politics.

This is not to suggest, however, that international legal orders, and emerging transnational legal regimes,[3] are somehow oblivious to or ignore the reality of TNCs. To the contrary, corporate liability is possible, at least in theory, under the jurisdiction of the International Criminal Court.[4] Likewise, the 1989 Basel Convention on the Control of Transboundary Movements of Hazardous Wastes and their Disposal, and other environmental treaties, suggest a willingness on the part of states to impose legal responsibility directly on corporations.[5] As well, corporations enjoy a plethora of rights under bilateral investment treaties (BITs),[6] often bolstered by the domestic law tendency to treat corporations as "persons" for constitutional purposes.[7] Overall, therefore, the "non-status" of corporations under international law allows them to enjoy rights without corresponding duties and thereby "have it both ways."[8] Indeed, large TNCs have emerged as transnational standard setters and law makers. Consequently, international law doctrine has done much to empower TNCs against states, but has thus far failed to demand any form of corresponding corporate accountability.[9]

This chapter is a foray into the debate over TNC liability in domestic courts for breaches of international law and related human rights abuses committed abroad.[10] It is one thing to suggest — as many have — that corporations should be rendered subjects of international law; it is quite another thing to articulate principles, let alone legal rules, capable of making this happen. The recent decision of the Supreme Court of Canada (SCC) in *Nevsun Resources Ltd v Gize Yebeyo Araya et al* highlights the importance of these questions — and the controversy surrounding them. In this case (considered in more detail later in this chapter and elsewhere in this volume), the court, in a split decision, allowed the plaintiffs to proceed to trial on a groundbreaking

---

2   See especially José E Alvarez, "Are Corporations 'Subjects' of International Law?" (2011) 9 Santa Clara J Intl L 1 [Alvarez, "Are Corporations 'Subjects' of International Law?"].

3   The notion of a transnational, as opposed to international, legal order is far from new. The term "transnational law" was coined in 1956 by Justice Philip Jessup of the International Court of Justice to refer to "all law which regulates actions or events that transcend national frontiers." See Harold Hongju Koh, *Transnational Litigation in United States Courts* (New York: Foundation Press, 2008) at 2.

4   See e.g. Leora Bilsky, *The Holocaust, Corporations, and the Law: Unfinished Business* (Ann Arbor, MI: University of Michigan Press, 2017).

5   See e.g. Alan E Boyle, "Making the Polluter Pay? Alternatives to State Responsibility in the Allocation of Transboundary Environmental Costs" in Francesco Francioni & Tullio Scovazzi, eds, *International Responsibility for Environmental Harm* (London, UK: Graham & Trotman, 1991) 363.

6   For a discussion of investor-state arbitration and its legal implications, see e.g. Chris Tollefson, "Games without Frontiers: Investor Claims and Citizen Submissions under the NAFTA Regime" (2002) 27 Yale J Intl L 141; Gus Van Harten & Martin Loughlin, "Investment Treaty Arbitration as a Species of Global Administrative Law" (2006) 17 Eur J Intl L 121; Benedict Kingsbury & Stephan Schill, "Investor-State Arbitration as Governance: Fair and Equitable Treatment, Proportionality, and the Emerging Global Administrative Law" (2009) IILJ Working Paper 2009/6.

7   For a historical account of how corporations secured civil rights in the United States, see Adam Winkler, *We the Corporations: How American Businesses Won Their Civil Rights* (New York: Liveright, 2018). The development of corporate rights under the Canadian Charter of Rights and Freedoms is analyzed in Chris Tollefson, "Corporate Constitutional Rights in the Supreme Court of Canada" (1993) 19:1 Queen's LJ 309.

8   Jonathan I Charney, "Transnational Corporations and Developing Public International Law" (1983) Duke LJ 748 at 767.

9   See e.g. Julian Arato, "Corporations as Lawmakers" (2015) 56:2 Harv Intl LJ 229.

10   See e.g. Simon Baughen, "Customary International Law and its Horizontal Effect? Human Rights Litigation Between Non-State Actors" (2015) 67 Rutgers L Rev 89; see also Elena Pariotti, "International Soft Law, Human Rights and Non-State Actors: Towards the Accountability of Transnational Corporations" (2009) 10 Human Rights Rev 139.

tort claim that seeks to impose liability on a Canadian corporation for violations of customary international law committed abroad.[11]

While there have been some significant and helpful theorizations of how corporations can be made subjects of international criminal law,[12] the literature addressing the underlying principles of how corporations could be held liable for torts based on customary international law is surprisingly sparse.

Perhaps the most comprehensive such attempt to date remains Steven Ratner's proposed theory of corporate responsibility for violations of international human rights law.[13] Reflecting on international human rights law and advocacy throughout the 1990s, Ratner observed a striking shift away from a focus on abuses committed by states toward a much closer scrutiny of the activities of business enterprises, TNCs in particular. According to Ratner, this shift in focus from states to corporations was a direct result of the developments encompassed by "globalization," including: increased investment by multinational corporations in developing countries; the popular perception that multinational corporations' economic power and influence was beginning to erode and, in some instances, outstrip the power of states; advances in global telecommunications that, among other things, simultaneously brought global attention to the inequitable living conditions of the citizens of less developed states while enhancing the capacity of non-governmental organizations (NGOs) to mobilize public opinion; actions and decisions of the World Trade Organization and International Monetary Fund having the effect of compelling states to be more welcoming to foreign investors; and, not least, the well-documented accounts of the activities of some of the world's most powerful corporations.[14]

In response to this shift in focus toward greater scrutiny of the activities of TNCs, Ratner explored whether and how the existing international legal process could directly impose human rights obligations on corporations. More specifically, he argued that international law can and should supply such obligations, and that the scope of those obligations ought to be delimited by the characteristics of corporate activities.[15]

Nearly two decades after Ratner's original reflection seems an opportune time to revisit some of the questions he raised, in particular in connection with the domestic liability of TNCs for international human rights abuses. In many ways, not much has changed. Our world remains beset by a profound "governance gap," whereby "[t]he root cause of the business and human rights predicament today lies in the governance gaps created by globalization — between the scope and impact of economic forces and actors, and the capacity of societies to manage their

---

11   *Nevsun Resources Ltd v Gize Yebeyo Araya et al*, 2020 SCC 5 [*Nevsun v Araya*], dismissing an appeal from the British Columbia Court of Appeal in *Araya v Nevsun Resources Ltd*, 2017 BCCA 401 [*Nevsun Resources Appeal Decision*].

12   See the discussion in Bilsky, *supra* note 4. See also James G Stewart, "The Turn to Corporate Criminal Liability for International Crimes: Transcending the Alien Tort Statute" (2014) 47:1 NYUJ Intl L & Pol 121.

13   Steven R Ratner, "Corporations and Human Rights: A Theory of Legal Responsibility" (2001) 11:3 Yale LJ 443.

14   *Ibid* at 447–48.

15   *Ibid* at 449.

adverse consequences. These governance gaps provide the permissive environment for wrongful acts by companies of all kinds without adequate sanctioning or reparation."[16]

In fact, this governance gap appears to be growing. According to the 2018 report of the Corporate Human Rights Benchmark,[17] an NGO whose mandate is to determine which of the world's largest corporations perform best on human rights issues, "The overall picture is deeply concerning; most companies score poorly on the Benchmark, indicating weak implementation of the UN Guiding Principles on Business and Human Rights."[18] According to the Corporate Human Rights Benchmark, these findings "should provide food for thought for governments considering the role of legislation in business and human rights and should also serve as a wake-up call for businesses and investors everywhere."[19]

How should international law respond to this endemic and enduring governance gap? In this chapter, we explore both the challenges associated with bringing TNCs more fully and coherently under the rule of international law, and the extent to which Ratner's approach may provide a useful tool to this end. To do this, we offer a preliminary assessment of how the framework might offer real-world judicial guidance through a consideration of three landmark tort law cases currently before Canadian courts that seek to hold Canadian-based mining companies liable for wrongs committed abroad.

The rest of the chapter unfolds as follows. The first part discusses the conundrum of categorizing corporations as international legal subjects by considering possible answers to the inextricably linked questions of "whether" and "how" to bring corporations under the umbrella of international law. The second part proceeds by setting out Ratner's proposed framework as a potential means of answering the "how" question, while the third part applies Ratner's framework to three Canadian human rights cases. In the conclusion, we suggest that the thorniest questions surrounding the potential of a transnational corporate law may well be neither whether nor how, but rather — or, at the very least, also — "who" and "where"? Indeed, we find that Robert Howse's response to Ratner is exactly right: an international lawyer has got to dream; it comes with the territory.[20]

---

16   *Report of the Special Representative of the Secretary-General on the Issue of Human Rights and Transnational Corporations and Other Business Enterprises: Protect, Respect and Remedy: A Framework for Business and Human Rights*, UNHRC, 8th Sess, UN Doc A/HRC/8/5 (2008) at para 3. See also Penelope Simons & Audrey Macklin, *The Governance Gap: Extractive Industries, Human Rights, and the Home State Advantage* (New York: Routledge, 2014).

17   Corporate Human Rights Benchmark, *Corporate Human Rights Benchmark 2018 Key Findings: Apparel, Agricultural Products and Extractive Companies*, online: <www.corporatebenchmark.org/sites/default/files/.../CHRBKeyFindings2018.pdf>.

18   *Ibid* at 4. The Corporate Human Rights Benchmark ranked 101 of the world's largest corporations in high human-rights-risk sectors. A quarter of the corporations included in the study scored less than 10 percent on the assessment, and "an alarming amount of companies score no points for human rights due diligence" (at 4). Notably, the weak implementation of the UN Guiding Principles was apparent from their very beginning. Endorsed in 2011, the Guiding Principles' lack of access to an effective remedy produced calls as early as 2013 for a legally binding international corporate accountability treaty, which constituted a damning indictment of an informal, pluralist and polycentric corporate-accountability mechanism. For a balanced discussion of both the potential and the inherent limitations of the Guiding Principles, see Sara L Seck, "Transnational Judicial and Non-Judicial Remedies for Corporate Human Rights Harms: Challenges of and for Law" (2013) 31:1 Windsor YB Access Just 177 at 194.

19   *Ibid* at 4.

20   Howse, *supra* note 1.

The Conundrum of Corporations as Legal Subjects under International Law

Our journey begins on a well-worn path. The question of whether TNCs should be recognized and treated as distinct legal subjects for the purposes of international law has preoccupied scholars and practitioners since the outset of the Cold War.[21]

It is a question of considerable heft and complexity. Our Westphalian state-centred system of global governance has long struggled "to adjust to the expanding reach and growing influence of transnational corporations."[22] Few would seriously dispute the existence of the large and growing governance gap between rights enjoyed by TNCs and the duties that can meaningfully be imposed upon them for the harms and damage they cause, in particular in the realms of human rights and the environment.

Attempts to grapple with the conundrum of reconciling the reach and influence of modern-day TNCs with a legal architecture designed for a much simpler era almost invariably lead to a consideration of the practicalities involved. The conceptual and normative threshold question of "whether" thus bleeds into ruminations on the question of "how."

Indeed, Fleur Johns claims there is a growing sense among contemporary international law scholars that first-principles debates about "the 'what' and the 'who' of international law" are less pressing — or, at least, less interesting — than "the 'how' of international legal action."[23] According to Johns, "Contemporary international lawyers tend to address the distribution of authority and responsibility in international law less through questions of international legal personhood than through particularized programmes of institutional or regulatory reform."[24]

This chapter focuses both on the nuts and bolts of putting international law to useful work, and the normative and conceptual questions that loom at the threshold of the conundrum. Indeed, to try to draw too neat a distinction between theory and practice, between means and ends, is ultimately self-defeating. The following pages offer reflections on the "whether" and the "how" questions, mindful of the extent to which these inquiries necessarily overlap, and consider the utility of drawing upon corporate-personhood theory as a means of informing the nuts-and-bolts determinations that must be made in order to hold TNCs to account under international law for human rights abuses.

The "Whether" Question

Given the interconnectedness of the "whether" and "how" questions, it is important to situate and carefully frame the threshold inquiry. One of the key reasons why the "whether" question arises

---

21   See e.g. Alvarez, "Are Corporations 'Subjects' of International Law?", *supra* note 2; Charney, *supra* note 8; Ratner, *supra* note 13.

22   John Ruggie, "Business and Human Rights: the Evolving International Agenda" (2007) 101 AJIL 819.

23   Fleur Johns, "Introduction" in Fleur Johns, ed, *International Legal Personality* (New York: Taylor & Francis, 2010) at 5.

24   *Ibid.*

in cases such as those canvassed later in this chapter is the endemic and enduring governance gap when it comes to the activities of TNC extractive industries.[25]

Under the Westphalian model, recourse for the victims of human rights abuses must be sought by prevailing upon either the host country or the home country to take action. Under established international law principles, this is because it is the state that has the duty to promote and protect human rights within its territory (host state) or under its control (home state).

The response of host states will invariably be uncooperative, or worse; as Stephen Kobrin points out, host states are typically the "perpetrator...the prime violator of human rights."[26] Likewise, TNCs' home states can rarely be counted upon to take remedial action, even in the most egregious cases. This regrettable result is usually a function of a constellation of factors, including international diplomacy, domestic political considerations (including the pervasive effect of regulatory capture), the chilling effect on regulatory action associated with international trade and investment agreements, and various other "how"-related considerations.

Under orthodox Westphalian state theory, the notion that TNCs should have independent rights and duties is anathema. Within the "edifice of modern international law," states are the only actors that matter.[27] The rules governing how states interact within this edifice are, in turn, a reflection of exercises of their sovereign will, "as evidenced explicitly in treaty law and implicitly in customary international law."[28]

Various objections are routinely raised against the notion that customary international law should recognize the reach and influence of modern TNCs, in particular those corporations involved in extractive activities in the developing world. Virtually all of these objections proceed from concerns about state sovereignty. One such objection is that a change of this kind is effectively constitutional in nature. Because it so profoundly alters the governing rules of the game, it is a change that courts should be highly reluctant to implement.[29] In particular, if TNCs are to be made potentially liable in domestic courts for human rights abuses as defined under customary international law, this liability must be brought to fruition by legislation or treaty. This is the approach recently taken by the US Supreme Court in the recent case of *Jesner v Arab Bank*.[30]

A related objection is the concern that to render TNCs liable for activities occurring within the territorial authority of host states amounts to neo-colonialism. This objection is regularly raised in various UN fora and undoubtedly forms part of the calculus considered by home states when they are called upon to sanction domestically registered TNCs for foreign wrongs.

A variety of rejoinders can be offered to these concerns. Arguably the most powerful is the fact that we no longer live in a Westphalian world, and have not for many decades. Since at

---

25   See e.g. Sara L Seck, "Revisiting Transnational Corporations and Extractive Industries: Climate Justice, Feminism, and State Sovereignty" (2017) 26:2 Transnat'l L & Contemp Probs 383; Jason MacLean, "*Chevron Corp. v. Yaiguaje*: Canadian Law and the New Global Economic and Environmental Realities" (2016) 57 Can Bus LJ 367.

26   Stephen J Kobrin, "Private Political Authority and Public Responsibility: Transnational Politics, Transnational Firms, and Human Rights" (2009) 19:3 Business Ethics Q 349 at 351.

27   *Ibid* at 352, citing AC Cutler, "Critical Reflections on the Westphalian Assumptions of International Law and Organization: A Crisis of Legitimacy" (2001) 27 Rev Intl Studies 133.

28   *Ibid*.

29   *Jesner v Arab Bank*, 138 S Ct 1386 (2018).

30   *Ibid*.

least the 1970s, the notion that TNCs exist at the pleasure of states, or even exercise powers that derive from states, has been broadly challenged.[31] Increasingly, TNCs and other actors, including some civil society organizations and other international organizations, are exercising autonomous or quasi law-making powers.[32] Moreover, often these powers are exercised in ways that supplant the traditional sovereign prerogatives of the state, while attracting high levels of systemic legitimacy. This has triggered a new generation of international law scholarship that seeks to document the transition away from a Westphalian world to one in which, to a large extent, authority and governance have been privatized.[33]

Evidence of this transition can be gleaned in a variety of areas of international law. Of particular significance is international criminal law. In this setting, the notion that individuals — including corporations — are legal subjects is now well ensconced. In this regard, proponents of expanded recognition of corporate legal personality frequently cite the post-World War II Nuremburg trials, during which German industrialists were prosecuted for various international law-based offences, including war crimes and crimes against humanity. While the defendants in these cases were individuals, the Nuremburg Tribunal made it clear that international law also contemplated corporate and organizational liability.[34]

The corporate form is likewise recognized as a subject of international law under various international labour agreements and conventions. Perhaps most notable of these is the foundational 1949 International Labour Organization convention enshrining the right of workers to organize and bargain collectively. Ratner argues that the early groundbreaking protections for workers' rights in their dealings with corporate employers "assume a special significance with respect to the possibility of duties on corporations in the human rights area," given the close relationship between labour rights and human rights (economic and social rights in particular).[35]

Corporations have been even more fully integrated into the architecture of international environmental law. This integration was prompted by necessity, in particular the drive to implement the emerging "polluter pays" principles of customary international law. Dating back to the 1960 Paris Convention on Third Party Liability for Nuclear Energy, a significant number of treaties or conventions have imposed liability on corporations for environmental damage.[36]

Proponents of expanded international law recognition of corporate liability also point to the 1997 Organisation for Economic Co-operation and Development (OECD) Anti-Bribery

---

31   See e.g. Joseph S Nye & Robert O Keohane, "Transnational Relations and World Politics: A Conclusion" (1971) 25:3 Intl Organization 721.

32   Cutler, *supra* note 27. See also José E Alvarez, *International Organizations as Law-Makers* (New York: Oxford University Press, 2006).

33   See John G Ruggie, "Reconstituting the Global Public Domain — Issues, Actors and Practices" (2004) 10:4 European J Intl Relations 499; see also John G Ruggie, *Just Business: Multinational Corporations and Human Rights* (New York: WW Norton, 2013).

34   See e.g. Bilsky, *supra* note 4; Ratner, *supra* note 13 at 475–76; Harold Hongju Koh, "Separating Myth from Reality about Corporate Responsibility Litigation" (2004) 7:2 J Intl Econ L 263 at 265 [Koh, "Separating Myth from Reality"].

35   Ratner, *supra* note 13 at 479; see also Kobrin, *supra* note 26 at 355–56.

36   As discussed above, perhaps the best known of these, and one that allows for the imposition of criminal liability on corporate wrongdoers, is the 1989 Basel Convention on the Control of Transboundary Movements of Hazardous Wastes and their Disposal. Nevertheless, international law commentators still tend to view this and related regimes as part of the "transboundary civil litigation" dimension of international law. See e.g. Boyle, *supra* note 5.

Convention. Under this OECD Convention, signatory parties are required to criminalize the bribery of foreign public officials, and to ensure that these prohibitions extend to the activities of corporations.[37] Similar prohibitions have been implemented by various other international agencies.[38]

While there is a clear and perceptible — or, at any rate, compellingly arguable — trend toward greater corporate accountability under international law, a far more robust trend has been the expansion of corporate legal rights and entitlements, including corporations' role in directly formulating their international rights and entitlements alongside corresponding limitations on state authority.[39] The area that has seen the most radical transformation is international investment law. Prior to the 1960s, corporations with foreign investments operated largely within the Westphalian model. As such, if a host country wrongfully interfered with that investment, the corporation had effectively no option but to try to persuade its home state to intervene on its behalf.

This picture began dramatically to change starting in the 1980s. In the intervening years, a massive international investment regime has been established that empowers foreign investors to compel host states to resolve outstanding disputes through mandatory arbitration.[40] Where a corporate investor can prove its rights as defined under a relevant regime have been violated, the presumptive remedy is a binding requirement that the host state pay damages.

In short, the treatment of TNCs within international law is, as Ratner charitably puts it, "somewhat inconsistent."[41] In some areas, most notably in the realm of environmental and anti-corruption law, corporations have been substantially but incompletely integrated into the corpus of international law, in particular where the duty imposed on them has a "vertical" dimension. A much greater ambivalence exists, however, with respect to the recognition of more "horizontal duties" that corporations might owe to other individuals as opposed to states. Meanwhile, in the crucial realm of investor rights in particular, the last 20 years have seen what some have described as a radical "constitutionalization" of corporate rights on the world stage.[42]

In reflecting on this inconsistency, Harold Hongju Koh offers a more blunt assessment, making what is effectively a "symmetry" argument: "The commonsense fact remains that if states and individuals can be held liable under international law, then so too should corporations....If corporations have rights under international law, by parity of reasoning, they must have duties as well."[43]

This symmetry argument in respect of the "whether" question, so pithily framed by Koh, is closely related to what might be termed the "personhood" argument. Here, the contention that is mounted is that just as corporations have largely secured legal recognition as persons under

---

37   Ratner, *supra* note 13 at 482.

38   *Ibid.*

39   Arato, *supra* note 9.

40   Alvarez, "Are Corporations 'Subjects' of International Law?", *supra* note 2 at 11.

41   Ratner, *supra* note 13 at 487.

42   David Schneiderman, *Constitutionalizing Economic Globalization: Investment Rules and Democracy's Promise* (New York: Cambridge University Press, 2008).

43   Koh, "Separating Myth from Reality", *supra* note 34 at 265.

domestic law, the same should prevail under international law. As has been authoritatively documented in the US context,[44] the discourse of corporate personhood has been used with considerable success to advance business interests, simultaneously expanding corporate rights while providing a pretext for resisting regulation. The US Supreme Court's 2010 decision in *Citizen's United* is widely regarded as yet another testament to the resonance of the "natural entity" of the corporation, a conception that imagines the corporation not as an aggregation of natural persons, nor as a state-created legal fiction.[45]

Increasingly, advocates of expanding corporate liability under international law for violations of human rights appear to be seeking to leverage and extend the domestic concept of corporate personhood. As with the symmetry argument, these claims have an element of circularity: the "is" — the objective reality of TNCs, whether as marketplace actors or within the jurisprudence of the US Supreme Court — should drive determinations about the "ought."

However, just as David Millon has cautioned in the domestic law context, José Alvarez warns that divining doctrine or policy prescriptions from *a priori* suppositions about the essential nature of the corporation is potentially a dangerous business.[46] Alvarez, much of whose scholarship has focused on BITs, worries that the risks of deeming corporations to be persons for international law purposes far outweigh the anticipated benefits in terms of enhanced accountability for human rights abuses and other violations of international law. In his view, if granted legal personality, writ large, for international law purposes, TNCs will parlay this into expanded entitlements against states under various trade, investment and regulatory regimes. For this reason, he rejects what he terms a top-down, personhood-based theorization of the legal basis for expanding TNC liability for human rights and other international law-based wrongs. Instead, Alvarez favours a more pragmatic, bottom-up approach that properly recognizes and is premised on what he calls the "facts on the ground": "including the reality that corporations operate under a social and not only a legal license; have unique systems of monitoring, information gathering, assessment and disclosure; may be made accountable through their own conceptions of 'due diligence' to shareholders and the wider public; and may owe differing human rights obligations depending on their sphere of business, their corporate structure, or their relationships with partners and suppliers...[this] conception of corporate responsibility/accountability is evidence-based and pragmatic. It is the very antithesis of *deducing* obligations from formal subject-hood or personhood."[47]

The "How" Question

Alvarez's plea for pragmatism is not only relevant to the "whether" question; it also offers a useful way to segue into the closely related question of "how." As noted above, Johns observed that, of late, international law scholars seem less interested in the "whether" question than its "how" counterpart. Perhaps this is because there is not much more that can be said about the former question, while the debate over the latter question is just beginning.

---

44   See especially the work of Morton Horwitz, David Millon and others. See also Winkler, *supra* note 7.

45   For a comprehensive discussion, see Winkler, *supra* note 7.

46   Alvarez, "Are Corporations 'Subjects' of International Law?", *supra* note 2 at 31; see also David Millon, "The Ambiguous Significance of Corporate Personhood" (2001), doi:10.2139/ssrn.264141.

47   Alvarez, "Are Corporations 'Subjects' of International Law?", *supra* note 2 at 32 [emphasis in original].

Before diving into the question of how TNCs can be more fully and effectively brought under the rule of international law, it is worthwhile to muse carefully over the "whether" debate, given the difficulty of considering these two questions in isolation.

Alvarez admonishes that the answer to the "how" question cannot be simply deduced in a top-down manner from the supposition of international corporate personhood. However, while Alvarez is certainly correct that any answer to this "how" question should rest on a firm conceptual foundation, less than a decade following his warning, it is difficult to imagine TNCs enjoying *more* rights and freedoms than they do at present, even without formal recognition of corporate personhood under international law. If one approaches the "how" question in a more pragmatic and evidence-based manner, as Alvarez recommends, the question of what that would look like still remains. In the quotation cited above, Alvarez offers some initial suggestions. Those suggestions closely track Ratner's core argument, discussed in the next section, that the scope of corporations' obligations under international law ought to be delimited by the characteristics of corporate activities and relationships.

Answering the "How" Question Using Ratner's Framework

What makes Ratner's article such a landmark is its pioneering attempt to grapple with this challenging and difficult question. Ratner argues that corporate international law obligations should flow from four sets of considerations: the corporate-state relationship; the nexus between corporations and affected populations; the particular legal rights at issue; and the position of human rights violators within the corporate structure.[48] We reprise these considerations below before proceeding in the next section to apply them to three recent cases in Canada.

The Relationship between Corporations and States

Ratner begins with the doctrine of state responsibility under international law. More specifically, Ratner rehearses the reciprocal, "mirror image" point that states can act and attract liability through a variety of actors, including corporations, while the obligations of corporations are significantly informed by the relationships with states. Ratner proceeds to consider three such sets of relationships: corporations as state agents;[49] corporations as complicit with states; and corporations as commanders. In the first of these relationships, the primary wrongful act is directly attributable to the state as principal, with the corporation incurring liability as its agent. In the latter two scenarios, the corporation incurs liability through its complicity in illegal state action by aiding and abetting, or in benefiting from the illegal conduct. That complicity may take the form of active involvement in the wrongdoing, or result from playing a more passive role that fails to prevent illegal conduct.

Analogizing from well-established principles of international law, Ratner derives the following corresponding corporate duties: "private corporations have duties to protect the human rights

---

48   Ratner, *supra* note 13 at 496–97.

49   An oft-cited example of corporate actors that would fall into this first category are the industrialist defendants that were put on trial at Nuremburg after World War II. See Bilsky, *supra* note 4.

of those under their control when they exercise quasi-state authority";[50] "if a business materially contributes to a violation of human rights by the government with knowledge of that activity, it should be held responsible as a matter of international law";[51] and a corporation should be liable for acts of those under its "effective authority and control": where it "knew, or consciously disregarded information which clearly indicated, that the subordinates were committing or about to commit such crimes," and where "the crimes concerned activities that were within the effective responsibility and control of the superior."[52]

Notably, for our purposes, Ratner further argues that corporate liability under international law should extend to those situations where a corporation allows government actors to violate rights.[53]

The Nexus between Corporations and Affected Populations

Drawing (loosely) on moral philosophy, Ratner proceeds by building on the principle — central in human rights theory and law generally — of equal respect for all humans and the related notion that, under certain circumstances, individuals owe greater duties to those *within* their associative sphere, which, in respect of corporations, is sometimes characterized as their sphere of influence.[54] From this, Ratner derives a version of the proximity (or neighbour) principle, which he defines as the extent to which a business enterprise and a population have formed a meaningful association. According to Ratner, all other things being equal, as this proximity lessens, so too the duties of the corporation lessen toward those individuals, and vice versa.[55] Proximity in this sense can flow from legal ties, physical proximity or possession of de facto control over a particular piece of territory.[56]

The Legal Rights at Issue

Once a corporation's relationship to the relevant government(s) and affected population(s) has been established, decision makers using Ratner's framework are to turn to the nature of the right(s) infringed. Ratner argues that the determination of corporate duties is based on a balancing of individual rights with business rights and interests, the latter informed by a consideration of the nature of the business activity in question.[57]

There are, however, certain rights that neither states nor corporations, notwithstanding the latter's rights and interests, can ever justifiably infringe: "Beyond balancing, certain rights with which the state may never interfere — such as the right to life and physical integrity and the

---

50   Ratner, *supra* note 13 at 500.

51   *Ibid* at 502.

52   *Ibid* at 506. Ratner proceeds to argue that "if my theory is to derive a set of duties applying to corporations generally rather than simply those duties that give rise to criminal liability, a lower standard of knowledge seems justifiable, one more akin to the negligence standard imposed on military commanders." *Ibid*.

53   *Ibid* at 524.

54   *Ibid* at 507–08. See also Jason MacLean, "Accountability" in Michael Kerr, Richard Janda & Chip Pitts, *Corporate Social Responsibility: A Legal Analysis* (Toronto: LexisNexis, 2009) 417 at 487–88.

55   Ratner, *supra* note 13 at 508. Ratner observes, however, that in respect of certain absolute rights, corporations may have "equal duties toward all" (*ibid* at 511).

56   *Ibid* at 525.

57   *Ibid* at 511.

rights against torture, slavery, or debt imprisonment — would be just as nonderogable against the corporation. The nature of those rights determines their nonderogability, such that no state or corporate interests can override them."[58]

Corporate Structures and Liability Attribution

Finally, Ratner's framework addresses the relationship between the structure of the corporate enterprise, on the one hand, and on the other the position of the human rights violator — or person(s) complicit with the government — within that structure. The task at this step of deriving corporate duties under international law is, in general terms, to "confront the reality of the corporate enterprise."[59] However, given the variety and, in certain cases, near-inscrutable complexity of corporate structures, including corporate groups, determining the locus of control and attributing the actions of the rights violator to the corporation may not always be an entirely straightforward exercise.[60] It is precisely for this reason that Ratner and others argue in favour of recognizing some form of enterprise liability for corporate groups having complex, multilayered structures and contractual relationships (for example, recognition of a rebuttable presumption of enterprise liability in respect of such structures, whereby liability follows the corporate structure's economic function rather than its legalistic form).

Related considerations of fault further complicate matters. Ratner argues that a corporation should be responsible for all of its constituent members acting under colour of corporate authority, without the necessity of having to separately establish fault on the part of the corporation. But Ratner concedes that in cases where severe sanctions are contemplated, the corporate enterprise's liability might reasonably be limited to those situations where it did not exercise due diligence in respect of its members and agents.[61]

Applying the Ratner Framework to Canadian Human Rights Cases

This section reflects on the real-world relevance of Ratner's framework by considering three high-profile torts cases that have been filed in Canadian courts: *Araya v Nevsun Resources*;[62]

---

58   *Ibid* at 515.

59   *Ibid* at 518.

60   Some commentators argue, however, that to even try to do so is to introduce "an intolerable level of uncertainty into the question of liability" and reduce "both the efficiency and fairness of corporate law." Mary Elizabeth Kors, "Altered Egos: Deciphering Substantive Consolidation" (1998) 59 U Pitt L Rev 381 at 437–38. In our view, such difficulties are often substantially overstated. See e.g. Jason MacLean, "The Cult of Corporate Personality: *Yaiguje v. Chevron Corporation*" (2014) 55 Can Bus LJ 281; Jason MacLean, "The Political Reality of Corporate Law" Can Bus LJ (forthcoming 2020).

61   Ratner, *supra* note 13 at 524.

62   *Nevsun Resources Appeal Decision, supra* note 11. For a preliminary analysis of the trial court's decision on a motion to strike, brought unsuccessfully by Nevsun Resources, see Jason MacLean, "The Enduring Evil of Slavery and the Emergence of Transnational Corporate Law: *Araya v. Nevsun Resources Ltd*" (2016) Toronto LJ, online: <www.tlaonline. ca/document/183/Toronto_Law_Journal-Nov2016.pdf>. In February 2020, a majority of the SCC ruled that the claims brought by the Eritrean plaintiffs in the case against the British Columbia-based mining company could proceed to trial. See *Nevsun v Araya, supra* note 11.

Choc v Hudbay Minerals Inc;[63] and *Garcia v Tahoe Resources Inc.*[64] Each of these suits seeks to impose liability on Canadian-based mining companies for human rights abuses arising in connection with mining operations being carried out abroad. While space limitations mean that we can only offer a very preliminary assessment of the utility of the Ratner framework in informing an analysis of these cases, the framework does appear to offer significant promise.

In two of these cases — *Hudbay* and *Tahoe* — the mining operations were based in Guatemala; in the third case, *Nevsun*, the operation was located in Eritrea. In the *Hudbay* and *Tahoe* cases, the plaintiffs are protesters who allege that they were the victims of assaults and other torts recognized under Canadian law committed by individuals for whose actions the Canadian mining companies should be held liable. In *Nevsun*, the plaintiffs are Eritrean nationals who were forced by the Eritrean military to work at a Canadian-owned mining operation located in Eritrea. Their claim is twofold: that the defendant company committed acts that amount to torts under existing Canadian law; and that the company should also be held liable for breaching peremptory norms of international law — including prohibitions on torture and slavery — through a complex business partnership with the Eritrean government.

The *Nevsun* case, discussed first, is particularly instructive in considering the Ratner framework's treatment of how the nature and proximity of the relationship between the TNC and the host state should influence liability determination. Likewise, the *Hudbay* and *Tahoe* cases help elucidate Ratner's analysis of how and to what extent the actions of those directly responsible for committing rights abuses should be attributed to associated corporate actors. Finally, all three cases are useful in exploring Ratner's remaining two factors: the nexus between the corporation and the affected populations, and the nature of the legal rights at stake in the litigation.

Nevsun Resources

In this case, Eritrean refugees allege that the Canadian mining company Nevsun Resources orchestrated a complex web of contractual relationships to develop the Bisha gold, copper and zinc mine in Eritrea. In particular, they allege that Nevsun, through its majority representation on — and effective control over — the board of the Eritrean Bisha Mining Share Company, engaged contractors and other partners to develop the mine, including, notably, the Eritrean military.[65] According to the Eritrean refugees-plaintiffs, the Eritrean military and companies owned by senior military officials used Eritrea's National Service Program of conscription to obtain forced labour from them and others remaining in Eritrea. Their claim is corroborated by the international NGO Human Rights Watch, which reported in the mid-2000s that Eritrean national conscripts were compelled to work on public infrastructure projects and farms owned by senior officials of the Eritrean military and the country's sole political party.[66]

---

63 *Choc v Hudbay Minerals Inc*, [2013] ONSC 1414 [*Hudbay Minerals*]. For a preliminary analysis of this decision on a motion to strike, brought unsuccessfully by Hudbay Minerals, see Jason MacLean, "One Small Step Toward Corporate Accountability: *Choc v. Hudbay Minerals Inc*" (2013) Toronto LJ. At the time of writing, this case remains mired in the documentary discovery stage.

64 *Garcia v Tahoe Resources Inc*, 2017 BCCA 39 [*Tahoe Resources*].

65 *Araya v Nevsun Resources Ltd*, 2016 BCSC 1856 at paras 26–28 [*Nevsun Resources Motion Decision*].

66 *Ibid* at para 28.

Human Rights Watch further reported in 2006 that individuals apprehended after fleeing conscripted national service in Eritrea were frequently tortured, a finding corroborated by a 2008 report of the US State Department and a subsequent report issued by Human Rights Watch in 2009, which further observed that those caught after attempting to escape conscripted military labour were detained without charge or trial, and were treated as deserters under Eritrean military law.[67]

As conscripts under the Eritrean state's National Service Program, the plaintiffs were assigned to work at the Bisha mine against their will, and under abhorrent and punitive conditions.[68] According to the evidence of the plaintiff, Gize Yebeyo Araya, punishments included beatings, being made to roll or run in hot sand, and having one's hands and feet tied together behind the back and being left in the sun for hours at a time.[69]

Nevsun vigorously resisted having the matter proceed to trial in British Columbia. It raised various arguments. These included a *forum non conveniens* motion (dismissed at the British Columbia Supreme Court, and not appealed) and a motion to strike (which failed in the British Columbia Supreme Court, the British Columbia Court of Appeal, and most recently in the SCC). Nevsun's motion to strike is particularly interesting for our purposes, in that it contended that it is plain and obvious that the plaintiffs' claim for violations of the peremptory norms of customary international law — *jus cogens* — prohibiting slavery, forced labour and torture cannot succeed because Nevsun is "immune" from liability because it is a corporation.[70] In a close five-to-four decision handed down in early 2020, a majority of the SCC forcefully rejected this argument. In the majority's view, while states "were classically the main subjects of international law," this no longer remains the case; increasingly the individual is being recognized as the "ultimate unit of all law."[71] Relying on academic authority, including an article authored by Koh cited earlier herein that documents this transition away from state-centrism,[72] in the majority's view it was by no means plain and obvious that "corporations today enjoy a blanket exclusion under customary international law" for direct or "complicity-based" liability for breaches of international law.[73]

Under Ratner's framework, Nevsun's close connections with the Eritrean state military and sole political party point to violations of paradigmatic complicity-based international law duties. While not alleging that it was acting as an agent of the state, the plaintiffs contend that the defendant is nonetheless liable for its complicity in illegal acts committed by the Eritrean state. The Eritrean refugees claim that Nevsun knowingly or negligently partnered with the Eritrean military and members of the state's ruling party to use the coercive powers of the state to develop a mining project. Indeed, the notoriety of the Eritrean military's abusive conduct and prior violations of peremptory norms of customary international law strongly tends to

---

67   *Ibid* at para 31.

68   *Ibid* at paras 44–46.

69   *Ibid* at para 46.

70   The plaintiffs have also pleaded that the defendant is liable under domestic nominate torts, including assault and battery, unlawful confinement and unjust enrichment. The right of the plaintiffs to pursue these torts was not in issue at the SCC.

71   *Nevsun v Araya, supra* note 11 at para 109.

72   Koh, "Separating Myth from Reality", *supra* note 34.

73   *Nevsun v Araya, supra* note 11 at para 113.

discount any possibility that Nevsun was unaware of its partners' practices. This notoriety likely also assists, perhaps not in clarifying, but in diminishing the legal importance of the otherwise characteristically complex nature of the contractual web connecting Nevsun with its various partners and subcontractors.

The manner in which the plaintiffs have pleaded their case also allowed them to mount a very tenable legal defence to the claim that their action is barred by operation of the "act of state" doctrine. Under this doctrine, the nature and even existence of which is a matter of considerable controversy, plaintiffs can be precluded from bringing a case if the claim requires the court to pronounce on the legality of state action. From the outset of the litigation, Nevsun relied heavily, and unsuccessfully, on the act of state defence. Its most recent setback came in the SCC, where the majority held that the doctrine was not part of Canada's common law. But even had the court held that the doctrine existed under Canadian law, the plaintiffs' position was that Nevsun could not invoke it here. According to the plaintiffs, this was because Nevsun's complicity was a stand-alone basis for imposing liability that did not require any predicate determinations as to the liability of the Eritrean state.

Hudbay Minerals

The allegations in this case arise out of the Fenix mining project conducted in Guatemala by a Canadian mining company, Hudbay Minerals Inc., and its wholly owned subsidiaries HMI Nickel Inc. (formerly Skye Resources Inc.) and Compañia Guatemalteca De Niquel. The plaintiffs, Indigenous Mayan Q'eqchi', allege that Hudbay and its subsidiaries negligently supervised their site security personnel, who are alleged to have gang-raped and murdered members of the Q'eqchi' and their relatives who were protesting against the project. The Q'eqchi' pleaded the following acts of direct negligence committed by Hudbay and its subsidiaries:

- Hudbay and Skye voluntarily assumed direct responsibility over key aspects of the on-the-ground security policy and personnel at the mining site, and issued an official corporate response to an ongoing farmland dispute involving local Mayan communities;

- Hudbay and Skye created a high risk of violence by retaining improperly trained and inadequately supervised site security personnel, who provided security services without the required authorization of the Guatemalan government;

- Hudbay and Skye retained ultimate control of the forced removal of Mayan subsistence farming communities, including those in which the Q'eqchi' plaintiffs resided; and

- Hudbay and Skye consistently acknowledged direct responsibility for, and control over, the security practices at the Fenix mining site by issuing public statements committing the companies to the implementation of detailed standards of conduct applicable to their security personnel, including commitments to adhere to Guatemalan and international law and comply with the international Voluntary Principles on Security and Human Rights[74] in respect of its security personnel and other contractors in Guatemala.[75]

Notably, Hudbay's president and chief executive officer during the relevant time frame made a public statement acknowledging that the development of the Fenix mining project required a *"relationship with the broader community,* whose efficient functioning and support are critical to the long-term success of the company in Guatemala."[76] In dismissing Hudbay's motion to strike the Q'eqchi' plaintiffs' claim because it failed to disclose a legal cause of action (owing to the absence of an extant duty of care applicable to Hudbay), the Ontario Superior Court of Justice explained that the "public statements alleged to have been made by the parent company [Hudbay] are one factor among others to be considered and *are indicative of a relationship of proximity between the defendants and the plaintiffs."*[77]

This claim directly against Hudbay highlights a different dimension of the Ratner framework than the complicity-based theory advanced in *Nevsun.* Here the liability flows not from the nature and proximity of the relationship between the corporation and the state, but rather from the nature and proximity of the relationship — in Ratner's terminology, the "nexus" — between the corporation and the affected local population. As such, this lawsuit seeks to impose liability on Hudbay based on its nexus — its proximity, both geographic and *legal* — to the Indigenous communities in Guatemala in which it operated. By engaging with these communities and making undertakings to them, the claim asserts that Hudbay brought the Indigenous rights-holders within its associative sphere of influence, giving rise to a duty of care that is actionable.

Ratner's principles of attribution are also relevant here. While at the time of the illegal actions Hudbay and Skye were separate legal entities, arguably what matters is whether and to what extent Hudbay's senior corporate officers exercised control over the security personnel alleged to have perpetrated the violent acts. Also to be weighed in the balance under the Ratner framework is the gravity of the harms perpetrated, which further militates in favour of holding Hudbay liable. Finally, while Ratner's framework suggests that competing interests must be balanced, it also makes clear that business interests cannot be allowed to condone nonderogable human rights of freedom of life and security — including physical integrity — of the person.

Tahoe Resources

In a strikingly similar case involving another Canadian-owned mining project in Guatemala, seven individuals protesting outside the gate to the Escobal mine site allege they were shot and seriously injured by the security personnel hired by the subsidiary of the controlling Canadian

---

74   The Voluntary Principles on Security and Human Rights is a set of guidelines for companies on how to conduct their security operations while respecting human rights. The Voluntary Principles Initiative, which is responsible for the development, implementation and monitoring of the Voluntary Principles, is a global, membership-based, multi-stakeholder platform established in 2000 by a group of national governments, corporate members, NGOs and a number of international organizations that serve as observers. Online: *Voluntary Principles on Security and Human Rights* <www.voluntaryprinciples.org/>.

75   *Hudbay Minerals, supra* note 63 at paras 67–70. In the motion to strike decision, there is some discussion regarding the corporate relationships among Hudbay and its subsidiaries. Skye, for example, owned the Fenix mining site during the time frame relevant to one of the actions joined together in this case, but not the others (para 43); subsequently, Skye and Hudbay amalgamated, and Hudbay assumed responsibility for Skye's liabilities. More importantly, the plaintiffs frame their case almost entirely in terms of Hudbay's *direct* liability, not its indirect liability though its subsidiaries (para 43).

76   *Ibid* at para 69 [emphasis added].

77   *Ibid* at para 68 [emphasis added].

mining company, Tahoe Resources Inc. The protestors pleaded that on the evening of the protest, which reflected strong local community opposition to the project, security personnel opened the gates to the mine and "opened fire on the protestors using weapons that included shotguns, pepper spray, buckshot and rubber bullets."[78] The protestors further pleaded that the shooting was planned, ordered and directed by Tahoe's security manager, Alberto Rotondo Dall'Orso, and that Tahoe "expressly or implicitly authorized the use of excessive force by Rotondo and other security personnel, or was negligent in failing to prevent Rotondo and other security personnel from using excessive force."[79]

In alleging that Tahoe directly controlled the conduct of Rotondo, who was employed by Tahoe's wholly owned subsidiary Minera San Rafael S.A. (MSR), a Guatemalan company, the protestors rely on Tahoe's and MSR's corporate social responsibility (CSR) initiatives, including:

- MSR's claim that, "As a demonstration of genuine commitment to the region and sensitivity to socio-economic issues in the communities in which MSR operates, numerous CSR initiatives have been implemented";[80]

- MSR's claim that "Tahoe's Board of Directors formed a Health, Safety, Environment, and Community Committee to oversee health, safety, environmental and other community issues at a high level";[81]

- Tahoe's establishment of a "CSR Steering Committee," which includes executive officers of Tahoe;[82]

- Tahoe's retention of CSR consultants to assist in complying with various business and human rights conventions;[83] and

- MSR's employment of local personnel to "build relations with the local community."[84]

Tahoe was initially successful at staying the protesters' action in the British Columbia Supreme Court on *forum non conveniens* grounds,[85] but the British Columbia Court of Appeal reversed the stay, finding that there was a real risk of an unfair process were the plaintiffs' claims to be heard in Guatemala instead of British Columbia.[86]

Under Ratner's framework, much like in the Hudbay case, the evidence suggests Tahoe brought the local community rights-holders into its associative sphere of influence through the declaration of its CSR standards and compliance commitments under international business and human rights instruments, and through its subsidiary's employment of local personnel to establish a relationship with the local community. The seriousness of the allegations of extreme

---

78   *Tahoe Resources, supra* note 64 at para 9.

79   *Ibid* at para 10.

80   *Ibid* at para 21.

81   *Ibid.*

82   *Ibid.*

83   *Ibid.*

84   *Ibid.*

85   *Ibid* at paras 1–2.

86   *Ibid* at para 126.

physical violence, and the corresponding nonderogable rights at issue, likewise point to a violation of international law by Tahoe.

Unlike the Hudbay case, however, the application of the principle of attribution appears to be somewhat less clear and more complex. This is illustrated both by the plaintiffs' alternative pleading regarding Tahoe's implicit authorization of the use of excessive force against the plaintiffs-protesters, and the fact that the security manager, Rotondo, was charged by a Guatemalan prosecutor with assault, aggravated assault and obstruction of justice, while no charges were laid against either Tahoe or its subsidiary MSR.[87] As a result, at trial it was anticipated that Tahoe would likely claim that Rotondo and those under his command were acting outside their contractual duties and beyond Tahoe's corporate control.

Ultimately, the matter did not go to trial. In early 2019, Tahoe was acquired by Pan American Silver, another Canadian mining company active abroad. Negotiations with the plaintiffs to resolve the case yielded a settlement in July 2019. In the settlement, Pan American Silver acknowledged on behalf of Tahoe that "the shooting on April 27, 2013, infringed the human rights of the protesters"; it also apologized to the victims and to the community. Financial terms of the settlement were not disclosed.[88]

In each of the three Canadian cases we have canvassed, Ratner's framework provides a highly serviceable legal scaffolding for raising aspirational international and transnational claims against corporations for their violations of human rights. His scaffolding seeks to address both the "whether" and "how" questions at the same time and in the same way, by grounding corporate duties and liabilities both in the nature of their relationships with states and affected populations, as well as in their own business decisions and practices. In our view, Ratner's framework is a sturdy one, constructed from the raw materials of international law itself. In that sense, however, it presents as a somewhat conservative foundation for what some still see as a radical objective. Moreover, it will not erect itself, suggesting that the thorniest questions are not — or at least not only — whether and how, but rather, who and where?

Conclusion

In this chapter we have sought to tackle two interwoven questions: a normative one — whether corporations should be directly liable for international human rights abuses — and a functional one — how this liability might be imposed, bearing in mind the principles and bodies of law, domestic and international, that could be harnessed to this end. It deliberately does not address the legal regimes or architecture that could plausibly host this transformation. The *Nevsun* case suggests the potential for some of these changes to occur through judicial interpretation informed by emerging government policies and academic scholarship. Of course, the enthusiasm embodied in the majority's reasons for entertaining new arguments and engaging with novel legal principles and arguments is not universally shared. In this regard, the dissenting reasons in *Nevsun* are highly instructive. The first pair of dissenters chastise the majority for selectively

---

87   *Ibid* at para 13.

88   Pan American Silver, "Pan American Silver Announces Resolution of Garcia v. Tahoe Case" (30 July 2019), online (blog): *Business & Human Rights Resource Centre* <www.business-humanrights.org/en/pan-american-silver-announces-resolution-of-garcia-v-tahoe-case>.

relying on academic sources, contending that, in their view, it is "plain and obvious" that "corporations are excluded from direct liability."[89] The second pair of dissenters likewise assert that the majority errs in concluding that "international human rights norms have horizontal application between individuals and corporations."[90]

Because of the uneven and unpredictable way norms evolve through the litigation process, other drivers for change become important. In this vein, in addition to domestic legal regimes and litigation, Ratner emphasizes the important role of other law-reform venues, including: corporate-initiated codes of conduct; NGO scrutiny; international soft law; and the establishment of a *binding* corporate code of conduct through the treaty process.[91] However, the potential of these venues to play this transformative role is and will continue to be constrained by powerful economic and political interests. As Ratner cautiously observed in 2001, "It is, of course, unexceptionable that if states are so uninterested in regulating the activities of corporate actors, they will neither create domestic regimes nor cooperate to prescribe more hard or soft international law."[92] The past two decades have more than borne out Ratner's realist outlook on the political prospects of an emergent transnational corporate law.

As Martti Koskenniemi sagely observes, demonstrating that "'it all depends on politics' does not move one inch towards a *better* politics."[93] Thus, as all good international lawyers must, Ratner dreamed of a way of circumventing the political economy obstacles to holding TNCs accountable for their violations of human rights. It is possible, he imagined, "that courts, domestic and international, that remain somewhat insulated from such economic pressures could jump-start this process through the sorts of rulings the European Court of Justice has issued regarding nondiscrimination in the private sector."[94]

This, in fact, is precisely the aspiration of the Eritrean refugees-plaintiffs' appeal to the SCC in *Nevsun*. Nor is their dream delusional. In dismissing Nevsun Resources' motion to stay the proceedings and strike out the plaintiffs' claim for failing to state a legal cause of action, the British Columbia Supreme Court concluded regarding the plaintiffs'"most serious"transnational corporate law claims that "a real issue exists, one which has a reasonable chance of success."[95] After all, as the court noted earlier in its judgment, "this is British Columbia; and it is 2016."[96] Writing for the British Columbia Court of Appeal, Madam Justice Newbury went a step further: "At the end of the day, I do not believe it can be said the plaintiffs' claims are *'bound to fail.'* We have seen that international law is 'in flux' and that transnational law, which regulates 'actions or events that transcend national frontiers' is developing, especially in connection with human rights violations that are not effectively addressed by traditional 'international mechanisms.'"[97]

---

89   *Nevsun v Araya, supra* note 11 at para 189.

90   *Ibid* at para 269.

91   Ratner, *supra* note 13 at 531–40.

92   *Ibid* at 543.

93   Martti Koskenniemi, "The Politics of International Law — 20 Years Later" (2009) 20:1 EJIL 7 at 8 [emphasis in original].

94   Ratner, *supra* note 13 at 544.

95   *Nevsun Resources Motion Decision, supra* note 65 at para 484.

96   *Ibid* at para 421.

97   *Nevsun Resources Appeal Decision, supra* note 11 at para 197 [emphasis in original].

As far as dreams are concerned, however, we are left with a nagging desire for something more. This is not in the least meant to suggest a lack of support for the claims for redress sought by victims from the Global South in Canadian courtrooms that we have analyzed above. Rather, it is to suggest that, given the sheer indeterminacy of the raw materials of international law making, seeking to impose on corporations legal obligations that are akin to those that are ostensibly and haphazardly applicable to states may be aiming *too low*. Is this really the best answer to "that interminable question: what is to be done?"[98] Recall that Ratner himself sought "to develop an approach to corporate responsibility that can be applied in numerous international fora, *not merely courts*."[99] But where, and by whom?

We do not pretend to have the answers to these questions, but neither do we despair. While it would be easy to dismiss much international law scholarship as wishful thinking, including the wish for legal and structural coherence,[100] international law's inherent fragmentation and indeterminacy also make it a perpetually incomplete project, one constantly in the making and remaking. Indeed, the SCC majority's use of international law scholarship in *Nevsun Resources* shows this to be true.

At the same time, no matter how informed by academic theory and research, litigation before the courts will not be sufficient. As we concluded the writing of this chapter, the English Court of Appeal released it decision in *Kadie Kalma & Ors v African Minerals Ltd & Ors*.[101] In its judgment, the English Court of Appeal not only confirmed that businesses operating abroad are legally entitled to avail themselves of host-state security forces, the court refused to draw on international standards of business and human rights to inform its inquiry into the existence of a legal duty of care owed by a TNC. Instead, the English Court of Appeal expressly re-inscribed the global governance gap. In refusing to ground a freestanding duty of care based on the Voluntary Principles on Security and Human Rights, the court commented that "there is nothing in the Voluntary Principles which make companies operating abroad generally liable for the unlawful acts of the police forces of the host countries in which they are operating: on the contrary, the Voluntary Principles are drafted on the basis that, whilst companies operating abroad may properly help to facilitate the law and order expected to be provided by host countries, it is the governments of those countries (*and not the companies*) who have 'the primary responsibility to protect human rights.'"[102]

The global governance gap that motivates this chapter is part and parcel of the "outcomes of international legal work," broadly conceived, involving the "projection of controversial, varied and impactive visions of the personal and the political."[103] This includes the work of law courts, but it does not end there. It also includes the work of NGOs and other civil-society actors,

---

98   Fleur Johns, *Non-Legality in International Law: Unruly Law* (Cambridge, UK: Cambridge University Press, 2013) at 222 [Johns, *Non-Legality*].

99   Ratner, *supra* note 13 at 451 [emphasis added].

100   For a critical take on this tendency of international law scholarship, see e.g. David Kennedy, *A World of Struggle: How Power, Law, and Expertise Shape Global Political Economy* (Princeton, NJ: Princeton University Press, 2016) at 253.

101   *Kadie Kalma & Ors v African Minerals Ltd & Ors*, [2020] EWCA Civ 144.

102   *Ibid* at para 151 [emphasis added].

103   Johns, *Non-Legality, supra* note 98 at 218, 220–21.

academics and, of course, law-making TNCs themselves — including their own members[104] — across multiple sites and scales of normativity. The trajectory of legal change is non-linear, unpredictable and uncertain, and will require the aspirations and actions of a plurality of change makers. The dreams of international lawyers alone will not suffice to inspire and inform international law reform.[105]

---

104 Corporations are not bounded, autonomous, rational agents, and calls for changes to corporate policies and actions can arise from their constituent members, including employees (see e.g. Amazon Employees for Climate Justice, online: *Twitter* @AMZNforClimate). For a discussion of the implications of this insight from relational legal theory, see e.g. Sara L Seck, "Relational Law and the Reimagining of Tools for Environmental and Climate Justice" (2019) 31:1 CJWL 151.

105 Howse, *supra* note 1.

2

THE CORPORATION AND MODERN CAPITALISM

Folk, Broke and Woke

Christopher C. Nicholls

Introduction

In the view of a number of modern pundits,[1] politicians,[2] professors[3] and even pontiffs,[4] it is axiomatic that modern capitalism is "broken." Evidence of this state of brokenness is said to be

---

1   See e.g. Ferris Eanfar, *Broken Capitalism: This Is How We Fix It* (Jericho, NY: AngelPay Foundation, 2017); Jonathan Carr, *Fixing Capitalism: Toward a Stable, Efficient Economy* (Xlibris Corp, 2002); "Fixing the Flaws in Today's Capitalism", *The Economist* (16 April 2018); David Leonhardt, "American Capitalism Isn't Working", *The New York Times* (2 December 2018); Joseph Stiglitz, *People, Power and Profits: Progressive Capitalism for an Age of Discontent* (New York: Norton, 2019).

2   See e.g. David Leonhardt, "Elizabeth Warren Actually Wants to Fix Capitalism", *The New York Times* (15 March 2019); Binyamin Applebaum, "Congressional Democrats Promise a 'Better Deal' for American Workers", *The New York Times* (24 July 2017) citing Senator Charles Schumer ("Old fashioned capitalism has broken down").

3   See e.g. Robert Reich, *Saving Capitalism* (New York: Vintage, 2016); Joel Bakan, *The Corporation* (Toronto: Viking, 2004); Harry Glasbeek, *Wealth by Stealth* (Toronto: Between the Lines, 2002); Paul Collier, *The Future of Capitalism* (New York: Harper, 2018); Colin Mayer, *Firm Commitment* (Oxford: Oxford University Press, 2013); Michael E Porter & Mark R Kramer, "Creating Shared Value: How to Reinvent Capitalism — and Unleash a Wave of Innovation and Growth", *Harvard Business Review* (January-February 2011) 62.

4   See Holy See Press Office, Summary of Bulletin, "'*Oeconomicae et pecuniariae quaestiones*': Considerations for an ethical discernment regarding some aspects of the present economic-financial system" (17 May 2018), online: <https://press.vatican.va/content/salastampa/en/bollettino/pubblico/2018/05/17/180517a.html>.

found in ever increasing income[5] and wealth inequality,[6] the excesses and corruption of modern business,[7] manipulation of the political system through questionable campaign finance practices and aggressive, generously funded lobbying, the unfair exploitation of vulnerable workers and vulnerable communities, and the degradation of the natural environment and exacerbation of climate change. Grand reworkings of the existing system — through the pursuit of "inclusive capitalism,"[8] "millennial socialism"[9] or some optimal, if elusive, "third way"[10] or "third pillar"[11] — have been proposed as necessary transformations (or perhaps welcome evolutionary developments) to address the "obvious" failures of the existing system.

One institution that has come under especially heavy fire from such critics is the business corporation. This quintessential capitalist entity has been accused of engaging in a relentless and often unscrupulous pursuit of profit at the expense of the community as a whole. Nor is the problem thought to be reducible to a matter of corrupt (but potentially replaceable) corporate leadership. It is the very design of the business corporation that is said to make it incorrigible.[12] The business corporation has thus been variously described as parasitic,[13] a "vampire squid,"[14] a "Frankenstein's monster,"[15] a "psychopathic creature"[16] and the "cancerous spine of the economy."[17]

Whether there is, in fact, objective evidence of meaningful decline or dysfunction in modern market-based economies is, needless to say, a matter of debate. A contrarian might speculate that the perception of at least some of the "problems" associated with modern capitalism or the modern business corporation could be the result of the cognitive bias David Levari et al. have

---

5   Recent reports, for example, have revealed especially significant disparities between the compensation levels of some senior executives of large publicly traded corporations and the average salaries of employees at those same organizations. See e.g. Anders Melin, Jenn Zhao & Jason Perry, "Tesla CEO's Pay Ratio Hits Stratosphere with $2.28 Billion Grant", *Bloomberg* (18 April 2019), online: <www.bloomberg.com/graphics/ceo-pay-ratio/#TSLA>. On the general topic of excessive senior executive compensation, see Lucian Bebchuk & Jesse Fried, *Pay Without Performance: The Unfulfilled Promise of Executive Compensation* (Cambridge, MA: Harvard University Press, 2004).

6   See generally Thomas Piketty, *Capital in the Twenty-First Century* (Cambridge, MA: Belknap Press, 2014).

7   See e.g. "The New Age of Corporate Scandals", *The Economist* (6 April 2019) at 51.

8   The term "inclusive capitalism" is particularly associated with the Embankment Project for Inclusive Capitalism. See the Embankment Project for Inclusive Capitalism Report, online: <www.ey.com/Publication/vwLUAssets/ey-at-embankment-project-inclusive-capitalism/$FILE/EY-the-embankment-project-for-inclusive-capitalism-report.pdf>.

9   See e.g. Kristian Niemietz, "Millenial Socialism: Same old, Same old" (2019) 39 Economic Affairs 424.

10   See e.g. Sally Wheeler, *Corporations and the Third Way* (Oxford: Hart, 2002); Cynthia A Williams & John P Conley, "An Emerging Third Way — The Erosion of the Anglo-American Shareholder-Value Construct" (2005) 38 Cornell Intl LJ 493; Ronald J Gilson, "Leo Strine's Third Way: Responding to Agency Capitalism" (2007) 33 J Corp L 47; Kent Greenfield, "The Third Way" (2014) 37 Seattle L Rev 749 [Greenfield, "Third Way"].

11   See Raghuram Rajan, *The Third Pillar: How Markets and the State Leave the Community Behind* (New York: Penguin, 2019).

12   As Noam Chomsky put it, for example, about those who participate in corporations, speaking in an interview featured in the film version of Joel Bakan's *The Corporation*, "In their institutional role, they're monstrous because the institution is monstrous."

13   Robert Creamer, "Time to Just Say No to Giant Corporate 'Parasites' — and Recognize Them for What They Are" *Huffington Post* (18 November 2009; updated 25 May 2011).

14   Collier, *supra* note 3 at 70. The use of the vampire squid as a metaphor for the modern mega corporation was first used in 2009 in reference to Goldman Sachs in Matt Taibbi, "The Great American Bubble Machine", *Rolling Stone* 1082/1083 (9–23 July 2009) 52.

15   See e.g. Jill E Fisch, "Frankenstein's Monster Hits the Campaign Trail: An Approach to Regulation of Corporate Political Expenditures" (1991) 32 Wm & Mary L Rev 587; Ed Finn, "The Corporate Frankenstein Monster: Plundering, Pillaging, and Polluting the Planet for a Profit", Canadian Centre for Policy Alternatives (1 April 2013); *Louis K Ligget Co et al v Lee, Comptroller et al*, 288 US 517 (1933) 548, 567.

16   Bakan, *supra* note 3 at 60.

17   Glasbeek, *supra* note 3 at 37.

identified as "prevalence-induced concept change in human judgment,"[18] that is, the tendency to mistakenly regard social problems as intractable and growing, paradoxically, because of the actual reduction in prevalence of those very problems, which causes people to take greater notice of the fewer such problems that actually remain.[19] However, this chapter does not engage in the complex debate over the net social costs or benefits of the modern capitalist system. It deals with a much narrower issue: namely, the extent to which the pro-social business corporation has reliable historical precedents. One proposed remedy to the presumed anti-social operation of the modern business corporation is to repurpose the corporation to pursue explicit "socially responsible" objectives. Key advocates of this position frequently seek to reassure skeptics that there is no material risk that such a change could lead to widespread and unpredictable economic harm because the socially responsible corporation was, in fact, the historical norm and actually prevailed during times of significant economic prosperity. This view of corporate history, however, is highly contestable, and proposals to dramatically shift the wealth-increasing goal of the business corporation should, therefore, be scrutinized with considerable wariness.

The Corporate New Deal

Some critics of the business corporation evidently view their fight against corporations merely as the first step in a broader campaign aimed at disrupting the entire free enterprise system.[20] Others, though, insist that they are, in fact, loyal stewards of capitalism who are only trying to purify the system's soul by driving out corrupting impurities[21] and restoring it to its original intended purpose. That purpose, they claim, was more properly understood in an earlier era, when corporations and the people who managed them appreciated the debt they owed to the government and to the society that granted them a "social licence" that made their very existence possible, and so followed a balanced mandate. Such corporations pursued "reasonable" profits,[22] to be sure, but never at the expense of dutiful consideration for the interests of the corporation's varied non-shareholder constituents, including employees, creditors, customers, suppliers, the natural environment, the local community, government and so on. Proponents of this latter view,

---

18 David E Levari et al, "Prevalence-induced Concept Change in Human Judgment" (2018) 360 Science 1465.

19 One of the specific examples given by Levari et al. relates to perceptions of global poverty. Although the percentage of the human population living in poverty has decreased monumentally over the past 200 years, with particularly dramatic reductions since the late twentieth century, many people mistakenly believe it is getting worse. Levari et al. cite Max Roser, "The short history of global living conditions and why it matters that we know it" (online: Our World in Data <ourworldindata.org>), which indicates that in 1820, more than 89 percent of the world's population lived in extreme poverty. By 1950, that number had fallen to 36.65 percent and continued to fall for the next 65 years, such that by 2015, less than 10 percent of the world's population lived in extreme poverty.

20 See e.g. Glasbeek, *supra* note 3 at 283; Lorri Nandrea, "Why Fixing Capitalism is Not Enough", Communist Party of USA (16 January 2019); Peter Coy et al, "Seven Fixes for American Capitalism", *Bloomberg Businessweek* (7 February 2019); Naomi Klein, *This Changes Everything: Capitalism vs. the Climate* (Toronto: Penguin Random House, 2014).

21 See e.g. Elizabeth Warren's unequivocal declaration, "I am a capitalist to my bones." Ted Rall, "The Left is Lukewarm on Elizabeth Warren", *The Wall Street Journal* (6 November 2018). See also Kent Greenfield, "Defending Stakeholder Governance" (2008) 58 Case W Res L Rev 1043 ("none of the scholars who are thoughtfully and carefully presenting arguments in favor of stakeholder governance attack capitalism at all" at 1052).

22 "Reasonable" profits, as Adolf Berle wryly noted some 60 years ago, are the "twentieth-century lawyer's parallel to canon-law thinking of the Middle Ages, when ethical considerations — notably that of a 'just price' — were the imperatives." See Adolf Berle, "Foreword" in Edward S Mason, *The Corporation in Modern Society* (Cambridge, MA: Harvard University Press, 1959) [Mason, *The Corporation in Modern Society*] ix at xii. See also Raymond de Roover, "The Concept of the Just Price: Theory and Economic Policy" (1958) 18 J Economic History 41. See also Hayek's related discussion of "reasonable wages," a concept that he also links to the "futile medieval search for the just price and the just wage." Friedrich A Hayek, *Law, Legislation and Liberty, Volume 2: The Mirage of Social Justice* (Chicago: University of Chicago Press, 1976) at 75.

therefore, include advocates of a view of the business corporation, and thus of corporate law, that is consistent with the explicitly pro-social approach championed by promoters of corporate social responsibility and environmental, social and governance standards,[23] including leaders of the B Corporation[24] and, more recently, the benefit corporation or public benefit corporation[25] initiatives or their British community interest company[26] cousins.

The embrace by corporations of broader social concerns seems to signal civilized enlightenment and modernity. In August 2019, the Business Roundtable (an association of chief executive officers [CEOs] of major US corporations), with much fanfare and self-congratulation, issued its new "Statement on the Purpose of a Corporation."[27] Signatories to this statement trumpeted their new-found commitment "to deliver value" to all of their stakeholders, "for the future success of our companies, our communities and our country." The statement itself was constructively ambiguous. It was the press release accompanying the statement that really drew the headlines. That release clearly signalled that members of the Business Roundtable, which had embraced "principles of shareholder primacy" since 1997, had turned over a new leaf.[28] They had come over from the dark side, it seems, and joined the modern people-before-profit camp of enlightenment. This corporate epiphany has been viewed by some as part of a wave of "new capitalism" that has been embraced as contemporary orthodoxy.[29] (The uncomfortable fact, of course, as Stephen Bainbridge was quick to point out in a wry tweet to the Business Roundtable, is that the Business Roundtable simply has no authority to "redefine the purpose of the corporation": "Only the Delaware courts can change the law of corporate purpose. And, as you ought to know, Delaware comes down square on the side of shareholder wealth maximization."[30]) Nor is it clear, as a recent *Wall Street Journal* op-ed by two business academics

---

23. See e.g. Global Reporting Initiative Standards, online: <www.globalreporting.org/standards/gri-standards-download-center>; Principles for Responsible Investing Initiative, online: <www.unpri.org/>.

24. B Corporation, online: <bcorporation.net/>; Sustainability Accounting Standards Board, online: <www.sasb.org/why-sasb/>.

25. See William H Clark et al, White Paper, *The Need and Rationale for the Benefit Corporation* (2013), online: <benefitcorp.net/sites/default/files/Benefit_Corporation_White_Paper.pdf>.

26. See Regulator of Community Interest Companies, *Annual Report 2017–18*.

27. Business Roundtable, "Statement on the Purpose of a Corporation", online: <https://opportunity.businessroundtable.org/ourcommitment/>.

28. Business Roundtable, Press Release, "Business Roundtable Redefines the Purpose of a Corporation to Promote 'An Economy That Serves All Americans'" (19 August 2019), online: <www.businessroundtable.org/business-roundtable-redefines-the-purpose-of-a-corporation-to-promote-an-economy-that-serves-all-americans>.

29. See e.g. "The Next Business Revolution", *The Economist* (2 November 2019) at 55; Marc Benioff, "We Need a New Capitalism", *The New York Times* (14 October 2019) ("Capitalism, as we know it, is dead"); World Economic Forum, "Davos Manifesto 2020: The Universal Purpose of a Company in the Fourth Industrial Revolution", online: <www.weforum.org/agenda/2019/12/davos-manifesto-2020-the-universal-purpose-of-a-company-in-the-fourth-industrial-revolution>; British Academy, "Principles of Purposeful Business", online: <www.ggs.uk.com/british-academy-principles-for-purposeful-business/>.

30. Stephen Bainbridge, "A tweet to the Business Roundtable re the law of corporate purpose" (19 August 2019), online: <www.professorbainbridge.com/professorbainbridgecom/2019/08/a-tweet-to-the-business-roundtable-re-the-law-of-corporate-purpose.html>.

has suggested, that the signatories of the Business Roundtable's virtuous manifesto necessarily represent beacons of modern corporate enlightenment.[31]

The Idealized Past

Criticism of large public corporations and proposals for a more benign explicitly pro-social enterprise alternative embody strong normative claims. But they also manifest a particular version of corporate history. That view suggests that the pro-social business corporation was once the accepted norm, and that such corporations operated successfully during a period of strong economic growth and prosperity. This version of history is important to the agenda of corporate reformers to the extent that it may calm fears that abandoning corporations' pro-shareholder focus could seriously endanger the prosperity of nations in which the corporation is the dominant form of business organization. If pro-social corporations were the historical norm until disrupted by a relatively recent aberrational neo-liberal shift, then we need neither fear such a return to the norm nor unfairly stigmatize its champions as stealth socialists.[32] This short chapter will not debate the competing merits of the pro-shareholder and explicitly pro-social models of the corporation. The focus will be, rather, on the narrow, contestable and frequently advanced claim that the pro-social corporation was the historical norm while the pro-shareholder corporation is merely a recent development reflecting a late-twentieth-century ideological shift.

US Senator Elizabeth Warren, for example, in a 2018 *Wall Street Journal* op-ed that accompanied the introduction of her bill, "The Accountable Capitalism Act," asserted, "For much of U.S. history…[c]orporations sought to succeed in the marketplace, but they also recognized their obligations to employees, customers and the community.…Late in the 20th century, the dynamic changed. Building on work by conservative economist Milton Friedman, *a new theory emerged* that corporate directors had only one obligation: to maximize shareholder returns."[33]

Cornell University professor the late Lynn Stout, one of the most vociferous opponents of the corporate shareholder primacy norm, offered a similar view of corporate law history:

> For the next half-century [following the 1932 publication of Adolf Berle and Gardiner Means's *The Modern Corporation and Private Property*], boards and executives of public corporations embraced a philosophy that has been called "managerial capitalism"

31　See Aneesh Raghunandan & Shiva Rajgopal, "Is There Real Virtue Behind the Business Roundtable's Signaling?", *The Wall Street Journal* (3 December 2019) A15. Raghunandan and Rajgopal revealed that the firms that were signatories to the August 2019 Business Roundtable statement reported a higher incidence of federal violations than non-signatory firms, bought back a larger proportion of their shares than non-signatory firms (thus engaging in a practice that has been particularly condemned by progressive critics of corporations), amassed larger market shares than non-signatory firms, and had weaker association between CEO compensation and firm performance than non-signatory firms. The authors, accordingly, conclude: "These findings suggest that Business Roundtable signatories aren't leaders in socially conscious environmental, social or governance practices or stakeholder orientation. Instead, the average signatory is more likely to enjoy a large market share, and has an incentive to pre-empt regulatory scrutiny that might expose rent-seeking behavior."

32　For example, the allegation that advocates of corporate social responsibility are, deliberately or inadvertently, promulgating socialism was made explicitly by Milton Friedman in "The Social Responsibility of Business is to Increase its Profits", *The New York Times Magazine* (13 September 1970) 32. More recently, *The Wall Street Journal*, in an editorial criticizing the Business Roundtable's August 2019 statement, suggested the statement was intended — but would fail — to stave off the rise of the "socialist left." See "The Stakeholder CEOs", *The Wall Street Journal* (20 August 2019) A14.

33　Elizabeth Warren, "Companies Shouldn't be Accountable Only to Shareholders", *The Wall Street Journal* (14 August 2018) [emphasis added].

or "managerialism." Rather than seeing themselves as mere agents of shareholders, corporate directors and professional executives — who usually worked for fixed fees and owned relatively little stock in the company — viewed themselves as stewards or trustees charged with guiding a vital social and economic institution in the interests of a wide range of beneficiaries. Certainly they looked out for investors' interests, but they looked out for the interests of employees, customers, and the nation as well.... In the decades following the publication of Jensen and Meckling's article ["Theory of the Firm: Managerial Behavior, Agency Costs and Ownership Structure"], managerial capitalism fell into academic disrepute. It was replaced by *a new business theory*: the theory of "shareholder primacy."[34]

Or, as Stout stated succinctly elsewhere, "Fifty years ago, if had you asked a director or executive what the purpose of the corporation was, he was likely to answer that the firm had many purposes: to produce satisfactory returns for investors, but also to provide good jobs to employees, make reliable products for consumers, and to be a good corporate citizen."[35]

Harwell Wells, similarly, has chronicled the rise of what he dubs "heroic" managerialism in the 1950s, an approach he associates with a view held by a "surprisingly wide swathe of individuals" at that time, who "saw the corporation as having developed into a 'social institution,' run by managers who had taken on responsibility to (at minimum) employees, consumers and shareholders, or (at maximum) all of society."[36] Wells explains that this "old" view gave way to the "new" law and economics approach in the 1970s and 1980s (although, he notes, "this transition from the old corporate law to the new"[37] may have been heralded by the work of Henry Manne in 1962).[38] Kent Greenfield has likewise asserted that, "Historically, the corporation was a public institution with public purposes; shareholder primacy is a *historically recent phenomenon*."[39] Or, as Greenfield has written elsewhere, "Even though corporate law once served as a mechanism for injecting some aspects of public interest into the corporation's structure and goals, *in recent decades* the focus of corporate law has narrowed to a fixation on shareholder rights and executive prerogatives."[40] In a 2018 article by Leonardo Davoudi, Christopher McKenna and Rowena Olegario, completed as part of the British Academy's Future of the Corporation program, the authors referred to the "period between 1950 and 1980," as "the heyday of worker-oriented, industrial paternalism."[41] All this changed by the 1990s, they say, when, quoting Archie Carroll et al., "the social contract between

---

34   Lynn A Stout, "On the Rise of Shareholder Primacy, Signs of its Fall, and the Return of Managerialism (in the Closet)" (2013) 36 Seattle UL Rev 1169 at 1171, citing Adolf A Berle & Gardiner C Means, *The Modern Corporation and Private Property*, with introduction by M Weidenbaum & Mark Jensen (New Brunswick, NJ: Transaction, 2005) [1932]; *ibid* at 1173 [emphasis added], citing Michael Jensen & William Meckling, "Theory of the Firm: Managerial Behavior, Agency Costs and Ownership Structure" (1976) 3 J Financial Economics 305.

35   Lynn Stout, "The Problem of Corporate Purpose" (2012) 48 Brookings Institution Issues in Governance Studies 1.

36   Harwell Wells, "'Corporation Law is Dead': Heroic Managerialism, Legal Change, and the Puzzle of Corporation Law at the Height of the American Century" (2013) 15 U Pa L Rev 305 at 331. Wells acknowledges that "there is also little evidence to support a claim that managers of large public corporations in the 1950s actually governed their firms for the benefit of multiple constituencies or cared less about profits than their predecessors or successors (they might have been complacent about them, but that is a different matter)." *Ibid* at 330. See also *ibid* at 330, n 112.

37   *Ibid* at 354.

38   See Henry Manne, "The Higher Criticism of the Modern Corporation" (1962) 62 Colum L Rev 399.

39   Kent Greenfield, "New Principles for Corporate Law" (2005) 1 Hastings Business LJ 87 at 88 [emphasis added].

40   Kent Greenfield, "Proposition: Saving the World with Corporate Law" (2008) 57 Emory LJ 948 at 948 [emphasis added].

41   Leonardo Davoudi, Christopher McKenna & Rowena Olegario, "The Historical Role of the Corporation in Society" (2018) 6:1 J British Academy 17 at 37.

America and the 'good corporation' was disappearing....The corporation's economic performance is no longer measured in jobs created but in financial wealth generated for shareholders."[42]

The narrative reflected in these passages, and others like them, is that the view of the role and purpose of the large publicly traded corporation underwent a significant shift at some point in the late twentieth century. The "old" (pre-1970s or perhaps 1980s) view was that of the community-minded managerial corporation. Then, following the ascendance of the neo-classical law-and-economics approach to corporate law, corporations apparently "broke bad." The "new" view of the corporation, which emerged in the 1970s (or perhaps 1980s),[43] was the single-minded law-and-economics shareholder primacy view. This new shareholder primacy view was regarded by many law and economics scholars as a sensible and even inevitable development; maximizing shareholder wealth, from this perspective, is seen not as contrary to serving societal interests, but rather as the specific means by which business corporations serve such interests. To understand how an apparently morally ambiguous sub-goal is actually essential to a beneficial social outcome, one might consider how criminal lawyers' single-minded vigorous defence of, or "resolute advocacy" for, their clients — regardless of such lawyers' personal views about the likely moral innocence of those clients — is the crucial means by which society's interest in criminal justice is pursued as it operates within the broader criminal justice system. We do not expect — or indeed allow — defence lawyers to "do the right thing" for society and ensure that their guilty clients are convicted. We require them, instead, to perform a narrow, specialized role, limited to advocating honestly, but vigorously, on behalf of their client. As other participants in the system also faithfully perform their specific roles, the interests of society are advanced. If the defence lawyer were, instead, to forego the "fixation" or "obsession" on advocacy in favour of carefully balancing the client's interests with a presumed explicitly "socially responsible" objective that could involve betraying his client to ensure conviction of those believed by the lawyer to be guilty, society would be seriously harmed.

So, too, it is argued that the shareholder wealth maximization norm, properly understood, is more socially responsible than the explicit pursuit by corporations of ostensibly pro-social goals. Where corporations must compete for capital, shareholder wealth maximization may be the only corporate goal that may be expected to succeed in the long run.[44] Nor, on this view, is this corporate objective, properly understood, likely to lead to a distortive or "myopic" focus on short-term gains at the expense of the long term, as critics frequently claim.[45] A corporation's current stock price

---

42   *Ibid* at 37, citing AB Carroll et al, *Corporate Responsibility: The American Experience* (Cambridge, UK: Cambridge University Press, 2012).

43   Some of the more prominent documents that may have contributed to the shift include: Friedman (*supra* note 32); Lewis F Powell, "Confidential Memorandum" to the Chairman of the Education Committee of the US Chamber of Commerce (23 August 1971) ["Powell Memorandum"]; Jensen & Meckling, *supra* note 34.

44   See e.g. Henry Hansmann & Reinier Kraakman, "The End of History for Corporate Law" (2001) 89 Geo LJ 439 [Hansmann & Kraakman, "End of History"].

45   There is no shortage of examples of critics who assail the "short-termism" of the modern corporation. See e.g. Dominic Barton, Jonathan Bailley & Joshua Zoffer, "Rising to the challenge of short-termism", FCLT Global, online: <www.fcltglobal.org/docs/default-source/default-document-library/fclt-global-rising-to-the-challenge.pdf>; Rebecca Carr & Tim Koller, "How to Build an Alliance Against Corporate Short-Termism", FCLT Global, online: <www.fcltglobal.org/docs/default-source/default-document-library/fclt-global-rising-to-the-challenge.pdf>; Martin Lipton, "The Threat to the American Economy and Society from Activism and Short-Termism", Wachtell, Lipton, Rosen & Katz, online: <https://corpgov.law.harvard.edu/2015/01/27/the-threat-to-the-economy-and-society-from-activism-and-short-termism-updated/>; Aspen Institute, *Overcoming Short-Termism: A Call for a More Responsible Approach to Investment and Business Management* (15 December 2009), online: <https://assets.aspeninstitute.org/content/uploads/files/content/images/BSPonlineBroch.pdf>; Lynne L Dallas, "Short-Termism, the Financial Crisis and Corporate Governance" (2012) 37 J Corp L 265; Kent Greenfield, "The Puzzle of Short-Termism" (2011) 46 Wake Forest L Rev 62.

is, by definition, a price that impounds the market's assessment of future earnings. Maximizing shareholder wealth, as reflected in the current market price for the corporation's shares, therefore ensures that all shareholders — irrespective of individual investment horizons — have a community of interest.[46] That wayward corporations are capable of engaging in egregious anti-social behaviour (as are wayward human beings) is not denied by advocates of shareholder primacy. However, it is argued that constraining such objectionable behaviour is better achieved by legislation or regulation than by reliance on vague and unenforceable norms of ethical managerial behaviour.[47]

Progressive scholars and activists nevertheless bemoan the presumed post-1970s shift in corporate teleology traced by Warren, Stout and others. They long, instead, for a legal embrace of the pro-stakeholder corporation, a conception of the corporation that is thought to appeal to a self-evident sense of fairness, compassion and decency, and which is occasionally bolstered by portrayals of an idealized past. Such proposals variously involve either a return to some form of idealized managerialism or the supposed innovation of enforcing mandatory pro-stakeholder or public benefit norms, rather than relying upon managerial munificence[48] — while resisting, often with sneering contempt, the regular resurgence of shareholder primacy apologists.[49] Importantly, an explicitly pro-social vision of the corporation, advocates of such proposals contend, need not be feared as a radical distortion of a capitalist institution, but should rather be welcomed as a sensible and humane reinvigoration of principles that have, it is argued, a much longer and more thoroughly proven pedigree than the recent upstart shareholder primacy doctrine.

While a relatively simple and linear "corporate fall from grace" narrative has many illuminating features, it suffers from at least three shortcomings. First, it understates the significance of the continuing, vigorous "classical"[50]/managerial dialectic that prevailed throughout much of the twentieth century, including during the very period in which managerialism is said to have prevailed. Second, it is difficult to reconcile with the fact that the emergence in the financial economic literature of the shareholder wealth maximization norm (in lieu of the profit-

---

46   See e.g. Robert C Clark, *Corporate Law* (Aspen, CO: Aspen Law and Business, 1986) at 18, n 46. For a detailed critique of the short-termism perspective, see Mark J Roe, "Stock Market Short-Termism: Impact" (2018) 167 U Pa L Rev 71. Reconciling the interests of "short-term" versus "long-term" investors is one of the key advantages of defining the corporate goal in terms of maximizing current shareholder wealth, rather than the largely undefinable goal of maximizing profits. See Franco Modigliani & Merton H Miller, "The Cost of Capital, Corporation Finance and the Theory of Investment" (1958) 48:3 Am Economic Rev 261; Gerard Debreu, *Theory of Value: An Axiomatic Analysis of Economic Equilibrium* (New Haven, CT: Yale University Press, 1959); Stephen A Ross, Randolph W Westerfield & Bradford D Jordan, *Essentials of Corporate Finance*, 7th ed (New York: McGraw-Hill/Irwin, 2011) at 10.

47   See e.g. Stephen M Bainbridge, "In Defence of the Shareholder Wealth Maximization Norm: A Reply to Professor Green" (1993) 50 Wash & Lee L Rev 1423. Critics note, however, that large corporations play an important role in the process of creating the very laws to which they are subject. See e.g. Christopher Stone, *Where the Law Ends* (New York: Harper & Row, 1975) 94ff. Nevertheless, as Nobel Prize-winning economist Jean Tirole has noted, the fact that laws may, for such reasons, be suboptimal does not support the argument for an increased role for corporate managerial discretion to pursue broader goals beyond shareholder value maximization since "nothing guarantees that [managers] will better reflect the 'collective will' than the courts or legislators." Jean Tirole, *The Theory of Corporate Finance* (Princeton, NJ: Princeton University Press, 2006) at 61.

48   See e.g. Greenfield, "Third Way", *supra* note 10 at 751. See also Warren's proposed *Accountable Capitalism Act*, which would require that all "large entities" (essentially firms engaged in interstate commerce with more than US$1 billion in gross receipts) obtain a federal charter that must include the purpose of "creating a general public benefit." US, Bill S 3348, *Accountable Capitalism Act*, 115th Cong, 2018, s 5(b)(2), online: <www.congress.gov/bill/115th-congress/senate-bill/3348/text>.

49   Perhaps the most influential and provocative reiteration of the logic of the pro-shareholder corporate mandate was Hansmann and Kraakman's "The End of History for Corporate Law" (*supra* note 44).

50   The word "classical" here is used in the sense of "the model of a decentralized, private, competitive capitalism, in which the forces of supply and demand, operating through the price mechanism, regulate the economy in detail and in aggregate." Francis X Sutton et al, *The American Business Creed* (New York: Schocken, 1962) at 33.

maximization assumption that had characterized earlier economic models of the business firm) occurred in the 1950s — that is, during the very era during which it is said that many or most corporations were *not* pursuing a shareholder-focused mission. Finally, at least in the Canadian context, the characterization of the managerial view as the old (pre-1970s) vision of the corporation and the shareholder primacy model as the new model does not seem to accord with many informed commentators' understanding and experience of the development of Canadian corporate law.

Corporate Folklore

Contextualizing corporations within an ideological, historical narrative is nothing new. In 1937, Thurman Arnold wrote *The Folklore of Capitalism*,[51] recounting how the business corporation had been persistently identified as an individual in an attempt to reconcile philosophically the inherent contradictions offered by the powerful role played by a group (or collective) enterprise in a system founded on principles of "rugged individualism."[52] Since then, economic and popular views of the business corporation have evolved. In the current era, the corporation's powerful economic and social roles are prompting demands for renewed theoretical justifications. Our understanding of the public corporation appears to involve a move from the folklore view that Arnold depicted to what might glibly be termed a modern "woke lore." This shift invokes, in part, an idealized but selective view of the managerial corporation of the 1950s and 1960s. That view may offer many psychic benefits to ease the cognitive dissonance of public-spirited beneficiaries of corporate largesse, but could ultimately prove problematic for the corporate wealth-generation function upon which much of the world has come to depend.

Managerialism

The concept of corporate managerialism is used in two closely related senses. The term is used, first, to refer to the emergence of a distinct managerial class characterized by professional corporate managers who were neither entrepreneurs nor significant shareholders of the corporations they came to lead. In this primary sense, managerialism describes an inevitable aspect of the phenomenon of the separation of ownership from control in the large public corporation. This separation of ownership from control was identified early in the twentieth century by Thorstein Veblen[53] and others, and famously documented by Berle and Means in their iconic work, *The Modern Corporation and Private Property*.[54] By the middle of the twentieth century, this separation had become institutionalized, with the rise of what Alfred Chandler identified as the function of "administrative coordination and allocation and the coming of a new subspecies of economic man — the salaried manager — to carry out this function."[55]

---

51   Thurman W Arnold, *The Folklore of Capitalism* (New Haven, CT: Yale University Press, 1937). Other modern law scholars have drawn on Arnold's trenchant and witty work to illuminate the study of contemporary law. See especially Marcel Kahan & Edward B Rock, "Symbolic Corporate Governance Politics" (2014) 94 BUL Rev 1998.

52   *Ibid* at 190.

53   Thorstein Veblen, *The Theory of Business Enterprise* (New York: Scribner, 1904) at 86.

54   Berle & Means, *supra* note 34.

55   Alfred D Chandler Jr, *The Visible Hand: The Managerial Revolution in American Business* (Cambridge, MA: Belknap Press, 1977) at 484.

The term "managerialism" is also used, in a secondary sense, to refer to certain defining institutional characteristics said to have accompanied the emergence of managerialism in the primary sense referred to above. Once it is observed that managers of large corporations are neither entrepreneurs nor major shareholders, then, as Berle and Means observed, neither the "traditional logic of property"[56] nor the "traditional logic of profits"[57] apply to ensure that managerial incentives align with those of the holders of the residual economic interest in the corporation. Thus, the issue that economic theory had to confront many years before the mid-century rise of managerialist rhetoric was the ascendance of a group of people — corporate managers — whose power did not arise from their ownership or entrepreneurial ability, but from the offices they held atop gigantic organizations. These corporate barons exercised significant economic power; some account of the legitimacy of that power was needed. An eponymous corporate titan such as Henry Ford might become personally wealthy and economically powerful owing to his entrepreneurialism and innovation. But the stature of a CEO who had built nothing, invented nothing, invested (almost) nothing — and who may have owed his position principally to his adroit manipulation of the "tournament"[58] of corporate promotion — posed a potential threat to the integrity of the free enterprise claims upon which the status of the large business corporation depended. In short, how could one justify wielding enormous economic power in the interests of pursuing profit when one had not created the business generating the profit? The free enterprise system should undoubtedly reward creators and builders, but why should it tolerate economic despotism from the hired help?

Accordingly, an alternative theory was required. Managerialism in this second sense seeks to provide such a theoretical underpinning for the operation of the large modern corporation in which the incentives of the managerial class are difficult to frame in traditional economic terms. The origin of managerial theory is curious. Today, Berle and Means' famous explication of the implications of the separation of ownership and control is often regarded as an important intellectual harbinger of modern agency theory,[59] premised on inevitable conflict between the interests of "owners" and managers. However, as many commentators have noted, Berle and Means' assessment of the consequences of the ownership/control divide was complex and more sanguine than that of many later theorists. They recognized the "control"/shareholder disconnect that would later be identified as the principal source of agency costs.[60] For Berle and Means, however, the separation of ownership and control did not simply represent a worrisome opportunity for greedy corporate managers to feather their own nests. It could, at least in some circumstances, foster the development of public-spirited corporations no longer fettered by the narrow-minded constraints of their shareholders. As passive investors — or mere "*rentiers*" — shareholders could not (or should not) expect the corporation to be run primarily for their benefit.[61] Consider Berle and Means' admonition that "it seems almost essential if the corporate

---

56   Berle & Means, *supra* note 34 at 293ff.

57   *Ibid* at 299ff.

58· See e.g. Edwin P Lazear & Sherwin Rosen, "Rank-Order Tournaments and Optimum Labor Contracts" (1981) 89 J Political Economy 841; Brian L Connelly, Laszlo Tihanyi, T Russell Crook & K Ashley Gangloff, "Tournament Theory: Thirty Years of Contests and Competitions" (2014) 40 J Management 16.

59   See e.g. Weidenbaum & Jensen, "Introduction" in Berle & Means, *supra* note 34 at ix.

60   Other agency problems within the corporation have also been identified. See e.g. John Armour, Henry Hansmann & Reinier Kraakman, "Agency Problems and Legal Structure" in Reinier Kraakman et al, *The Anatomy of Corporate Law*, 2nd ed (Oxford: Oxford University Press, 2009) 35.

61   See e.g. Berle & Means, *supra* note 34 at 311–12.

system is to survive — that the 'control' of the great corporations should develop into a purely neutral technocracy, balancing a variety of claims by various groups in the community and assigning to each a portion of the income stream on the basis of public policy rather than private cupidity."[62] This observation seems to invoke the model of the public-serving corporation (or "managerial paternalism"[63]) that has been said to characterize the golden era corporations. But this was an aspirational statement, not a description of the world as Berle and Means found it.[64] Still, the prospect of divining a theory to support a community-focused managerial credo seemed to offer a way of defusing the threat posed by the spectre of rapidly increasing managerial power.

But would it be possible to fashion a theory as coherent and convincing as the traditional "classical" framework based upon the "endocratic"[65] managerial corporation, "the soulful corporation,"[66] the "well-tempered corporation,"[67] the "metro corporation"[68] or perhaps the corporation viewed as "conscience-carrier of twentieth century American society"?[69] *The Economic Theory of 'Managerial' Capitalism*, by Robin Marris,[70] represents a significant contribution to this literature. But throughout the 1950s and 1960s there were a number of other attempts,[71] scholarly and popular, to articulate a socially defensible theory of the for-profit managerial corporation that was not riddled with inherent contradictions and that could address the sort of unsatisfactory characterization of the animating corporate principle that Merrick Dodd had derided in 1935 as an improbable reliance upon "vicarious acquisitiveness."[72]

Many of these efforts reflect a common theme. Managerialism was said to imply both an inescapable consequence of corporate growth and a philosophy of corporate governance: at the descriptive level, decision making in large industrial corporations had effectively devolved to managers who, as a practical matter, were not subject to any effective accountability to shareholders; such self-perpetuating and largely insulated corporate managers purportedly understood their governance role to involve the balancing or mediating of the interests of various corporate stakeholders, of which shareholders were only one. It is this sense of managerialism that Hansmann and Kraakman described as "the managerial paternalism popular in the 1950s."[73] And it is this paternalistic version of managerialism that has been invoked

---

62   *Ibid* at 312–13.

63   Henry Hansmann & Reinier Kraakman, "Reflections on the End of History for Corporate Law" in AA Rasheed et al, eds, *The Convergence of Corporate Governance* (London, UK: Palgrave Macmillan, 2012) 32.

64   There were precursors to the archetypal public-spirited mid-century managerial corporation in the early years of the twentieth century, including, notably, the General Electric Company under the leadership of Owen D. Young. See Adolf A Berle, *Studies in the Law of Corporation Finance* (Chicago: Callaghan & Company, 1928) at 1; E Merrick Dodd, "For Whom Are Corporate Managers Trustees?" (1932) 45:7 Harv L Rev 1145 at 1154; Adolf Berle, "For Whom Corporate Managers *Are* Trustees: A Note" (1932) 45 Harv L Rev 1365 at 1372; Ida M Tarbell, *Owen D. Young: A New Type of Industrial Leader* (New York: Macmillan, 1932).

65   Eugene V Rostow, "To Whom and for What Ends Is Corporate Management Responsible?" in Mason, *The Corporation in Modern Society, supra* note 22 at 46.

66   Carl Kaysen, "The Social Significance of the Modern Corporation" (1957) 47 American Economic Rev 311 at 314.

67   Richard Eels, *The Meaning of Modern Business: An Introduction to the Philosophy of Large Corporate Enterprise* (New York: Columbia University Press, 1960).

68   *Ibid.*

69   B Lewis, "Economics by Admonition" (1959) 49 American Economic Rev 384.

70   Robin Marris, *The Economic Theory of 'Managerial' Capitalism* (London, UK: Macmillan, 1967) [1964].

71   See generally text accompanying notes 79 to 88 below.

72   E Merrick Dodd, "Is Effective Enforcement of the Fiduciary Duties of Corporate Managers Practicable?" (1935) 2 U Chicago L Rev 194 at 195, 200.

73   Hansmann & Kraakman, "End of History", *supra* note 44.

approvingly by Lynn Stout and Elizabeth Warren. (Some commentators advocate a variant of managerialism in which, somehow, directors and managers would not merely be permitted but mandated to balance the interests of competing stakeholders. But — in the absence of conflict or bad faith — any such supposed mandatory scheme would necessarily collapse into complete managerial discretion in any event, since courts would have no way to challenge any good faith "balancing" justified by a corporation's managers without purporting to second-guess managers' business judgment, contrary to wisely established legal doctrine and profoundly threatening to the success and even, potentially, the survival of businesses.)

Powerful managers were incentivized both by social mores and the need to establish legitimacy to signal concern for employees' welfare, customer satisfaction and the prosperity and safety of the communities in which they operated. These pro-stakeholder, pro-social attitudes were aimed at building cohesion at a time when the legitimacy of the professional manager's status was being scrutinized and questioned. But the idea that for-profit business corporations should properly perform a major role as community leaders and philanthropists was always susceptible to valid criticism. What special (or indeed any) expertise did business leaders have for setting the course for community development or prioritizing charitable needs? If the principal purpose of indulging in such activities was simply to stave off government interference in business[74] (or to defuse widespread popular challenges to the power held by corporate executives), why were such activities expected to be of any real long-term benefit to the community? If the corporate manager's role was to balance competing social needs, how was the mandate of the corporate executive different from that of the government bureaucrat? Why, then, to take the argument to its chilling extreme, might government itself not usefully take over the "means of production"?[75]

The emergence of agency theory in the 1970s was embraced by free market advocates not least because it restored the idea of the profit-making firm to its rightful place within the overall economic system and provided a coherent framework within which to understand the legitimacy of shareholder wealth maximization. But the theory explained and legitimated the goal; it did not create it. The best and most socially useful corporations throughout history had always maximized wealth, although politically astute business leaders may have frequently engaged in apologetic, defensive behaviour or duplicitous pseudo-pro-social camouflage. Agency theory also legitimized managerial authority by positing the contestability of management positions. Managers were not simply self-perpetuating oligarchs. They were subject to market forces — in competitive markets for labour, for capital, for products and, perhaps most significantly, in the market for corporate control.[76] Therefore, the survival of managers rested on merit. Managerial merit necessarily meant effectiveness in running the corporation successfully; a corporation could succeed only if it was thriving in competitive markets; and success in competitive markets depended on producing goods and services that consumers wanted, and

---

74   See e.g. *The Wall Street Journal*, *supra* note 32.

75   As Milton Friedman put it (*supra* note 32), a corporate executive who is pursuing "socially responsible" goals rather than seeking to maximize profit "becomes in effect a public employee, a civil servant, even though he remains in name an employee of a private enterprise."

76   Robin Marris (*supra* note 70 at 30ff) identified how the threat of hostile takeover bids could serve as an effective check on managers. Henry Manne helped position this particular market constraint at the forefront. Henry Manne, "Mergers and the Market for Corporate Control" (1965) 3 J Political Economy 110. Jonathan Macey and Geoffrey Miller once asserted that "the market for corporate control lies at the heart of the American system of corporate governance." Jonathan R Macey & Geoffrey P Miller, "Corporate Governance and Commercial Banking: A Comparative Examination of Germany, Japan and the United States" (1995) 48 Stan L Rev 73.

upon retaining productive employees by offering attractive compensation. Thus, the success of a manager derived from the corporation's success in improving society by satisfying consumer wants, creating opportunities for employees and suppliers, and so enriching the communities in which they operated. Managers were therefore neither self-perpetuating nor solely self-serving; they were simply enjoying rewards commensurate with their business achievements. And in the absence of negative externalities,[77] their success coincided with net societal benefit.

The Arguable Dominance of Managerialism

The public-spirited stakeholder-constituency managerial view of the large business corporation was undoubtedly discussed in the United States, during the 1950s in particular. However, it is not entirely clear that it represented the overwhelmingly dominant view of the large public corporation throughout that period that some of its modern admirers assert. This observation is important not simply for reasons of historical accuracy, but because of the claim frequently made by opponents of the shareholder primacy norm that the financial progress of the 1950s could be attributed to the widespread adoption of this more enlightened model of the corporation — as though the 1950s could be seen as a natural experiment in "doing well by doing good."[78]

Certainly, there were a number of frequently cited works produced in the post-World War II era supporting the proposition that capitalism had entered a new developmental phase and that pro-social managerial capitalism was the new dominant paradigm. Such works include James Burnham's *The Managerial Revolution: What Is Happening in the World Now*;[79]Alfred P. Chandler's *The Visible Hand*; Edward S. Mason's "The Apologetics of Managerialism";[80]*Fortune* Magazine's *U.S.A.: The Permanent Revolution*;[81] Howard S. Bowen's *The Social Responsibilities of the Businessman*;[82] and some, although not all,[83] of the essays in Edward S. Mason's 1959 publication, *The Corporation in Modern Society*.[84] Richard Eels, writing in 1960, alluded to the argument that the "traditional" corporation, in which managers' goals did "not include any such objective as the promotion of the general welfare,"[85] might be considered "antiquated." Marris, too, recognized that, practically speaking, managers were free to pursue the social interests of corporate stakeholders other than shareholders, such as employees, but he suggested that

---

77   If a corporation is not required by law to internalize the negative externalities generated by its operations, there can be no assurance that a corporation's business will result in net societal benefit. Critics of the modern corporation fear that legislators and regulators cannot be relied upon to enact and enforce adequate laws, owing to, among other things, "*the role of corporations in making the very law that we trust to bind them.*" Stone, *supra* note 47 at 94 [emphasis in original]. It is not clear, however, why failure by democratically elected and publicly accountable governments is thought to be solvable by reliance on the munificence of corporate managers who are neither democratically elected nor accountable to the general public. On this latter point, see Tirole, *supra* note 47.

78   See e.g. Warren, *supra* note 33: "This [corporate social responsibility] approach worked. American companies and workers thrived." See also Stout, *supra* note 34 ("Judged by that standard, managerial capitalism seemed to generate good results. American corporations dominated the global economy, producing innovative products for their consumers, secure jobs for their employees, and corporate tax revenues for their government....This compares very favorably indeed with the sorts of returns shareholders have received more recently" at 1171).

79   James Burnham, *The Managerial Revolution: What Is Happening in the World Now* (London, UK: Putnam, 1942).

80   Edward S Mason, "The Apologetics of Managerialism" (1958) 31 J Business 1.

81   Editors of *Fortune, U.S.A.: The Permanent Revolution* (New York: Prentice Hall, 1951).

82   Howard S Bowen, *Social Responsibilities of the Businessman* (New York: Harper, 1953).

83   See, for example, Eugene Rostow's strong endorsement of long-term profit maximization as the appropriate goal of the corporation. Rostow, *supra* note 65 at 46.

84   Mason, *The Corporation in Modern Society*, *supra* note 22.

85   Richard Eels, *The Meaning of Modern Business* (New York: Columbia University Press, 1960) at 40.

this practical freedom existed despite what he understood to be the prevailing legal duty of directors to serve the corporation's shareholders by maximizing profits.[86] For Marris, it seemed clear that corporate managers were indeed maximizing something: "the rate of growth of the firm they are employed in subject to a constraint imposed by the security motive."[87] Marris also made one additional, rather non-contentious, observation: in the managerial corporation, where executives are not entrepreneurs, there is nevertheless some choice in the matter. "Given imperfect markets and hence an element of transcendence, traditional capitalists are able to choose products because they like them, or at least like producing them."[88]

There are, however, several reasons to view the claim that managerialism dominated the view of the large corporation prior to the 1970s with at least some circumspection. First, it was during the 1950s — the very era in which it is generally claimed that the shareholder primacy norm was in retreat — that the modern concept of the corporate goal of shareholder wealth maximization, rather than profit maximization, was originally articulated and developed.[89] Second, there is some contemporary evidence that suggests that although managerialism may have been an important mid-century ideological rival of the wealth- or profit-focused business corporation, it was not necessarily a dominant ideology. For example, in *The American Business Creed*, an important and frequently cited study of post-World War II business ideology first published in 1956,[90] the authors identified two "strands" of the prevailing business creed: the "classical" and the "managerial."[91] They linked the emergence of the managerial view to the "discrepancy between the classical model of small and weak business proprietorships and the real world of great corporate enterprises."[92] Unlike modern writers, however, they did not suggest that the managerial strand had become the dominant strand in the 1950s. Instead, they document the revealing observation that adherents of each of the two strands of capitalism harboured sharply different views of American business history. Adherents of the classical view saw the current era as the continuation of a largely homogeneous past. Managerial proponents, on the other hand, viewed the current era as representing "a radical break with the past."[93]

A similar study of the opinions of business leaders from the 1920s to the 1960s was conducted by Herman E. Krooss.[94] Krooss's study is somewhat more supportive of the view that the "socially responsible" managerial corporation reflected the spirit of the age in the early post-World War II era. There is some question, however, as to whether some claims of social responsibility during that era were no more than common sense recognitions that, of course, to maximize shareholder wealth in the long term, a business needs to retain a happy, productive work force and satisfied customers,

---

86   Marris, *supra* note 70 at 2. For the distinction between maximizing "profits" and maximizing shareholder wealth, see note 89 below.

87   *Ibid* at 47.

88   *Ibid* at 59.

89   See e.g. Modigliani & Miller, *supra* note 46 (under conditions of uncertainty, "The profit outcome...has become a random variable and as such its maximization no longer has an operational meaning....[T]he alternative approach, based on market value maximization, can provide the basis for an operational definition of the cost of capital and a workable theory of investment" at 263–64). See also Debreu, *supra* note 46 at 100 (demonstrating that maximizing share value [evidenced by corporate share price] becomes the tractable goal of a corporation under conditions of uncertainty).

90   Sutton et al, *supra* note 50.

91   *Ibid* at 9.

92   *Ibid* at 358.

93   *Ibid* at 35.

94   Herman E Krooss, *Executive Opinion: What Business Leaders Said and Thought on Economic Issues 1920s–1960s* (Garden City, NY: Doubleday, 1970).

and operate within a viable, prosperous community.[95] Moreover, it is possible that Krooss may occasionally have too-readily accepted sanctimonious public relations statements as sincere commitments,[96] or that he may have mistaken the emergence of several impressive mountains for a rise in general elevation. Nonetheless, Krooss does suggest that the businessmen of that era did not fit the economist's model of profit-maximizer. He claims that, as early as the 1920s, an idealistic approach to business had come to be identified as the "New Capitalism,"[97] a view, he says, that was controversial at the time and, in any event, yielded to an increased emphasis on the profit motive following the onset of the Great Depression.[98] By the 1950s, he asserts, although economists continued to employ models assuming that businesses were operated to maximize profits, these models did not reflect what business executives themselves understood as their mission. As Krooss explains: "If economic theorists knew and taught that the businessman's objective was to maximize profits, that was more than most businessmen knew. Indeed, only a few were sure what their primary objective was; but most were quite sure it was not to maximize profits."[99]

By contrast, in addition to many other unequivocal rejections of this alternative model of capitalism published during the period,[100] Wilbur Katz, writing in 1958, in the midst of the supposed golden era, called the "social responsibility" theory of the business corporation a new theory, and went on to dismiss it, saying, "Apart from these provisions for charitable contributions, the new concept of social responsibility has had almost no elaboration. It is not merely that the theory has had no further influence on the actual statutes, but in a quarter of a century, neither the originators of this philosophy nor their disciples have sketched with any detail or persuasiveness the lines of possible practical application. And the few suggestions which have been made justify skepticism as to the seminal quality of the new theory."[101]

Finally, one may note that it was during this same era that some of the most high-profile individual shareholder activists — promoting a view of strong shareholder accountability — were most engaged and by many accounts widely admired, including corporate gadflies such as Wilma Soss,[102] David Livingston[103] and Lewis D. Gilbert[104] (who claimed to have coined the term "shareholder democracy"[105]).

---

95   This notion, embodied in the hackneyed phrase "enlightened self-interest," or, perhaps, "enlightened shareholder interest" is indeed alluded to in some of the executives' statements Krooss documents. *Ibid* at 53.

96   As noted earlier, it is not clear that corporations making the strongest claims for the value of corporations pursuing explicitly pro-social goals rather than maximizing shareholder value are, in fact, more pro-social than their less vocally sanctimonious peers. See Raghunandan & Rajgopal, *supra* note 31.

97   *Ibid* at 42.

98   *Ibid* at 45.

99   *Ibid* at 333.

100 See e.g. Theodore Levitt, "The Dangers of Social Responsibility", *Harvard Business Review* (September-October 1958) 49. See also Rostow, *supra* note 65; Lewis, *supra* note 69; JD Glover, *The Attack on Big Business* (Boston: Harvard Graduate School of Business Administration, 1954). See also Ayn Rand's famously provocative work of fiction, *Atlas Shrugged* (New York: Random House, 1957).

101 Wilbur G Katz, "The Philosophy of Midcentury Corporate Statutes" (1958) 23 L & Contemp Probs 177 at 190.

102 When Wilma Soss died in 1986, her obituary in *The Los Angeles Times* provided highlights of her remarkable and colourful career as a shareholder activist. "Wilma P. Soss, Corporations' Nemesis, Dies at 86", *The Los Angeles Times* (18 October 1986) E7.

103 See David Livingston, *The American Stockholder* (New York: JB Lippincott, 1958).

104 See Lewis D Gilbert, *Dividends and Democracy* (Larchmont, NY: American Research Council, 1956).

105 See Livingston, *supra* note 103 at 68.

Socially Responsible Corporations: Old or New?

Whatever may be the validity in the United States of the story of the shift from the "paternalistic" or "heroic" managerialism of corporations in the early post-World War II era to the narrow shareholder focus of the latter years of the twentieth century, it appears, in any event, that this order of events was not universal. In particular, it seems that no such clear shift occurred in Canada or the United Kingdom. In fact, there are some suggestions that corporate practice and even corporate law may have moved in precisely the opposite direction.

As early as 1931, for example, F. W. Wegenast, in his seminal treatise on Canadian corporate law, quoted with approval Lord Lindley's statement: "The duty of directors to shareholders is so to conduct the business of the company as to obtain for the benefit of the shareholders the greatest advantages that can be obtained consistently with the trust reposed in them by the shareholders and with honesty to other people."[106]

More recently, Beverley McLachlin, former chief justice of the Supreme Court of Canada, in a speech delivered in May 2018, suggested that in Canada, matters were the other way around. Corporations used to be governed only for shareholders, but this old-fashioned view subsequently yielded to a broader corporate mission:

> The classic concept of a commercial corporation — the one I was taught in law school[107] and the one that is still being taught in some business schools — holds that the sole purpose of a corporation is to produce a return on shareholders' investment. It followed that the sole concern of CEOs and board directors was to ensure that the return to shareholders was maximized and assured for the future.
>
> The modern concept of a commercial corporation is more complex….[C]orporate governance is no longer only about ensuring short- and long-term return to shareholders. Other constituencies are part of the corporate picture.[108]

The suggestion that shareholder primacy, in Canada, was the old (pre-1970s) norm is also supported by a cryptic comment in the 1971 Dickerson Committee Report,[109] the document that preceded the enactment of the Canada Business Corporations Act.[110] Referring to proposed language in the new corporate statute that would oblige directors and officers to act "in the best interests of the corporation," the Dickerson Committee acknowledged that this phrase would be subject to interpretation. They declined to offer an explanation, preferring to leave

---

106   FW Wegenast, *The Law of Canadian Companies* (Toronto: Carswell, 1979) at 360.

107   The former chief justice graduated from law school in 1968, eight years before the publication of Jensen and Meckling's article, which Lynn Stout suggested heralded the beginning of the movement toward shareholder primacy, (*supra* note 34), before the beginning of the 1970s, in which Harwell Wells suggests the shareholder primacy era began to emerge (*supra* note 36), and three years before the publication of the Powell Memorandum (*supra* note 43). Given the close interconnection between the US and Canadian economies, including the fact that many of the largest Canadian corporations are also cross-listed on US stock exchanges, it seems implausible that Canadian and US public corporations could, in fact, have been pursuing materially different corporate objectives prior to the 1970s or 1980s.

108   Beverley McLachlin, "Enhancing Governance in Uncertain Times" in *Director Journal* (Toronto: Institute of Corporate Directors, 2018) 19.

109   Robert WV Dickerson, John L Howard & Leon Getz, *Proposals for a New Business Corporations Law for Canada*, vol 1, Commentary (Ottawa: Information Canada, 1971).

110   RS 1985, c C-44 [*CBCA*].

the meaning to evolve through judicial interpretation. However, they expressed the hope that the malleable language they had chosen would permit courts to "escape from the constraints of what has somewhat charitably been described as the 'anachronistic' view that has developed in the English courts."[111] Although the Dickerson Committee offered no explanation of this "anachronistic" view, they did cite their source of this observation: the then-current edition of L. C. B. Gower's *The Principles of Modern Company Law*.[112] The anachronistic view to which Gower was objecting was the view that the best interests of a company meant no more than the best interests of the shareholders.[113] This "unenlightened" and anachronistic view certainly accords with the sense of English law conveyed in such law school warhorses as *Parke v Daily News Ltd*[114] and *Hutton v West Cork Railway Co*.[115]

English corporate law scholar Len Sealy, writing in 2001, also affirmed that in the English corporate law chronology, shareholder primacy was not a late-twentieth-century innovation, but rather preceded the development of a broader stakeholder-constituency view. As he put it, "Until fairly recently, it would not have occurred to anyone to doubt that in [the context of directors' duty to act in the interests of the company] 'the company' meant 'the shareholders, collectively' or 'the shareholders, present and future,' for no other interest group was recognised as having any stake in the corporate enterprise."[116]

However, he notes, public opinion has changed. It is now, in his view:

> ...widely accepted that the claims of other interest groups, such as the company's workforce, its customers and suppliers, may call to be recognised quite as much as those of the people who are no more than passive investors in the enterprise; and there are those who would go further, and require the 'responsible company' of today and its directors to have regard to wider considerations, such as the community, the environment, charitable and other good causes and the national interest. The law does, of course, meet some of these demands by specific legislation: employment laws, insolvency laws, environmental laws, and so on. But company law has responded only tentatively to the pressure for change.[117]

In Sealy's view, in fact, "judges have largely been content to utter moralising or hortatory dicta without making any serious attempt to frame new rules of law."[118] In any event, he notes, addressing the issue in the context of directors' duties could lead to manifold and irresolvable conflicts.

---

111 Dickerson, Howard & Getz, *supra* note 109 at para 241.

112 LCB Gower, *The Principles of Modern Company Law,* 3rd ed (London, UK: Stevens, 1969) at 522.

113 *Ibid.*

114 [1962] Ch 927.

115 (1883) 23 Ch D 654.

116 LS Sealy, *Cases and Materials in Company Law,* 7th ed (London, UK: Butterworths, 2001) at 259.

117 *Ibid.*

118 *Ibid.*

The current Companies Act 2006 (UK) is sometimes identified as a statute that embraces consideration of non-shareholder interests.[119] Certainly, the report that preceded revisions to the statute implemented in 2006 trumpeted the notion that factors such as a company's "relationships with its employees, customers and suppliers, its need to maintain its business reputation, and its need to consider the company's impact on the community and the working environment…are of growing importance for companies in a modern economy."[120] The final text of the directors' duties provision in the legislation, however, makes clear that while directors must, indeed, have regard to a number of specifically listed non-shareholder considerations, these matters are to be considered in the context of the director's duty to "act in the way he considers, in good faith, would be most likely to promote the success of the company *for the benefit of its members* [i.e., the shareholders] *as a whole.*"[121] Moreover, section 170(1) of the Companies Act 2006 states that the directors' duties specified in sections 171 to 177 "are owed by a director of a company to the company." Thus, whatever obligations to non-shareholder interests section 172 arguably creates, such obligations do not appear to be owed directly to such non-shareholders and, presumably, would not be enforceable by them either. Since a detailed consideration of the Companies Act is entirely beyond the scope of this chapter, nothing further will be said here.

The Modern Era and the Emergence of the "Woke" Corporation

Perhaps objection to the shareholder wealth-maximizing corporation is owing, in part, to fear that acknowledging the legitimacy of such a model might somehow be performative. That is, in the view of some, endorsing an enterprise premised on the unabashed pursuit of financial self-interest is not merely an exercise in accepting, and so usefully harnessing, human nature "as we know it,"[122] but may actually foster selfishness and greed, in the way that it has occasionally been suggested that exposing economics students to economic models premised on the ubiquity of human self-interest exacerbates the selfishness of those students.[123] When it comes to self-interest, in other words, perhaps the wealth-maximizing business corporation is not merely a harness, but a spur. Shareholder primacy skeptics may thus prefer the approach suggested in 2009 by Nobel laureate in economics Elinor Ostrom: "Designing institutions to force (or nudge) entirely self-interested individuals to achieve better outcomes has been the major goal posited by policy analysts for governments to accomplish for much of the past half century. Extensive empirical research leads me to argue that instead, a *core goal of public policy should be to facilitate the development of institutions that bring out the best in humans.*"[124]

---

119   Andrew Keay, for example, states that "the enlightened shareholder value ('ESV') principle was enacted in law that became operative on 10 October 2007 and 6 April 2008." Andrew Keay, *The Enlightened Shareholder Value Principle and Corporate Governance* (London, UK: Routledge, 2013) at vii.

120   United Kingdom, White Paper, *Modernising Company Law* (2002), ch 3, s 3.8, Cm 5553.

121   *Companies Act 2006* (UK), c 46, s 172(1) [emphasis added].

122   Frank Knight, *Risk, Uncertainty and Profit* (New York: Harper & Row, 1965) at 270.

123   See e.g. Robert H Frank, Thomas Gilovich & Dennis T Regan, "Does Studying Economics Inhibit Cooperation?" (1993) 2:7 J Economic Perspectives 159.

124   Elinor Ostrom, "Beyond Markets and States: Polycentric Governance of Complex Economic Systems" (2010) 100 American Economic Rev 641 at 665. [Revised version of Ostrom's 2009 Nobel Lecture; emphasis added.]

A number of well-meaning attempts have been made to work within the boundaries of traditional corporate norms and reconcile the goals of shareholder primacy and corporate social responsibility. The most familiar of these efforts include versions of the "enlightened shareholder self-interest" or "doing well by doing good" bromides. Other, more refined, attempts to square the shareholder primacy/public interest circle have recently been offered by thoughtful commentators such as Todd Henderson and Arnup Malani,[125] and Oliver Hart and Luigi Zingales.[126] One might well wonder why such rationalizations are thought necessary. Why, after all, would anyone oppose a view of the corporation as a pro-social responsible corporate citizen? The answer might lie in what has been dubbed "do-gooder derogation."[127] Alternatively, critics may share the wariness of Lord Wedderburn, who dismissed the "enlightened self-interest" notion as belonging to an unsatisfactory and not entirely coherent "fudge school."[128] More likely, however, the principal reason for opposing the rejection of straightforward shareholder primacy is that such a rejection implies a broader rejection of the value of free markets, a demonizing of business (by suggesting that for-profit business does not, in and of itself, provide value to society, unless it also embraces an explicit non-commercial "socially responsible" mission),[129] and a troubling and potentially economically harmful preference for allocating resources on some basis other than through negotiation in competitive markets and, worse, at the discretion of unaccountable agents.

It does appear, however, that momentum currently favours a broader, pluralist conception[130] of the corporation. The list of corporate pro-social initiatives continues to proliferate in what might be dubbed a twenty-first-century attempt to move from "broke" capitalism to "woke" capitalism.[131] Courts have also lent some support to this development. The US Supreme Court, for example, has acknowledged that the corporation does not pursue profits alone (although this observation occurs within a passage that suggests a curious misunderstanding of the impetus for the creation of the benefit corporation).[132] In Canada, the Supreme Court has suggested that the business corporation

---

125 Todd Henderson & Arnup Malani, "Corporate Philanthropy and the Market for Altruism" (2009) 109 Colum L Rev 571.

126 Oliver Hart & Luigi Zingales, "Companies Should Maximize Shareholder Welfare Not Market Value" (2017) 2 J L, Finance & Accounting 247.

127 Julia A Minson & Benoît Monin, "Do-Gooder Derogation: Disparaging Morally Motivated Minorities to Defuse Anticipated Reproach" (2012) 3 Social, Psychological & Personality Science 200.

128 Lord Wedderburn, "Trust, Corporation and the Worker" (1985) 23 Osgoode Hall LJ 203 at 227.

129 Milton Friedman noted this concern in "The Social Responsibility of Business is to Increase its Profits", *supra* note 32 at 124.

130 See e.g. Rick Molz, "The Theory of Pluralism in Corporate Governance" (1995) 14 J Business Ethics 789.

131 See e.g. Embankment Project for Inclusive Capitalism, *supra* note 8; United Nations, Human Rights, Office of the High Commissioner, "Guiding Principles on Business and Human Rights: Implementing the United Nations 'Protect, Respect and Remedy' Framework" (2011), online: <www.ohchr.org/documents/publications/GuidingprinciplesBusinesshr_eN.pdf>; British Academy, "Future of the Corporation", online: <www.thebritishacademy.ac.uk/publications/journal-british-academy/6s1>. See also the "social licence" provisions in the Australian Stock Exchange's proposed update of the ASX Corporate Governance Council's Principles and Recommendations, released for public consultation in May 2018, online: <www.asx.com.au/documents/asx-compliance/consultation-paper-cgc-4th-edition.pdf>. See also Ross Douthat, "The Rise of Woke Capital", *The New York Times* (28 February 2018).

132 In *Burwell v Hobby Lobby Stores, Inc*, 573 US 134 S Ct 2751 (2014), Associate Justice Samuel Alito, in the majority opinion, wrote, "While it is certainly true that a central objective of for-profit corporations is to make money, modern corporate law does not require for-profit corporations to pursue profit at the expense of everything else, and many do not do so....In fact, recognizing the inherent compatibility between establishing a for-profit corporation and pursuing nonprofit goals, States have increasingly adopted laws formally recognizing hybrid corporate forms. Over half of the States, for instance, now recognize the 'benefit corporation,' a dual-purpose entity that seeks to achieve both a benefit for the public and a profit for its owners." In fact, the principal impetus for benefit corporations was to overcome the concern that directors of traditional corporations could be found liable for breach of their fiduciary duties if they were to pursue goals other than shareholder wealth maximization. See e.g. Benefit Corporation, "What Is a Benefit Corporation?", online: <https://benefitcorp.net/what-is-a-benefit-corporation>; see also Clark et al, *supra* note 25 at 7, 8.

should act as a "good corporate citizen,"[133] or a "responsible corporate citizen,"[134] terms which may be light in substantive content, but are nevertheless of considerable symbolic significance. And the recent amendment to the Canada Business Corporations Act to add section 122(1.1)[135] seems to reflect Parliament's recognition of the value of allowing — although, significantly, not mandating — directors to consider a number of factors beyond maximizing shareholder or enterprise value.

It should not be forgotten, however, that, notwithstanding judicial nods to non-shareholder interests, the pivotal case of *BCE v 1976 Debentureholders*[136] ultimately involved a decision by the Supreme Court to approve a transaction that had been explicitly undertaken with the aim of maximizing shareholder value. Nevertheless, suggestions that models of the corporation that deviate from a wealth-maximization norm merely provide a modern version of a long-enduring and economically successful enterprise form appear to be based on very slender evidence.

Conclusion

Business corporations are not philanthropic institutions. Yet, provided they operate in competitive markets and can be required to internalize the negative external effects of their operations, they benefit society without explicitly pursuing non-financial goals. Like many modern institutions of business and finance, however, the business corporation has come under considerable scrutiny as perceptions of excesses and failures, along with a host of broader economic and environmental concerns, have prompted calls for increased public accountability. Improvements and refinements to the business corporation may well be important and useful. However, it is important to be mindful of the possibility that the growing popularity and influence of initiatives invoking the promise of a kinder, gentler managerial-style corporation may rely on a simplified or even distorted view of corporate history, intended to dampen opposition to untested and potentially harmful transformative changes to the prevailing corporate model. While Thurman Arnold was certainly no advocate of the hard-headed, profit-maximizing corporation of his day, his work does serve as a sobering reminder of the dangers to human development and prosperity of pursuing a confected philosophical idea rather than acknowledging and grappling with a more nuanced and uncomfortable reality.

Author's Note

Some portions of the section entitled "Socially Responsible Corporations: Old or New?" draw on material from an earlier work. See Christopher C Nicholls, *Corporate Law* (Toronto: Emond Montgomery, 2005).

---

133   [2008] 3 SCR 560 at para 66.

134   *Ibid* at para 82.

135   *CBCA, supra* note 110.

136   The proxy circular describing the arrangement for which court approval was sought by BCE referred to the goal of the transaction as "enhancing" or "maximizing" shareholder value more than a dozen times. See BCE Inc, "Notice of Special Shareholder Meeting and Management Proxy Circular" (7 August 2007), online: <www.sedar.com>. Thus, notwithstanding the Supreme Court's comments on the value of non-shareholder interests, it must not be forgotten that the Supreme Court did approve this arrangement, fully understanding that it was expressly and unequivocally intended to pursue the goal of maximizing shareholder value.

3

IMPLICATIONS OF A SOPHISTICATED SHAREHOLDER BASE IN PUBLIC CORPORATIONS

Anita Indira Anand

Introduction

The growing prevalence of institutional shareholders — including hedge funds and pension funds — has significantly impacted capital markets around the world. These investors are neither characterized by the passivity of retail shareholders, nor willing to place corporate control in the hands of corporate managers alone. Rather, they are sophisticated, often seeking governance changes in addition to a return on their investment. They may be short-term investors who seek to purchase control of an underperforming corporation, or long-term investors who seek stable investments on behalf of beneficiaries to whom they owe a fiduciary duty. While these types of investors can differ significantly, one commonality is clear: they are not content to sit on the sidelines, allowing corporate managers and boards alone to determine the corporation's course.

As sophisticated shareholders increasingly eschew a passive approach to governance in public corporations, our thinking about their role within the corporation must similarly adapt. In this vein, we can isolate a trio of important roles that sophisticated shareholders play. To begin, given their size and greater access to resources, they carry out an important monitoring function in corporate governance. In addition, beyond monitoring, their ability to affect governance in the corporation is growing through their increased use of the proxy contest process enshrined in corporate law. Finally, these activist campaigns have led to the formation of activist groups, known as "wolf packs," that act in coordination with each other to initiate governance and other reforms.

These trends in institutional investor activity are evident in capital markets around the world where sophisticated investors have become dominant. In the United States, in the 1960s, individual investors held 84 percent of all publicly listed stocks.[1] Today that number has dropped to less than 40 percent — possibly less than 30 percent.[2] In Canada, by the late 1990s, institutional trading accounted for two-thirds of all trading on the Toronto Stock Exchange (TSX),[3] and currently 15 percent of all assets in the Canadian financial system are held by pension funds.[4] In the European Union, financial assets held by institutions grew by more than 150 percent between 1992 and 1999,[5] and in the United Kingdom individual equity holdings have fallen more than 40 percent in the last 50 years.[6] A similar trend has occurred in Japan as well: as of 2011, only 18 percent of all public equity in Japan was held by individual investors.[7]

In short, we have witnessed a paradigm shift from passive to active ownership in public corporations. As the prevalence of sophisticated shareholders in capital markets grows, it becomes increasingly important to consider the economic and legal influence that these shareholders have on capital markets. This chapter argues that the rise of a sophisticated shareholder class leads to three main consequences, two of which are in the vein of recommended legal reforms. First, given wolf pack behaviour among sophisticated shareholders in the capital markets, regulators should leverage existing disclosure regimes that apply to blockholders to address their coordinated activity. Second, regulators should actively facilitate shareholder engagement with corporate affairs by fostering a "stewardship culture," thereby encouraging all market participants to benefit from a marketplace in which sophisticated institutions seek out, and look to create, well-governed corporations. Third, achieving the first two of these objectives lessens the need for a fiduciary duty among shareholders *inter se*.

The second section of this chapter examines key themes relating to increased shareholder activism that emerge from the academic literature. The third section assesses the current legal mechanisms in place to address these issues and identifies existing gaps in the applicable legal regime. The fourth section highlights current legal and policy initiatives under way to address these challenges, and the final section proposes some policy developments to address these challenges.

---

1   Serdar Çelik & Mats Isaksson, "Institutional Investors and Ownership Engagement" (2013) 2 OECD J Financial Market Trends 93 at 96, online: *Organisation for Economic Co-operation and Development* <www.oecd.org/corporate/institutional-investors-ownership-engagement.pdf>.

2   *Ibid*; Paul Borochin & Jie Yang, "The Effects of Institutional Investor Objectives on Firm Valuation and Governance" (2017) 126:1 J Financial Economics 171; Jennifer G Hill, "Good Activist/Bad Activist: The Rise of International Stewardship Codes" (2018) 41:2 Seattle UL Rev 497 at 499.

3   Jeffrey G MacIntosh, "Institutional Shareholders and Corporate Governance in Canada" (1996) 26:2 Can Community LJ 145 at 148.

4   Guillaume Bédard-Pagé et al, *Large Canadian Public Pension Funds: A Financial System Perspective* (2016) Bank of Canada Financial System Rev 33, online: <www.bankofcanada.ca/wp-content/uploads/2016/06/fsr-june2016-bedard-page.pdf>.

5   Stuart Gillan & Laura T Starks, "Corporate Governance, Corporate Ownership, and the Role of Institutional Investors: A Global Perspective" (2003) Weinberg Centre for Corporate Governance Working Paper No 2003-01 at 3.

6   Çelik & Isaksson, *supra* note 1 at 96.

7   *Ibid*.

Background and Academic Literature

The academic literature relating to sophisticated shareholders is voluminous. It revolves around three main themes: the rise of activism; the important monitoring role that institutional investors play; and the growth of wolf pack behaviour.

The Rise of Shareholder Activism

While sophisticated shareholders are arguably better suited than individual investors to monitor corporations, recent literature elucidates a number of concerns associated with their monitoring activity.

Institutional Investors with Large Holdings

The common starting point for analysis of shareholder activity in the capital markets is the separation of ownership and control in capital markets, which can lead to a divergence between the interests of a firm's management and those of its shareholders.[8] These divergent interests give rise to agency costs — costs incurred by shareholders to monitor managers' actions and ensure they are acting in the best interests of the firm. Institutional investors are often better able to incur these monitoring costs, and they have the time and resources to engage in monitoring activities.[9] Certainly, these institutions hold considerable assets.[10]

In 2008, Canada's eight largest pension funds managed a combined CDN$600 billion in total assets. By 2018, this figure had ballooned to CDN$1.4 trillion, cementing the economic heft of these institutional players. The scope of this investment speaks to these institutions' willingness and capacity to promote and maintain an effective corporate governance regime at the firms in which they have invested.

Institutional investors also benefit from connections to each other. Various network connections, such as those formed between institutions that operate in the same geographic area or own a stake in the same portfolio company, lower the cost of gathering information.[11] And, as William Bratton and Joseph McCahery have explained, institutional investors are able to invest more patiently because they are better able to access and use information about a firm's operations.[12]

In comparison to retail investors, institutional investors often hold a larger stake in a firm, giving them greater incentive to monitor management.[13] Further incentive may derive from institutional investors' — in particular, large mutual funds' — reluctance to divest even poorly

---

8   Adolf Berle & Gardiner Means, *The Modern Corporation and Private Property* (New York: MacMillan, 1932) at 6.

9   Iman Anabtawi & Lynn Stout, "Fiduciary Duties for Activist Shareholders" (2008) 60:5 Stan L Rev 1255 at 1276.

10   Organisation for Economic Co-operation and Development (OECD), *OECD Institutional Investors Statistics 2018* (Paris: OECD, 2018) at 26.

11   Luca Enriques & Alessandro Romano, "Institutional Investor Voting Behaviour: A Network Theory Perspective" (2019) 1 U Ill L Rev 223 at 243.

12   William W Bratton & Joseph A McCahery, "Comparative Corporate Governance and the Theory of the Firm: The Case Against Global Cross Reference" (1999) 38:3 Colum J Transnat'l L 213 at 226 [Bratton & McCahery, "Comparative Corporate Governance"].

13   Robert C Illig, "The Promise of Hedge Fund Governance: How Incentive Compensation Can Enhance Institutional Investor Monitoring" (2008) 60:1 Ala L Rev 41 at 49.

performing shares.[14] Institutional investors' monitoring behaviour is evidenced by data from Institutional Shareholder Services (ISS). ISS Voting Analytics shows that the average percentage of shares outstanding that were voted at corporations' annual meetings in 2015 for the election of directors was 68.7 percent.[15] Given that the largest 50 institutional investors hold an average of 44.2 percent of shares in a corporation, this voting data suggests that these large institutional investors cast a majority of these votes.[16] In this sense, the presence of institutional investors helps to reduce some of the agency issues between managers and shareholders.

That said, a recent study found no evidence "that greater ownership by passive mutual funds is associated with more activism by non-passive institutions [or individual shareholders]."[17] On the contrary, the presence of large institutional investors appears to lower rates of activism, because of the monitoring function that those institutions perform.[18] Of course, an institutional shareholder will incur these monitoring costs only if doing so is in its own self-interest; increased informational symmetry and freedom to make longer-term investments often lead to the pursuit of greater market share at the expense of an optimal rate of return.[19] Hence, the incentive to monitor stems from the size of a shareholder's stake, rather than from an ability to generate quick returns; the larger the position that a shareholder owns, the greater the incentive to monitor (as the shareholder has more to lose in the case of poor governance practices).

However, it is important to note that institutional investors often take sizeable ownership positions (and are blockholders) in multiple firms. As Jun-Koo Kang et al. note, on average, an institutional investor serves as a blockholder in five different firms at the same time.[20] This raises the question of how a multiple-blockholding position impacts institutional investors' monitoring behaviour. On the one hand, some argue that multiple blockholdings split institutional investors' attention, making monitoring less effective.[21] In addition, if institutional investors are subject to constraints on monitoring, managers use the opportunity to pursue their own private benefits.[22] On the other hand, some argue that multiple blockholdings *enhance* sophisticated shareholders' monitoring capabilities because their additional experience and governance-relevant information served to reduce the overall monitoring costs for these shareholders.[23] In fact, from an empirical

---

14   Ian R Appel, Todd A Gormley & Donald B Keim, "Passive Investors, Not Passive Owners" (2015) 121:1 J Financial Economics 111 at 113; Roberta Romano, "Public Pension Fund Activism in Corporate Governance Reconsidered" (1993) 93:4 Colum L Rev 795 at 833.

15   Lucian Bebchuk, Alma Cohen & Scott Hirst, "The Agency Problems of Institutional Investors" (2017) 31:1 J Economic Perspectives 89 at 93.

16   *Ibid.*

17   Appel, Gormley & Keim, *supra* note 14 at 128.

18   *Ibid.*

19   Bratton & McCahery, "Comparative Corporate Governance", *supra* note 12 at 227.

20   Jun-Koo Kang, Juan Luo & Hyun Seng Na, "Are institutional investors with multiple blockholdings effective monitors?" (2018) 128:3 J Financial Economics 576 at 576.

21   *Ibid.*

22   *Ibid.*

23   *Ibid.*

perspective, Kang et al. find that institutional investors with more blockholdings are more active and effective monitors than investors with fewer blockholdings.[24]

Institutional Investors with Small Holdings

Not all institutional investors will necessarily take a blockholding position. "Institutional investor" is a very broad term, and the characteristics of the shareholders that fall under this umbrella vary significantly.[25] For example, pension and mutual funds face legal and market pressures to diversify their portfolios and typically hold a relatively small percentage in any one firm.[26] With only a small stake in a firm, these funds will likely not monitor the firm closely or become deeply involved in the firm's affairs, as the benefits of doing so do not outweigh the costs.[27] Lucian Bebchuk, Alma Cohen and Scott Hirst find that, outside of activist hedge funds, shareholders are incented to be passive rather than active monitors.[28] Often, these passive institutions will outsource voting decisions by following a proxy advisory firm's untailored voting recommendation, which is based on the adviser's own general analysis of optimal governance measures.[29] The incentives for index funds to be active monitors are particularly low, which raise concerns as these funds become more common.[30] While the increasing prevalence of index funds is beneficial for investors, since it takes out the cost of financial intermediation, it also has potentially adverse consequences on corporate governance, including a loss of voter independence.[31]

Shareholder Activism and Agency Issues

As the number and power of institutional investors grows, what, if any, new duties should be imposed on shareholders?

Inter-shareholder Agency Issues

With the shift from retail investors to large institutional investors as major players in the capital markets, there has been a corresponding increase in the concentration of equity ownership.[32] As a result, today's institutional shareholders collectively hold more power than they did in the past. This has led to agency concerns among shareholders, in particular in countries such as the United States and Canada.[33] These regulatory regimes place less emphasis on shareholders'

---

24   *Ibid* at 602. It is these monitoring benefits that blockholders confer upon other shareholders, and capital markets more generally, that lead some to object to tightened disclosure roles for blockholders. On this point, see Lucian A Bebchuk & Robert J Jackson, Jr, "The Law and Economics of Blockholder Disclosure" in William W Bratton & Joseph A McCahery, eds, *Institutional Investor Activism: Hedge Funds and Private Equity, Economics and Regulation* (Oxford: Oxford University Press, 2015) 617 [Bratton & McCahery, *Institutional Investor Activism*].

25   Çelik & Isaksson, *supra* note 1 at 95–96.

26   Anabtawi & Stout, *supra* note 9 at 1278.

27   *Ibid.*

28   Bebchuk, Cohen & Hirst, *supra* note 15 at 99–101.

29   *Ibid* at 109; Stephen Choi, Jill Fisch & Marcel Page, "The Power of Proxy Advisors: Myth or Reality?" (2010) 59 Emory LJ 869 at 871–72; George W Dent, Jr, "A Defence of Proxy Advisors" (2014) Michigan State L Rev 1287 at 1292–93.

30   Bebchuk, Cohen & Hirst, *supra* note 15 at 108–09.

31   *Ibid*; Michael C Schouten, "The Mechanisms of Voting Efficiency" (2010) Colum Bus L Rev 763 at 828–29. But this is not to say that passive investors are necessarily disengaged from issues of corporate governance. For an argument that passive institutions can, and often do, take an interest in governance reforms, see Jill E Fisch, Asaf Hamdani & Steven Davidoff Solomon, "The New Titans of Wall Street: A Theoretical Framework for Passive Investors" (2020) 168 U Pa L Rev 17.

32   Bebchuk, Cohen & Hirst, *supra* note 15 at 89.

33   Anabtawi & Stout, *supra* note 9 at 1275.

obligations vis-à-vis other shareholders.[34] In fact, in Canada, the positive law does not articulate any duties owed among shareholders *inter se*.[35] Yet as the number of institutional investors grows, and as these investors take on larger ownership stakes in firms, the potential for agency costs among shareholders rises. These costs are amplified by developments in proxy laws and the creation of shareholder advisory services, which together have helped shift the balance of power in firms away from management to shareholders.[36]

It is unsurprising that with this power shift, shareholder activism is on the rise, especially among hedge funds. Hedge funds are the most active of the sophisticated shareholders, while pension funds tend to take a backseat in activism campaigns.[37] Hedge funds may become active because they are dissatisfied with the firm's governance practices.[38] They seek out firms in need of operational changes and believe that making these changes will lead to an increase in firm value.[39] Accordingly, their campaigns are typically focused on short-term profits;[40] few hedge funds hold on to their shares for more than one to two years.[41] Critics argue that in the pursuit of short-term earnings, hedge funds will undermine the long-term returns of the company.[42] In response, proponents of hedge fund activism argue that these campaigns generate long-term benefits for the organization[43] and that successful campaigns benefit all shareholders.[44]

Does a short-term "get in, get out" approach benefit the fund at the expense of the corporation?[45] Does short-term behaviour serve as a reason for imposing a fiduciary duty among shareholders? A fiduciary duty may not be suitable in all jurisdictions. For example, the circumstances in Canada to date reduce the need for such a duty.[46] That may be symptomatic of the limited Canadian-specific information available on hedge funds' impact on corporate performance and shareholder returns.[47] What is known is that, although the investment landscape has been steadily shifting over the last two decades, offensive shareholder activism, characteristic of hedge funds, remains relatively unusual in Canada.[48] The main reason for this is the nature of the Canadian market: most Canadian companies are too closely held for hedge funds to

---

34   *Ibid* at 1261.

35   *Brant Investments Ltd v KeepRite Inc et al*, [1991] OJ No 683, 1 BLR (2d) 225 [*Brant*].

36   *Ibid.*

37   Anabtawi & Stout, *supra* note 9 at 1276. There have been, however, recent examples of pension funds becoming increasingly active. See e.g. Brent Jang & Jacquie McNish, "CPPIB Backs Pershing Square in CP Proxy Row", *The Globe and Mail* (11 May 2012).

38   Leo E Strine, Jr, "Who Bleeds When the Wolves Bite? A Flesh-and-Blood Perspective on Hedge Fund Activism and Our Strange Corporate Governance System" (2017) 126 Yale LJ 1870 at 1892.

39   *Ibid.*

40   *Ibid.*

41   John C Coffee, Jr & Darius Palia, "The Wolf at the Door: The Impact of Hedge Fund Activism on Corporate Governance" (2016) 41:3 J Corp L 545 at 572.

42   *Ibid* at 594.

43   Lucian A Bebchuk, Alon Brav & Wei Jiang, "The Long-Term Effects of Hedge Funds Activism" (2015) 115:5 Colum L Rev 1085 at 1089. For a discussion of the unique characteristics that allow hedge funds to augment a firm's value, see Alon Brav et al, "Hedge Fund Activism, Corporate Governance, and Firm Performance" in Bratton & McCahery, *Institutional Investor Activism, supra* note 24, 261.

44   Bebchuk, Cohen & Hirst, *supra* note 15 at 106.

45   *Ibid* at 107.

46   *Brant, supra* note 35; Paul Martel, *Business Corporations in Canada: Legal and Practical Aspects* (Toronto: Carswell, 2020) at 15-5A.

47   Brian Cheffins, "Hedge Fund Activism Canadian Style" (2014) 47 UBC L Rev 1 at 6 [Cheffins, "Canadian Style"].

48   *Ibid* at 5.

acquire a sufficient stake.[49] Owing at least in part to that reality, Canadian institutional investors, the investing activities of which are also focused on Canadian businesses, have acquired a reputation for "quiet and collaborative intervention" rather than public proxy fights.[50] That is to say that Canadian hedge funds often *do* have an existing stake in a target company before trying to effect a change.[51] They also tend to hold slightly larger minority positions than their American counterparts and tend to hold their positions longer.[52] Admittedly, only a small minority of Canadian hedge funds currently have the resources to obtain a substantial stake in a typical TSX-listed company.[53] Nevertheless, hedge fund activity has increased dramatically in Canada, including both local and foreign investors.[54] There is also growing consensus that hedge fund activism is here to stay.[55] Therefore, concerns about inter-shareholder agency are not without justification.

The confluence of these legitimate concerns about inter-shareholder agency costs and Canadian courts' unwillingness to identify a fiduciary duty as among shareholders means this debate is a live one.[56] Those opposed to such a duty argue that controlling shareholders have no legal power over the property of other shareholders, and thus a fiduciary duty is inappropriate. They also contend that controlling shareholders have justly acquired their position of influence, and minority shareholders have opted into their tenuous position at the point at which they buy shares. Finally, they argue that a fiduciary duty may problematically present a reason to avoid investing in public corporations, since it creates additional risk in the form of legal liability.

Ultimately, though, it is not clear that a fiduciary duty is required in the Canadian context or in other common law jurisdictions with similar capital market characteristics. There is a strong case to be made that *ex ante* safeguards and robust *ex post* remedies adequately safeguard minority shareholder interests in the status quo. As the Ontario Court of Appeal in Canada noted in *obiter* in *Brant*, the oppression remedy is a particularly potent tool that enables minority shareholders to protect their interests. Its availability cuts against the claim that a fiduciary duty among shareholders is a necessary condition to safeguard the interests of minority shareholders. Beyond this remedy, we must appreciate the role played by the normative force of socially accepted guidelines for shareholder conduct. Guidelines can safeguard minority shareholders by supplying their majority counterparts with reasons, both selfish and other-regarding, to act for the betterment of the firm as a whole.

---

49   *Ibid* at 36–37; Kobi Kastiel, "Against All Odds: Hedge Fund Activism in Controlled Companies" (2016) 60:1 Colum Bus L Rev 60 at 74.

50   Janis Sarra, "Shareholders as Winners and Losers Under the Amended Canada Business Corporations Act" (2003) 39:1 Can Bus LJ 52 at 66; Cheffins, "Canadian Style", *supra* note 47 at 56.

51   Cheffins, "Canadian Style", *supra* note 47 at 8.

52   Dionysia Katelouzou, *Hedge Fund Activism, Corporate Governance and Corporate Law: An Empirical Analysis across 25 Countries* (PhD Dissertation, University of Cambridge Faculty of Law, 2013) at 139 [unpublished]; Dionysia Katelouzou, "Myths and Realities of Hedge Fund Activism: Some Empirical Evidence" (2013) 7:3 Va L & Business Rev 459 at 479.

53   Cheffins, "Canadian Style", *supra* note 47 at 56.

54   *Ibid* at 54.

55   Dionysia Katelouzou, "Worldwide Hedge Fund Activism: Dimensions and Legal Determinants" (2015) 17:3 U Pa J Bus L 789 at 794 [Katelouzou, "Worldwide Hedge Fund Activism"].

56   Anita Anand & Christopher Puskas, "Enforcing Shareholder Duties: Legal and Economic Rationales for Shareholder Duties and their Enforcement" in Hanne S Birkmose & Konstantinos Sergakis, eds, *Enforcing Shareholders' Duties* (Cheltenham, UK: Edward Elgar, 2018).

Agency Issues vis-à-vis Beneficial Investors

On top of these inter-shareholder agency concerns, institutional shareholders may owe fiduciary duties to clients whose assets they manage. Some scholars have argued that institutional investors compete on relative performance, seeking to deliver only competitively superior performance for stakeholders, while minimizing costs.[57] If an institutional investor incurs costs to improve a portfolio company's performance, the investor's performance may worsen relative to its competitors. Thus, some academics have questioned whether institutional investors always act in the best interests of their clients.[58]

Bebchuk, Cohen and Hirst consider whether the decisions made by the investment managers at these institutions are always optimal for the beneficial investors.[59] Generally, investment managers incur non-recoverable costs from stewardship activities such as proxy contests or other activist campaigns.[60] For example, under the current regulations that govern mutual funds, personnel and management expenses incurred by investment managers cannot be charged directly to the portfolio.[61] So, if an investment manager initiates a proxy fight opposing a firm's management, any costs incurred would come out of the fees charged to investors.[62] Furthermore, investment managers may be influenced by their own private motivations that reduce their willingness to monitor and vote against firms.[63]

While Bebchuk, Cohen and Hirst's concerns relate mainly to mutual funds, similar concerns arise in the case of hedge funds as well. Leo Strine argues that human investors are indirect investors in hedge funds: when hedge funds make high-risk investment decisions, it is the individuals who indirectly assume this risk.[64] That possibility may be particularly acute in the case of an underperforming fund. Under the "carried interest" model, managers' compensation depends entirely on the profit they generate, notwithstanding the typical requirement that fund managers invest a significant portion of their own money in their respective funds.[65] Thus, Bebchuk, Cohen and Hirst suggest that investment managers at hedge funds are more incentivized to make decisions that are advantageous for the beneficial investor by engaging in positive monitoring and stewardship activities.[66] Hedge funds also tend to take more concentrated positions in corporations, meaning that an increase in firm value has a stronger positive effect on the fund's portfolio compared to a mutual fund, thereby providing additional incentive.[67] In sum, hedge funds might be more inclined than mutual funds to monitor firms and engage in activism because of the different compensation scheme and concentrated position they hold.

---

57   Ronald J Gilson & Jeffrey N Gordon, "The Agency Costs of Agency Capitalism: Activist Investors and the Revaluation of Governance Rights" (2013) Colum L Rev 863 at 889–90.

58   Bebchuk, Cohen & Hirst, *supra* note 15 at 109–10.

59   *Ibid* at 94–95.

60   *Ibid* at 97.

61   *Ibid*.

62   *Ibid*.

63   *Ibid* at 101.

64   Strine, *supra* note 38 at 1936.

65   Illig, *supra* note 13 at 73. There is also evidence, drawn from the private equity context, that investors today prioritize and often secure "investor-favorable" fee and profit arrangements. For a discussion of this point, see Joseph A McCahery & Erik PM Vermeulen, "Recasting Private Equity Funds After the Crisis" in Bratton & McCahery, *Institutional Investor Activism*, *supra* note 24, 599 at 609–10.

66   Bebchuk, Cohen & Hirst, *supra* note 15 at 105.

67   *Ibid*.

Wolf Packs

As the prevalence of shareholder activism has increased, so, too, has the number of instances of shareholders working together to effect change in firms. When multiple institutional investors coordinate with each other to target a particular firm, this informal network of investors is often referred to as a wolf pack.[68] These networks are frequently comprised of hedge funds that individually may hold only a small percentage of ownership in a firm, but can function together like a single shareholder with a sizeable percentage of equity.[69] Whether these networks must disclose their positions depends on whether they are acting jointly or in concert, which is a question of fact that has not been extensively addressed in case law.[70] Consequently, these networks could exert significant influence on target firms without necessarily triggering disclosure requirements to which individual shareholders are subject. For that reason, it is difficult to know the precise extent to which this activity occurs. However, in a 2015 article, Dionysia Katelouzou revealed that out of 432 activist campaigns studied in 25 countries outside the United States, 54 of the campaigns involved one or more wolf packs; of those 54, only six were caught by acting-in-concert legislation and subjected to filing requirements.[71] While wolf packs can have benefits in terms of monitoring and improving corporate governance, the fact that they are able to form raises questions about the proper application of disclosure rules. The presence of a wolf pack may be relevant information to other investors, and investors should not have to make decisions in the absence of material information.[72]

Legal Mechanisms and Gaps

As the above discussion suggests, legal mechanisms are in place to address issues relating to institutions that invest on behalf of others. However, gaps in the law still exist, leaving some challenges unaddressed.

Shareholder Engagement Regulations

Certain jurisdictions have enacted regulations to encourage institutional investors to engage in more active monitoring of firms. For example, in the United States, institutions that are subject to the Employee Retirement Income Security Act (ERISA) have an obligation to exercise their voting rights on all shares under management.[73] The engagement of these institutions is mandatory. In addition, a number of jurisdictions, including Australia, Germany, Japan

---

68   Anita Anand & Andrew Mihalik, "Coordination and Monitoring in Changes of Control: The Controversial Role of 'Wolf Packs' in Capital Markets" (2017) 54:2 Osgoode Hall LJ 377 at 377. For an examination of the particular conditions that invite wolf pack behaviour, and the conclusions about regulatory decision making that follow, see Anita Anand, "Shareholder-Driven Corporate Governance and Its Necessary Limitations: An Analysis of Wolfpacks" (2019) 99 BUL Rev 1515.

69   *Ibid* at 386.

70   Ontario Securities Commission, *National Instrument 62-103: The Early Warning System and Related Take-Over Bid and Insider Reporting Issues* (1 April 2017), ss 2.1–4.8, online: <www.osc.gov.on.ca/documents/en/Securities-Category6/ni_20170401_62-103_early-warning-system-take-over-bids.pdf>; *Genesis Land Development Corp v Smoothwater Capital Corp*, 2013 ABQB 509 at para 24 [*Smoothwater Capital*]; Anand & Mihalik, *supra* note 68 at 393.

71   Katelouzou, "Worldwide Hedge Fund Activism", *supra* note 55 at 845.

72   Anand & Mihalik, *supra* note 68 at 393

73   Çelik & Isaksson, *supra* note 1 at 108. See also Alan Kandel & David Eckhardt, "Proxy Voting and Interpretive Bulletin 2016-01" (3 April 2017), online (blog): *Technology, Manufacturing & Transportation Industry Insider* <www.tmtindustryinsider.com/2017/04/proxy-voting-and-interpretive-bulletin-2016-01/>.

and Switzerland, have regulations requiring institutional shareholders to disclose their voting policies.[74]

The European Union also recognizes the importance of institutional investors as monitors (and their current underperformance in this role). In 2017, a proposal by the European Commission to amend the Shareholder Rights Directive was passed; it called for increased transparency from institutional investors and asset managers regarding their approach to shareholder engagement.[75] The proposal stated that sophisticated shareholders should either develop and publicly disclose their shareholder engagement policy, or explain why they have not done so.[76] The objective would promote investor awareness, encourage shareholder engagement and strengthen institutional investors' "accountability to stakeholders and to civil society."[77]

However, these regulations and proposals do not fully address the question of how to encourage institutional investor engagement and monitoring activities. The voting obligation under the ERISA is applicable only to those institutions that manage employee benefit plan assets, and therefore may not capture a number of institutional investors. Furthermore, an institution can exercise its voting rights without actively engaging with or monitoring the firm. If active monitoring is not in the institution's self-interest, the institution may take a more passive approach and vote on its own, perhaps according to a proxy advisory firm's recommendation. Given that institutional and other investors routinely rely on proxy advisory firms' recommendations, the question arises: should proxy advisory firms be regulated? This question is examined below.

Disclosure Regulations and Wolf Packs

Existing disclosure regulations aim to ensure that firms and shareholders can know when an investor takes a sizeable stake in a company. The disclosure may signal to the firm, as well as its other shareholders, that an activism campaign is imminent. For example, in the United States, after acquiring a five percent or greater ownership in a company, an investor is required to file a Schedule 13D disclosing their ownership.[78] In Canada, the equivalent threshold for filing an early warning report is 10 percent.[79] Both jurisdictions also have rules regarding collective action by shareholders, which impose constraints on wolf pack formation. Shareholders acting as·a "group" (in the United States) or "jointly or in concert" (in Canada) must disclose when the group's ownership exceeds five or 10 percent, respectively. In most cases, these disclosure regulations ensure that other shareholders are aware of an institutional investor's presence. However, as mentioned above, wolf packs are often able to skirt the "group" definition and

---

74   Çelik & Isaksson, *supra* note 1 at 108.

75   EC, *Directive (EU) 2017/828 of the European Parliament and of the Council of 17 May 2017 amending Directive 2007/36/EC as regards the encouragement of long-term shareholder engagement*, [2017] OJ, L 132/1 [*Directive 2017/828*].

76   *Ibid*; see also Therese Strand, "Short-Termism in the European Union" (2015) 22:1 Colum J Eur L 15.

77   *Directive 2017/828*, *supra* note 75.

78   US Securities and Exchange Commission, "Fast Answers — Schedule 13D", online: <www.sec.gov/fast-answers/answerssched13htm.html>.

79   Canadian Securities Administrators, "CSA Notice of Amendments to Early Warning System" (25 February 2016) at 3, online: *Ontario Securities Administration* <www.osc.gov.on.ca/documents/en/Securities-Category6/csa_20160225_62-104_early-warning-system-take-over-bids.pdf>.

thereby avoid these disclosure requirements.[80] In these cases, neither the firm nor its other shareholders are aware of the wolf pack until the lead investor launches its campaign. There is also variation in how courts interpret these regulations. In some cases, a court will find that a wolf pack does not constitute a group,[81] while in others "jointly or in concert" has been interpreted more broadly to apply to the wolf pack.[82]

Shareholder Fiduciary Duty

While there is no legislated fiduciary duty among shareholders, some courts in the United States have recognized a duty of loyalty in specific circumstances. For example, courts have held that majority shareholders owe a duty of loyalty to minority shareholders that prevents them from making economic gains from a corporation at the expense of the minority shareholders.[83] In the case of *Jones v HF Ahmanson & Co*, the California Supreme Court held that "any use to which they [the majority shareholders] put the corporation or their power to control the corporation must benefit all shareholders proportionately."[84] However, in markets such as the United States where ownership is highly dispersed, activist institutions that are extracting benefits from firms are often not majority shareholders. Thus, the question of whether *all* shareholders of a firm should owe loyalty duties to each other still remains unanswered.

How Are the Challenges Being Addressed?

Proxy Advisory Firm Regulation

Proxy advisory firm regulation has been a topic of significant discussion in both Canada and the United States, as the influence of these firms grows. In 2015, the Canadian Securities Administrators released a new policy regarding proxy advisory firms that provides recommended best practices and disclosure to promote transparency.[85] Similarly, the US Securities and Exchange Commission chairman has highlighted the need for greater regulation of proxy advisory firms in order to increase transparency.[86] Given the growing influence of these firms and the number of institutional investors that have come to rely on them when deliberating about how to vote, greater oversight seems like a reasonable step. More transparency regarding the process by which proxy advisory firms come to their recommendations would allow institutional investors to make more informed voting decisions, thereby bolstering the monitoring function that proxy advisory firms serve. Enhancing proxy adviser transparency would also support institutional shareholders' responsibilities to those investors whose money they manage, as these investors (the "beneficial"

---

80   Katelouzou, "Worldwide Hedge Fund Activism", *supra* note 55 at 845. Marcel Kahan and Edward Rock, while slightly downplaying the prevalence of this disclosure-evading conduct, nonetheless also hold that the term "group" is overly vague and invites reform. Marcel Kahan & Edward B Rock, "Hedge Funds in Corporate Governance and Corporate Control" in Bratton & McCahery, *Institutional Investor Activism*, *supra* note 24, 151 at 185.

81   See e.g. *Hallwood Realty Partners LP v Gotham Partners LP*, 286 F (3d) 613 (2d Cir 2002).

82   See e.g. *Smoothwater Capital*, *supra* note 70 at para 24.

83   Anabtawi & Stout, *supra* note 9.

84   *Jones v HF Ahmanson & Co*, 1 Cal (3d) 93 at 108 (1969).

85   Canadian Securities Administrators, News Release, "Canadian Securities Regulators Publish Guidance for Proxy Advisory Firms" (30 April 2015), online: <www.osc.gov.on.ca/en/NewsEvents_nr_20150430_proxy-advisory-firms. htm>. See also Anita Anand, "The importance of regulatory oversight of proxy advisory firms", *The Globe and Mail* (23 May 2018).

86   US Securities and Exchange Commission, Press Release, "Statement on Shareholder Voting by Commissioner Robert J Jackson, Jr" (14 September 2018), online: <www.sec.gov/news/public-statement/statement-jackson-091418>.

holders) could more clearly determine whether the proxy advisory firm's recommendations align with the beneficiaries' interests.

Another issue to bear in mind is that some proxy advisory firms sell consulting services to companies. This practice raises a conflict of interest problem as a proxy advisory firm may be asked to evaluate a company's proposal to shareholders while simultaneously providing that company's management with some type of consulting service, potentially on the very proposal it is evaluating. Thus, in theory, proxy advisory firms may recommend voting in favour of management proposals on which they were consulted either to demonstrate the efficacy of their consulting business or as a "quid pro quo" arrangement. Proxy advisory firms claim to manage this conflict of interest through firewall measures between the services they offer, but the question remains as to whether voluntary firewalls are sufficient to eliminate the conflict. Regulation may be a better option to eliminating this conflict and instill confidence in the proxy advisory firms' recommendations.

That said, there are also legitimate concerns with regulating proxy advisory firms too heavily. As Bebchuk, Cohen and Hirst point out, if proxy advisory services are too restricted, it may become prohibitively expensive for firms to provide these services.[87] Without proxy advisers monitoring corporate governance, it is unclear whether (and to what extent) institutional investors will fill the gap and perform their own monitoring functions.[88] Indeed, some scholars argue that proxy advisers have been instrumental in increasing informational symmetry. Faced with outside monitoring, the argument goes, management would be compelled to explain its conduct and to solicit shareholders' views in order to persuade shareholders to vote in its favour.[89] If proxy advisory services were overly restricted, institutional investors would be more likely to return to the Wall Street Rule — "vote with management or sell" — than to incur the monitoring costs associated with an informed vote.[90] That possibility is particularly present if institutional investors are inclined to vote with management.[91] Thus, a balance needs to be struck between allowing proxy advisory firms the freedom to fulfill their important monitoring functions while also ensuring that there is transparency in the recommendations they provide.

Stewardship Codes

To address gaps regarding shareholder voting regulations, some jurisdictions have created stewardship codes. For example, the UK Stewardship Code sets out guidelines for institutional investor engagement, which include monitoring investee companies, establishing clear guidelines relating to the escalation of stewardship activities, being willing to act collectively if necessary, and having a clear policy on voting activity.[92] In Canada, the investor-led Canadian Coalition for Good Governance (CCGG) has also published stewardship principles. The

---

87   Bebchuk, Cohen & Hirst, *supra* note 15 at 109.

88   *Ibid.*

89   Dent, *supra* note 29 at 1295.

90   *Ibid* at 1288, 1305–306.

91   *Ibid* at 1305; Bernard S Black & John C Coffee, "Hail Britannia? Institutional Investor Behavior under Limited Regulation" (1994) 92:7 Mich L Rev 1997 at 2059–60. The concern is that institutional investors may have an inherent conflict of interest, because they may be managing the pension plans of the issuers or be trying to gain access to them. Similarly, institutional investors associated with merchant banks may not want to jeopardize their banking business by opposing management at firms that use their banking services.

92   *The UK Stewardship Code* (UK), 2012 at 4–5.

CCGG's Stewardship Principles outline institutional investors' role in "exercising voting rights and monitoring and engaging with companies on issues that might have an impact on the company's value."[93] According to Jennifer Hill, stewardship codes "represent a generalized response to John Plander's global financial crisis lament — 'where were the shareholders?'" and "reflect the view that engagement by institutional investors is an integral part of any corporate governance system."[94]

In other words, stewardship codes stand for the principle that the institutions responsible for widening the gap between individual investors and management should be the very institutions responsible for bridging that gap.[95] While these codes arguably capture the fundamentals of active engagement better than voting requirements, they are only collections of guidelines. They function on a "comply or explain" basis (in the case of the UK Stewardship Code) or are voluntary and not monitored for compliance (as with the CCGG's principles).[96] Thus, they ultimately rely on the market's regulating itself, by sanctioning with low share prices those firms that inexplicably deviate from corporate governance standards.[97] Brian Cheffins argues that even if institutional investors were *willing* to take up the mantle of monitoring investee firms, diverse share ownership poses a significant hurdle. Stewardship demands a certain degree of consensus among monitors; unless one shareholder has a sufficiently large stake to command management's attention, management may dismiss shareholders' disparate and divergent interests in favour of its own plan.[98]

Also problematic is the point that stewardship codes are premised, at least in part, on the assumption that shareholders are rational actors; yet the consequences of shareholder irrationality (in the 2008 financial crisis, for example) largely motivated the creation of these codes.[99] In response to some of these challenges, the UK Financial Conduct Authority has undertaken consultations and published a discussion paper on potential stewardship improvements.[100] In particular, the Financial Conduct Authority is exploring how regulations can be used to complement the existing stewardship code in order to raise stewardship standards and thereby improve market integrity.[101]

---

93   Canadian Coalition for Good Governance, "CCGG Stewardship Principles" (2017), online: <https://admin. yourwebdepartment.com/site/ccgg/assets/pdf/stewardship_principles_public.pdf> ["CCGG Stewardship Principles"].

94   Hill, *supra* note 2 at 506.

95   David William Roberts, "Agreement in Principle: A Compromise for Activist Shareholders from the UK Stewardship Code" (2015) 48:2 Vand J Transnat'l L 543 at 549.

96   "CCGG Stewardship Principles", *supra* note 93.

97   Anita Anand, "An Analysis of Enabling vs Mandatory Corporate Governance Structures Post Sarbanes-Oxley" (2005) 31:1 Del J Corp L 229 at 235–36.

98   Brian Cheffins, "The Stewardship Code's Achilles' Heel" (2010) 73:6 Mod L Rev 1004 at 1020.

99   Demetra Arsalidou, "Institutional Investors, Behavioural Economics and the Concept of Stewardship" 6:6 L & Financial Markets Rev 410 at 413–14.

100   Financial Conduct Authority, "Building a Regulatory Framework for Effective Stewardship" (January 2019) Discussion Paper DP19/1, online: <www.fca.org.uk/publication/discussion/dp19-01.pdf> at 28–29.

101   *Ibid* at 4.

Are Further Reforms Needed?

Improving Wolf Pack Regulation

Considering the sizeable ownership share that these activist packs are able to amass, and the resulting impact they can have on corporations, it is appropriate to consider wolf packs to be blockholders and regulate them as such.[102] Possible legal reforms may include the amendment of securities regulation to tighten the definition of "group" or "acting jointly or in concert" and requiring any institutional investors consciously working together to file disclosure.[103] Short of legislative amendments, a change in how courts interpret group disclosure regulations could have a similar impact. If courts are more receptive to recognizing a wolf pack as a group, legislative changes may be unnecessary.[104] Furthermore, some organizations and academics believe that the 10-day window between when the five percent ownership stake is acquired and when it must be disclosed should be tightened.[105] Proponents of this change argue that in today's modern financial markets, where shares can be amassed quickly and the size of this stake can be masked in other forms of ownership (for example, derivatives or equity swaps), the regulation is not serving its intended purpose of alerting investors when there is a potential change in corporate control.[106]

Promoting a "Stewardship Culture"

Research by the Organisation for Economic Co-operation and Development suggests that there is more to investor engagement than mere regulation.[107] An institutional shareholder's level of engagement is influenced by a number of determinants, including the purpose of the institution, its fee and portfolio structures, and its political or social objectives.[108] If it is in the institution's self-interest to monitor, then the institution is more likely to engage in these activities. Thus, improving investor engagement will likely involve more than changing existing regulations or introducing new ones. By focusing on creating a stewardship culture that balances enabling, encouraging and requiring shareholder engagement, better engagement may be achieved.

A number of factors can contribute to the creation of a stewardship culture. For example, creating a code, following the United Kingdom's lead, that publicizes country or industry stewardship standards, and making shareholder engagement easier, may provide more support in this area than mandatory engagement.[109] Along these lines, some scholars have suggested

---

102   Anand & Mihalik, *supra* note 68 at 391.

103   Stephen Bainbridge, "Responding to wolf pack activism by hedge funds" (6 April 2015), online (blog): *Stephen Bainbridge's Journal of Law, Religion, Politics, and Culture* <www.professorbainbridge.com/professorbainbridgecom/2015/06/responding-to-wolf-pack-activism-by-hedge-funds.html>.

104   *Ibid.*

105   Coffee & Palia, *supra* note 41 at 597–98.

106   Daniel Gallagher, "Activism, Short-Termism, and the SEC" (Remarks at the 21st Annual Stanford Directors' College of Stanford Law School, Stanford, California, 23 June 2015), online: *US Securities and Exchange Commission* <www.sec.gov/news/speech/activism-short-termism-and-the-sec.html#_edn18>; Henry TC Hu, "Financial Innovation and Governance Mechanisms: The Evolution of Decoupling and Transparency" (2015) 70:2 Bus Lawyer 347.

107   Çelik & Isaksson, *supra* note 1.

108   *Ibid.*

109   Charles M Nathan, "On Governance: Institutional Investor Engagement: One Size Does Not Fit All" (18 July 2018), online (blog): *The Conference Board* <www.conference-board.org/blog/postdetail.cfm?post=6826>.

creating an internet-based review and rating facility, not unlike Yelp, for corporate governance.[110] Encouraging passive institutional investors to engage more and to support long-term firm value creation could also address some of the hedge fund "short-termism" concerns, as institutional investors would respond more vigorously to activism campaigns if they believe they are not in the best interests of the corporation.[111]

Bebchuk, Cohen and Hirst suggest that amendments to mutual fund fee regulations could also promote a stewardship culture and better incentivize mutual funds to engage with corporations. As discussed above, current regulations that prevent investment managers from charging stewardship expenses to their funds, or from tying fees to increases in portfolio value, disincentivize investment managers from engaging in stewardship activities.[112] While the justification of these regulations may lie in the protections that they provide to beneficial investors, it is important to recognize that these protections do not come without a cost. Regulators may wish to explore adjustments to these rules in order to better incentivize investment managers to undertake stewardship activities.[113]

In a similar vein, Robert Illig sees a solution to institutional investor under-engagement in hedge fund-style compensation structures.[114] Specifically, he argues that the carried interest model described above offers a practical way to align shareholder and management interests, with minimal need for legislative intervention.[115] Providing compensation when an institutional shareholder increases the value of its holdings in absolute terms (rather than relative to a particular market index), and withholding compensation in the alternative, would motivate shareholder engagement while guarding against compensation for fund managers that simply benefit from a general market upturn.[116] Illig concedes that banks and insurance companies would not make good "corporate disciplinarians" because of their close ties to the rest of the corporate world, but he is optimistic about mutual funds and the like.[117] Of course, performance-based incentives might not be ideal for every type of institutional investor, given the diversity in investment approaches among such investors and the fact that many large Canadian pension funds manage their investments in-house.

Empirical evidence exists to support Illig's theory in the form of "delta." Delta is the amount by which managers' wealth increases if the value of their firm increases by one percent.[118] Based on a sample of almost 5,000 hedge funds, from 1994 to 2010, Shuang Feng et al. estimated the median delta for hedge fund managers at US$1.98 million.[119] By contrast, Yixin Liu and David Mauer estimated the median delta for chief executive officers, during a similar period, to be

---

110   Eva Micheler, "Facilitating Investor Engagement and Stewardship" (2013) 14:1 Eur Bus Org L Rev 29 at 46–47.

111   Robert C Pozen, "Institutional Investors and Corporate Short-Termism" (24 August 2015), online (blog): *Harvard Law School Forum on Corporate Governance* <https://corpgov.law.harvard.edu/2015/08/24/institutional-investors-and-corporate-short-termism/>.

112   Bebchuk, Cohen & Hirst, *supra* note 15 at 96.

113   *Ibid* at 108.

114   Illig, *supra* note 13 at 45.

115   *Ibid* at 73.

116   *Ibid* at 74.

117   *Ibid* at 65.

118   Houman B Shadab, "Hedge Fund Governance" (2013) 19:1 Stan JL Bus & Fin 141 at 181.

119   Shuang Feng, Nikunj Kapadia & Mila Getmansky Sherman, "Flows: The 'Invisible Hands' on Hedge Fund Management" (2011) at 18, online: *SSRN* <http://ssrn.com/abstract=1929205>.

only US$205,000.[120] Houman Shadab points to these figures to support the proposition that hedge fund manager compensation is more performance-dependent than corporate manager compensation, and also appears to incentivize higher performance.[121]

Fiduciary Duty between Shareholders?

While stewardship codes are useful, imposing a fiduciary duty among shareholders is likely unnecessary. One reform suggested by Iman Anabtawi and Lynn Stout to address institutional investor activism and the risk of short-termism is a new interpretation of the fiduciary duty that can arise between majority and minority shareholders.[122] Rather than suggesting a duty that is triggered by a shareholder's majority stake in a firm, Anabtawi and Stout propose that control be defined more expansively to include the variety of ways in which institutional investors can influence corporations without being majority owners.[123] Whenever a shareholder's action is a determinative cause of a corporation's conduct and that shareholder has a material, personal interest in the transaction or strategy that it is promoting, a fiduciary duty would be triggered.[124]

If implemented, this novel idea could have a chilling effect on the benefits of shareholder activism. Shareholder activism confers benefits upon those parties who have an interest in the effective management of a corporation, especially over the medium and long term. These benefits flow from activist investors' monitoring of managers and boards. Activist investors, motivated to observe management's competence and empowered to secure change, keep management and boards accountable to shareholders. The imposition of a fiduciary duty owed *among* shareholders risks upsetting the delicate equilibrium of activist self-interest and managerial accountability. In effect, such a duty may bid up the price of occupying the position from which activists can monitor, and potentially change the composition of, management. This state of affairs means a victory won by advocates of an inter-shareholder fiduciary duty is a frustratingly pyrrhic one. While an avenue for deterring and rectifying shareholder malfeasance is created, a useful symmetry between self-interest and collective shareholder benefit is likely disturbed.

The availability of the statutory oppression remedy also calls into question the necessity to impose a fiduciary duty owed among shareholders *inter se*.[125] Such a duty arguably would be rendered superfluous by Canada's corporate statute, which provides judicial relief against conduct that is oppressive, injurious or abusive against a collection of parties that includes shareholders of the corporation. As Jeffrey MacIntosh has argued, the oppression remedy plays the ameliorative role that is typically cited as the rationale for imposing a shareholder fiduciary duty. The oppression remedy is a mechanism for redress in circumstances where a controlling shareholder deploys corporate resources in a way that injures their minority counterparts. This redress is available for minority shareholders in both widely held and closely controlled companies.

---

120   Yixin Liu & David C Mauer, "Corporate Cash Holdings and CEO Compensation Incentives" (2011) 102:1 J Financial Economics 183 at 188.

121   Shadab, *supra* note 118 at 181.

122   Anabtawi & Stout, *supra* note 9 at 1295.

123   *Ibid.*

124   *Ibid* at 1296.

125   For a detailed explanation of this argument, see Anand & Puskas, *supra* note 56.

Conclusion

The growing prevalence of institutional investors has changed the capital market landscape, raising a number of new issues that must be addressed. These issues include the role of stewardship codes, the monitoring role of institutional investors and the emergence of wolf pack activism. While legal mechanisms to address some of these issues are in place or being proposed, there are still gaps to be filled. It is unclear whether, in the absence of law, the market itself will allow the beneficial aspects of shareholder activism to develop on their own.

Author's Note

The author thanks Richard Kennedy and William Maidment for their valuable research assistance, and the Social Sciences and Humanities Research Council of Canada for funding.

4

THE REVIEW OF GLOBAL MERGERS

Exploring the Status Quo and Its Uncertain Future

Edward Iacobucci

Introduction

Commerce in many goods is global; competition policy is domestic. This creates inevitable tensions: How should domestic competition policy deal with local effects of conduct taking place abroad? How should domestic competition policy authorities account for the decisions, or potential decisions, of foreign competition policy authorities? How do firms comply with multijurisdictional antitrust? The list of potential frictions is long.

There have been various strategies, both implemented and proposed, to account for the lack of territorial overlap between market conduct and the jurisdictional reach of competition policy. Some have called for international antitrust harmonization,[1] which would minimize conflict

---

1   See e.g. Diane P Wood, "International Harmonization of Antitrust Law: The Tortoise or the Hare?" (2002) 3 Chicago J Intl L 391; David W Leebron, "Claims for Harmonization: A Theoretical Framework" (1996) 27 Can Bus LJ 63.

across jurisdictions. Others have taken a more laissez-faire approach, seeking to protect the autonomy of individual jurisdictions to choose their own approaches to competition policy.[2]

In the second part of this chapter, I briefly review the arguments for and against harmonization. I reiterate a conclusion that I and co-authors have defended in previous work: harmonization would be a mistake. I also review previously made recommendations to address the frictions that local competition policies inevitably create in an era of global commerce, observing that certain principles can go a long way in reducing these frictions in most contexts. There is, however, one context that is especially thorny: mergers policy.

The standard remedies for anti-competitive mergers are injunctive in nature. While in some contexts local injunctions are available — for example, merging parties may be required to divest local assets to potential competitors — in other cases a merger will invite either an approval as is or a rejection. I will call these latter cases "intrinsically global mergers." Such intrinsically global mergers do not necessarily result from geographic antitrust markets that are global in scope, although they may. Rather, even if competitive conditions varied across jurisdictions and local markets, it may be that there are no practical local remedies to address local concerns about competition. If, for example, Google were to acquire Bing, it would be impractical to order the merger prevented in Canada but allowable in the European Union: it would either be approved or rejected. Such binary outcomes create stresses in the international system, since a single jurisdiction making an order against a merger could prevent a merger that, conceivably, all other affected jurisdictions approve. There could, in theory, be a "race to the strictest," with international mergers being governed by the most stringent approach across multiple jurisdictions.

Here, I will focus on mergers that are either intrinsically global in their entirety, or at least there is an irreducible kernel of the merger that is intrinsically global. Local divestitures or other conduct-oriented remedies, in other words, are limited in their efficacy, and significant competitive outcomes depend on whether the merger goes ahead or not.

The third part of this chapter considers how international mergers policy has played out in practice. It offers reasons to explain why, in fact, interjurisdictional tensions over mergers policy have been muted. When global mergers with potentially anti-competitive effects are proposed, there are, at this point, only two jurisdictions that matter in practice: the European Union and the United States. I review reasons why other jurisdictions, even ones with sophisticated competition policy, are likely to defer to the European Union and the United States. First, small jurisdictions could run a risk by making an order against an intrinsically global merger if other jurisdictions approve. It could be that the profits derived from that jurisdiction are dominated by the gains to the merging parties from the merger, which would imply that the optimal strategy for the merging parties is to go ahead with the merger and take steps simply to withdraw from the objecting country. Second, smaller jurisdictions may not have the expertise associated with the scale of EU and US competition authorities, and may rationally defer to the larger authorities. Third, there are *realpolitik* considerations. Small jurisdictions may want to avoid

---

2   See e.g. Edward Iacobucci & Michael Trebilcock, "National Treatment and Extraterritoriality: Defining the Domains of Trade and Antitrust Policy" in Richard A Epstein & Michael S Greve, eds, *Competition Laws in Conflict: Antitrust Jurisdiction in the Global Economy* (Washington, DC: AEI Press, 2004) [Iacobucci & Trebilcock, "National Treatment and Extraterritoriality"]; Edward Iacobucci, "The Interdependence of Trade and Competition Policies" (1997) 21:2 World Competition 5.

political conflict with the European Union and the United States because of the possible costs of a damaged relationship with either power. As a consequence, an equilibrium has emerged that depends, for the most part, on deference to the United States and the European Union in the face of intrinsically global mergers. The third section of this chapter considers the costs and benefits of this outcome.

The last section considers the stability of the status quo. The forces that shape the status quo may be jarred considerably in the coming years. There is a basic reason for concerns about future instability: the possibility of increased reliance on non-economic considerations to determine mergers outcomes. As political considerations gain prominence, inter-jurisdictional variation will predictably grow, and such variation will challenge the relatively cooperative status quo. The final section considers what this might imply for competition policy on intrinsically global mergers, predicting that tensions will grow in the coming years.

The Case for Domestic Competition Policy

In a series of papers, some co-authored with Michael Trebilcock, I have defended the proposition that despite the global reach of modern commerce, competition policy should be locally determined.[3] Efforts to compel harmonization are unlikely to be successful, and in any event are not desirable. This section first outlines the good reasons why domestic competition policy may vary, and then addresses the potential tensions that may arise. A general adoption of antidiscrimination rules goes a long way to reduce these tensions; harmonization is neither necessary nor appropriate to reduce considerably the costs of local antitrust.

The Advantages of Local Competition Policy

There are several good reasons why domestic competition policies might vary from jurisdiction to jurisdiction. First, economic conditions vary. For example, recognizing that borders are not frictionless for the movement of goods and services, firms within a small jurisdiction may have a more difficult time achieving scale than firms in large countries.[4] This could invite variations in how competition policy is formulated and applied. An efficiencies defence, one that permits anti-competitive conduct if accompanied by productive efficiency, may be more justifiable in a relatively small jurisdiction than in a large one. It is perhaps not surprising, then, that Canada, a medium-sized jurisdiction, has such a defence, while the United States does not.

Second, attitudes about economically optimal competition policy vary. There is endless debate about many aspects of competition policy, ranging from the basic precepts of policy (for example, should policy protect consumer welfare or total welfare?) to specific enforcement questions (for example, should competition policy enforce access to essential facilities?). No one can claim to have all the answers to the question of what approach to competition policy brings about the greatest economic benefits. In such a context, harmonization would force the adoption of a view of optimal policy that is not only unlikely to be shared across jurisdictions, but unlikely to be correct.

---

3   Michael J Trebilcock & Edward M Iacobucci, "Designing Competition Law Institutions: Values, Structure, and Mandate" (2010) 41:3 Loy U Chicago LJ 455; Iacobucci & Trebilcock, "National Treatment and Extraterritoriality", *supra* note 2.

4   See e.g. Michal S Gal, *Competition Policy for Small Market Economies* (Cambridge, MA: Harvard University Press, 2003).

Third, attitudes about the appropriate political ambitions of competition policy vary. For example, the European Union idiosyncratically looks to competition policy to break down privately constructed impediments to the European common market.[5] South Africa includes remedying racial disadvantage as one of the objectives of its competition policy.[6] Canada explicitly relies on competition policy to allow small and medium-sized businesses to compete.[7] Such political ambitions, while rarely at the centre of competition cases, are legitimate concerns of different jurisdictions, reflecting local norms and institutions, and would be stifled by harmonization efforts.

The Costs and Risks of Local Competition Policy

Local competition policy creates costs and risks. Some of the costs are mundane, but important: in the absence of global competition enforcement, firms must comply with the authorities in multiple jurisdictions. A global merger, for example, may be required to notify dozens of competition authorities. Such compliance costs for business are not trivial. In addition, global mergers that require multijurisdictional review also create costs for the multiple authorities reviewing the same merger.

More fundamentally, firms must attempt to comply with various competition authorities that take different approaches to the same conduct. Some jurisdictions, for example, may take a permissive approach to resale price maintenance; others may not. For a firm crafting a global strategy, there may be business and organizational challenges in pursuing strategies that are permitted in some jurisdictions but forbidden in others. At the limit, there could be conflicts where a firm would be required to do X in one jurisdiction, while simultaneously being required to do not-X in another jurisdiction. Fortunately, this extreme case is unlikely in the competition context, pursuant to which business conduct of a certain type may or may not be permitted, but is rarely required. Inconsistencies in competition law across jurisdictions create not only enforcement costs and uncertainties, but also affect business strategies: where a practice is banned in one jurisdiction, a firm may avoid its use in all jurisdictions, even if it is viewed as permissible and economically efficient in other jurisdictions.

The costs of varying competition laws are potentially higher if jurisdictions engage in strategic behaviour. There is a risk that jurisdictions will adopt policies that are skewed by self-interest in interjurisdictional commerce.[8] For example, Country A may permit price-fixing cartels as long as the cartels sell only to foreign buyers. Such an example is not fanciful: Canada, the United States and the European Union all exempt export cartels for reasons that must turn on jurisdictional self-interest at the expense of global welfare. More subtly, a country with firms that are dominant in global markets may take a more permissive approach to abuse of dominance generally, but that approach is only locally optimal because of the benefits of harming foreign buyers by dominant firms. This kind of beggar-thy-neighbour motivation for interjurisdictional variation in the legal treatment of certain conduct is clearly problematic: domestic regimes may seek to maximize domestic welfare, including benefits for producers, at the expense of foreign consumers and global welfare.

---

5   *Consten SaRL and Grundig GmbH v Commission*, Case 56/64 [1996] ECR 299.

6   Michael Wise, "Competition Law and Policy in South Africa" (2004) 5:4 OECD J Competition L & Pol'y 7.

7   *Competition Act*, RSC 1985, c C-34, s 1.1.

8   See e.g. Iacobucci, *supra* note 2; Iacobucci & Trebilcock, "National Treatment and Extraterritoriality", *supra* note 2.

Effects-based Jurisdiction

As Michael Trebilcock and I have articulated in previous work, there are ways to address the concerns created by parochial competition policy. We have advocated a non-discrimination principle for competition regimes, in which countries would agree not to treat foreign actors differently from domestic ones.[9] For example, allowing export cartels while forbidding local ones effectively treats foreigners differently from local citizens and would violate the principle of non-discrimination.

The urgency for the non-discrimination approach is mitigated by other responses to beggar-thy-neighbour policies. In particular, and most importantly, while exporting countries may permit conduct that exploits foreign consumers, this does not mean that importing countries do not have a say. Even if anti-competitive conduct takes place abroad, competition jurisdictions can and do penalize this conduct. Cases such as *Hartford Fire*[10] established that the key consideration for jurisdiction is the location of the effects of the conduct: if conduct has domestic effects, domestic policy applies. So even if a price-fixing cartel is permitted by the exporting country, the importing country can penalize it. To be sure, this solution is not perfect. Enforcement across borders may be challenging, for one. But it does go some distance in reducing concerns about beggar-thy-neighbour policy.

The effects-based approach also addresses good faith differences in the optimal approach to competition policy. If there is a practice that some jurisdiction regards as potentially abusive of dominance — resale price maintenance, for example — while another jurisdiction does not, each can take its own approach within its borders, and businesses can adjust their behaviour, jurisdiction by jurisdiction, accordingly. As observed above, this is not ideal, as businesses may prefer to pursue a single strategy across countries, but it accommodates variation across competition policies without creating conflicts of laws.

The solution of relying on the jurisdiction where effects take place cannot avoid certain conflicts. In particular, remedies must be able to be targeted regionally for the inbound-commerce approach to remedy potential conflicts. In many cases in competition policy, this is not problematic. If a cartel sells into Country A, Country A can impose damages and orders not to price-fix when selling to Country A consumers. If a dominant firm adopts problematic loyalty programs for customers in Country B, Country B can require the cessation of such practices in Country B. But there is one context where this is especially problematic: mergers policy.

In most cases, the review of a merger by a competition authority leads to one of two conclusions: either permit the merger, or do not. To be sure, there may be local conditions imposed — for example, Country A could require local divestitures before approving the merger — but ultimately will say yes (with conditions) or no to the merger. Consider the implications of this approval/disapproval approach to mergers policy in a global context. A global merger — that is, a merger that inevitably has global implications — will be reviewed by many, possibly dozens, of competition authorities. Such authorities will consider domestic law when evaluating the merger and will decide to approve (or not) accordingly. This has potentially very negative consequences

---

9   Iacobucci & Trebilcock, "National Treatment and Extraterritoriality", *supra* note 2.

10   *Hartford Fire Insurance Co v California*, 509 US 764 (1993).

for global welfare. In essence, there will be a race to the strictest, with the jurisdiction that is least tolerant of mergers determining whether the merger goes ahead or not. This implies that the preferred approach of the other jurisdictions, better tailored to local political and economic preferences and circumstances, cannot apply. Even if all jurisdictions had the same objective, and differed only in the adoption of means to achieve them, the power of the strictest jurisdiction to prevent a merger almost certainly implies a sub-optimal global approach: the outlier jurisdiction is probably wrong in its approach.

In the following sections, I consider how conflicts between domestic competition policies over global mergers have been neutralized in practice, with, on balance, positive implications for global welfare. I then review how this equilibrium may be upset in the coming years.

The Reasons for, and Advantages of, Hegemonic Mergers Authorities

The previous section identified the dangers of domestic competition authorities reviewing global mergers. There is a risk of a race to the strictest, which not only prevents domestic authorities from implementing locally preferred policies, but also means that an outlier (and, thus, probably misguided) jurisdiction will have outsized influence over global mergers policy. In practice, however, intrinsically global mergers have not been subject to an obvious race to the strictest, with one jurisdiction exercising outsize influence. Rather, two jurisdictions are the important ones: the United States and the European Union. Despite ostensible reviews by a host of authorities, jurisdictions other than the United States and European Union do not prevent intrinsically global mergers outright. For some mergers, there have been local remedies including local divestitures, but small jurisdictions do not make orders preventing a global merger. This section first explores why this is likely the case, and then turns to the positive welfare impact of the current de facto regime of deference to the European Union and United States.

Explaining Deference

There are several reasons why smaller jurisdictions defer to the European Union and United States when it comes to reviewing global mergers. The first is economic. A multi-jurisdictional merger will be the goal of companies seeking to gain profit from the merger, whether through increased efficiencies, better global reach, anti-competitive profits, or any of dozens of other possibilities. The merged entity will realize those profits across the jurisdictions in question. If there emerges a jurisdiction that threatens to make an order against a merger, the merging firms face a trade-off. One possibility is to give up on the merger and forgo the profits associated with it. A different approach is to go ahead with the merger, realize profits from all the jurisdictions that would permit the merger, but retreat from the jurisdiction that would have disallowed it. That is, the merged entity can simply stop selling in the jurisdiction in question, and relocate any assets belonging to the merged entity. Aside from practical reality, even at the level of principle, it cannot be a violation of competition policy for a firm to stop selling in a jurisdiction. On the effects doctrine noted above, a merged entity that does not have any anti-competitive impact in a local jurisdiction because of a refusal to sell in that jurisdiction cannot violate local law. Given the potential for increased profits from the merger in all the other jurisdictions in which the merging parties continue to do business, it could well be profitable for the merging parties to retreat entirely from the smaller profits associated with the objecting jurisdiction.

Consider, then, the perspective of a small jurisdiction that has concerns about the competitive impact of a merger, but recognizes that it is an outlier in this respect. If a large jurisdiction makes an order against the merger, the small jurisdiction's decision makes no difference. On the other hand, if it is the only jurisdiction making an order against the merger, it risks the exit of the merging parties altogether, something that could easily be a rational strategy for the merged entity if the profits associated with the jurisdiction are small, and the potential gains from a merger elsewhere are large. While the first-best world from the perspective of the small jurisdiction might be that the would-be merging parties continue to compete in the jurisdiction, it could be better to allow the parties to merge and sell in the jurisdiction than to have them exit.

Anticipating that they potentially risk self-defeating outcomes by attempting to block a global merger that other jurisdictions approve, it is rational for smaller jurisdictions to defer to larger ones.

On the other hand, if larger jurisdictions object to the merger, while smaller ones approve, the approval of the smaller jurisdictions makes no difference to the outcome. The parties can either merge or not merge, and will live with the decision of the large jurisdiction not allowing the merger: they have too much economically at stake to seek to avoid the order not to merge by exiting from the large jurisdictions; better to forgo the gains from the merger than to forgo the gains from selling into the large jurisdictions. In such a case, the smaller jurisdictions have no choice: the more restrictive the large jurisdictions are, the less of a say they have over merger outcomes.

There is an intermediate possibility, in which there is more than one smaller jurisdiction that would block a merger that larger jurisdictions would allow. Even in this case, however, it may be rational for the smaller jurisdiction not to make an order against the merger, and instead leave other jurisdictions to make such a call. If enough other jurisdictions make an order, the merging parties may choose to abandon the merger rather than exit a significant number of smaller jurisdictions, in which case, for an individual jurisdiction, it makes no difference whether it also issues an order. Only in one case does the decision of a small jurisdiction matter: if the jurisdiction deciding to make an order against the merger is pivotal to the decision to abandon the merger. This circumstance would presumably be improbable. Given that investigating mergers is costly, it is unlikely to be rational to invest much in such an investigation.

In summary of the argument thus far, smaller jurisdictions are rational to defer to large jurisdictions in evaluating global mergers: if the large jurisdictions object, then the merger will not occur and the decision of the small jurisdiction has no impact; if the small jurisdiction is the lone objector, then it risks the merging parties exiting in the face of an order against the merger; and even if there is a group of small, objecting jurisdictions, the decision of any single smaller jurisdiction is unlikely to have an impact on the decision to merge, so there is little gain in making an order to offset the costs of the investigation.

The second argument about the rational deference of smaller jurisdictions to larger ones resonates with, but is distinct from, the first. There is a danger that even if the small authority successfully blocks a merger, larger, non-merging jurisdictions will impose costs on the objecting jurisdiction. Disputes over merger review have flared up from time to time between similarly politically powerful jurisdictions in the European Union and the United States, with the United States approving, for example, the GE/Honeywell merger, and the European Union forbidding it.[11] Observing the tensions that these disputes have generated, small jurisdictions may rationally wish to avoid provoking more politically powerful jurisdictions who could punish the objector either within antitrust, or by other political means, on everything from trade to security cooperation to diplomatic assistance. In short, there are very real *realpolitik* considerations that rationally deter smaller jurisdictions from flying in the face of consensus and attempting to block unilaterally an intrinsically global merger.

There is a third set of reasons that help explain why small jurisdictions defer to large ones and do not attempt on their own to block global mergers: administrative efficiency. While there are important variations in competition policy across jurisdictions, most existing authorities rely on a similar set of economic considerations in reviewing mergers. At root, jurisdictions attempt to determine whether the merger will lessen competition sufficiently such that an order against it is appropriate. There are variations in criteria for evaluating whether the merger will lessen competition across jurisdictions, but these tend, in many cases, to lead to similar outcomes. Most importantly, in every jurisdiction, many, many more mergers are approved than are not. That is, in most cases, the parties will pre-notify, the authorities will spend resources on reviewing the merger, and the merger will go ahead as originally planned, without antitrust challenges.

In contrast, there is a much smaller number of merger cases in which competition authorities make an order. Even in these cases, however, the similarities across competition jurisdictions in their approach to merger review are far greater than the differences. All jurisdictions will examine the relevant market(s) in question, identify relevant competitors and ask whether the merger will affect competitive conditions *ex post* sufficiently that an order should be made.

This is not to say that there are not variations. There are. The European Union, for example, tends to be suspicious of mergers that create large, powerful merged entities, even if the merging parties do not necessarily compete head-to-head, while the United States will focus on competitive circumstances to evaluate mergers. Canada has an efficiencies defence to mergers, as another example, while most other jurisdictions do not have one (or at least do not have a meaningful one that is likely to affect the outcome of the review). Occasionally, these differences in principle result in differences in practice. Again, GE/Honeywell provides an example, with the United States approving and the European Union disapproving the merger. But in the bulk of cases, similar outcomes are likely, even if there are differences in policy.

Given that existing policies are not that different from one another, there is an administrative efficiency explanation for deference to larger jurisdictions in the review of global mergers. If policies were completely identical, it would be obviously administratively inefficient for multiple jurisdictions to actively review a merger. With the variation in policies that exists in practice, on the other hand, it may or may not make sense for any given jurisdiction to scrutinize carefully a merger. The benefit of local scrutiny is that local preferences are more likely to be influential, but the cost is that local authorities and the parties must invest in the local investigation.

---

11   European Commission, Press Release, IP/01/939, "The Commission prohibits GE's acquisition of Honeywell" (3 July 2001).

Where policies across jurisdictions are similar, the better outcome may be that one jurisdiction investigates carefully and extensively, and other jurisdictions largely defer to that process.

Such an outcome makes even more sense if a jurisdiction has lower costs in investigating than others. In such a case, efficiencies from lower investigation costs from having only one jurisdiction investigate are more likely to trump the efficiencies from having the merger review reflect local preferences.

It is plausible that there are significant economies of scale at competition policy enforcement agencies. A very small jurisdiction, for example, is less likely to find it cost-justifiable to employ a significant staff of full-time economists that would either work with outside experts, or on their own, to conduct an empirical analysis of a market and a proposed merger's probable impact. In addition, the larger the jurisdiction, the greater experience agency staff will have with merger and other kinds of competition analysis. It is reasonable to expect that larger jurisdictions will, all things being equal, have lower enforcement costs than smaller ones.

Given that larger jurisdictions will have lower costs in reviewing mergers, it is probable that they will be more likely to review a global merger than smaller jurisdictions. There are local benefits and costs from reviewing a merger. Larger jurisdictions are more likely to have more significant local benefits from deciding whether to approve a merger or not, as there is likely to be a larger economic stake in the outcome for a large jurisdiction than for a small one. Moreover, larger jurisdictions are more likely to have economies of scale at the enforcement agency, which implies that their costs are likely to be lower. It is reasonable to expect, then, that larger competition jurisdictions are more likely to find it cost-justifiable to investigate a global merger thoroughly.

There is a caveat associated with the cost-benefit reasons for a smaller jurisdiction's deference to larger jurisdictions. There may be a free-rider temptation on the part of larger jurisdictions, especially if their competition regimes are similar to others. That is, while local benefits may exceed local costs *conditional on no other jurisdiction reviewing the merger*, it may be even better for the larger jurisdiction to defer to another sophisticated jurisdiction that reviews the merger.

There are several reasons why the potential free-rider problem is not a problem in practice. First, large jurisdictions anticipate that there are economically rational reasons for small jurisdictions not to go against the will of a larger one, such as the risk that merging parties vacate the jurisdiction, or the risk of retaliation from an aggrieved large jurisdiction. Large jurisdictions would only attempt to free-ride on other large jurisdictions. This, for the moment, means that only the United States and European Union are likely to be the significant agencies reviewing intrinsically global mergers.

As between the European Union and United States, there is much more likely to be coordination and cooperation than free-riding attempts to defer to each other. Each jurisdiction has its own views of competition, which, while fundamentally similar to one another, do vary. Given the large economic stakes for each jurisdiction from intrinsically global mergers, the European Union and United States are likely to find it worthwhile to investigate on their own, and share what they find with the other jurisdiction in the hopes of influencing the outcome in a manner favourable to their own jurisdiction. While such attempts at coordination do not always succeed, it is probable that both the European Union and United States benefit from the investigation and attempt to influence the other.

The Rationality and Efficiency of the Status Quo

All three sets of reasons for the deference of smaller to larger antitrust jurisdictions help explain the status quo in the review of intrinsically global mergers and, moreover, help justify it. The United States and European Union are clearly the most significant jurisdictions in the review of global mergers in practice. Small jurisdictions, perhaps out of economic rationality and a concern that merging parties will abandon their jurisdiction, perhaps out of *realpolitik* concerns, perhaps for efficiency reasons, do not challenge mergers on their own in practice, but rather defer to the United States and European Union.

This outcome of US/EU hegemony is almost certainly welcome from a global welfare perspective. While policies vary across competition jurisdictions, they do not fundamentally differ, which means that the lack of influence of local jurisdictions over merger reviews is unlikely to present significant costs.

This is especially so when one considers the up or down nature of merger remedies. Given that intrinsically global mergers[12] are either approved or they are not, there is simply no state of the world in which all local preferences can be reflected in a nuanced way in the outcome of the merger review. The loss of local influence is therefore inevitable, regardless of the particular configuration of global merger enforcement. The only question is which regime(s) decide(s) the matter.

Given the similarities in approach at present, and given that local influence cannot be accommodated in all-or-nothing merger reviews in any event, antitrust enforcement over intrinsically global mergers is better left to the lowest-cost enforcers. Given their scale and expertise, the most efficient agencies are very likely to be those in the European Union and the United States. This is the outcome that we observe in practice, and is appropriate. Smaller jurisdictions effectively benefit from the enforcement offered by the European Union and United States.

There is an additional reason why the status quo is efficient. Not only are the European Union and the United States most likely to be the most expert, but they are also the ones with the largest economic stakes in globally significant mergers, at least as a general matter. To the extent, then, that there are variations in local preferences for antitrust policy across jurisdictions, it is most efficient that the preferences of the jurisdictions with the greatest economic stakes in the merger be reflected in the outcome. The status quo, with its deference to the United States and European Union, achieves this.

Challenges to the Status Quo

The story to this point is largely upbeat about the current state of international review over intrinsically global mergers. Most jurisdictions may pursue local remedies to address local concerns, but leave the basic decision to allow (or disallow) the intrinsically global merger to the European Union and the United States. As I have explained, there are administrative and

---

12   There may be local remedies for local issues, but I am focusing on the question of intrinsically global mergers, whose effects are similar across geographic locations.

other efficiencies associated with the practical confinement of merger review to these major jurisdictions.

There is, however, reason to suspect that there will be strains on the status quo in the coming years. While other factors may have a role in challenging EU and US hegemony, including the probable emergence of China as a significant antitrust jurisdiction, it is apparent that the emphasis on economic criteria in antitrust matters is under siege as political considerations gain prominence, at least in public discourse. If political considerations, as opposed to economic ones, grow in importance, this could have a significant impact on the status quo.

It is well known and documented that politics has long influenced antitrust. Canada, for example, adopted a competition statute in 1889,[13] which at the time was understood, in part, to offset the political and economic consequences of a robust program of tariffs then prevailing. The European Union, in a more coherent approach, adopted pan-European competition policy as part of the program of political integration that followed World War II and clearly had political motivations: jurisdictions did not want private restraints on trade to replace now-abolished, publicly established restraints on trade [14] South Africa relies on competition policy, in part, to address historical racial injustice.[15]

But while it is not difficult to identify examples of jurisdictions having political goals for competition policy, it is harder to discern globally significant cases in recent times in which a political goal ran counter to the economic considerations underlying the review of a merger or other conduct, and the case was decided on political grounds *despite* economic considerations cutting in the other direction. Some in the United States, to be sure, have expressed concerns that the European Union has decided cases on a political, protectionist basis (GE/Honeywell, for example),[16] but there is not strong evidence that the European Union treats global mergers differently from domestic ones.[17]

While it is far too early to say what the impact will be, there is momentum in some quarters for antitrust to take a much more explicitly political, rather than economic, approach. In particular, concerns about the rise of globally powerful technology platforms have invited calls for antitrust, and/or perhaps other regulation, to respond to a perceived problem with concentrated economic and political power. For example, prominent calls for Facebook to be broken up, including recently by a co-founder,[18] are not premised strictly, or even necessarily at all, on market power in advertising markets, but rather on the concerns that its size and access to data make it a politically powerful entity.

Such calls to use antitrust as a tool to respond to political concerns are not without problems. The problem, as Daniel Crane has identified,[19] is that one should not abandon carefully

---

13   *An Act for the Prevention and Suppression of Combinations formed in the Restraint of Trade*, SC 1889, c 41.

14   See e.g. Michelle Cini, "The European Merger Regime: Accounting for the Distinctiveness of the EU Model" (2002) 30:2 Policy Studies J 240; Hubert Buch-Hansen & Angela Wigger, "Revisiting 50 years of market-making: The neoliberal transformation of European competition policy" (2010) 17:1 Rev Intl Political Economy 20.

15   Wise, *supra* note 6.

16   For discussion of US criticism of the EU decision, see e.g. Michael Elliott, "The Anatomy of the GE-Honeywell Disaster", *Time Magazine* (8 July 2001), online: <http://content.time.com/time/business/article/0,8599,166732,00.html>.

17   Anu Bradford, Robert J Jackson Jr & Jonathon Zytnick, "Is EU Merger Control Used for Protectionism? An Empirical Analysis" (2018) 15:1 J Empirical Leg Studies 165.

developed economic and legal criteria in favour of vaguely articulated concerns about political power. This is not necessarily to say that political concerns about Facebook and other platforms are not legitimate, but it is to doubt that antitrust is the solution, rather than some other policy instrument better calibrated to address political power.

But whatever one's views of recent calls for the greater politicization of antitrust, it remains the case that they are growing in prominence. It is predictable that they will have an influence on antitrust on the ground in the coming years.

Such a development would threaten the status quo. Currently, the United States and European Union take fundamentally similar economic approaches to merger review. Given that it would be difficult for any jurisdiction to settle on clear and uncontroversial approaches to using antitrust to regulate political power, at least in the short to medium term it is reasonable to expect significant variation across the United States and European Union about politics and antitrust. This alone would upset the status quo.

In addition, however, I have described the causes of deference to the European Union and United States as having both economic motivations and justifications. Economic, cost-benefit analysis, by definition, recedes in policy significance where non-economic, political values are at stake. If a country is concerned about the distortion of democracy allegedly caused by a large tech firm, it may be willing to risk that firm's exit from the jurisdiction altogether by taking an interventionist approach to antitrust, rather than defer to a permissive approach taken in other countries.

The potential rise of non-economic, political influences over antitrust policy presents the risk of significant upheavals in competition policy in a variety of important ways. The point I emphasize here is that it risks disturbing the status quo that has emerged in respect of intrinsically global mergers. Rather than deferring to the two largest jurisdictions, smaller jurisdictions may sacrifice the efficiencies of deference in order to pursue non-economic goals that are furthered by orders against global mergers, even if such orders result in the exit of the merging parties from the jurisdiction. And there would inevitably be a greater probability of disagreement between the large jurisdictions in any event: as the economic consensus over basic antitrust objectives recedes in importance, it is unlikely that a consensus over political goals will emerge, and certainly not in the short run. Expect concerns over multi-jurisdictional review of mergers, and the corresponding risks of the race to the strictest, to grow alongside any growth in the influence of politics over antitrust. The economically defensible status quo may not last much longer.

II.
ACCOUNTABILITY FRAMEWORKS TAKING SHAPE

5

"COYOTE AND THE CANNIBAL BOY"

Secwépemc Insights on the Corporation

Rebecca Johnson and Bonnie Leonard

Introduction

In this chapter, we take up the invitation to share Canadian perspectives on the globalized rule of law, with a focus on the corporation in international, transnational and domestic law and governance. We have chosen to focus on a number of key concerns. How might we understand and respond to the corporation as a very particular kind of legal person, one that plays an increasingly significant role in global governance? What challenges emerge in considering "the best interests of the corporation" and the related fiduciary duties of its corporate directors? What is the work of directors' duties of care and corporate social responsibility, in particular within the context of extractive industries in a world of shared limits? Indigenous legal orders, we argue, need to be part of contemporary conversations about such questions. Our exploration is grounded and informed by three key assertions. First, Indigenous legal orders exist and operate in the world. Second, contemporary state-based legal orders are embedded in histories of colonization, frequently built on the (ongoing) denial of Indigenous legalities, autonomies and sovereignties. Third, such denial is not inevitable. Indigenous and non-Indigenous people alike can act otherwise in their engagement with Indigenous law, legal theorizing and legal resources. These engagements are important, and they need to operate not only as theoretical possibilities, but also as embedded and embodied practices.

In order to model the kind of work we believe is both possible and necessary, we particularize our discussion. Our focus will be on the forms through which consumptive economic power has sometimes been concentrated, and about possible strategies for monitoring or holding such power in check. We place our conversation within the context of the *Secwépemc* legal order, and explore one specific legal resource, the 1909 telling of the Secwépemc oral narrative, "Coyote and the Cannibal Boy." This storied legal resource is a rich example of Secwépemc legal theorizing, and is an important "tool for thinking."[1] Through an exploration of Secwépemc storied legal thinking, we hope to encourage active engagement with Indigenous legal orders more generally, and to model in very specific ways how such engagement may assist us in collectively addressing contemporary legal questions raised by, for example, the pervasiveness of corporate structures in our lives.

Beginning with Some Questions about Corporations

Let us begin, then, by situating our engagement against the backdrop of contemporary public conversations about the corporation as an economic, social and political actor. In these conversations, the corporation figures sometimes as hero, sometimes as villain and often as inevitable.[2] There are different ways to tell the history of the corporate form, but whether one looks to classic texts such as *The King's Two Bodies*,[3] or contemporary explorations such as *The Corporate Commonwealth*,[4] one can observe that the corporate form has been a dominant mechanism through which wealth has been gathered, consolidated and moved. Through the East India Company or the Hudson's Bay Company, one can note how the emergence of the corporate form has moved in parallel with histories of colonization and empire. In the cinematic world, the theme of the corporation as embedded in toxic globalization is well established, whether one looks to the Tyrell Corporation of *Blade Runner* fame, or the Water & Power

---

1   Louis Bird, *Telling Our Stories: Omushkego Legends and Histories from the Hudson Bay* (Toronto: University of Toronto Press, 2005).

2   Scholars have focused attention on how these corporate structures operate in multiple sites, and how they might best be understood, governed, monitored or reformed. See e.g. William K Carroll, *Corporate Power in a Globalizing World: A Study in Elite Social Organization* (Don Mills, ON: Oxford University Press, 2004); Claire A Cutler, *Private Power and Global Authority: Transnational Merchant Law in the Global Political Economy* (Cambridge, MA: Cambridge University Press, 2003); Allan Hutchinson, *The Companies We Keep: Corporate Governance for a Democratic Society* (Toronto: Irwin Law, 2005); Janis Sarra, ed, *Corporate Governance in Global Capital Markets* (Vancouver: University of British Columbia Press, 2003). On the rhetoric of inevitability, and theories of corporate and marketized identities in our times, see Wendy Brown, *Undoing the Demos: Neoliberalism's Stealth Revolution* (New York: Zone Books, 2015).

3   Ernst H Kantorowicz, *The King's Two Bodies: A Study in Medieval Political Theology*, vol 20, *Past and Present* (Princeton: Princeton University Press, 1957).

4   Henry S Turner, *The Corporate Commonwealth: Pluralism and Political Fictions in England, 1516–1651* (Chicago: University of Chicago Press, 2016).

Corporation of *Tank Girl*.[5] Joel Bakan suggests that this fear is not surprising, given that the structure of the corporation itself is one that generates a pathological pursuit of power.[6]

Academic and popular literature both encourage reflection on how we understand the corporation as a legal person, with agency, interests and ways of being responsible to others.[7] Through an act of incorporation, a given corporation is legislatively declared to be a natural person or, perhaps more accurately, "to have the capacity, rights, powers and privileges of a natural person."[8] We have new stories of origin. But this legal person is not, like the human person, constrained by the rhythms and demands of biological life. At the moment of incorporation, it emerges with full capacity, somewhat like Athena springing from the head of Zeus. Untethered to biology and temporality, there is no necessary limit to how large the corporation can grow, nor to how long it can live. This untethering is part of what gives power to the corporate form: it can enable action that extends beyond the limits of time and scale. It also poses different challenges.

The corporation, lacking a body in the conventional sense, can act in the world only through the bodies of human agents or intermediaries. And so, intention and action might be distributed across a number of human and non-human actors.[9] The corporation itself (unlike its human agents) has no soul to be damned and no body to be jailed.[10] This poses challenges in governance. Standing as fiduciaries, the directors have the obligation to give effect to the corporate will, acting only "in the best interests" of the corporation. But how are those interests best aligned? And before that, how are they to be identified? Are there any limits to what those interests might be? What are the implications of the profit motive being so central to those interests? If there is a structural hunger at the heart of the corporation, what is the place of directors in working with that hunger? How is this hunger to be moderated, channelled or controlled? Does this hunger pose different challenges based on the size of the corporation? Does scale matter? The possibility of perpetual life invites different questions if one imagines the corporation as living a kind of "angelic time" or as located in a shadow world of the living dead.[11] What might the Secwépemc legal order have to say about these questions?

---

5   An IMDB search for "corporation" retrieves 411 titles. Specifying "evil corporation" generates 143 films.

6   Joel Bakan, *The Corporation: The Pathological Pursuit of Profit and Power* (Toronto: Penguin Canada, 2004); see also Harry Glasbeek, *Wealth by Stealth: Corporate Crime, Corporate Law, and the Perversion of Democracy* (Toronto: Between the Lines, 2002).

7   We note here Paddy Ireland's work, exploring the slow process through which the understanding of a company as "they" was transformed to an understanding of the corporation as an "it," as an entity capable of an origin story. See PW Ireland, "The Rise of the Limited Liability Company" (1984) 12 Intl J Soc L 239; Paddy Ireland, Ian Grigg-Spall & Dave Kelly, "The Conceptual Foundations of Modern Company Law" (1987) 14:1 JL & Soc'y 149.

8   There are, of course, different regimes for the creation of corporate personhood. In British Columbia, the creation of a legal person is present in the practices of incorporation that produce both the corporation and the cooperative, whether organized under federal or provincial jurisdiction. See e.g. *Canada Business Corporations Act*, RS 1985, c C-44, s 15; *British Columbia Business Corporations Act*, SBC 2002, c 57, s 30; *British Columbia Co-operative Associations Act*, SBC 1999, c 28, s 19. In Quebec, the corporate person is identified as a "moral person" rather than as a "legal person."

9   Steven Bittle, *Still Dying for a Living: Corporate Criminal Liability After the Westray Mine Disaster* (Vancouver: University of British Columbia Press, 2014).

10   Edward, First Baron Thurlow (1731–1806), the Lord Chancellor during the impeachment of Warren Hastings, stated: "Corporations have neither bodies to be punished, nor souls to be condemned, they therefore do as they like." Cited in John Poynder, *Literary Extracts*, vol 1 (1844) at 268.

11   We have been inspired here by the work of Martha-Marie Kleinhans, "The Angelic Time of the Legal Person" (Paper delivered at the "Liquid Lives, Wholesome Selves" conference, Centre for Law, Gender & Sexuality, Westminster University, London, February 2007).

Shifting Gears – Sharing a Secwépemc Story

The Secwépemc, which in Secwépemctsín means "spread out people," have for at least 10,000 years known the south-central interior of British Columbia as their homeland.[12] Secwépemcúlecw (the land of the Secwépemc people) is vast, extending across 180,000 km. Secwépemc law continues to be practised. That law has its own long and rich tradition governing legal relationships, not only between Secwépemc and other peoples, but also with animals, plants, water and land. As is the case with other Indigenous legal orders in North America, the Secwépemc have their own history of legal pluralism and transnational law.[13] Secwépemc law has its layered and textured legal resources for governance and engagements with families, communities, economies, lands, non-human life, property, succession, citizenship, boundaries, diplomacy, war, peace and international entanglements. It has resources that provide space and tools for identifying, thinking about and responding to the full range of challenges in our past and current worlds.

One of these resources is "Coyote and the Cannibal Boy,"[14] an English version of which appears in a collection of Secwépemc stories shared with James Teit,[15] and gathered into a 1909 monograph, *The Shuswap*. Because we take seriously the act of storytelling as intellectual and legal practice, let us begin with the story itself. You may, if you wish, imagine this story being told at night, in the woods, around a crackling fire. You may imagine yourself sitting by Teit as he listens to his old friend Sixwi'lexken ("Big Billy") tell the story in his own language, Secwépemctsín. Or you may, if you wish, imagine yourself in the middle of the day, sitting in a rather sterile classroom full of law students, halfway through the semester in your Business Associations course, listening to the professor announce that they are going to tell you a Secwépemc story. You might think to yourself that you are not certain you could find Secwépemc territory on a map, or wonder what connections you can make from the story to the course materials. Or perhaps you grew up in the area, and can imagine yourself walking on the sage-scented hills of Kamloops, cooling your feet in the waters of Shuswap Lake, or watching salmon on their migratory voyages in any number of rivers. In any case, you set down your pen to listen.

---

12   For a rich exploration of the Secwépemc world, see Marianne Ignace & Ronald E Ignace, *Secwépemc People, Land, and Laws — Yerí7 Re Stsqʼeyʼs-Kucw* (Montreal & Kingston: McGill-Queen's University Press, 2017).

13   This is unsurprising, given the number of neighbouring nations, which includes the Sekani and Cree to the north, Cree and Stoney to the east, the Ktunaxa (Kootnei), Okanagan, N'laka'pumux (Thompson) and St'at'im (Lillooet) to the south, and the Tsilqot'in and Dakelh (Carrier) people to the west. There is an acceptance of multiple legal orders, with a focus on work in collaboration with others in order to deal with shared problems. The record includes long histories of treaties with other neighbouring Indigenous nations to end disputes and settle boundaries. See Ignace & Ignace, *supra* note 12, ch 8, 288ff, "Treaties, Wars, and Intermarriage." In the Indigenous context specifically, it has been argued that much of Indigenous law can be understood as "transnational." See James (Sákéj) Youngblood Henderson, "Mi'kmaw Tenure in Atlantic Canada" (1995) 18:2 Dal LJ 196 at 238; James (Sákéj) Youngblood Henderson, "First Nations' Legal Inheritances in Canada: The Mi'kmaw Model" (1996) 23 Man LJ 1 at 24–25. On transnational law more generally, see David Armitage, *Foundations of Modern International Thought* (Cambridge, MA: Cambridge University Press, 2013) at 6, 18, 42–45.

14   "Coyote and the Cannibal Boy", told by Sixwi'lexken (Big Billy) from the Upper Fraser River area (Canoe Creek), recorded in James Teit, *The Jesup North Pacific Expedition, Memoir of the American Museum of Natural History*, vol IV, part VIII, *The Shuswap* (Leiden & New York: EJ Brill & GE Stechert, 1909) at 640–41.

15   James Teit was a Shetlander who moved to the interior of British Columbia in 1884, married a Nlaka'pamux woman, and became a fluent speaker. He was a key figure in both early anthropology and Indigenous rights activism in British Columbia. For more about Teit, see Wendy Wickwire, *At the Bridge: James Teit and an Anthropology of Belonging* (Vancouver: University of British Columbia Press, 2019). On Teit's attention to gender, see Wendy Wickwire, "Women in Ethnography: The Research of James A. Teit" (1993) 14:4 Ethnohistory 539.

"Coyote and the Cannibal Boy"

As Coyote was passing near the house of some people, he saw a boy, whom he captured. He put him on his shoulders and walked away with him as fast as he could. Now, Coyote had a small boil or sore at the root of his neck, or somewhere between his shoulders; and the boy, seeing it, picked the skin off and commenced to probe it. Coyote said, "Don't do that! It hurts." But the boy said, "I am only opening the sore to let the matter out, so that it may soon get well." Thus the boy opened up the sore four times, until it bled and became large; and each time Coyote remonstrated with him, for it was painful. At last he reached home with the boy, and the people asked him where he had gotten him, and what he intended to do with him. Coyote answered, "Oh! I stole him. When he grows, he will do everything for me. He is my slave." The people said, "If he belongs to any tribe nearby, his friends may attack us, and try to get him back." Coyote did not know that the boy was a cannibal's son.

That night Coyote made his bed and put the boy in it, covering him over with a blanket, and lay down alongside of him. In the same bed, on Coyote's other side, lay a woman with whom he was familiar. Shortly after going to bed, Coyote turned his back to the boy, and, laying his head on the woman's breast, he soon fell fast asleep. Then the boy put his mouth to Coyote's sore and sucked out all his blood and flesh, leaving nothing but the bones and skin. The boy swelled out very much, and had a thirst for human blood and flesh. Therefore he arose and killed all the people, and ate them, excepting one man who happened to wake up, and who made his escape. As the boy ate the people, he kept on growing, until, by the time he had finished his meal, he had attained the proportions of a man of gigantic bulk and enormous weight. Now, following the tracks of the man who had escaped, he soon began to draw near him. As he ran along, he repeatedly uttered the cry, "A'ak!" and the man, hearing him coming, threw earth behind him, thus retarding the cannibal's progress. Four times he retarded him thus, but at last the cannibal came close up to him again.

Then the man hastily made a fire, and, taking a marmot's bone, a porcupine's bone, a wolf's bone, and a grisly bear's bone, he put them into the fire. Taking them out again, he sharpened their points, and transformed them into four dogs, placing those made of the marmot and porcupine bones in front, and the other two a little farther back, while he himself sat down behind all. He made the dogs lie down quietly, with their jaws resting on their front feet, and leaving enough space for a person to pass between them. The cannibal approached, and asked the man to call in his dogs, that he might pass. The man answered, "Pass between them: there is plenty of room. They are very quiet dogs, and have never been known to bite anybody." The cannibal walked in between them, and, when he had passed the first two, all the dogs attacked him simultaneously and tore him to pieces. They devoured him, and licked his blood off the ground. Then the man returned home, and found Coyote still alive, but in such a weak condition that he could not walk. The man hunted deer, killed many, and fed Coyote until he regained his flesh and strength, and became quite well again. The man and Coyote lived together for a long time.

With the story once told, let us pause to place a number of our own preliminary questions on the table. First, how might we think of the cannibal boy in this story? Can he help us think about the nature of the corporation? Second, how might the relationship between Coyote and the cannibal boy help us think about the relationship between the corporation, its shareholders and its directors? Does the boy's status as both cannibal and child invite us to think about how we theorize fiduciary duties and duties of care between corporations and their directors? How do the people in this story stand in for "stakeholders," and how might we understand both the risks they encounter and the ways they might participate in the work of governance? What strategies are available when the behaviour of the cannibal/corporation threatens the community as a whole? How might we unpack the potential of the marmot, porcupine, wolf and bear bones/dogs as allies, procedures or resources to contain the danger? Finally, what might we learn from the final piece of the story, where Coyote is nursed back to health? Keep these questions in mind, and we will return to them later in the discussion. But first, let us say a bit more about the three key assertions that ground our argument, and about how one can engage with a story such as this.

Visibilizing the Existence and Continuing Relevance of Indigenous Law

Indigenous peoples, like all other peoples, in North America or elsewhere in the world, have always lived within traditions structured through law. We put to the side arguments that suggest Indigenous peoples have lived outside of structures of law, or that speak of those relations as resting only in culture or tradition. In our view, such arguments rest on a narrow understanding of law, or of the multiple forms through which legal orders find expression and structure. Nation-to-nation relations (whether within the Indigenous, Canadian, transnational or international arenas) are built on a foundational understanding that multiple legal orders exist in the world, and that people can learn from and work across these orders. Legal pluralism is, quite simply, a fact.[16] And the Secwépemc legal order is, stated with equal simplicity, a fact.

It is unfortunately still the case that statements such as these remain controversial in some quarters. The history of empire and colonization lurks as the shadow character in many domestic discussions about Indigenous law, where there is a continued blindness (or resistance) to acknowledging and working with Indigenous legal orders.[17] This domestic blindness to Indigenous law is also visible in the international realm, where Indigenous peoples are too often pushed to the margins of the debate, fighting for recognition or inclusion in conversations about the spaces in which life is lived.[18] We begin here simply to acknowledge the challenges against which contemporary discussions often proceed.

Even in the face of the difficulties, however, we hold to our third proposition: engagement with Indigenous laws is both possible and important. Just as Indigenous peoples have done the hard work of learning how to understand and work with the legal mechanisms of the colonial state,

---

16   Paul Schiff Berman, *Global Legal Pluralism: A Jurisprudence of Law Beyond Borders* (New York: Cambridge University Press, 2012). For a nuanced treatment of this insight in the context of India, see Pooja Parmar, *Indigeneity and Legal Pluralism in India* (New York: Cambridge University Press, 2015).

17   In one articulation of the problem, Canada put in place jurispathic laws, "laws that would not recognize or tolerate any other laws but themselves." See Hadley Friedland et al, "Porcupine and Other Stories: Legal Relations in Secwépemcúlecw" (2018) 48:1 RGD 153 at 157 [Friedland et al, "Porcupine"].

18   This is frustratingly visible in article 46 of the United Nations Declaration on the Rights of Indigenous Peoples (GA Res 295, UNGAOR, 61st Sess, Supp No 49, UN Doc A/Res/61/295, 46 ILM 1013 [2007]), which states that the integrity of sovereign states cannot be impaired by the Indigenous rights articulated within the document. For an exploration of the ways that Inuit peoples try to find spaces of engagement within jurispathic systems in the circumpolar Arctic, see Gordon Christie, "Indigeneity and Sovereignty in Canada's Far North: The Arctic and Inuit Sovereignty" (2011) 110:2 South Atlantic Q 329.

it is both necessary and possible for the reverse to happen.[19] Our commitment to this belief is founded in the experience of engaging in such work. Over the past several years, the Shuswap Nation Tribal Council and the Indigenous Law Research Unit at the University of Victoria have worked in partnership on two collaborations. One of these focused on lands and resources, and the other engaged with Kwséltkten/Secwépemc-kt (relations of kinship and belonging).[20] Both projects are part of ongoing work around and with Secwépemc law, aiming to identify and articulate law "in a form that would be cognizable across legal culture."[21]

In doing this work, there are many legal resources one can turn to. There are many forms and structures in which Indigenous law is both laid down and can be drawn up: language, land, stories, songs, art, protocols, dreams, deliberative practices, elders, oral histories, conventions, artefacts, trial transcripts and more.[22] As is the case in each legal order, there are also practices and conventions of interpretation that can shape and guide the ways one identifies and engages with the different sources from which law flows.[23] In working with the richness of these legal resources, one can more easily move beyond the presumption that Indigenous law is primarily about a list of rules, and take up instead Indigenous law's capacity to open avenues for dealing with important and recurrent human challenges.

---

19   For a discussion of the simultaneous danger and necessity of such work, see Jeffery G Hewitt, "Decolonizing and Indigenizing: Some Considerations for Law Schools" (2016) 33:1 Windsor YB Access Just 65. For a discussion of why all people need to be involved in such projects, see Four Arrows, "The Indigenization Controversy: For Whom and By Whom?" (2019) 10:18 Critical Education 1.

20   See the report on the first of these: *Secwépemc Lands and Resources Law Research Report*, online: <www.uvic.ca/law/assets/docs/ilru/SNTC%20Law%20Book%20July%202018.pdf>. For a longer discussion of the shape of these partnerships, see Friedland et al, "Porcupine", *supra* note 17. We note here the important role of the Secwepemc Elders Council in supporting this work and pressing it forward.

21   Friedland et al, "Porcupine", *supra* note 17 at 158.

22   There is a rich literature exploring law in language, landscape, ceremony and art. A sampling that has been helpful in our own work includes: Hannah Askew, "Learning from Bear-Walker: Indigenous Legal Orders and Intercultural Legal Education in Canadian Law Schools" (2016) 33 Windsor YB Access Just 29; Andrée Boiselle, *Law's Hidden Canvas: Teasing out of the Threads of Coast Salish Legal Sensibility* (PhD Dissertation, University of Victoria, 2017) [unpublished]; John Borrows (Kegedonce), *Drawing Out Law: A Spirit's Guide* (Toronto: University of Toronto Press, 2011); Lindsay Borrows, "*Dabaadendiziwin:* Practices of Humility in a Multi-Juridical Legal Landscape" (2016) 33 Windsor YB Access Just 149; Ruth Buchanan & Jeffery G Hewitt, "Treaty Canoe" in Jessie Hohmann & Daniel Joyce, eds, *International Law's Objects* (Oxford: Oxford University Press, 2018) 491; Christie, *supra* note 18; Robert Yelkátte Clifford, "WSÁNEĆ Legal Theory and the Fuel Spill at SELEKTEL (Goldstream River)" (2016) 61:4 McGill LJ 775; Hadley Friedland, *The Wetiko Legal Principles: Cree and Anishinabek Responses to Violence and Victimization* (Toronto: University of Toronto Press, 2018); Alan Hanna, "Making the Round: Aboriginal Title in the Common Law from a Tsilhqot'in Legal Perspective" (2015) 45:3 Ottawa L Rev 365; Darcy Lindberg, "Miyo Nêhiyâwiwin (Beautiful Creeness): Ceremonial Aesthetics and Nêhiyaw Legal Pedagogy" (2018) 16/17 Indigenous LJ 51; Naomi Metallic, "Becoming a Language Warrior" in Marie Battiste, ed, *Living Treaties: Narrating Mi'kmaw Treaty Relations* (Sydney, NS: Cape Breton University Press, 2016) 241; Aaron Mills, "The Lifeworlds of Law: On Revitalizing Indigenous Legal Orders Today" (2016) 61:4 McGill LJ 847; Sarah Morales, "STL'UL NUP: Legal Landscapes of the Hul'qumi'num Mustimuhw" (2016) 33:1 Windsor YB Access Just 103; Val Napoleon, *Ayook: Gitksan Legal Order, Law and Legal Theory* (PhD Dissertation, University of Victoria, 2009) [unpublished]; Nancy Sandy, "*Stsquy'ulécw Re St'exelcemc* (St'exelcemc Laws from the Land)" (2016) 33 Windsor YB Access Just 187; Emily Snyder, *Gender, Power, and Representations of Cree Law* (Vancouver: University of British Columbia Press, 2018); Lara Ulrich & David Gill, "The Tricksters Speak: Klooscap and Wesakechak, Indigenous Law, and the New Brunswick Land Use Negotiation" (2016) 61:4 McGill LJ 979.

23   It is helpful to distinguish questions about legal resources (the places one looks to learn and teach law), from questions about sources of law (that is, the various authorities from which law flows). There is a rich discussion of the various sources (authorities) of law in John Borrows, *Canada's Indigenous Constitution* (Toronto: University of Toronto Press, 2010). See especially *ibid*, ch 2, "Sources and Scope of Indigenous Legal Traditions" at 22.

We have drawn heavily on stories as one resource for legal learning, one way that legal histories, principles and cases are written.[24] Stories are not the only place that law is inscribed, but they are important vehicles for both learning and sharing law, since they have the capacity to carry questions, carry histories, carry theories, and make space for people to begin imagining and understanding themselves as occupying the lifeworlds in which legal structures are constructed. Stories may be particularly helpful at the intersection of new learning. John Borrows, pointing to story methodology, notes that Anishinaabe people tell stories to open spaces for instruction and inquiry, where it is expected that stories (like words) have several meanings.[25] These challenges include the forms and structures through which an economy operates, the forms through which collective action can be organized, ways peoples interact with each other in a world of shared limits, and include questions about, for example, how the corporation might operate in our contemporary societies.

Engaging in Storywork

Western-trained legal actors sometimes tend to approach Indigenous stories in the way they would read one of Aesop's fables, looking to the story for the moral or rule that is offered to guide future conduct. Such an approach rests on an incomplete view of the pedagogy of Indigenous storytelling as a practice of law.[26] Stories are more than lists of rules; they are tools for thinking. In the context of strongly decentralized legal orders, patterns of recording and operationalizing law require robust skills of legal interpretation.[27] Just as there is a range of accepted interpretive practices for reading law within common law and civil law orders, there is a range of interpretive practices that can assist people in working with the storied legal resources of Indigenous legal orders.[28]

There are multiple avenues for respectful and productive engagement and, as is the case with all legal orders, increasing literacy can be built and nourished through engagement over time. The very brevity of some stories is part of their power; they carry great riches without being overwhelming. They can be returned to again and again, and can offer up different insights in different situations.

As is the case with all legal orders, one is asked to inhabit the text or story. In the context of storied resources, the listener is invited to move through the story, to occupy it from a number of different subject positions. What is to be explored, in our story, where the reader/listener

---

24   For an elaboration of the methodology behind this storied form of work, see Hadley Friedland & Val Napoleon, "Gathering the Threads: Developing a Methodology for Researching and Rebuilding Indigenous Legal Traditions" (2015) 1:1 Lakehead LJ 16; Val Napoleon & Hadley Friedland, "An Inside Job: Engaging with Indigenous Legal Traditions through Stories" (2016) 61:4 McGill LJ 725.

25   See e.g. John Borrows, *Law's Indigenous Ethics* (Toronto: University of Toronto Press, 2019), Preface. See also Elsie Paul in collaboration with Paige Raibmon & Harmony Johnson, *Written as I Remember It: Teachings (ʔəms taʔaw) from the Life of a Sliammon Elder* (Vancouver: University of British Columbia Press, 2014).

26   For a rich exploration of Stó:lō pedagogies and methodologies of storywork, see Jo-ann Archibald Q'um q'um Xiiem, *Indigenous Storywork: Educating the Heart, Mind, Body, and Spirit* (Vancouver: University of British Columbia Press, 2008).

27   For a helpful exploration of learning how to read such stories, see Julie Cruikshank, *The Social Life of Stories: Narrative and Knowledge in the Yukon Territory* (Lincoln: University of Nebraska Press, 1998); Julie Cruikshank, *Do Glaciers Listen? Local Knowledge, Colonial Encounters, & Social Imagination* (Vancouver: University of British Columbia Press, 2005).

28   Val Napoleon, "Thinking About Indigenous Legal Orders" in René Provost & Colleen Sheppard, eds, *Dialogues on Human Rights and Legal Pluralism* (Dordrecht: Springer, 2013) 229.

imagines themselves as Coyote, as the people of the village, as the woman at whose breast Coyote sleeps, as the man who escapes death and is pursued, as the dogs brought into existence? It can be read to ask about good and bad behaviour. It can also invite us to consider more complicated relationships of causation, connection and obligation. It can assist us in looking for patterns in the world, and invite us to imagine what shifts in behaviour or structure might enable us to maintain conditions of care, safety and continuity.

These stories unfold most powerfully in the context of shared listening, and practices rooted in conversation and dialogue. Complicated stories enable one to ask questions, to be alive to the many factors at play in a situation, in order to better determine the range of responses that might be both appropriate and possible. In short, we look to the story not simply for "the right answer," but for a richer engagement with the problem that the story poses. Note that this also invites multiple stories to be pulled into interaction with each other.[29] The stories draw the past and present into conversation to help us imagine steps in the direction of future action and thought. In this way, storywork may help us ask ourselves better questions.[30]

There is significant flexibility in working with story. Storywork is strengthened by thinking about the interpretive bounds that are part of the meaning-making process. Here, more aspects of a story come to life where it is read in the context of the legal theory that shapes the order. It may be useful to comment briefly on a few pieces of the interpretive framework within which this story came to be produced, told and retold. First, the story draws in two important characters: Coyote (*Sḱelép*) and a cannibal. Their co-presence evokes the *stsptekwll* and Sḱelép transformer stories. It resonates with stories such as "Coyote Travels the Land," a story that involves events happening as long as 12,000 years ago, where the Secwépemc ancestors took possession of the land, vanquished the "cannibals" and made Secwépemcúlecw safely accessible to the generations after them.[31] These ancient stories are marked on the land and lay down three fundamental laws for the Secwépemc: "the Secwépemc law of sovereignty within Secwépemcúlecw, the law that defines rights of access and rights to resources, and the law that acts as an impetus to make treaties among nations."[32]

There are other Coyote stories that are situated in more contemporary times. Many of these play with the transcending of social and moral boundaries, and involve Coyote making visible the consequences of behaviour that makes a person a nuisance to the community. This sometimes involves the person who defies the norms of acceptable social behaviour, and sometimes involves the person who is unable to recognize the boundaries they have crossed.[33] These stories operate in many layers. As Marianne Ignace and Ronald Ignace put it, "[A]s living *trickster* stories, their attraction to present generations is their timelessness....[T]hey link the past with the present, continuing to engage our emotions, notions of contradictions, and ambiguities of life through

---

29   Chimamanda Ngozi Adichie's insights on "The Danger of a Single Story" are apposite here. TEDGlobal, 2009, online: <www.ted.com/talks/chimamanda_ngozi_adichie_the_danger_of_a_single_story>.

30   On this challenge, see Rebecca Johnson, "Questions about Questions: Law and Film Reflections on the Duty to Learn" (2020) 50 Northern Rev 83.

31   Ignace & Ignace, *supra* note 12 at 59–60.

32   *Ibid* at 59.

33   *Ibid* at 60. They note that this concept has an analogue to the Canadian concepts of nuisance, both in its private sense (i.e., trespass) and public sense (i.e., criminal).

multiple layers of reality and experience."[34] Where Coyote appears in a story, we can anticipate that something is likely to go sideways, and there are important things to be learned.

Part of the context of working with a story might also mean thinking about the time and place that it was told, as well as the audience for and purpose of the telling. This version of the story was shared as part of an active engagement between men from two different legal orders, in the early 1900s. The Secwépemc were politically astute, and also dealing with the very real questions of land dispossession, extractive mining enterprises and epidemics of life-threatening disease. This story is not only an engagement with the past, but also with what was then the contemporary present. As Wendy Wickwire pointed out in her work in the 1980s with Okanagan storyteller Harry Robinson, Coyote stories are powerful sites of engagement. She shows us that "Robinson's Coyote, for example, is important not for what he represents in the deep past, but for his fluid relationships with non-Aboriginal peoples from the beginning of time to the present."[35] Indigenous peoples, she argues, have long shared stories with outsiders not simply as ways of preserving culture, but as forms of engagement. Stories are ways of teaching about legality, of inviting outsiders to see themselves in conversation with a legal order and to take up the ways they are implicated in shared experience. In the telling of this story, it would seem that both Sixwi'lexken and Teit believed there were good reasons for non-Secwépemc people to read themselves into this Secwépemc resource. So let us now return to our story, and walk through it again, thinking together about how the story might help us ask additional questions about the corporation, its nature, its best interests (and its desires), and those with whom it is in relations.

A Return to "Coyote and the Cannibal Boy"

The story begins with a very specific form of desire: Coyote's desire for an easier way of life. He seeks someone (some form) that will do his bidding. Imagining the advantages of having a slave for this purpose, he captures the boy and walks away with him on his shoulders. There is little investigation at this point in the story. One wonders at both his desire for a slave and his presumption that the boy he has captured will indeed be in a position to fill this role. Coyote is explicit about both his actions and his desire. When asked about what he has done, Coyote announces to the people, "I stole him. When he grows, he will do everything for me. He is my slave." The question of the boy's own will or purpose is irrelevant, as Coyote sees the relationship as one of master and slave. Coyote believes that he will be the decision maker; the boy, carried on Coyote's back, is harnessed to Coyote's will. If the boy moves, it is through Coyote's footsteps. In this articulation, if the boy/corporation has a distinct identity, it is structured such that Coyote is the directing mind. Coyote has also identified that the boy is not yet in a position to do the work necessary, in using the words "when he grows." And so, the story invites us to ask about how the boy will grow, and about how he will learn the skills he needs.

But Coyote has not turned his mind to the capacity of the boy to follow his instructions, or to act in accordance with Coyote's desires. The boy retains some agency in this new relationship, although the only place it can be enacted is on the top of Coyote's shoulders. As he is carried, the boy picks the skin off the boil on Coyote's neck and begins to probe it. Coyote tells the boy

---

34   *Ibid.*

35   Wendy Wickwire, "Stories from the Margins: Toward a More Inclusive British Columbia Historiography" (2005) 118 J American Folklore 453 at 453.

to stop: "Don't do that! It hurts." The boy responds with a justification, arguing that the pain is useful or necessary: "I am only opening the sore to let the matter out, so that it may soon get well." This interaction is repeated four times, the sore becoming larger and more painful.[36] Given explicit direction on four occasions, the boy nonetheless continues in a pattern of action that causes pain and/or discomfort, justifying the action rather than stopping. At this point, we are invited to consider the extent to which instructions ("don't do that") and information ("it hurts") are not enough to alter the pattern that is already emerging between Coyote and the boy. What other forms of training or tutelage might be necessary?

When Coyote arrives home with the boy, the people, wanting to know more about the boy's history, lineage or provenance, ask questions that Coyote seems to skip over. Coyote is asked how he came by the boy, and what he intends to do with him. In the face of Coyote's explanation, the people express their concerns: "If he belongs to any tribe nearby, his friends may attack us, and try to get him back." Here, the people are attentive to the possibilities of danger to the whole posed by Coyote's individual action, and they make their concerns visible. In doing so, they raise questions about the impact of Coyote's taking that extend beyond Coyote's purposes. That is, they make visible the risk that they all might suffer as a group as a result of Coyote's desire for a slave. There is some foreshadowing here, since harm does come to the community, albeit not in the precise way they feared. The story does not, however, see the community intervening to exclude Coyote and the boy, or to prevent the boy's arrival. We see an articulation of concern, coupled with what seems like an acknowledgement of Coyote's autonomy. Put otherwise, we see the community articulating concern with Coyote's actions, suggesting that Coyote should act otherwise, and Coyote ignoring or dismissing the warning.

It is only at this point in the story that we, as readers, learn that the boy is a cannibal. One might ask how the story might have been different if Coyote or the people had known the boy was a cannibal. It is worth noting that cannibals appear not infrequently in Secwépemc stories, and cannibals are not always killed upon encounter. Often the question is how cannibals and non-cannibals might live in proximity without extensive harm. The stories do make visible that the cannibals have a thirst for consumption that poses a potential threat. So where cannibals are in the area, it seems crucial to remain attentive and to be careful to minimize the ways cannibals can harm others, or to warn others to take care in those spaces.[37]

In our story, as the community prepares to sleep, Coyote appears to act on his responsibilities for the boy: he makes a bed, puts the boy in it, covers him with a blanket and lays down by him. However, Coyote is soon distracted by his interest in the woman beside him, and so turns his back on the boy. Coyote's focus is pulled from obligation to personal desire. And while Coyote sleeps, the boy acts on his own desires and hunger, sucking out the blood and flesh, leaving nothing but Coyote's bones and skin.

---

36 This is a pattern visible in many of the stories, linking to a number of principles operating at the level of pedagogy, epistemology, metaphysics and cosmology. It suggests attention to all four directions (including past, present, the concrete world and the spiritual), four seasons and more. Its significance also suggests that the boy's act of harm has repeated itself in all four directions. For more on patterns of four as an element of Indigenous legal reasoning, see Borrows, *Law's Indigenous Ethics*, *supra* note 25 at 214.

37 This topic is taken up in a discussion of "The Cannibal and the Fishes" in *Secwépemc Lands and Resources*, *supra* note 20 at 92. A number of these stories are collected in Teit, *supra* note 14. See e.g. "The Cannibals and the Fishes" at 670 (where Swan maintains ongoing relations with the cannibals for an extended period of time); "Coyote and the Hunting Cannibal" at 632 (where the cannibal is taught to hunt for deer rather than for people); "The Gambler's Son and Red-Cap" at 727 (where the man's father-in-law is a cannibal).

The next move shows us how his growth amplifies his hunger. What may have begun as "a failure to restrain" shifts into more intentional acts: the boy begins to kill and eat the sleeping people, growing as he does. We also see that the problem has moved beyond that involving only Coyote and the boy. As the boy grows in size, the impacts are experienced by others in the community. We note here that the story demonstrates collective impacts of individual decision making, in ways that remind us that this is not precisely a "moral story." The story is describing a problem of scale: as the boy grows larger, so does his hunger and his desire to consume, until he has consumed nearly everything and everyone in the community. The story thus poses questions about the possibilities of containment when the boy has grown so big, inviting questions about "globalizing forces" and the energies that might move them. What, then, is the man to do in the face of a force that seems unstoppably driven by a desire for consumption and growth, in particular, where the vulnerability of others in the community has left the man with few alternatives for collaborative action?

Here, the story invites us to consider distance as a strategy for safety. The man flees. But the hunger and desire of the boy are so significant that they leave no space for the man simply to live elsewhere. The man is pursued. And just as Coyote had attempted four times at the beginning of the story to get the cannibal boy to stop picking at his neck, here we see the man four times attempting to create space between himself and the cannibal boy. We see the man attempting to make barriers between them, but the cannibal persists: "The man, hearing him coming, threw earth behind him, thus retarding the cannibal's progress. Four times he retarded him thus, but at last the cannibal came close up to him again."

Let us reflect for a moment on the portion of the story where the man heats and sharpens four bones, transforming them into dogs. Here we have a turn that, for some Western-trained readers, may appear as a kind of magical or mystical intervention, something that draws largely on the spiritual (a site that, for many, appears inaccessible). But when one takes up the narrative as a tool for thinking — one designed to address the challenges of the present — it is easier to work within the space of metaphor and creativity it delineates. The man takes up four specific bones: marmot, porcupine, wolf and bear. We are pointed in the direction of insights and teachings laid out in additional stories involving these kin.[38] The story tells us that the bones are not transformed without preparation: the man must work with the bones, heating them in the fire and sharpening the points. We are invited to consider how each bone leans in the direction of important strategies for conflict management, problem solving and accountability.

Note that the dogs respond to the man's instructions. We are told, "He made the dogs lie down quietly, with their jaws resting on their front feet, and leaving enough space for a person to pass between them." One can imagine this as a kind of trick, but can also see this as a kind of preparation, where the dogs are placed not as a barricade or blockade, but so as to enable a line of protection against certain kinds of possible harms. Note again that the dogs have not been sent out to hunt down or attack the cannibal. They are waiting on the road, and not interfering with other kinds of movement.

---

38   For a larger discussion on the interconnection and interdependence between humans, land and non-human beings, who are understood as Ḱwseltkteneẃs (relatives to one another), see *Secwépemc Lands and Resources*, *supra* note 20 at 38. See also Ignace & Ignace, *supra* note 12.

Our point is that the story does not simply suggest that the desired outcome is the destruction of the boy. Indeed, the bones chosen point in the direction of other possibilities. The dogs in front, the first line of defence, are the marmot and the porcupine. While neither of us has deep familiarity with stories of marmots, cultural keeper (and magnificent storyteller) Ralph William McBryan reflected on the specific ways that marmots support conditions of safety, by popping up in many places, keeping watch. The inclusion of marmot on the frontline of defence invites reflection on the need for warnings, for ways to notice when something poses a potential risk. Marmot asks us to consider systems of monitoring and reporting. Alongside the dog from the marmot bone, the man sets the dog transformed from the porcupine.

Porcupine is an important actor in a powerful story in which two communities in conflict are able to change their relationship to create peaceful and mutually beneficial relations.[39] The inclusion of the porcupine bone points toward strategies of diplomacy, negotiation and mutual understanding. It asks us to consider whether there are processes through which the man and boy might be able to alter their relationship with each other. Indeed, by including porcupine, this story requires the reader to turn their attention to the perspective of the cannibal boy. Here, it is worth recalling that the story began with the kidnapping of the boy. The relationship with Coyote was based on the assumption that the boy would be a slave. The question of the boy's will, or needs, or being, were not interrogated. He is taken away from his home, given sets of instructions that largely take the form of a list of "don't statements," and is left unmonitored, governed only by his hunger. The placement of the dogs on the road disrupts the reader in assuming too quickly that the cannibal boy is necessarily a monster to be destroyed. It leaves open a space in which two groups might do the harder work of making sense of the other's being, and assessing the ways each can act to respect their differences and build a relationship that sustains both. Stories about porcupine may point in the direction of skills of diplomacy and the work of creating changed relations between people whose ways of living are causing harm to others.[40]

But in our story, the cannibal boy does not take up the lessons of porcupine. Instead, he continues toward the man, and thus into the space of wolf and bear. Again, there are many stories that are drawn into the frame. There is much in the wolf stories that speaks to leadership, and the placement of wolves in the pack to ensure the protection of the young, the elderly and the vulnerable. There is also much in these stories that speaks to the use of resources (and the ways they provide food not only for their pack but for many other beings). And stories of bear speak powerfully to strength and the protection of family. How might these stories help us think about the responsibilities and obligations of leaders, of directors, and shareholders? Do the bones open conversations for thinking about insights held in other stories that can be drawn into the frame? The many stories about wolves and bears invite attention to characteristics and strategies related to protection, to teamwork, to loyalty, as well as to the importance of seeing one's obligation not only to feed oneself, but also to attend to what one leaves for others.[41]

---

39   For an extended exploration of this story, see Friedland et al, "Porcupine", *supra* note 17.

40   See "The Story of Porcupine" in Teit, *supra* note 14 at 658.

41   This is visible in stories such as "Story of Tcotcu'lca; or, The Hunter Who Became a Wolf" in Teit, *supra* note 14 at 718, and "Coyote and Wolf", *ibid* at 637.

In this story, the boy's voracious appetite is stopped only by his death. Stopping the danger, in this context, involves drawing on higher principles and strategies carried in the bones of other legal resources. It involves a mobilization of Secwépemcúlecw, the land itself. Note that it is also possible to see, in the work of the dogs tearing apart and consuming the boy, an economic aspect of the story. We see the return of the cannibalized/hoarded resources to Secwépemcúlecw (if one thinks of both Coyote and the people eaten as ancestors/resources coming from and belonging to the land). The cannibal had consumed the people, consumed the resources of all and, in turn, was consumed by the dogs, dogs that were drawn from the bones of other ancestors. Resources are thus returned to the land.

The story does not drive to the conclusion that all cannibals are to be destroyed. Rather, it provides a mapping of strategies and relationships that can be drawn on in order to find spots of intervention in stories of unrestrained hunger. That is, the bones of this story invite us to consider the work that is necessary to prevent other stories from going in this direction. Indeed, it is important that the story does not end with the death of the cannibal boy. It continues. We are told that the man returns home. There, he finds Coyote "still alive, but in such a weak condition that he could not walk. The man hunted deer, killed many, and fed Coyote until he regained his flesh and strength, and became quite well again."

Those trained in the Canadian legal system (with its emphasis on punishment and retribution) may find themselves feeling unsatisfied by this turn of events. Coyote brought the cannibal to the community, leaving nearly everyone dead. Why, then, is Coyote to be nurtured back to health? Such an ending can seem frustrating to one who inherits a legal lens that focuses on causation and "just desserts." But this turn helps to make visible that the story's focus is not on guilt and culpability, although it does let us see actions and results that can be described as good or bad. Certainly, what we see is the man modelling a kind of behaviour that was not present in the earlier parts of the story. It is behaviour that speaks to the importance of deep principles of relationality.

For better or worse, Coyote is kin. And, in many contexts, something more. While one can read Coyote as "akin to a human person," he is also a character that can be read in connection to the land itself: he is linked to and associated with territory in ways that make it possible to draw other connections, to understand his body as standing in for the land and its resources. Here, then, the story invites us to think about a very particular kind of hunger that the cannibal boy is experiencing, a hunger for resources. We are then invited to think about how the boy extracts resources from the land until there is nothing but a hollowed-out shell. One can draw parallels to histories of extraction of resources, be it in the context of mining, water, timber or fish. We thus see that the boy depletes the environment. He swells out, but remains driven by his persisting and increasing hunger.

There is something that shifts if one takes this approach and thinks of the cannibal boy's first harm (his draining the flesh and blood from Coyote) as being akin to an extraction of the resources of the land, a depleting of the land itself. The man, in returning home, acknowledges that work must be done to restore Coyote/the land in the face of all that was extracted. And we are shown the man doing the work necessary to revive Coyote: he hunts, makes broth and works to slowly nourish Coyote back to full health. It is a story that suggests the work of a fiduciary involves a number of steps. The man shows a commitment to home. He returns home, to the site of so many extractions. The cannibal boy had consumed all and then walked away. We see here the opposite. The man models the attentive watchfulness that is necessary to identify the places where life persists, even in the face of what seems to be total loss. The man hunts for what is necessary to assist in recovery (compare this to the cannibal boy picking off skin to supposedly heal a boil). The man also begins with broth, modelling the ways that recovery is never immediate, but may require a slower reintroduction to old ways of eating or being. He continues in this work patiently, over time, until Coyote is quite well again. The story concludes by telling us that the two then lived together for a long time. There is a measure of important truth in this articulation, as opposed to "happily ever after." This story ends not with a conclusion, but with a reminder of the kinds of attention and care that are necessary in order to live together, and to continue to live in worlds in which cannibalistic desires continue to be real.

At the end of the day, how do we create the conditions for safe and ongoing community in a world in which the corporate form is central to how our economies operate and, increasingly, how our social and political lives are structured? The story plays out the logic of consumption, unrestrained consumption, consumption without limits. It takes up the desire for a slave who can do the work of community. It is worth asking if the corporate form is not such a being. The story invites us to consider our desire for a legal person that can be made our slave, that might carry the responsibilities and obligations of our work. It invites us to think carefully and responsibly about what is necessary to safely have cannibal forms as part of the community. Perhaps we can imagine a cannibal boy who lives in a good way with others. But can we imagine that it would be enough for Coyote to say to the cannibal boy, "Just restrain your hunger"? Is it like telling an addict to control their own addiction? Do we see something similar in debates around corporate social responsibility? If we imagine the corporation as a cannibal boy, it also raises the question of what it means to act in the best interests of the cannibal boy. In acting as a fiduciary to a cannibal, is one seeking to change its nature? To transform it into something other than what it is? A kinder, gentler cannibal? Or is one seeking to maximize the utility of a slave while minimizing its potential dangers?

Importantly, the story also invites the reader to take seriously the parallels between the cannibal boy and the rest of us. It invites us to take our corporate structures just as seriously, and to reflect on the ways that the work of transformation and restraint may be a necessary part of doing this work. The story invites us to see this work as not simply "outside of us," but as work that draws us into the frame. The story invites us to think about the hungry desires of not only Coyote and the cannibal boy but also of ourselves.

There is undoubtedly more to be said, and there could be more conversations about other ways to read, amplify or limit the ways we have talked about the story. This exploration of "Coyote and the Cannibal Boy" offers us many pathways for thought. It is a structure for thinking about important policy and legal challenges for the work ahead. In thinking about the role of the corporation in law and governance, what do we need to know about a corporation's history, its purposes? What is served by its growth? What kinds of limits are necessary to contain that growth? What is the role of the fiduciary? What are the relationships between those the corporation is expected to serve, and others in a community who live in proximity to hungry desire? These questions are important ones at a time and place in which attention spreads to the international and the transnational, places that operate as a mixed space between hierarchically ordered centralized legal systems and decentralized legal orders. Indigenous legal orders and Indigenous legal resources need to be part of the conversation.

"Coyote and the Cannibal Boy" is a powerful story for these times, as we consider questions about corporate forms — forms with a life unlike that of human persons — in the face of hungry desire that is a very real part of human life. Coyote, as a legal actor in this story, provides the distance necessary for us to observe the Wetiko tendencies at the heart of human desiring.[42] In a globalizing world, how do we construct systems of restraint appropriate to the challenges of the corporate form? This piece of legal storytelling offers a space to consider what structures, approaches and strategies might best enable us to negotiate the spaces ahead. It reminds us that Indigenous legal resources can provide us with pathways for thinking that will better enable us to work in community for life-sustaining solutions.

Authors' Note

We proceed with gratitude to the Shuswap Nation Tribal Council and the Secwépemc Elders Council for their encouragement and support in doing this work, and to the many storytellers we have listened to over the years, those whose tellings have been written down in books and on the land, and those who continue, in the present, to shape and tell stories of Secwépemc practices of life and law. It is a privilege to have friends and colleagues willing to read and comment on earlier versions of these ideas. In particular, we thank Juliana F. Alexander, Jess Asch, John Borrows, Lindsay Borrows, Gillian Calder, Arta Johnson, Bonnie Johnson, Mary Johnson, Sunny LeBourdais, Hester Lessard, Ralph William McBryan, Val Napoleon and Mark Zion.

---

42   See Friedland, *supra* note 22.

6

CLIMATE CHANGE

A New Bellwether of Corporate Accountability for Systemic Risks

Edward J. Waitzer and Douglas Sarro

Introduction

Global warming is likely to reach 1.5°C above pre-industrial levels by as soon as 2030 if it continues at its current rate, according to a 2018 report by the Intergovernmental Panel on Climate Change (IPCC).[1] Preventing further warming, the IPCC adds, would require substantial and rapid reductions in greenhouse gas emissions.[2] In adding climate change to its list of key Canadian financial stability risks for 2019, the Bank of Canada highlighted research indicating that Canada is "warming significantly faster than the rest of the world."[3]

---

1   Myles Allen et al, "Summary for Policymakers" in *Special Report: Global Warming of 1.5°C* (Geneva: Intergovernmental Panel on Climate Change, 2019) [IPCC] 3 at 4, online: <www.ipcc.ch/site/assets/uploads/sites/2/2019/05/SR15_SPM_version_report_LR.pdf>.

2   *Ibid* at 12.

3   Bank of Canada, *Financial System Review—2019* (Ottawa: Bank of Canada, 2019) at 28.

The scale of the reductions contemplated by the IPCC would mean incurring significant and politically controversial costs in the short-term[4] — costs our political institutions appear to be unwilling to incur. That climate change crosses jurisdictional boundaries raises another issue: the costs of climate change are borne globally, while the costs of responding to climate change are borne locally. Governments have perverse incentives to free-ride on the climate change mitigation efforts of others and opt out of solutions and targets they perceive as politically costly.

It has been argued that in eras of "thin political markets," where political processes and institutions appear unable to protect the public interest, private actors have a responsibility to help fill the gap.[5] The corporate sector's long-term interest in responding to climate change is clear: the ability to mobilize capital and generate wealth depends on the continued availability of natural resources and the continued vitality of political and civil institutions. This dependence also provides a basis for imposing responsibilities on the corporate sector to address urgent challenges to natural and social systems. Courts have become an increasingly important channel for imposing and elaborating on these responsibilities, using norms of "reasonableness," including the doctrine of "reasonable expectations," to forge new legal pathways.

In this chapter, we continue a line of inquiry that has focused on the emerging role for judicial activism in breaking structural log jams inherent in our political systems today and helping to re-focus corporate directors and officers on the ultimate purpose of capitalism: to respond to a society's expressed needs. We highlight legal pathways toward modernized corporate accountability frameworks, grounded in norms of reasonableness, that may be pursued to trigger and accelerate corporate action in response to the climate crisis. To the extent climate litigation helps to develop these pathways, it may provide a template for addressing other systemic risks (risks that threaten the stability of our financial system and the real economy).

We begin this chapter by briefly discussing how legal concepts grounded in norms of reasonableness differ from norms grounded in rationality. We then turn to discuss how legal duties and remedies are evolving in corporate and securities law, incorporating norms of reasonableness, with a focus on their implications for corporate directors' and officers' monitoring of and responses to climate risk.

Reasonableness and Rationality

Rules emphasizing "reasonableness" suppose that decision makers act with reference to others in society and show concern for the common good. They stand in contrast to rules that merely encourage rationality — the maximization of self-interest.[6] John Rawls illustrated the distinction, noting that a group could take a stance that "was perfectly rational given their strong bargaining position, but [that] was nevertheless highly unreasonable, even outrageous."[7]

---

4   IPCC, *supra* note 1; see also Coral Davenport, "Major Climate Report Describes a Strong Risk of Crisis as Early as 2040", *New York Times* (7 October 2018), online: <www.nytimes.com/2018/10/07/climate/ipcc-climate-report-2040.html>.

5   Rebecca Henderson & Karthik Ramanna, "Do Managers Have a Role to Play in Sustaining the Institutions of Capitalism?" (2015) Brookings Institution Center for Effective Public Management, Initiative on 21st Century Capitalism Series, online: <www.brookings.edu/wp-content/uploads/2016/06/BrookingsInstitutionsofCapitalismv5.pdf>.

6   Steve Lydenberg, "Reason, Rationality and Fiduciary Duty" (2014) 3 J Business Ethics 365.

7   John Rawls, *A Theory of Justice* (Cambridge, MA: Harvard University Press, 1971) at 290.

A recent analysis by Roy Shapira and Luigi Zingales of the 2017 DuPont settlement,[8] in which the company paid more than US$670 million to settle claims over emissions of a toxic chemical used in the making of Teflon, provides additional colour. Shapira and Zingales point out that even though preventing pollution would have cost less than the damages caused by pollution, the corporate decision to pollute — which in this case was made in a deliberate manner and informed by management's *ex ante* cost-benefit analyses — was rational, at least from the perspective of maximizing the short-term financial interests of shareholders.[9] The immediate costs of polluting were borne by others and any damages, penalties, or reputational harm for which the company or its managers ultimately might be accountable were discounted by the probability of detection, the time lags between the decision to pollute and the detection of pollution (and between detection and enforcement), as well as by the likelihood that class action counsel would seek to recover quickly by settling monetary claims.[10]

Canadian courts have drawn on "reasonable expectations" as a scaffold for achieving fairness across a number of areas of the law.[11] By definition, reasonable expectations mean something more than the current law. As the Supreme Court of Canada put it in *BCE Inc v 1976 Debentureholders*, a leading case on corporate law duties and remedies, they "look…beyond legality to what is fair, given all of the interests at play" to address conduct that is "wrongful, even if it is not actually unlawful."[12] Despite its broad application, the standard has been used to achieve consistent objectives: first, to promote fair treatment of affected stakeholders by responding to actions that cause unnecessary or disproportionate harms to others; second, to preserve the vitality of legal and regulatory frameworks by responding to actions that, even if in technical compliance with these frameworks, produce results that subvert the purposes of these frameworks.

Legal Duties and Remedies

As of January 2020, there were more than 1,400 climate change impact cases filed around the world.[13] While most are claims against governments, many relate to the actions or omissions of companies or their directors or officers relating to carbon emissions or climate risk more broadly.[14] Plaintiffs have asserted a number of theories of liability originating in both private and public law.[15]

---

8   DuPont, Press Release, "DuPont Reaches Global Settlement of Multi-District PFOA Litigation" (13 February 2017), online: <bit.ly/2A4ylpZ>.

9   Roy Shapira & Luigi Zingales, "Is Pollution Value-Maximizing? The DuPont Case" (2017) National Bureau of Economic Research Working Paper No 23866 at 2-3, online: <https://ssrn.com/abstract=3037091>.

10   *Ibid* at 20–21.

11   See Edward J Waitzer & Douglas Sarro, "Protecting Reasonable Expectations: Mapping the Trajectory of the Law" (2016) 57 Can Bus LJ 285 [Waitzer & Sarro, "Reasonable Expectations"].

12   *BCE Inc v 1976 Debentureholders*, 2008 SCC 69, [2008] 3 SCR 560 at para 71 [*BCE*].

13   Sabin Centre for Climate Change Law, "Climate Change Litigation Databases", online: <http://climatecasechart.com/search/>.

14   Joana Setzer & Rebecca Byrnes, *Global trends in climate change litigation: 2019 snapshot* (London, UK: Grantham Research Institute on Climate Change and the Environment & Centre for Climate Change Economics and Policy, 2019) at 4, online: <www.lse.ac.uk/GranthamInstitute/wp-content/uploads/2019/07/GRI_Global-trends-in-climate-change-litigation-2019-snapshot-2.pdf>.

15   See Maria L Banda & Scott Fulton, "Litigating Climate Change in National Courts: Recent Trends and Developments in Global Climate Law" (2017) 47 Environmental Law Reporter 10121.

In this section, we focus on the duties of care and loyalty owed by directors and officers to the corporations they serve, as well as three of the relevant remedial provisions under corporate and securities law: the oppression remedy, remedies arising from public corporations' disclosure obligations under securities law, as well as courts' ability to "pierce the corporate veil" to address conduct that would otherwise frustrate the purposes of legal or regulatory regimes.

We describe how these duties and remedies appear to be developing in ways that require corporations and their leadership to have due regard for climate risk as well as the climate impacts of corporate actions in order to show that they are acting "reasonably." This means monitoring for and reporting on the relationship between climate risk and a company's activities (facilitating both board oversight of climate risk and accountability to institutional investors, which are increasingly focusing on climate risk as part of their investment decision-making processes),[16] and proactively managing these risks to help lead a transition to a greener economy.

Duties of Care and Loyalty

Corporations range in size from one-person businesses to widely held, complex, transnational enterprises. They operate countless lines of business, working within a web of legal frameworks, socio-political contexts and market circumstances. It would be difficult, if not impossible, to create an exhaustive set of one-size-fits-all rules governing the supervision of these enterprises.

Instead, statutory corporate law imposes two open-ended, adaptive duties on corporate directors: a duty to manage, or supervise the management of, the business and affairs of the corporation and, in doing so, to exercise the care, diligence and skill that a reasonably prudent person would exercise in comparable circumstances (*the duty of care*);[17] and a duty to act honestly and in good faith with a view to the best interests of the corporation (*the duty of loyalty*).[18] The content of these duties varies depending on the nature of the corporation at issue and the circumstances it faces. It has evolved over time to reflect changes in the expectations (and consequential responsibilities) placed on directors and officers.

The courts have also adapted these duties to reflect the challenges boards of directors face in overseeing large enterprises that, by reason of their size and complexity, can have outsized, at times difficult to predict and potentially irreversible impacts on stakeholders and financial, environmental and social systems more broadly. In particular, courts have increasingly read three obligations as flowing from the duties of care and loyalty: a duty to monitor the management of the corporation to effectively address risk and misconduct; a duty to treat stakeholders fairly; and a duty to act ethically. We consider each in turn.

A Duty to Monitor

It is unrealistic to expect that directors will have the time or resources to actively manage a large, complex business. In *Caremark*,[19] the Delaware Court of Chancery responded to this reality by fashioning a new accountability mechanism reflecting the role one can reasonably

---

16   See PRI, *Principles for Responsible Investment* (2019), online: <www.unpri.org/download?ac=6303>; Larry Fink, "Larry Fink's Annual Letter to CEOs: A Sense of Purpose", BlackRock (2018), online: <www.blackrock.com/corporate/investor-relations/larry-fink-ceo-letter>; see also the text accompanying notes 24–25.

17   See e.g. *Canada Business Corporations Act*, RSC 1985, c C-44, ss 102(1), 122(1)(b) [*CBCA*].

18   See e.g. *ibid*, s 122(1)(a).

19   *In re Caremark International Inc Derivative Litigation*, 698 A2d 959 (Del Ch 1996) [*Caremark*].

expect directors to play in this context: the duty to monitor. This means directors must: "assur[e] themselves that information and reporting systems exist in the organization that are reasonably designed to provide to senior management and to the board itself timely, accurate information sufficient to allow management and the board, each within its scope, to reach informed judgments concerning both the corporation's compliance with law and its business performance."[20]

In a February 2018 enforcement action against Wells Fargo, the US Federal Reserve emphasized directors' responsibility for risk oversight.[21] The action linked Wells Fargo's compliance breakdowns to failures in board oversight and emphasized the Wells Fargo board's responsibility for ensuring management has a robust risk management system to support the company's strategy.[22] While the duties of bank directors are in some ways more demanding than those of other corporate directors, the view that risk oversight is a key element of directors' role is widely held,[23] indicating the Wells Fargo enforcement action's relevance for corporate directors more broadly.

A number of the world's largest institutional investors have echoed this sentiment, in particular as regards environmental and social risks.[24] As stated in a 2018 public letter by the chairman and chief executive officer of BlackRock Inc.: "In the current environment…stakeholders are demanding that companies exercise leadership on a broader range of issues. And they are right to: a company's ability to manage environmental, social, and governance matters demonstrates the leadership and good governance that is so essential to sustainable growth."[25]

"Leadership" means going beyond strict compliance with existing regulatory requirements. Recent litigation in the Delaware courts involving directors of Duke Energy indicates the potential for the duty to monitor to require attention to the environmental implications of corporate actions. In this litigation, it was alleged that Duke Energy's directors violated their duty to monitor by supporting a business strategy that purposely shirked environmental laws and relied on a captured state regulator to protect it from liability. While not resulting in personal liability on the part of directors, this outcome was not unanimous: in dissent, Chief Justice Leo Strine reasoned that the plaintiffs' pleadings gave rise to an inference that "it was the business strategy of Duke Energy, accepted and supported by its board of directors, to run the company in a manner that purposely skirted, and in many ways consciously violated, important environmental laws.…Duke's executives, advisors, and directors used all the tools

20   *Ibid* at 970. See also *Re Barings plc (No 5)*, [1999] 1 BCLC 433 at 489; *Lexi Holdings Plc v Luqman & Ors*, [2009] EWCA Civ 117 at para 37 (articulating similar obligations under UK law).

21   Board of Governors of the Federal Reserve System, News Release, "Responding to widespread consumer abuses and compliance breakdowns at Wells Fargo, Federal Reserve restricts Wells' growth until firm improves governance and controls. Concurrent with Fed action, Wells to replace three directors by April, one by year end" (2 February 2018), online: <www.federalreserve.gov/newsevents/pressreleases/enforcement20180202a.htm>.

22   Letter from the Board of Governors of the Federal Reserve System to the Board of Directors of Wells Fargo & Company (2 February 2018), online: <www.federalreserve.gov/newsevents/pressreleases/files/enf20180202a2.pdf>.

23   See e.g. Mark Beasley, Bruce Branson & Bonnie Hancock, *The State of Risk Oversight: An Overview of Enterprise Risk Management Practices*, 9th ed (Raleigh, NC: ERM Initiative in the Poole College of Management at North Carolina State University, 2018), online: <www.aicpa.org/content/dam/aicpa/interestareas/businessindustryandgovernment/resources/erm/downloadabledocuments/aicpa-erm-research-study-2018.pdf>.

24   For example, more than 2,000 asset owners, representing more than US$80 trillion of assets, have signed onto the Principles for Responsible Investment, which include commitments to "seek appropriate disclosure on ESG issues by the entities in which we invest" and to incorporate ESG issues into their "ownership policies and practices" and their "investment analysis and decision-making processes." PRI, *supra* note 16.

25   Fink, *supra* note 16.

in their large box to cause Duke to flout its environmental responsibilities, therefore reduce its costs of operations, and by that means, increase its profitability. This, fiduciaries of a Delaware corporation, may not do."[26]

To date, Delaware courts have refused to impose personal liability arising from alleged failures to meet the duty to monitor unless the directors' actions went beyond inattention to the level of bad faith — conduct that implies that the directors are knowingly acting for reasons other than the best interest of the corporation. Much of the scholarship surrounding the duty to monitor has suggested that this standard may be almost impossible for most plaintiffs to meet, citing, among other things, a series of lawsuits brought against directors of major financial institutions in the wake of the global financial crisis for excessive risk taking that were dismissed due to failure to meet this high bar.[27]

Courts' articulation of clear expectations as to what constitutes best practice in this area may nonetheless signal the trajectory of the law and influence directors' behaviour prospectively. The reputational harms that come from being "named and shamed" in litigation, even if personal liability ultimately does not follow, may also influence directors' behaviour. When it comes to climate and other systemic risks, influencing directors' behaviour prospectively is more important than after-the-fact personal liability: the point is to change directors' behaviour before severe social and environmental harms occur, rather than to penalize directors after the fact.

In 2019, the US Department of Justice issued new guidance for prosecutors in evaluating corporate compliance programs,[28] focusing on whether the program was effective at the time of an offence and is effective at the time of a charging decision or proposed resolution. It asks the questions to which a board should be expected to be attuned: Is the compliance program well designed? Is it implemented effectively? Does it work in practice?

The duty to monitor emerged in response to the changing nature of directors' responsibilities within large corporations. They can reasonably be expected to ensure systems are put in place that allow them to monitor corporate strategy and how related risks are being managed. Institutional investors have emphasized their expectation that boards will monitor for environmental, social and other systemic risks, providing a potential pathway for further development of the law in this direction.

A Duty to Treat Stakeholders Fairly

As noted above, the duty of loyalty requires directors and officers to act honestly and in good faith with a view to the best interests of the corporation. Historically, this duty was narrow in scope — it focused on avoiding conflicts of interest and furthering the economic interests of shareholders.[29] Over time, however, the duty has broadened in scope, with greater recognition of both the significant effects corporate actions can have on other stakeholders and corporations'

---

26   *City of Birmingham Retirement and Relief System v Good*, 2017 WL 6397490 (Del Dec 15, 2017).

27   See e.g. Eric J Pan, "A Board's Duty to Monitor" (2009) 54:10 NYL Sch L Rev 717 at 727; Louis J Bevilacqua, "Monitoring the Duty to Monitor" (2011) NYLJ at 2; Renee M Jones & Michelle Welsh, "Toward a Public Enforcement Model for Directors' Duty of Oversight" (2012) 45 Vand J Transnat'l L 343 at 359.

28   US, Department of Justice, Criminal Division, *Evaluation of Corporate Compliance Programs* (Updated April 2019), online: <www.justice.org/criminal-fraud/page/file/93751/download>.

29   See Richard F Devlin & Victoria Rees, "Beyond Conflicts of Interest to the Duty of Loyalty: From *Martin v Gray* to *R v Neil*" (2005) 84 Can Bar Rev 433; Edward J Waitzer & Douglas Sarro, "The Public Fiduciary: Emerging Themes in Canadian Fiduciary Law for Pension Trustees" (2012) 164 Can Bar Rev 163 at 184.

reliance on the political, social and environmental systems in which they are embedded and on which they depend for their continued vitality. The duty today encompasses a positive obligation to promote the long-term success of the corporation, having due regard for the interests of all stakeholders.

In the United Kingdom, this shift was fostered by statutory reform. The Companies Act 2006 reformulated the duty of loyalty as a duty to act in good faith to "promote the success of the company for the benefit of its [shareholders] as a whole," having due regard for, among other things, impacts on the community, the environment and employees.[30]

In Canada, this shift came about via judicial decisions. In *Peoples*,[31] the Supreme Court of Canada stated that "in determining whether they are acting with a view to the best interests of the corporation it may be legitimate, given all the circumstances of a given case, for the board of directors to consider, *inter alia*, the interests of shareholders, employees, suppliers, creditors, consumers, governments and the environment."[32] In *BCE*, the court went further, stating that the duty of loyalty includes a "'fair treatment' component" requiring directors to balance stakeholders' conflicting interests fairly, in a way that reflects these stakeholders' reasonable expectations.[33]

While the Delaware courts' interpretation of the duty of loyalty continues to reflect a shareholder-centric viewpoint, this viewpoint is oriented to the long term[34] — a time horizon in which the interests of shareholders and other stakeholders tend to converge. In any event, the *G20/OECD Principles of Corporate Governance* provide that a board should have some structure in place for stakeholder consultation as part of its decision-making processes.[35] Whether as a means of ascertaining the long-term interests of shareholders or in recognition of stakeholders' separate interests in the corporation and its actions, the connection between attention to stakeholders and fulfilling the duty of loyalty is becoming increasingly clear.

A Duty to Act Ethically

A related development has been the integration of ethical considerations into the duty of loyalty. The Delaware courts have concluded that the duty of loyalty incorporates norms of good faith and obedience to law, with Chief Justice Strine's dissent in the Duke Energy case indicating that these norms may be interpreted to mean not only fostering compliance with existing law, but also monitoring for and addressing activity that appears to "skirt" environmental and other regulatory obligations. The UK Companies Act requires that directors have regard for "the desirability of the company maintaining a reputation for high standards of business conduct."[36] In *BCE*, the Supreme Court of Canada characterized the duty of loyalty as a "duty to act in the best interests of the corporation, *viewed as a good corporate citizen*."[37]

---

30   *Companies Act 2006* (UK), c 46, s 172(1).

31   *Peoples Department Stores Inc (Trustee of) v Wise*, 2004 SCC 68, [2004] 3 SCR 461.

32   *Ibid* at para 42.

33   *BCE, supra* note 12 at para 36.

34   *TW Servs, Inc v SWT Acq Corp*, 1989 WL 20290 at 7 (Del Ch 2 March 1989).

35   Organisation for Economic Co-operation and Development (OECD), *G20/OECD Principles of Corporate Governance* (2015) at 5, online: <www.oecd.org/daf/ca/Corporate-Governance-Principles-ENG.pdf>.

36   *Companies Act 2006, supra* note 30, s 172(1)(e).

37   *BCE, supra* note 12 at para 81 [emphasis added].

These standards imply that directors should cause corporations to not only comply with existing law, but to act ethically. This reflects the broader goal that duties of loyalty are in many cases intended to achieve. Duties of loyalty arise in relationships of trust (referred to as "fiduciary relationships"), where one party holds discretionary power over another and undertakes to exercise that power in the interest of the other party.[38] These relationships of trust are essential to the functioning of key social and economic institutions, and, as explained by the Supreme Court of Canada in *Hodgkinson*,[39] duties of loyalty are intended to foster and preserve the trust that sustains these institutions: "[T]here can be a public interest in reassuring the community — not merely beneficiaries — that even the appearance of improper behaviour will not be tolerated. The emphasis here seems, in part at least, to be the maintenance of the public's acceptance of, and of the credibility of, important institutions in society which render 'fiduciary services' to the public."[40]

Corporate and Securities Law Remedies

Oppression

The oppression remedy allows certain corporate stakeholders to seek redress for actions that amount to "oppression," "unfair prejudice" or "unfair disregard" of their interests.[41] When enacted as part of the Canada Business Corporations Act in 1975, it was quickly recognized as the "broadest, most comprehensive and most open-ended shareholder remedy in the common law world…unprecedented in its scope."[42] In *BCE*, the Supreme Court highlighted the remedy's potential as an instrument through which directors' duty to treat stakeholders fairly may be enforced.[43]

That said, the remedy's effectiveness is hampered by the somewhat muddled statutory language describing which stakeholders can access the remedy. Under the federal statute, the definition of "complainant" (those with standing to bring a claim) is open-ended (including any "person who, in the discretion of a court, is a proper person to make an application"),[44] but the statute also provides that the harm complained of must be suffered by a security holder, creditor, director or officer of the corporation to fall within the scope of the remedy.[45] The reason for this gap is not apparent, and was not addressed, at the time the statute was enacted. Nor is it consistent with the Supreme Court's discussion of the oppression remedy as a means of protecting stakeholder interests in *BCE*.

Elsewhere, we have suggested that correcting the confusion arising from the existing statutory structure should be a legislative priority.[46] A simple fix would be to provide that harms to any "stakeholder" (as opposed to "any security holder, creditor, director or officer") can give rise to an

---

38   *Alberta v Elder Advocates of Alberta Society*, 2011 SCC 24, [2011] 2 SCR 261 at para 36.

39   *Hodgkinson v Simms*, [1994] 3 SCR 377.

40   *Ibid* at 422.

41   See e.g. *CBCA, supra* note 17, s 241.

42   Stanley M Beck, "Minority Shareholders' Rights in the 1980s" in *Special Lectures of the Law Society of Upper Canada — Corporate Law in the 80s* (Toronto: Law Society of Upper Canada, 1982) 311 at 312.

43   *BCE, supra* note 12 at para 82.

44   *CBCA, supra* note 17, s 238.

45   *Ibid*, s 241.

46   Edward J Waitzer & Douglas Sarro, "In Search Of Things Past And Future: Judicial Activism And Corporate Purpose" (2018) 55:3 Osgoode Hall LJ 791.

oppression claim. This change would not require boards to weigh stakeholder interests equally, or mean that all stakeholders would stand on an equal footing when making an oppression claim. *BCE* makes clear that corporate decision making is context-specific, with some stakeholders' interests looming larger in some contexts than in others.[47]

While legislative reform has the advantage of signalling to boards that the scope of the oppression remedy has expanded, an alternative is to effect a similar result through the courts. One such pathway would be for stakeholders to find ways in which their interests align with those of one or more security holders or creditors and enlist them to pursue the litigation. This type of litigation strategy may stimulate engagement between companies, their institutional investors and other stakeholders, thereby reducing some of the current pressure to pursue the short-term interests of certain shareholders at the expense of the long-term interests of other stakeholders.

Disclosure Obligations

Climate risk disclosure represents another, rapidly growing, basis for liability. Public companies generally are required under securities laws to disclose information about material (i.e., significant) risks to the company's business. Guidance from securities regulators,[48] as well as analyses by major institutional investors such as BlackRock,[49] provide strong evidence of the materiality of climate risks for many businesses.[50]

A company's duty to disclose material risks and directors' duty to monitor go hand-in-hand: the company's execution of the former duty provides evidence that directors have met the latter duty, and vice versa. It should therefore be unsurprising that cases are emerging in which directors of public corporations have been held responsible for failing to make proper inquiries as to whether climate-related risk factors have been accounted for,[51] or for failing to adequately monitor climate-related issues that had an adverse impact on corporate performance.[52]

As these risks are likely to escalate as climate change progresses, reliance on historical exposures alone in measuring climate risk is likely insufficient.[53] Future risks may, for example, include exposures to potential stranded assets — assets that become obsolete or non-performing ahead of their expected economic life — such as oil reserves that could be required to remain in the ground as a result of future climate change, carbon regulation or energy market transitions.[54]

---

47   *BCE, supra* note 12 at paras 81–88.

48   See e.g. SEC Release Nos 33-9106; 34-61469; FR-82, Commission Guidance Regarding Disclosure Related to Climate Change (8 February 2010); Canadian Securities Administrators (CSA) Staff Notice 51-333, "Environmental Reporting Guidance" (27 October 2010); CSA Staff Notice 51-358, "Reporting of Climate Change-related Risks" (1 August 2019).

49   BlackRock Investment Institute, "Adapting portfolios to climate change: Implications and strategies for all investors" (2016), online: <www.blackrock.com/corporate/literature/whitepaper/bii-climate-change-2016-us.pdf>.

50   Cynthia A Williams, "Disclosure of Information Concerning Climate Change: Liability Risks and Opportunities" (2017) Commonwealth Climate and Law Initiative Working Paper Series at 15–16, online: <hennickcentre.ca/wp-content/uploads/2017/11/CCLI-DisclosurePaper-October-30.pdf>.

51   *ASIC v Loiterton* (2004), 50 ACSR 693, [2004] NSWSC 897.

52   *ASIC v Rich* (2004), 50 ACSR 500 (NSWSC).

53   See Mercer, *Investing in a time of climate change* (Paris: Mercer, 2015) at 6.

54   *Ibid* at 55, 62.

In late 2015 and early 2016, more than a dozen US state attorneys general initiated investigations into whether ExxonMobil and its auditors had committed securities fraud by publicly emphasizing that the risks and impacts of climate change are inherently uncertain, even though it had conducted significant internal investigations demonstrating their scientific certainty.[55] A resulting lawsuit by the New York State Attorney General was dismissed in December 2019 after the court concluded that the company's disclosures to investors were not materially misleading,[56] but a parallel lawsuit by the Massachusetts Attorney General (which, unlike the New York lawsuit, alleges the company misled both investors and consumers) remains ongoing.[57]

In November 2016, a separate class action was commenced against ExxonMobil and a number of its directors, alleging securities fraud in their misrepresentation of the company's assessment and management of climate change-related financial risks, including stranded asset exposures.[58] In the following weeks, ExxonMobil announced that it was likely to write down approximately 4.6 million barrels from its North American "proven reserves" — about 20 percent of total proven reserves at year end, on the basis that they would not be economically recoverable under Securities and Exchange Commission (SEC) definitions at then current prices.[59] The lawsuit continues to proceed in federal court, after a federal judge in Texas denied ExxonMobil's motion to dismiss in August 2018.[60]

It should be noted that mandated disclosure under securities laws extends liability for an omission that creates the erroneous impression that the risk is not material or if the information is "presented in such a way as to obscure or distort [its] significance."[61] In August 2016, the UK environmental law advocacy group ClientEarth filed complaints with the UK Financial Reporting Council regarding the adequacy of the risk disclosures made by two oil and gas companies, Cairn Energy Plc and SOCO International Plc, in their annual reports.[62] The claims asserted that the companies breached their disclosure obligations by failing to report on material risks to their strategies and business models associated with climate change. The companies subsequently changed their reporting practices to provide for disclosure regarding these risks.

In November 2014, the New York State Attorney General announced a settlement with Peabody Coal in which it determined that by filing annual reports citing only favourable International Energy Agency (IEA) projections in support of its coal demand growth projections, without also disclosing the existence of other, less favourable IEA scenarios, Peabody's filings were

---

55   Paul Barrett & Matthew Philips, "Can ExxonMobil Be Found Liable for Misleading the Public on Climate Change?", *Bloomberg Businessweek* (7 September 2016).

56   *People v Exxon Mobil Corp*, No 452044/2018 (NY Sup Ct 2019).

57   Complaint, *Commonwealth v Exxon Mobil Corp*, No 19-333 (Mass Sup Ct).

58   See Robbins Geller Rudman & Dowd LLP, Press Release, "Robbins Geller Rudman & Dowd LLP Files Class Action Suit Against Exxon Mobil Corporation" (7 November 2016), online: <www.prnewswire.com/news-releases/robbins-geller-rudman--dowd-llp-files-class-action-suit-against-exxon-mobil-corporation-300358768.html>.

59   ExxonMobil, Press Release, "ExxonMobil Earns $2.7 Billion in Third Quarter of 2016" (28 October 2016), online: <https://news.exxonmobil.com/press-release/exxonmobil-earns-27-billion-third-quarter-2016>.

60   *Ramirez v Exxon Mobil Corp et al*, Civil Action No 3:16-CV-3111-K (ND Tex 2018).

61   *In Re Worldcom Inc Securities Litigation*, 303 F Supp 2d 385 (SDNY 2004) at 441 (quoting *Meyer Pincus & Assocs PC v Oppenheimer Co*, 936 F 2d 759, 2d Cir 1991) at 761.

62   ClientEarth, Press Release, "ClientEarth complaint prompts transformed climate reporting by oil and gas firms" (28 April 2017), online: <https://clientearth.org/clientearth-complaint-prompts-transformed-climate-reporting-oil-gas-firms/4/>.

incomplete, false and misleading, in contravention of New York's Martin Act.[63] Peabody Energy did not admit or deny the allegations.[64]

High-level, boilerplate disclosure of stranded asset and other risks should be deemed inadequate in light of these developments. The June 2017 recommendations of the Financial Stability Board's Task Force on Climate-related Financial Disclosures (TCFD), with respect to climate risk governance, strategy, risk management and disclosure, appear likely to inform future regulatory and judicial action.[65] The recommendations provide guidance on those forms of financial analysis and disclosure that are likely to be required for corporations to present a fair view of their financial position, in terms of both performance and prospects.[66]

Emerging market practice also appears likely to inform courts' and regulators' expectations as to climate risk disclosure. A recent survey of 15 of the largest oil and gas companies listed on the New York Stock Exchange revealed that, taken in aggregate, each of the 11 disclosure recommendations made by the TCFD was being acted on.[67]

The Bank of Canada's 2019 *Financial System Review* singles out the assessment of climate-related risks (and opportunities) as one of the main vulnerabilities to financial stability.[68] Noting that limited understanding and mispricing of climate-related risks could increase transaction costs to a low-carbon economy, the Bank of Canada intends to work with other central banks and supervisors on bridging data gaps. It also notes the importance of achieving robust and internationally consistent climate- and environment-related disclosure.[69] This, as well as equivalent statements by other financial regulators, will inform courts in assessing how boards satisfy their duty to monitor and how investment fiduciaries integrate environmental, social and governance factors into their portfolio management practices.

The Limits of Limited Liability

A basic tenet of corporate law is the concept of limited liability — that a shareholder's liability is limited to its equity investment in the corporation. This concept has long been viewed as central to the mobilization of capital and risk taking. Over time, however, courts have used equitable principles to pierce the corporate veil and statutes have established exceptions to the principle of limited liability — imposing liability on parent corporations and individual directors and officers — to respond to abuses of the corporate form and, increasingly, the problems that arise when limited liability incentivizes behaviour that is privately profitable but socially costly.[70]

---

63 *In the Matter of Investigation by the New York State Attorney General of Peabody Energy Co*, 2015, Assurance No 15-42, Assurance of Discontinuance, online: <http://ag.ny.gov/ pdfs/Peabody-Energy-Assurance-signed.pdf>.

64 *Ibid.*

65 Task Force on Climate-related Financial Disclosures, *Final Report: Recommendations of the Task Force on Climate-related Financial Disclosures* (2017), online: <www.fsb-tcfd.org/wp-content/uploads/2017/06/FINAL-TCFD-Report-062817.pdf>.

66 *Ibid.*

67 Edward J Waitzer, "Data Gap: Governments across Canada need to catch up when it comes to increased climate risk disclosure", *Corporate Knights* (Summer 2018) 64.

68 Bank of Canada, *supra* note 3.

69 *Ibid.*

70 Anat R Admati, "A Skeptical View of Financialized Corporate Governance" (2017) 31:3 J Economic Perspectives 131 at 131.

A recent study used industrial emissions to look at the trade-offs of limited liability in the parent-subsidiary context, finding that stronger parent liability protection (i.e., strong rules insulating the parent corporation from liability for environmental cleanup costs incurred by its subsidiaries) was associated with an increase in subsidiary ground emissions of five to nine percent.[71]

While courts have traditionally pierced the veil in response to a perceived abuse of the corporate form that amounts to a "deliberate" or "fraudulent" evasion of the law,[72] a series of Canadian and American decisions appear to have gone further, to respond to instances in which the corporate structures at issue had either the purpose or the *effect* of undermining a legal or regulatory regime.[73]

For example, in *Downtown Eatery*,[74] the Court of Appeal for Ontario pierced the corporate veil to let a former employee recover for wrongful dismissal. Although the court saw nothing "unlawful or suspicious" in the complex corporate structure that otherwise would have prevented recovery,[75] it concluded that "[t]he definition of 'employer' in this simple and common scenario should be one that recognizes the complexity of modern corporate structures, but does not permit that complexity to defeat the legitimate entitlements of wrongfully dismissed employees."[76] Accordingly, it adopted a broad definition of "employer" that allowed the employee to pierce through the entity that formally employed him (which had no assets) to recover against related, better-capitalized entities.

Some cases have begun to illustrate how courts may be prepared to pierce the corporate veil to remedy environmental wrongs. In *Choc v Hudbay Minerals Inc*,[77] on a preliminary motion, the Ontario Superior Court of Justice concluded that a Canadian parent company could be held liable for torts allegedly committed by a subsidiary in Guatemala, if the subsidiary is proven to have been (as was asserted by the plaintiffs) acting as an agent for the parent.[78]

Yaiguaje v Chevron Corp,[79] however, appears to represent a step backward. This case concerned whether Indigenous peoples in Ecuador who were affected by extensive environmental pollution caused by oil exploration and extraction by a subsidiary of Chevron Corporation, having won judgment against Chevron for these harms in the Ecuadorian courts, may enforce that judgment against Chevron's Canadian subsidiary. A majority of the Court of Appeal for Ontario declined to pierce the corporate veil on the basis of a narrow approach to the doctrine,

---

71   Pat Akey & Ian Appel, "The Limits of Limited Liability: Evidence from Industrial Pollution" (Paper presented at the 13th Annual Mid-Atlantic Research Conference in Finance, June 2018, draft last updated 7 September 2018) [unpublished], online: <https://papers.ssrn.com/sol3/papers.cfm?abstract_id=3083013>.

72   Thomas G Heintzman & Brandon Kain, "Through the Looking Glass: Recent Developments in Piercing the Corporate Veil" (2013) 28 BFLR 525.

73   See e.g. *Sun Capital Partners III, LP v New England Teamsters and Trucking Indus Pension Fund*, 724 F 3d 129 (1st Cir 2013); *Pension Benefit Guar Corp v Asahi Tec Corp*, 2013 No 10-1936 (ABJ) (DDC 2013); *Alcoa Inc*, SEC Release No 34-71261, 2014 WL 69457 (2014). These examples are discussed in Edward J Waitzer & Douglas Sarro, "Fiduciary Society Unleashed: The Road Ahead for the Financial Sector" (2014) 69 Bus Lawyer 1081 at 1082.

74   *Downtown Eatery (1993) Ltd v Ontario* (2001), 54 OR (3d) 161 (Ont CA), leave to appeal to SCC refused, [2002] 1 SCR vi.

75   *Ibid* at para 35.

76   *Ibid* at para 36.

77   (2013), 116 OR (3d) 674, 2013 ONSC 1414 (Ont Sup Ct J).

78   *Ibid* at para 49.

79   (2018), 141 OR (3d) 1, 2018 ONCA 472 (Ont CA), leave to appeal to SCC refused, 2019 CarswellOnt 5162.

and the Supreme Court of Canada denied leave to appeal the court's decision. Justice Ian Nordheimer's concurring opinion, however, remains worth noting: it pointed to the potential reach of the remedy, noting that prior case law "enunciate[s] a principle that the law should not allow even legitimate corporate structures to work an 'injustice.'"[80] Justice Nordheimer added that applying the remedy in a flexible way allows courts to "harmoniz[e] law with the needs and requirements of evolving social structures and relationships."[81] It remains to be seen whether Justice Nordheimer's opinion will influence subsequent case law.

Similar issues are playing out in courts around the world. For example, in April 2019, the UK Supreme Court dismissed an appeal from Vedanta Resources of decisions of the High Court and Court of Appeal that, based on evidence that Vedanta controlled a Zambian subsidiary, it could owe a duty to third parties affected by the subsidiary's activities.[82] Various jurisdictions are already clarifying national law on the expectations of multinationals with respect to environmental law. For example, France recently passed a law placing the onus on companies to prevent risks from their global activities.[83]

The jurisdiction to pierce the corporate veil can be thought of as a particular application of the principle that one should not be permitted to act in a way that undermines the integrity of legal relationships and institutions, a principle that underlies the legal concept of reasonable expectations.[84] In this manner, it has become an instrument to accelerate the judicial legitimization of social norms and encourage good corporate citizenship. It also reinforces the duty of directors to effectively monitor risks and mitigate social and environmental harms.

A Note of Caution

We have highlighted a number of opportunities to mould legal rules and standards to mandate that companies and their directors and officers measure and mitigate systemic risks such as climate change, but we recognize that these opportunities come with significant obstacles. Think of climate change litigation in the context of the tobacco and asbestos litigation that preceded it. While ultimately successful, the tobacco and asbestos litigation campaigns have proven to be hugely expensive, gruelling and lengthy. Tobacco litigation is now well into its seventh decade, almost a century after scientists began to focus on the link between cigarette smoking and lung cancer and more than half a century after the US Surgeon General determined that cigarette smoking contributed substantially to mortality from certain specific diseases and to the overall death rate.[85]

---

80   *Ibid* at para 107.

81   *Ibid* at para 113 (citing Leonard I Rotman, "The 'Fusion' of Law and Equity?: A Canadian Perspective on the Substantive, Jurisdictional, or Non-Fusion of Legal and Equitable Matters" (2016) 2 Can J Comp Cont L 497 at 503–504).

82   *Vedanta Resources Plc & another v Lungowe & others*, [2019] UKSC 20. In the interim, the Zambian government has named a provisional liquidator to run the subsidiary and production has been halted.

83   In France, the Corporate Duty of Vigilance law establishes an obligation for parent companies to identify and prevent adverse human rights and environmental impacts resulting from their own activities, activities of companies they control or of subcontractors and suppliers with whom they have an established commercial relationship. Online: <www.assemblee-nationale.fr/14/ta/ta0924.asp>.

84   See Waitzer & Sarro, "Reasonable Expectations", *supra* note 11 at 302–03.

85   US, Department of Health and Human Services, *The Health Consequences of Smoking—50 Years of Progress: A Report of the Surgeon General* (Rockville, MD: US Department of Health and Human Services, 2014) at 3, 19.

Furthering the goals of environmental and other social movements through the courts is particularly challenging. Funding the litigation can be difficult, as the claims often do not give rise to damages. Climate change litigation, in particular, raises special challenges with respect to causation — responsibility for climate change is dispersed among many public and private actors, and the causes and consequences of climate change may be distant in both geography and time — although scientific advances and recent judicial decisions provide pathways to overcoming these challenges. More importantly, however, the legal issues raised are not simply about compliance with existing legal norms, but rather about generating new normative frameworks that alter the political context.[86]

Yet the ultimate success of asbestos and tobacco litigation suggests that climate risk litigation will join these campaigns as part of an evolving template for invoking judicial relief in respect of a broad range of long-term risks to human health and welfare, many of which are increasingly perceived as directly affecting or falling within the ambit of fundamental human rights.[87] Courts' intervention to require parties to mitigate and compensate for harms associated with climate change would be consistent with their willingness to use doctrines such as reasonable expectations and fiduciary obligations to require powerful public and private actors not only to *avoid acting illegally*, but to *act fairly* — in particular, by treating others fairly and upholding the integrity of legal regimes (and, through them, social institutions).[88]

Conclusion

The governor of the Bank of England, Mark Carney, has characterized climate change as a "tragedy of the horizon," in that failing to address climate change "impos[es] a cost on future generations that the current generation has no direct incentive to fix." He adds: "The horizon for monetary policy extends out to two or three years. For financial stability it is a bit longer, but typically only to the outer boundaries of the credit cycle — about a decade. In other words, once climate change becomes a defining issue for financial stability, it may already be too late."[89]

While his remarks focused on short-termism within financial and capital markets, the likely impacts of climate change fall far beyond the typical four-year democratic electoral cycle as well. It therefore should be unsurprising not only that parties have identified political failures to address climate risk adequately, but also that parties are turning to the courts (as well as markets) to remedy these failures.

This chapter highlights legal pathways toward modernized corporate accountability frameworks grounded in norms of reasonableness. As reviewed above, the duties of loyalty and care are increasingly viewed as imposing obligations on directors and officers to monitor for and address systemic risks and to treat stakeholders fairly. The Canadian oppression remedy provides an

---

86   Gerald Torres, "Legal Change" (2007) 55:2 Clev St L Rev 135 at 138.

87   See Climate Change, Justice and Human Rights Task Force, *Achieving Justice and Human Rights in an Era of Climate Disruption* (London, UK: International Bar Association, 2014) (drawing a link between climate change, human health and human rights law).

88   Edward Waitzer & Douglas Sarro, "Reasonable Expectations and Fiduciary Obligations: Legal Pathways to Longer-Term Thinking" in Dominic Barton, Dezsö J Horváth & Matthias Kipping, eds, *Re-Imagining Capitalism: Building a Responsible Long-Term Model* (Oxford: Oxford University Press, 2016) 226.

89   Mark Carney, "Breaking the Tragedy of the Horizon: Climate Change and Financial Stability" (Speech delivered at Lloyd's of London, 29 September 2015), online: <http://bit.ly/1YMQmit>.

avenue for stakeholders to enforce their interest in being treated fairly. Public company disclosure requirements provide a mechanism for monitoring whether and how directors and officers are delivering on their duty to monitor. Piercing the corporate veil offers stakeholders the potential to cut through complex corporate structures to remedy harms that otherwise would undermine the credibility and effectiveness of legal and regulatory frameworks. While these pathways are not without obstacles, they may yet prove instrumental in driving corporations to be more proactive in responding to climate and other systemic risks.

7

MADE IN EVERYWHERE

Transformative Technologies and the (Re)codification of CSR in Global Supply Chains

Lucas Mathieu and Richard Janda

Introduction

Global supply chains, rather than individual corporations alone, are in many ways the true locus of corporate social responsibility (CSR) for multinational enterprises (MNEs). Yet the companies that form these supply chains can often escape state regulatory oversight. A race to the bottom, reinforced by regulatory entrepreneurship and the willingness of poorer states to benefit from hosting various parts of the chain without themselves having significant regulatory capacity, together limit the possibility of assuring the accountability and transparency of companies' activities throughout global supply chains.[1]

---

1   Larry Catá Backer, "Regulating Multinational Corporations: Trends, Challenges, and Opportunities" (2015) 22:1 Brown J World Affairs 153.

The intersection between two ideas — global supply chain governance and CSR — has been the subject of much discussion.[2] Indeed, some would argue that supply chains should be understood holistically and that CSR standards must be applied at the level of supply chains.[3] This chapter addresses the link between these two ideas and a third current trend: the rise of new information and communication technologies, and in particular the Internet of Things (IoT), blockchain and artificial intelligence (AI). We will illustrate how these technologies are already being used to strengthen the capacity of companies to monitor their CSR performance in global supply chains and will argue that they can and should be further exploited to this end.

In the first part of the chapter, we will map and identify current issues in assessing and implementing CSR in global supply chains. Second, we will discuss the potential impact of the IoT, blockchain and AI in helping MNEs address those technical and conceptual issues. Third, we will discuss the existing incentives for both MNEs and other actors to implement these technologies in supply chains. Finally, we will acknowledge that these positive developments are not without their own new set of risks.

Issues in the Assessment and Implementation of CSR within Global Supply Chains

First Challenge: The Need for Cross-level and Cross-scale Assessment of CSR

CSR can appear to be a diffuse, even impracticable concept, given the multiplicity of actors, norms and goals that underpin it. Yet the polysemous quality of the term corresponds to the true difficulty of rendering transnational firms accountable for the claims of the large array of stakeholders subject to the impacts of their activities. There is no single way to measure CSR. By way of analogy, one might recall the conclusions of the Stiglitz-Sen-Fitoussi Report, ordered by then French President Nicolas Sarkozy, which put into question the validity of GDP as the single, central unit of economic measurement, and which called for the adoption of a "dashboard" of indicators, including those relating to quality of life and sustainable development.[4] In short, CSR is vulnerable to a risk of illegitimacy if it becomes prone to what Bruno Latour has called an "oligopticon" effect — one produced by a device for seeing some, but not all, human activity — where the metrics used for assessment allow for the traceability of only a subset of the relevant claims and needs.[5]

---

2   See Mette Andersen & Tage Skjoett-Larsen, "Corporate social responsibility in global supply chains" (2009) 14:2 Supply Chain Management Intl J 75; Organisation for Economic Co-operation and Development (OECD), *OECD Guidelines for Multinational Enterprises* (Paris: OECD, 2011); Kish Parella, "Improving Social Compliance in Supply Chains" (2019) 8:22 Notre Dame L Rev 729; Julia Patrizia Rotter, Peppi-Emilia Airike & Cecilia Mark-Herber, "Exploring Political Corporate Social Responsibility in Global Supply Chains" (2014) 125:4 J Business Ethics 581; Stefan Ulstrup Hoejmose, Johanne Grosvold & Andrew Millington, "Socially responsible supply chains: power asymmetries and joint dependence" (2013) 18:3 Supply Chain Management Intl J 277.

3   Backer, *supra* note 1 at 156.

4   Joseph Stiglitz, Jean-Paul Fitoussi & Amartya Sen, *Report by the Commission on the Measurement of Economic Performance and Social Progress* (2008), online: <https://ec.europa.eu/eurostat/documents/118025/118123/ Fitoussi+Commission+report>.

5   Bruno Latour, *Reassembling the Social: An Introduction to Actor-Network-Theory* (Oxford: Oxford University Press, 2005) at 181.

Consequently, it can be argued that there is a need for diverse CSR measurement tools in line with the pluralist approach often favoured by ecological economics and conceptions of sustainable development.[6] Among the tenets of ecological economics is that an integrated, holistic approach should be taken to socio-ecological systems, both as regards the deployment of disciplines in the sciences, social sciences and humanities,[7] and as regards multiple scales ("the spatial, temporal, quantitative, or analytical dimensions used to measure and study any phenomenon") and levels (the "units of analysis that are located in the same position on a scale") of analysis.[8]

CSR has itself been conceptualized as flowing from sustainable development,[9] thus a cross-scale and cross-level framework would help to avoid the blind spots of an oligopticon. The challenge for the assessment of CSR is to integrate multiple dimensions and levels of accountability for the social and environmental impact of companies.[10]

If a cross-scale and cross-level approach is needed for CSR generally, that is even more obviously so as regards global supply chains. The assessment of CSR across a global supply chain cannot be limited, on the spatial scale, to responsibility in the domicile of any single company, or indeed to the state level on the jurisdictional scale. Thus, for example, Loblaw Companies Ltd., which runs a Canadian grocery chain, in the end acknowledged responsibility for having its source of supply for clothing items in the collapsed Rana Plaza factory in Bangladesh.[11] In an oligopticon view of its responsibility, the Canadian company was distinct from the Bangladesh supplier, and the grocery chain with ancillary clothing products did not need to take on standards for the textile sector. Yet Loblaw apparently understood, as did its consumers, that such partial views of responsibility were inadequate.

In sum, the assessment of CSR in global supply chains will inevitably draw upon the various jurisdictional and normative frameworks at every relevant scale and level, from extraction to production to distribution to consumption, with reciprocal responsibility for all actors throughout.

---

6   See Robert Costanza, "What is Ecological Economics?" (1989) 1 Ecological Economics 1 at 2. See also Bert de Vries, *Sustainability Science* (New York: Cambridge University Press, 2013) at 142.

7   Peter Brown & Peter Timmerman, eds, *Ecological Economics for the Anthropocene: An Emerging Paradigm* (New York: Columbia University Press, 2015).

8   Hsing-Sheng Tai, "Cross-Scale and Cross-Level Dynamics: Governance and Capacity for Resilience in a Social-Ecological System in Taiwan" (2015) 7:2 Sustainability 2045 at 2047, citing Clark C Gibson, Elinor Ostrom & TK Ahn, "The concept of scale and the human dimensions of global change: A survey" (2000) 32:2 Ecological Economics 217. See also David W Cash et al, "Scale and Cross-Scale Dynamics: Governance and Information in a Multilevel World" (2006) 11(2): Ecology & Society 8.

9   Michael Kerr, Richard Janda & Chip Pitts, *Corporate Social Responsibility: A Legal Analysis* (Toronto: LexisNexis, 2009).

10   See Alain Supiot, *Governance by Numbers: The Making of a Legal Model of Allegiance*, Hart Studies in Comparative Public Law, vol 20, translated by Saskia Brown (Portland, OR: Hart, 2017).

11   See Loblaw media statements; see especially 24 October 2013, online: <https://media.loblaw.ca/English/media-centre/company-statements/company-statements-details/2013/Loblaw-Update-to-Rana-Plaza-Compensation/default.aspx>. However, note the subsequent Canadian litigation; see also David J Doorey, "Rana Plaza, Loblaw, and the Disconnect Between Legal Formality and Corporate Social Responsibility" (13 September 2018), doi:10.2139/ssrn.3265826.

Second Challenge: The Lack of Transparency and Accountability for CSR in Global Supply Chains

Two main impediments to the implementation of CSR in global supply should be underlined. The first is raised by the view that CSR is purely voluntary, i.e., that companies are responsible solely to shareholders for financial performance and take on any other responsibilities *ex gratia* in order to build goodwill. The second is raised by the structure of global supply chains, which have technical impediments to accountability and transparency.

The Voluntary Nature of CSR

While the exact status of CSR may vary from country to country,[12] the dominant shareholder model still relies on Milton Friedman's idea that the only true responsibility of a company is to generate profit.[13] Although it may be possible to make the case for CSR from within the dominant shareholder model by arguing that CSR contributes to profit,[14] since both the public and investors give consideration to company ethics and sustainability, CSR is nevertheless often still understood as a matter of public relations rather than an essential element of the company's business.

The consequence of this weak status for CSR is that although CSR can be linked to the general fiduciary obligations of corporate directors and officers, it tends to be viewed as corporate behaviour that will emerge as a response to appropriate incentives rather than as flowing from "hard law."[15] Even if CSR can be rooted in formal legal obligations, it remains relevant and necessary to find the right set of incentives as well. This is especially true as regards obligations stemming from the operation of global supply chains, as illustrated by the Loblaw litigation alluded to above.[16]

Accountability and Traceability in Global Supply Chains

Incentives should be designed to overcome the gaps in monitoring and oversight of global supply chains produced by the patchwork of national legal regimes.[17] After all, regulation of global supply chains appears to be outside the traditional power of the nation state.[18] Indeed,

---

12 Canada, *People's Department Store v Wise (Trustee of)* 2004 SCC 68, and *BCE Inc v 1976 Debentureholders* 2008 SCC 69 laid the ground for a legal notion of good corporate citizenship, countering the shareholder-centric Delaware model. In China, the government has incorporated CSR into article 5 of its Company Law. See *Company Law of the People's Republic of China* (revised 2013), online: *Invest in China* <www.fdi.gov.cn/1800000121_39_4814_0_7.html>. In 2017, France adopted the *Loi relative au devoir de vigilance des sociétés mères et des entreprises donneuses d'ordre* (online: *LegiFrance* <www.legifrance.gouv.fr/affichTexte.do?cidTexte=JORFTEXT000034290626&categorieLien=id>), which requires parent corporations and corporations that direct subsidiaries or sub-contractors in supply chains to exercise vigilance with respect to human rights and environmental abuses. Corporations that fail to exercise proper oversight of their supply chains can be subject to significant fines. See also Pauline Abadie, "Le juge et la responsabilité sociale de l'entreprise" (2018) Recueil Dalloz 302, for the argument that this law will further the role and power of judges regarding CSR cases in France.

13 Milton Friedman, "The Social Responsibility of Business is to Increase its Profits", *The New York Times Magazine* (13 September 1970). It should be noted here that this shareholder model may differ in the European context. See Klaus J Hopt, "Comparative Corporate Governance: The State of the Art and International Regulation" (2011) 59:1 Am J Comp L 1.

14 Philipp Schreck, *The Business Case for Corporate Social Responsibility: Understanding and Measuring Economic Impacts of Corporate Social Responsibility* (Heidelberg: Physica-Verlag Heidelberg, 2009).

15 For a review of the legal foundations of CSR in Canada, see Richard Janda & Juan C Pinto, "National Report on Human Rights, Due Diligence and Reporting: Canada Country Report" in Lukas Heckendorn & Johanna Fournier, eds, *Regulating Human Rights Due Diligence for Corporations: A Comparative View* (Zurich: Edition Schulthess, 2017).

16 See Doorey, *supra* note 11.

17 See generally Backer, *supra* note 1.

18 See Andreas Georg Scherer & Guido Palazzo, "The New Political Role of Business in a Globalized World: A Review of a New Perspective on CSR and its Implications for the Firm, Governance, and Democracy" (2011) 48:4 J Management Studies 899.

the basic unit that is the object of state regulation is typically the company rather than the polycorporate supply chain.[19]

The global reach of supply chains allows MNEs to limit their legal and fiscal obligations by engaging in forum shopping and lobbying.[20] This permits them to escape accountability for the actions of their suppliers while having considerable influence on the governance of lower levels of the supply chain.[21] Yet companies are rarely held liable for the actions and decisions of their suppliers, sometimes even if these are linked to blatant human rights abuses.[22] There are thus significant gaps in the legal structure of corporate accountability for the social and environmental impact of suppliers whom they strongly influence.

Global supply chains also raise issues of traceability.[23] Traceability is defined by Petter Olsen and Melania Borit as "the ability to access any or all information relating to that which is under consideration, throughout its entire life cycle, by means of recorded identifications."[24] Even sophisticated organizations can lack ready access to product traceability. In December 2016, Walmart's vice president of food safety, Frank Yiannas, picked up a package of sliced mangoes at a store near company headquarters and ordered his team to find out how quickly they could determine where it came from. It took them an entire week.[25] All in all, the capacity to trace the origin and impact of goods throughout the chain, both for managerial and ethical purposes, is a major challenge in global supply chains characterized by a multiplicity of actors, markets and jurisdictions.

Technical and Conceptual Challenges: Potential Solutions Drawing on New Information and Communication Technologies

The first part of this chapter identified several challenges, summarized here for convenience:

- producing a holistic approach to CSR conceptualization and evaluation methodology that takes into account the multiple scales and levels of global supply chains;

- incentivizing companies across supply chains to adopt CSR policies; and

- fostering accountability and traceability throughout supply chains.

---

19   Backer, *supra* note 1 at 6–7. See also Darren Rosenblum, "Traveling Corporations and the Futility of Walls" (2019) 93 Tul L Rev 645. For an earlier analysis, see José Engrácia Antunes, *Liability of Corporate Groups: Autonomy and Control in Parent-subsidiary Relationships in US, German and EU Law: An International and Comparative Perspective* (Deventer: Kluwer, 1994).

20   Backer, *supra* note 1; Elizabeth Pollman & Jordan M Barry, "Regulatory Entrepreneurship" (2017) 90 S Cal L Rev 383.

21   See Ulstrup Hoejmose, Grosvold & Millington, *supra* note 2 (on the power asymmetry between different levels of global supply chains).

22   See *Kiobel v Royal Dutch & Co*, 569 US 108 (2013).

23   See generally Yong H Kim & Gerald F Davis, "Challenges for Global Supply Chain Sustainability: Evidence from Conflict Minerals Reports" (2016) 59:6 Academy Management J 1896.

24   Petter Olsen & Melania Borit, "How to define traceability" (2013) 29:2 Trends Food Science & Technology 142 at 148.

25   Alec Guzov, "Walmart: From supply chain to blockchain", Harvard Business School Digital Initiative (10 November 2017), online: <https://rctom.hbs.org/submission/walmart-from-supply-chain-to-blockchain/>.

This part will explore various ways in which the IoT, blockchain and AI could help address these challenges. First, we will survey how these new technologies can help respond to the challenges for CSR posed by global supply chains. Next, we will offer examples of developments made possible by the use of blockchain and the IoT for supply chain traceability and transparency. Finally, we will explore how AI can enable companies to use the data accumulated through the IoT to minimize the supply chain's environmental and social impact.

New Digital Technologies and Supply Chain Sustainability

The IoT, blockchain and AI have the potential to transform the conceptualization, evaluation and implementation of CSR in global supply chains. By their nature, they enable the cross-scale and cross-level holistic approach to CSR that was discussed in the first part of this chapter. They provide the means to recodify CSR throughout global supply chains.

The IoT allows for a continuous stream of data from physical objects that are connected to the internet. It thus enables exactly what a cross-level and cross-scale approach requires: a way to link, in a holistic way, the different levels of geographical scale, and to work simultaneously in physical, digital and jurisdictional dimensions. Put less abstractly, the IoT simplifies the analysis of a supply chain's entire social and environmental impact by connecting its actors and tracking the physical movement of its parts. Although the integration of the IoT within global supply chains is still limited at a technical level,[26] it could, in principle, respond to the challenge raised by ecological economics that we understand supply chains as socio-ecological (and technological) systems.

Blockchain technology also contributes to answering this challenge. By creating secured and public transaction traceability, blockchain technology offers the potential for a platform shared by all the members of the global supply chain and open to outside scrutiny. It can create incentives for companies to respect their CSR engagements and offer logistical help for decentralized governance at the level of the supply chain. Linked to the IoT, blockchain represents a way to safeguard and share the data accumulated across the supply chain.

Finally, AI (and machine learning algorithms in particular), can also enter this holistic approach to sustainable supply chain management by adding sophisticated tools to analyze the large quantities of data available to companies throughout the chain. AI may not only allow the identification of patterns of environmental and social impact in supply chains, but might also eventually help engineer ways through which companies could reduce the risk of generating social and environmental impacts in supply chains.

We turn now to practical illustrations of corporate initiatives using these technologies that could pave the way for more robust CSR across global supply chains.

See-through Supply Chains: The Impact of the IoT and Blockchain Technology on CSR and Self-regulation

The IoT and blockchain raise the prospect of business accountability and transparency in "see-through" supply chains. We will first offer two examples of supply chains reorganized around

---

26   See World Economic Forum System Initiative on Shaping the Future of Environment and Natural Resource Security, *Building Block(chain)s for a Better Planet* (2018), Fourth Industrial Revolution for the Earth Series at 15.

these two technologies and then explain how these changes have the potential to incentivize CSR through accrued transparency and accountability.

In 2016, Provenance, a UK company, sought to respond to many issues raised by labour and environmental concerns about the fishing of yellowfin and skipjack tuna in Indonesia.[27] The fishing industry is plagued by instances of forced labour and illegal fishing, giving rise to problems of sustainable resource management and protection of the environment.[28] Facing a growing demand for traceability through the tuna supply chain, Provenance acknowledged that its existing supply chain lacked transparency and began using blockchain technology to record the trajectory of each fish, from fisher to consumer. Provenance stated publicly that it sought to "share the same truth between all stakeholders — fishermen, factories, certifiers and consumers, without giving any of them a backdoor to the system."[29] To do so, Provenance established a system in which an external non-governmental organization (NGO) verified the efficiency of Indonesian fishers' fair trade practices. The fishers were then equipped with cellphones, which allowed the registration on the blockchain of each transaction through which individual items would change hands: from the producer to the supplier, supplier to the factory, and factory to consumers. Provenance also created a public access portal to the blockchain to allow consumers to track the origin of each item, down to the very fishers who introduced them in the chain.[30]

In a similar gesture, retail giants Walmart and Carrefour both recently introduced blockchain- and IoT-based food supply chain management programs, hoping to resolve issues of water management, traceability and food poisoning that had arisen in the past.[31] In an experiment, the Walmart team created a physical identification tag for mangoes harvested in Mexico. The tag allowed the tracking of mangoes throughout decontamination, transport, customs and storage, as well as identification for customers in Walmart stores.[32] John Keogh reports that whereas "it took almost 7 days to execute a mock recall [on the basis of existing formal regulatory requirements]... [it took] 2.2 seconds using their specific Blockchain configuration."[33] Carrefour, a European counterpart to Walmart, introduced a similar project in 2018 for its own food supply chain.[34] Both programs bring together the IoT (through near field communications technology,

27   Provenance, *From shore to plate: Tracking tuna on the blockchain* (16 July 2016), online: <www.provenance.org/tracking-tuna-on-the-blockchain#blockchains>.

28   *Ibid*, s II ("A broken system: When your fish supper supports slavery"). See also MSC Fisheries Standards, online: <www.msc.org/standards-and-certification/fisheries-standard>.

29   Provenance, *supra* note 27, s III ("Blockchains present a global, inclusive solution for traceability").

30   See *ibid*, s II for two graphs illustrating the blockchain-enabled control of the supply chain by consumers.

31   See Olga Rharif, "Walmart tackles food safety with test of blockchain technology", *Bloomberg* (18 November 2016), online: <www.bloomberg.com/news/articles/2016-11-18/wal-mart-tackles-food-safety-with-test-of-blockchain-technology>. See also Guzov, *supra* note 25.

32   See Robert Hackett, "Why Big Business Is Racing to Build Blockchains", *Fortune* (22 August 2018), online: <http://fortune.com/2017/08/22/bitcoin-ethereum-blockchain-cryptocurrency/>.

33   For a critical analysis of blockchain's potential to guarantee food authenticity and quality, see John G Keogh, "Blockchain, Provenance, Traceability & Chain of Custody" (17 August 2018), online: *My Food Trust* <www.myfoodtrust.com/2018/08/17/blockchain-provenance-traceability-chain-of-custody/>.

34   See "Carrefour lauches Europe first food blockchain", online: *Carrefour* <www.carrefour.com/current-news/carrefour-launches-europes-first-food-blockchain>. Provenance later supported a similar project for Unilever and the growing of tea plants; see Supply Chain Movement, "Unilever trials blockchain to improve supply chain sustainability" (11 January 2018), online: <www.supplychainmovement.com/unilever-trials-blockchain-improve-supply-chain-sustainability/>.

that is, the "tagging" of real-life items for radio identification)[35] and blockchain as a way to secure the registration of food items in a uniform system throughout the food supply chain.[36]

These examples demonstrate the possibility for blockchain and the IoT to be used as instruments in the development of traceability and sustainability in global supply chains. The Provenance project on the management of the tuna supply chain showed how proper use of blockchain could allow effective communication from every actor in the chain, as well as the democratization of the information relative to the goods transferred throughout the chain. Furthermore, the Provenance supply chain clearly works as a cross-scale and cross-level holistic system: it links the different levels of the supply chain by location and numerically.[37] By doing so, it offers a platform to produce more effective CSR monitoring of the presence of human trafficking, unsustainable fishing practices and the general lack of accountability on the part of suppliers.

Finally, by giving companies access to considerable amounts of additional data on the entire supply chain, the IoT and blockchain offer the beginnings of the response to the difficulty inherent in evaluating the impact of company practices. Provided companies are willing to give access to this data, it can provide rich sources of information for sustainability indexes to achieve more compelling assessments of the environmental and social impact of companies throughout the supply chain. The (meta)data encoded in the bar code, QR code (see Figure 1) [the full name is the Quick Response code] or RFID [radio frequency identification] of the final product is no longer limited to stating "Made in Country X" to convey its origin. A t-shirt can now tell the user of every place and every process through which it took its final form and thus how it was "Made in Everywhere."

Figure 1: Metadata of a Product Embedded in a QR Code That Is Itself Embedded in the Product

35   See Danny Pigini & Massimo Conti, "NFC-Based Traceability in the Food Chain" (2017) 9:10 Sustainability 1910.

36   See also a pilot project to use blockchain technology to certify the verification of a textile supply chain and to link the certificate to T-shirt QR codes: Anja Wilde, "CSR In The Supply Chain — Traceability Of Clothing@Kik", online: *More Than Digital* <https://morethandigital.info/en/csr-in-the-supply-chain-traceability-of-clothingkik/>.

37   Tai, *supra* note 8.

Better Social and Environmental Management of International Supply Chains through the Use of AI

In this section, we discuss the potential for AI to allow for better social and environmental engineering of supply chains. We then touch upon its potential to offer partial solutions to what we had characterized as the oligopticon problem: the existing surveillance of only some of the relevant sources of responsibility.

AI as a Tool to Minimize the Social and Environmental Impact of Companies

The IoT and blockchain, when used in conjunction with machine learning, can allow socially minded companies to better identify and predict their environmental and social impacts. To quote from IBM: "AI can rapidly and comprehensively read, understand and correlate data from disparate sources, silos and systems. It can then provide real-time analysis based on interpretation of that data."[38]

This is especially interesting because it suggests that AI could help not only to identify better social and environmental practices for companies, but also be used to modify the structure of supply chains themselves. By allowing for their optimization — notably in order to participate in a circular economy — AI could, in principle, offer tools to design supply chains that are more socially and environmentally responsible.

Some companies have begun to gain a better grasp of their social and environmental impact through the use of machine learning. A 2018 report from the Ellen MacArthur Foundation in the United Kingdom gave several examples in which AI was able to "help build and improve the reverse logistics infrastructure required to 'close the loop' on products and materials by improving the processes to sort and disassemble products, remanufacture components, and recycle materials"[39] in a circular economy. In one example drawn from the report, a company used AI to identify plant-based substitutes for animal products.[40] In another, AI was used to find new metal materials with low levels of toxicity in order to respect circular economy principles.[41] These examples suggest a promising direction for AI: the analysis of data from across the entirety of the supply chain, independent of the geographical or even cultural differences among its different levels, with a view to reducing or eliminating negative externalities.

AI as a Tool to Avoid the Risks of an Oligopticon

The emerging power of AI also suggests answers to the problem of CSR as an oligopticon. By having access to vast amounts of data on the physical characteristics and performance of a supply chain, machine learning opens the prospect of accounting for all of its levels and scales at once, in real time.

To go even further, companies may be able to identify the potential impact of their activities — and that of their supply chains — in fields or spheres that were not even part of their initial commitment to CSR. For example, IBM has marketed its Watson AI as able to "predict"

---

38   IBM, "Supply Chain Analytics", online: <www.ibm.com/dk-en/supply-chain/supply-chain-analytics>.

39   Ellen MacArthur Foundation & Google, with McKinsey & Company, "Artificial intelligence and the circular economy: AI as a tool to accelerate the transition."

40   *Ibid* at 25.

41   *Ibid* at 12.

disruptions in supply chains by monitoring "all aspects of the supply base including…relevant news, events, and raw material shortages, as well as suppliers and route integrity."[42] Similarly, AI company TransVoyant makes the following claim: "From sensors, satellites, radar, video cameras, smartphones and other devices that make up the Internet of Things (IoT), we collect over one trillion events each day, giving us one of the largest repositories of real-time big data in the world. Our proprietary machine learning algorithms analyze these massive big data streams in real-time to produce live and predictive insights that help companies to achieve competitive advantage and government agencies to save lives."[43]

Of course, machine learning should not be understood as a "magic wand."[44] It is still at its inception and faces many technical obstacles.[45] However, it seems to offer the possibility not only to help companies minimize the social and environmental impact of supply chains, but also to allow them to "mine the universe" to predict the future impacts they might have. Without overstating the power of machine learning, this could be understood as part of the answer to some of the conceptual issues raised by the complexity of defining CSR and engaging in multivariate evaluation of firm performance. Indeed, the power of AI to identify and predict disruption in the supply chain suggests that it could help trace impacts at scales and levels that were not previously anticipated, thus potentially confining the risks of producing an oligopticon in the conceptualization and evaluation of CSR.

Incentives Provided by New Technologies to Enhance CSR Disclosure Standards

Previously, we looked at new technologies as tools that could help companies develop better conceptions and implementation of CSR throughout supply chains. Technology, however, does not implement itself — and as noted in the first part of this chapter, the challenges to CSR in supply chains are not only technical, but relate as well to the significant incentives companies can have to resist increasing transparency. This third part discusses the ways in which companies can be incentivized to develop technology-driven CSR strategies.

New Incentives for the Development of CSR through the Knowledge-as-Service Model

The use of the IoT and blockchain could work to close the "structural hole"[46] between consumers and their sellers. By involving consumers in the supply chain and allowing them to track the origin of and processes giving rise to goods, see-through supply chains can do more than offer companies better opportunities to manage traceability. They also represent an opening

---

42   IBM, "IBM Supply Chain Insights with Watson: Leverage artificial intelligence to mitigate supply chain disruptions", Solution Brief at 5, online: <www.ibm.com/downloads/cas/YLEKOE53>.

43   TransVoyant, online: <transvoyant.com/predictive-analytics-space/>. This example and the specific case uses advertised by the company (online: <www.transvoyant.com/hello-world-2/>) are premised on supply chain optimization for profit, but could, by way of analogy, be exported to optimize the environmental or social impact of the supply chain.

44   Steve Banker, "Things to know about artificial intelligence of supply chain management", *Forbes* (1 January 2019) at para 15, online: <www.forbes.com/sites/stevebanker/2019/01/01/20-things-to-know-about-artificial-intelligence-for-supply-chain-management/#7e81e6a35371>.

45   *Ibid* at 9.

46   Robert A Phillips, "Ethics and Network Organizations" (2010) 20:3 Business Ethics Q 533 at 538, quoted in Provenance, *supra* note 27, s VII ("Pilot phase 3: The consumer experience and building an interface for trust").

for consumers as citizens to make sustainable choices, consumers who, in turn, represent an "external pressure factor"[47] for the adoption of CSR.

As a general matter, since the price of products does not reflect the externalities generated through the production process, there is what Ronald Coase identified as a problem of social cost, one that is specifically linked to all the transactions involved in connecting impacts to use.[48] According to Coase, consumers will purchase products that generate harm for others without bearing those consequences in mind because of the costs associated with identifying and managing all of those transactions. In principle, if transaction costs associated with identifying externalities could be brought to close to zero, this would mean that harmful impacts could be assessed and aligned with the price mechanism, at least to the degree that consumers would be willing to pay to avoid harms that are attributable to their purchases.

Consumers are not the only actors that can face new incentives if externalities can be traced throughout supply chains. If, in addition, harmful impacts crystallize into risk factors for investors (for example, single-use plastics become understood as a business risk for the plastics industry),[49] the traceability of supply chains can increase investor incentives to reduce the impacts of their portfolios.

Traceability can lead companies to respond to such shifting incentives by creating entire business models based on knowledge-as-service. Deloitte developed this idea in a 2015 report.[50] According to the report, the integration of the IoT within the supply chain could be turned into a business model — consumers may be willing to pay more to benefit from the knowledge inherent in the real-time information provided by the IoT.[51] The knowledge-as-service model could be the marketing incentive for CSR.[52] The example from the Provenance tuna supply chain is telling: if citizens/consumers find value in being able to discriminate their consuming choices according to the impacts products generate, then the use of the IoT and blockchain as tracking devices for management purposes could create a virtuous circle that generates further incentives for companies to adopt sustainable practices throughout their supply chains, promote traceability and transparency, and work toward enhanced evaluation and implementation of CSR policies.

---

47   See David Eriksson & Göran Svensson, "Elements affecting social responsibility in supply chains" (2015) 20:5 Supply Chain Management Intl J 561.

48   Ronald Coase, "The Problem of Social Cost" (1960) 3 JL & Econ 1.

49   See Justin Trudeau, Prime Minister of Canada, News Release, "Canada to ban harmful single-use plastics and hold companies responsible for plastic waste" (10 June 2019), online: <https://pm.gc.ca/en/news/news-releases/2019/06/10/canada-ban-harmful-single-use-plastics-and-hold-companies-responsible>; Pauline Skypala, "Investors must look hard at the future of plastics", *Financial Times* (15 July 2019), online: <www.ft.com/content/0a21d8b6-42af-3b99-b320-c6131b07be86>.

50   Joe Mariani, Evan Quasney & Michael E Raynor, "Forging links into loops: The Internet of Things' potential to recast supply chain management" (2015) 17 Deloitte Rev 122.

51   *Ibid* at 126.

52   See Zaheer Khan, Yong Kyu Lew & Byung Il Park, "Institutional legitimacy and norms-based CSR marketing practices: Insights from MNCs operating in a developing economy" (2015) 32:5 Intl Marketing Rev 463. See also Rojanasak Chomvilailuk & Ken Butcher, "The impact of strategic CSR marketing communications on customer engagement" (2018) 36:7 Marketing Intelligence & Planning 764.

Code-embedded CSR as a Way to Bridge the Trust Gap with Consumers

Traceability and transparency can also feed into an ambitious possibility enabled by the IoT and blockchain, namely to put into place "smart contracts" governing CSR undertakings.[53] In a blog post, Phil Gomes, CEO of a smart contracts company, presents the following algorithm structure:

> By way of example, consider the following contract logic:
> If the profitability of the firm is> [X]%, AND
> IF the firm's supply chain is certified by [insert reliable NGO here] as at least [Y]% fair trade, AND
> IF you are a holder of preferred stock as of [date], THEN
> Said shareholders will receive [$Z] per share in their electronic wallets
> within a day of the firm's quarterly earnings announcement.[54]

The logic underlying this algorithm is that blockchain technology, by automating contracts, could enforce CSR by incorporating it within the methodology for effectuating transactions. This idea has already given rise to an entire business model. Companies have started to create smart contract protocols as a way to improve branding for socially minded companies. For example, Medium is a company that offers to build a range of undertakings, such as charitable donations, into smart contracts.[55] Identifying the fact that many consumers lack trust in the businesses they interact with, Medium offers to build that trust by creating smart contracts that force companies to execute their CSR obligations, thus reassuring their clients.[56]

This forced accountability is different from the general transparency brought about by blockchain. Smart contracts offer the possibility of going further than creating additional and accessible data on companies: they can render CSR undertakings executable, taking accountability to another level.

Moreover, the possibilities raised by smart contracts are not limited to company-consumer relationships. Accountability is also possible among companies seeking to engage in socially responsible behaviour with their suppliers. If blockchain allows for secure and efficient tracking of goods, then companies could more easily enforce their own CSR policies by incorporating their codes of conduct into blockchain-enforced traceability and transparency.[57]

---

53   For a definition and explanation of smart contracts, see Lauren Henry Scholz, "Algorithmic Contracts" (2017) 20 Standford Tech L Rev.

54   Phil Gomes, "Using the Blockchain and Smart Contracts for CSR: The Social Purpose Case for Using Bitcoin's Core Technology", *LinkedIn* (15 October 2015), online: <www.linkedin.com/pulse/using-blockchain-smart-contracts-csr-phil-gomes/>.

55   Massimo Lomuscio, "Smart Social Contracts, unstoppable promises on the Blockchain" (4 February 2018), online: *Medium* <https://medium.com/reason/what-are-smart-social-contracts-the-new-business-model-for-the-blockchain-d3a27025fc4b>.

56   *Ibid.*

57   Nick Heinzmann & Pierre Mitchell, "Icertis Blockchain Framework: A Glimpse of CLM's Expanding Footprint into the Supply Chain" (4 March 2019), online: *Spend Matters* <https://spendmatters.com/2019/03/04/icertis-blockchain-framework-a-glimpse-of-clms-expanding-footprint-into-the-supply-chain/>.

Mercedes-Benz recently put into place a project of this sort. The company sought to ensure that every actor in Mercedes's supply chain signed and acknowledged the Mercedes supplier code of conduct. At the same time, some suppliers in the chain sought to preserve anonymity and Mercedes was willing to keep its contractual information limited to its first-tier manufacturers. It thus put into place a smart contract allowing for the signature and certification of the Mercedes code of conduct at each level of the supply chain, while preserving anonymity throughout the supply chain.[58] This allowed key relevant terms — such as code of conduct undertakings and, in some circumstances, the identity of suppliers — to move up the chain while protecting other terms requiring more anonymity, such as price points.[59]

Industry and State Norms Governing Traceability and Transparency

The increasing capacity to trace provenance and impacts is already beginning to manifest itself in the evolution of industry standards. In 2014, the United Nations Global Compact, together with Business for Social Responsibility, released *A Guide to Traceability: A Practical Approach to Advance Sustainability in Global Supply Chains*, which identifies 25 collaborative standards across 35 business sectors that have developed traceability certification.[60] Industry traceability standards are also beginning to incorporate use of blockchain.[61]

Governments are already involved in seeking to promote the development of AI for supply chain traceability.[62] They have also begun to issue general traceability standards. For example, in 2002, the European Union implemented the General Food Law, which requires food and feed businesses to trace the provenance and destination of their products and to provide this information to regulators in close to real time.[63] This kind of regulation can function in tandem with industry standards. For example, the GS1 industry standard originated in an effort to standardize the use of barcodes in the retail industry as a whole.[64] GS1 has developed a Global Traceability Standard for various food products, which allows food regulators to send a "GS1-centric message" to retailers that can result in a stop-sale protocol being implemented at cash registers across the country within 30 minutes, when necessary.[65]

Government traceability requirements, which are in the nature of disclosure rules, do not prescribe specific practices for businesses and correspond to efforts those businesses are already making to oversee their supply chains. In principle, therefore, they do not encounter the kind of

---

58   *Ibid.*

59   *Ibid* at "Icertis Blockchain Framework: What it does."

60   See UN Global Compact and Business for Social Responsibility, *A Guide to Traceability: A Practical Approach to Advance Sustainability in Global Supply Chains* (2014), online: <www.unglobalcompact.org/docs/issues_doc/supply_chain/Traceability/Guide_to_Traceability.pdf>.

61   See e.g. OriginTrail, "an ecosystem dedicated to making supply chains work — through championing standards supporting a universal data exchange…and ensuring data immutability by utilizing the blockchain technology", online: <https://origintrail.io/about-us>.

62   In December 2018, the Government of Canada launched Scale AI, whose stated mission is to "boost productivity across industries in Canada through the integration of AI with supply chains." Online: <https://scaleai.ca/about-us/>.

63   EC, *Commission Regulation 178/2002 of 28 January 2002, laying down the general principles and requirements of food law, establishing the European Food Safety Authority and laying down procedures in matters of food safety*, [2002] OJ, L 31/1.

64   GS1, "Mission and History", online: <www.gs1us.org/what-we-do/about-gs1-us/mission-history>.

65   See Keogh, *supra* note 33.

industry pushback that command-and-control regulation typically encounters. The "light touch" provided by a traceability requirement can nevertheless lead to stronger legal accountability of suppliers of goods at the transnational level. Since goods can be tracked through physical identification and an inherently public and unalterable blockchain database, states can regain a degree of supervision over MNEs by requiring them to give access to their supply chain management data.[66] The use of blockchain by companies to maximize the efficiency of their supply chain — as in the Walmart example — exerts additional pressure to adopt tougher CSR standards, since companies are, in effect, stopped from "looking the other way" at their suppliers' unsustainable practices. After all, they are able to track whether such practices have entered their supply chains.[67]

The legislation adopted by France to ensure vigilance over human rights and environmental standards in supply chains goes beyond simply mandating traceability. It also requires upstream companies in the chain to: map out human rights and environmental risks in the chain; implement procedures for regular verification of their subsidiaries, sub-contractors and suppliers; take steps to mitigate risks and prevent grave harm; create a system for signalling and receiving alerts when harmful impacts take place; and have a follow-up mechanism to evaluate the effectiveness of measures taken.[68] As the French legislation gets tested, it could become a bellwether for regulation elsewhere.

CSR Risks of New Technologies

In this last part, we explore the changes that AI, blockchain and the IoT will make to our conception of CSR itself. We suggest that the challenges linked to new technologies (such as data protection and cyber security) have already become one more field of CSR. We conclude with a brief discussion of the risks posed by incommensurability in CSR evaluation.

CSR Issues Spawned by the New Technologies of Information and Communication

Of all the main categories of CSR recognized in the literature — the environment, fair labour practices, human rights, Indigenous justice, consumer issues, and community involvement and development[69] — none fully contains the issues raised by the use of digital technologies. The first and most obvious of these issues is the privacy of the actors involved in collecting the massive quantities of data necessary for optimal use of the IoT and AI. The fiduciary role of corporations extends to protecting the vulnerability of those who share data through the

---

66   See Russ Stoddard, "How the blockchain could transform sustainability reporting" (24 April 2018), online: *GreenBiz* <www.greenbiz.com/article/how-blockchain-could-transform-sustainability-reporting>.

67   Julia Rotter, Peppi-Emilia Airike & Cecilia Mark-Herbert, "Exploring Political Corporate Social Responsibility in Global Supply Chains" (2014) 125:4 J Business Ethics 581 at 584.

68   See *Loi relative au devoir de vigilance des sociétés mères et des entreprises donneuses d'ordre, supra* note 12. The first case testing the legislation was brought forward on December 12, 2019. See Camille Bauer, "Justice première utilisation de la loi sur le devoir de vigilance des entreprises" (12 December 2019), online: *l'Humanité* <www.humanite.fr/justice-premiere-utilisation-de-la-loi-sur-le-devoir-de-vigilance-des-entreprises-681738>. See also Les Amis de la Terre France & Survie, "Les manquements graves à la Loi sur le devoir de vigilance des entreprises : le cas Total en Ouganda" (June 2019), online: *Survie* <https://survie.org/IMG/pdf/rapport_totalouganda_at_survie2019.pdf>.

69   International Organization for Standardization, "Guidance on social responsibility" (2010), ISO 26000:2010(en), online: <www.iso.org/obp/ui/#iso:std:iso:26000:ed-1:v1:en>.

supply chain, including ultimate consumers.[70] Data privacy and protection have thus become an increasingly important part of CSR, and indeed have become the main issue area to which executives expect to increase the allocation of resources over the next two years, according to the State of Corporate Citizenship Report.[71] Of course, the concern is particularly pressing in the case of global supply chains, through which data is, by its nature, readily transferable and can be moved through different jurisdictions having different legal standards, which in turn might allow companies to minimize their legal obligations through forum shopping and regulatory lobbying.

The second related issue arises out of the cyber security risks posed by algorithmic norms. The disastrous end of the Decentralized Autonomous Organization in 2016,[72] or the hacking of the Ethereum blockchain in 2017 following a human error in the creation of hash keys for some user accounts,[73] gave rise to the loss of several million dollars enabled by the algorithmic "laws" that had been put in place on the platform. It follows that the democratization of blockchain — and by extension, of the IoT and AI — throughout everyday activities, at all levels of global supply chains, creates an additional responsibility for businesses to address the cyber security concerns associated with the use of technologies. Although cyber security could be understood as implicit in broader categories of CSR, such as consumer protection or human rights, it may become its own separate category for oversight.[74]

Real-time Law Confronts Incommensurability

The traceable assessment of CSR social and environmental impacts in supply chains also brings to the fore the question of whether such impacts are inherently unmeasurable. Is it possible to give a measurable value to a visually pleasing landscape, access to a resilient climate, or even a feeling of job security? True, there are "willingness to pay" proxies, and life-cycle analyses can be expanded to include multifactorial approaches.[75] Yet any attempt to define a common measure of value and thus compare all factors on a single scale or index could give rise to potential injustice, as each of the goods or claims has an inherent value defended by a different normative and social sphere.[76] One could argue, for example, that the failure to monitor labour practices in

---

70   See Horace McPherson, "Data privacy — Protecting This Asset Is a Priority" (1 May 2014), online: *ISACA* <www.isaca. org/resources/isaca-journal/past-issues/2014/data-privacy-protecting-this-asset-is-a-priority>.

71   Susan McPherson, "8 Corporate Social Responsibility (CSR) Trends To Look For In 2018", *Forbes* (12 January 2018), online: <www.forbes.com/sites/susanmcpherson/2018/01/12/8-corporate-social-responsibility-csr-trends-to-look-for-in-2018/>.

72   See Nathaniel Popper, "A Hacking of More than $50 Million Dashes Hopes in the World of Virtual Currency", *The New York Times* (18 June 2016), online: <www.nytimes.com/2016/06/18/business/dealbook/hacker-may-have-removed-more-than-50-million-from-experimental-cybercurrency-project.html>. For an explanation of decentralized autonomous organizations in general (as opposed to the Decentralized Autonomous Organization that named itself after the concept and is referred to in the previous article), see David Olarinoye, "What is a decentralized autonomous organization (DAO)?" (3 July 2018), online: *Invest In Blockchain* <www.investinblockchain.com/decentralized-autonomous-organization-dao/>.

73   Andy Greenberg, "A 'Blockchain Bandit' Is Guessing Private Keys and Scoring Millions", *Wired* (23 April 2019), online: <www.wired.com/story/blockchain-bandit-ethereum-weak-private-keys/>.

74   See Scott Shackelford, "Cybersecurity as Social Responsibility: Business, Music, and the Symphony of Cyber Peace" (2017) Indiana University Kelley School of Business Research Paper Series No 17-69.

75   See Cécile Bulle et al, "IMPACT World+: a globally regionalized life cycle impact assessment method" (2019) 24 Intl J Life Cycle Assessment.

76   See *Stanford Encyclopedia of Philosophy*, online: <https://plato.stanford.edu/entries/value-incommensurable/>; see especially *ibid*, "Social choices and institutions" and discussion of the work of Michael Walzer, notably *Spheres of Justice* (New York: Basic Books, 1983).

a supply chain cannot be compensated by good environmental practices: a company that relies on child labour cannot redeem itself through recycling.

Thus, the technological possibilities brought forward by the Fourth Industrial Revolution may accentuate the question as to whether CSR should attempt to integrate, through the use of common metrics, notions that are, by definition, incommensurable.[77] If common metrics are used as diagnostic tools that assist in a more differentiated analysis (the dashboard of indicators we referred to earlier), they could be deployed responsibly. Indeed, a second-order assessment of CSR should pay attention to whether metrics are treated as ends or means: do companies simply report on and satisfy themselves with numerical rankings, without probing the claims that arise from incommensurable impacts? Furthermore, does the transparency they provide to users of data allow third parties to engage in differentiated analysis?

Conclusion: Conceptualizing CSR in Globalized Supply Chains

Globalized supply chains all but escape the control of state law. On their own, states can barely track supply chains that are polycentric and transnational, and if expectations for oversight are centred on the state, that creates space for the neglect of companies' social and environmental obligations. At the same time, it is a considerable challenge simply to define and evaluate precisely how to measure social and environmental impacts. The discourse on CSR is shared by a multiplicity of actors, including international organizations, states, academia and, of course, companies, and its boundaries remain uncertain. New information and communications technologies — the IoT, blockchain and AI — offer emerging avenues for addressing the problems inherent in measuring CSR, such as how best to assemble data from complex systems involving an array of environmental, economic and social impacts. They also hold the promise of better traceability and accountability among actors at all levels of global supply chains.

However, any technology is only a tool — it does not autonomously generate social norms. Although we have sought to show how these technologies could be and, indeed, are being arrayed so as to allow companies to expand their accountability for CSR throughout supply chains, they will still need to be implemented universally by the multiplicity of actors that form supply chains today. Even if that were accomplished, formal and informal norms to govern the use of data and the response to real-time signals of impact will have to emerge and evolve. CSR in global supply chains will become the constellation of such norms, enabled by traceability in real time.

Although we have attempted to identify ways in which CSR can take shape in this new setting, how MNEs are exercising and will exercise agency in shaping norms of corporate behaviour is a broader issue that would require a separate investigation.[78] Furthermore, the implementation of these new technologies will give rise to additional CSR issues, from data privacy and cyber security to normative questions concerning incommensurabilities among the various metrics

---

77   On incommensurability, see generally Supiot, *supra* note 10.

78   See e.g. Business Roundtable, "Statement of Purpose of a Corporation" (2019), online: <https://opportunity. businessroundtable.org/wp-content/uploads/2019/08/BRT-Statement-on-the-Purpose-of-a-Corporation-with-Signatures.pdf>.

being used to assess the data gathered. These issues boil down to problems of data and technology governance. How MNEs exercise agency in forming norms, and how data and technology are governed, will together open further questions concerning the nature and transformation of the law in this realm. Real-time traceability of social and environmental impacts is beginning to generate a new normative architecture that will recodify the very process of seeking sources of law.[79]

---

79   See Lawrence Lessig's initial, famous and subsequently revised effort to conceptualize how cyberspace transforms law. Lawrence Lessig, *Code: Version 2.0* (New York: Basic Books, 2006), online: <http://codev2.cc/download+remix/Lessig-Codev2.pdf>.

8

WÂHKÔTOWIN AND RESTORING HUMANE RELATIONALITY WITHIN THE TRANSNATIONAL CORPORATION

Darcy Lindberg

> To the Cree, stories are animate beings….In this respect, one could ask, what
> do stories do when they are not being told? Do they live in villages?…Do they tell
> each other to each other? Some Cree say this is true….A symbiotic relationship exists:
> If people nourish a story properly, it tells them useful things about life.
>
> — Howard Norman[1]

Rediscovering Our Relations through Stories

There are many ways *nêhiyaw* (Plains Cree) peoples conceive of and use *acimowina* (stories). As Howard Norman points out above, stories are fundamentally social beings, requiring our attention to live good lives. Their reach is long. They show us our connection and obligations

---

1   Howard Norman, "Crow Ducks and Other Wandering Talk" in David M Guss, ed, *The Language of the Birds: Tales, Texts, & Poems of Interspecies Communication* (San Francisco: North Point Press, 1985) 18 at 19.

with human and non-human beings and things that are not in our immediate lifeworld. In this way, acimowina cause us to consider how we relate to each other, and what legal expectations and obligations we have to each other inter-societally. Thus, acimowina provide nêhiyaw peoples with a frame to apply questions of legal obligations to peoples and things within other nations and societies.

Stories are also rigorous and pliable. Our older stories, *âtayôhkêwina*, the ones that tell us of the creation of the nêhiyaw world, have present-day applicability. As complex intellectual tools, our older stories can be applied to future and abstract challenges, offering solutions that maintain a fidelity to *nêhiyaw pimâtisiwin* (Plains Cree way of living).[2] This chapter explores the application of nêhiyaw pimâtisiwin to complex legal challenges. Specifically, it is concerned with the responsibility of the corporation transnationally in situations where its operation has contributed to environmental degradation and disaster within Indigenous territories. The jurisdictional challenges of enforcing corporate liabilities when their practice stretches across multiple nation-state jurisdictions remains a significant barrier to the good living of Indigenous peoples globally.

In this chapter, I consider our *wâhkôtowin* obligations — the laws that govern our relationships to human and non-human agents — as a potentially powerful principle to address these harms. As a foundational legal principle that influences the social and legal lives of nêhiyaw peoples, wâhkôtowin's relational ethic — one that considers kinship with human and non-human beings and things as a precondition of our legal obligations to each other — offers a conceptual avenue toward the redress of harms caused by corporations from other states. As an experiment in the future applicability of Indigenous legal ordering in transnational corporate law, this chapter will forward this argument in three parts. First, I will provide more background on wâhkôtowin, its epistemological roots within nêhiyaw societies, and its positioning within a web of constitutive principles that give rise to nêhiyaw law. This will be contextualized through the story of the creation of Buffalo Lake, a nêhiyaw narrative that, when examined through a legal lens, provides significant teachings on human obligations to new lands and jurisdictions. In the second portion, I apply wâhkôtowin and related laws to the principle of corporate separateness, and the challenge it places upon meaningful retribution, restoration and reparation for inter-jurisdictional harms. Corporate separateness, in its use to protect domestic corporations from the liabilities of subsidiaries that have committed ecological harms and human rights violations in other jurisdictions, is a well-worn tool in avoiding both legal and humane obligations to others. The challenges provided by corporate separateness are representative of how environmental justice is handcuffed by the international (and thus interjurisdictional) nature of corporate practice. As I argue, wâhkôtowin approaches this challenge from a different angle, where the obligations of a corporation are as vital as its rights to engage in whatever endeavour they undertake. Finally, I will briefly examine the future of Indigenous legal principles and traditions, their potential for intervening transnationally, and the constitutive reimagining that needs to occur to access the wealth of resources within Indigenous legal orders. To move beyond the speculative answers

---

2   As John Borrows notes, "The transmission of oral traditions in [Indigenous] societies is bound up with the configuration of language, political structures, economic systems, social relations, intellectual methodologies, morality, ideology, and the physical world"; stories for Indigenous societies are multi-faceted intellectual devices that inform many areas of Indigenous social relations. See John Borrows, "Listening for Change: The Courts and Oral Traditions" (2001) 39:1 Osgoode Hall LJ 1 at 21–24. For a more sustained look at the use of stories for their legal information within Indigenous societies, see Hadley Friedland & Val Napoleon, "An Inside Job: Engaging with Indigenous Legal Traditions through Stories" (2016) 61:4 McGill LJ 725.

this chapter puts forward, wâhkôtowin must be widely understood, adopted and applied. As this chapter argues at its conclusion, this application is possible through constitutive reimagining.

Restor(y)ing Our Relations: The Creation of *Paskwâwimostos Sakihikan* (Buffalo Lake)

Many of our stories are, quite literally, considerations of social and legal responsibilities when we come upon new grounds. These considerations help create new jurisdictions for *nêhiyaw* law, aiding in outlining new obligations to the peoples, non-human beings and other agents and things of the new territory. Our âtayôhkêwina, our origin stories, tell of our original relationships with specific places within *nêhiyaw askiy* (Plains Cree territory). These stories become aligned with these specific places with each retelling, so much so that we consider some as natural and inherent as the *asiniy* (rock) and *sipiy* (river) in our landscapes. They also teach us of new lands and waters, and how to conduct our relations when we come into contact with new peoples, beings and things. Consider the âtayôhkêwin of *paskwâwimostos sakihikan* (Buffalo Lake). I offer one version of the story here:[3]

> *Kayas (a long time ago), there was a time when a group of nêhiyawak (Plains Cree peoples) were struggling to find food. This was around the time when paskwâw-mostos (buffalo) were disappearing from the prairies. One hunter, knowing he would need assistance to find buffalo, engaged in ceremony for four days, seeking guidance for a successful hunt on behalf of the community. Finally, upon the fourth evening, he dreamt about a place further west on the prairies where he would find a buffalo. Setting off the next day with another hunter, they travelled for another four days. On the fourth day, they came upon the hill and, faithful to his dream, they found a sole buffalo on the other side. With care, the hunter approached and was able to pierce the animal with an arrow. The buffalo sprang away, leaving a trail of blood as it ran further across the prairies.*

> *The hunters followed this blood trail for another four days. Finally, they came to a spot where the buffalo had finally succumbed to its injury. Pulling the arrow from the buffalo, the two men were surprised to see water springing from the wound, rather than blood. They watched this for some time. The water formed a puddle, then a small pool, and then eventually a pond. The hunter who dreamt the buffalo left to gather the rest of the people. This took another four days. When he returned with them, they were surprised to see that the pond had turned into a large lake, in the shape of a buffalo. Understanding that the lake was a gift from kisê-man'to, (the creator) the people knew it would be a place of generosity toward them. And the lake provided — it brought all sorts of animals, including buffalo, from the prairies to its banks. It allowed large grasses, shrubs and trees to form at its shores. The lake became a place of abundance, and nourished the people for many years.*

---

3   As an example of the pliability of our stories, I have employed this story in public talks and prospective papers to describe how Plains Cree laws explain the danger of using abstractive language in our legal ordering with regard to lands, waters and other non-human beings and things.

This portion of the story describes the creation of Buffalo Lake for the benefit of the people.[4] This exemplifies a common motif within nêhiyaw âtayôhkêwina: that, in comparison to other beings, humans are pitiful and require the active intervention of non-human beings and things for survival. As a reciprocal act, because of the gifts that non-human beings and things provide humans, we are obligated to *miyo wicehtowin* (good relations or harmony) with these non-human beings and things. Or, as the story of the creation of Buffalo Lake concludes:

> One winter, many years later, the people were crossing the lake to visit relatives who had settled on the other shore. While they were crossing, a young boy came across a buffalo horn sticking through the ice. You see, the people used to run buffalo into the shallows of the lake for a more successful hunt. They must have hunted so much that year that one buffalo must have slipped past their attention and eventually floated to the centre of the lake before freeze-up. The young boy wanted the horn, and he begged his mosôm (grandfather) for it. Understanding that it would be a transgression to take it, the mosôm said no. But, as young ones have a special gift for, the boy was able to work the tenderness of his mosôm until the grandfather finally relented. Taking his hatchet, the boy hit the ice around the horn to retrieve it. Instead of freeing the horn, the ice cracked up, first around the two, then around the rest of the community. While some were able to scramble across the ice to the other side and others back to the shore they came from, some were lost in the water.

It was my oldest brother who first told this story to me when I was seven or eight years old. Over time, the fantastical elements of the story have given way to a deeper contemplation of what obligations the story impresses upon me, and guides my future behaviours. At its base, this story originally caused me to recognize the *inspirited* nature of the land, and how we are obligated to reckon with the autonomy of those who are inspirited (animals, plants and other non-human beings and things) in our laws when we hunt.[5] It also taught me the dangers of how we conceive and talk about the ecological world. With the consequences of misusing a keystone relation narrated in the story (the wasting of buffalo), the creation story of Buffalo Lake is a tidy example of the meta-principle of *ohcinêwin* (transgressions against non-human beings and things) in operation.[6] The carelessness of previous hunts causes the retribution at the end of the story. Further, remembering the obligation within nêhiyaw law that we *speak* properly about the environment (*ohcinêmowin*),[7] we can reflect on the story and our present-day tendency to categorize our animal kin as commodities or as subservient to humans. Thus, the creation story of Buffalo Lake allows us to reflect on ohcinêwin and ohcinêmowin in present-day contexts, and guides us in alternatives to the colonial language of the Canadian-state law, and the resulting attitudes toward lands, waters, animals and other non-human beings.

Even from the brief version of the story shared above, it is clear that narratives are rich resources for nêhiyaw peoples. Narrative is an intergenerational intellectual device that allows for "new knowledge" to be "incorporated into the practices and intellectual traditions" of nêhiyaw

---

4   Buffalo Lake is in central Alberta. There is another version of this story told by the Dene people to describe the separation of the T'suu T'ina people from their northern kin.

5   I am using "inspirited" here as a placeholder for nêhiyaw conceptions of the spiritual dimensions of the ecological world that are discussed further in this chapter.

6   Sylvia McAdam, *Nationhood Interrupted: Revitalizing Nêhiyaw Legal Systems* (Saskatoon: Purich, 2015) at 44.

7   Pauline Johnson, *E-kawôtiniket 1876: Reclaiming Nêhiyaw Governance in the Territory of Maskwacis through Wâhkôtowin (Kinship)* (PhD Dissertation, Western University, 2017) [unpublished] at 155.

societies.[8] As a foundational principle within nêhiyaw social, economic, spiritual and legal systems, the relationality expressed in the story — between humans, buffalo and *nipiy* (water) — is one of the constitutive elements that constellate nêhiyaw social life.

If we examine the creation story of Buffalo Lake for its expression of wâhkôtowin, it can tell us much about the abstract nature of the principle of corporate separateness, the injustices that corporate separateness can cause, and the potential for nêhiyaw laws in intervening in such injustice. On its face, it may be difficult for a reader, especially those unfamiliar with nêhiyaw intellectual traditions, to make such connections.[9] Exploring wâhkôtowin further, we can see the link. Commonly understood as the "laws governing all relations,"[10] it has both general understandings and specific obligations. Maria Campbell provides a broad view of wâhkôtowin:

> Today [wâhkôtowin] is translated to mean kinship, relationship, and family as in human family. But one time, from our place it meant the whole of creation. And our teachings taught us that all of creation is related and inter-connected to all things within it. Wâhkôtowin meant honoring and respecting those relationships. They are our stories, songs, ceremonies, and dances that taught us from birth to death our responsibilities and reciprocal obligations to each other. Human to human, human to plants, human to animals, to the water and especially to the earth. And in turn all of creation had responsibilities and reciprocal obligations to us.[11]

David McPhee similarly notes wâhkôtowin's broadness: "Wah-ko-to-win is how we are related to one another, and how things relate to one another. We all exist within larger relationships and these relationships are the foundation for everything else....In relationships there are roles that each party has. It is critical to recognize there is also responsibility as part of relationships."[12]

Sylvia McAdam furthers this understanding of wâhkôtowin extending beyond human-to-human relationships. She describes her father, Francis McAdam Saysewahum, sharing his understanding of wâhkôtowin: "Long ago after the human beings were created, they were allowed to walk with the animals and talked amongst each other like relatives. Even the trees, plants, all manner of life was able to communicate with each other. That was the beginning of understanding wâhkôtowin and the laws surrounding it....We still remember we are related to all of creation, [an understanding] that is still followed to this day."[13]

Finally, Matthew Wildcat states that wâhkôtowin can be broken into three parts: "First it references the act of being related — to your human and other than human relatives. Second, it is a worldview based on the idea that all of existence is animate and full of spirit. Since everything has spirit it means we are connected to the rest of existence and live in a universe

---

8   Friedland & Napoleon, *supra* note 2 at 742.

9   See Winona Wheeler, "Cree Intellectual Traditions in History" in Alvin Finkel, Sarah Carter & Peter Fortna, eds, *The West and Beyond: New Perspectives on an Imagined Region* (Edmonton: Athabasca University Press, 2010).

10   Harold Cardinal & Walter Hildebrandt, *Treaty Elders of Saskatchewan: Our Dream Is That Our Peoples Will One Day Be Clearly Recognized as Nations* (Calgary: University of Calgary Press, 2000) at 14.

11   Maria Campbell, "We need to return to the principles of Wahkotowin", *Eagle Feather News* (November 2007) at 5, online: <http://aboriginalasasktellwebhosting.com/Resources/November-2007.pdf>.

12   Hadley Friedland, *Reclaiming the Language of Law: The Contemporary Articulation and Application of Cree Legal Principles in Canada* (PhD Dissertation, University of Alberta, 2016) [unpublished] at 164.

13   McAdam, *supra* note 6 at 47.

defined by relatedness. Third, there are proper ways to conduct and uphold your relationships with your relatives and other aspects of existence."[14]

Wâhkôtowin, like other principles within nêhiyaw legal ordering, does not occupy a hierarchal position, but rather is connected to and works in concert with other related principles. As an example of decentred ordering, the non-hierarchal nature of nêhiyaw legal traditions is reflected in nêhiyaw legal theory. Within *nêhiyawewin* (the Plains Cree language), the word for law is *wiyasiwêwina*. This is often described as the act of weaving.[15] It utilizes the word *wiyasowe*, meaning "a meeting," and the suffix *-wina*, indicating a "collection of ideas."[16] Both of these interpretations, the meeting of a collection of ideas and the act of weaving, reinforce the collective nature and deliberativeness of nêhiyaw legal processes. For example, wâhkôtowin is linked to laws of *pastahowin*, or "something that violates natural law";[17] ohcinêwin, or the consequences for violating our obligations to the ecological world;[18] and the accompanying legal principle, ohcinêmowin, which guides our speech toward the ecological world,[19] with each serving as strength for the operation of the other. Thus we have an obligation to act in good relations, but also to speak well of our relationships. I offer this as a contemplation of how Canadian law speaks of the *other* — both non-Canadian peoples and non-human beings and things — and how that transgresses nêhiyaw laws. This has significant implications for corporate law principles.

Wâhkôtowin as an Affirmation of Human and Non-human Agency

Stories like the creation of Buffalo Lake also guide us in our relationships to new lands and territories. Fundamental to this is the understanding that the land, even void of human habitation, is inhabited by other animal nations and the multitude of inspirited beings and things. This makes treaty making, in its human and non-human variations, a vital legal process when reconstituting upon new lands and waters, much like what is described in the creation story of Buffalo Lake. Fundamental to this belief is how nêhiyaw peoples understand the *ahcâhk* (spirit), in whom an ahcâhk resides, and how this affects our obligations to beings and things are subject to such inspirited living. As such, the ahcâhk fundamentally underpins the relational orientations of nêhiyaw legal processes. Our ahcâhk connects us equally with other living beings and things within the inanimate world. Within nêhiyaw world view, everything in creation is animated by some form of ahcâhk.[20] The link between our individual intellectualism and our spirituality is described as *acahkomâmitonihcikan*, or the spirit-mind.[21] The spirit-mind is not

---

14   Matthew Wildcat, "Wahkohtowin in Action" (2018) 27:1 Const Forum Const 13 at 14.

15   Johnson, *supra* note 7 at 152.

16   Leona Makokis, *Leadership Teachings from Cree Elders: A Grounded Theory Study* (Saarbrucken, Germany: Lambert, 2009) at 56.

17   John Borrows, *Canada's Indigenous Constitution* (Toronto: University of Toronto Press, 2010) at 85.

18   *Ibid.*

19   See Johnson, *supra* note 7 at 155.

20   *Ibid* at 172.

21   Art Napoleon, *Key Terms and Concepts for Exploring Nihiyaw Tâpisinowin the Cree Worldview* (MA Thesis, University of Victoria, 2014) [unpublished] at 26.

limited to humans. While there are beliefs that some species share a collective ahcâhk,[22] it is a common understanding that plants and animals, like humans, have individual ahcâhk.[23] Recognizing the ahcâhk held by other human and non-human agents impresses a nêhiyaw version of constitutive equality among peoples. As we all are given our ahcâhk from the same source — *man'to iskotêw* (Creator's flame) — there is an inherent equality to our existence. Acknowledging the ahcâhk of plants, animals, lands and waters implies a similar equality for the ecological world. It calls for a consideration of the autonomy and sovereignty of beings who are subject to an ahcâhk. As Jerry Saddleback notes, the inspirited nature of land requires that "we take care of…[â]skiy…in the same compassionate manner that she takes care of us," where "[l]aw states that there should always be a conscientious effort in continuity of taking care of the interlinked balance" with âskiy "for our required sustenance and livelihood."[24]

The beliefs and teachings within nêhiyaw intellectual traditions of the inspirited nature of both humans and non-human agents informs how we should express our wâhkôtowin obligations — or, to put it another way, how we relate to others. As I will argue below, this colours how we view the principle of corporate separateness.

Gift/Obligation Praxis and Nêhiyaw Constitutionalism

While these brief explorations of wâhkôtowin and the ahcâhk may require further deliberations through observation of and even immersion within nêhiyaw ways of living, to understand their application to international legal relations, we can begin to see how nêhiyaw peoples view new obligations to agents on new lands. This is similar to what Brian Noble describes as a "treaty ecology." He describes treaty ecology as "living with the land and its diverse living inhabitants, and so to live together as peoples there as well. [It is] a praxis of treaty, animated by an ecology of sharing in the land and its fruits, of exchange, reciprocity, mutual obligation, extended relations through ceremonial-material encounter among persons, animal-persons, animal collectives, and people's collectives."[25]

While acknowledging the consumptive nature of humanness — we are consumptive beings in our need to rely upon our non-human kin for nourishment, shelter and labour — a treaty ecology sets out obligations to maintain that this is a reciprocal relationship. Gifting is one such obligation. A significant and central practice to nêhiyaw societies, gifting has long been

---

22   See Blair Stonechild, *The Knowledge Seeker: Embracing Indigenous Spirituality* (Regina: University of Regina Press, 2016) at 63.

23   For example, the Rock Cree of Northern Manitoba believe that animals existed before humans in a state of *ahcahkowiwin*, where animal nations lived out their own cultural values and practices. See Robert Brightman, *Grateful Prey: Rock Cree Human-Animal Relationships* (Regina: University of Regina Press, 1993).

24   Jerry Saddleback, "Cree Testimony on Water", International Organization of Indigenous Resource Development, Stakeholder Communication to the Office of the High Commissioner for Human Rights, on request, further to Decision 2/104 on Human Rights and Access to Water, United Nations Human Rights Council, online: <www2.ohchr.org/english/issues/water/contributions/civilsociety/IOIRD_Alberta.pdf>.

25   Brian Noble, "Treaty Ecologies: With Persons, Peoples, Animals, and the Land" in Michael Asch, John Borrows & James Tully, eds, *Resurgence and Reconciliation: Indigenous-Settler Relations and Earth Teachings* (Toronto: University of Toronto Press, 2018) 318.

institutionalized within nêhiyaw ceremonies.[26] Aside from the *mâhtâhitowin* ceremony (the giveaway, or literal translation, "gifts exchanged are a blessing"), minor giveaways occur at memorials, round dances, graduations and other significant events.[27] As a reciprocal exchange for gifts from non-human beings and things, giveaways are an integral practice for wâhkôtowin.[28]

Giveaways and gifting rely upon interactions with non-human beings and things as well. Our *matotisân* (sweat lodge ceremony) involves gifting beyond our human relations. When holding (or asking for a person to put up) a matotisân, we are obligated to bring gifts for the human *oskâpêwis* or helpers (usually clothing and/or honoraria), our animal relations who may visit the ceremony (usually through prints, and sometimes food), *k'se man'to* (through tobacco), our ancestors who aid us in the lodge (through sweetgrass, sage and other medicines), and other participants (through food). This ensures that all the relations involved have been gifted for their involvement. Beyond a symbolic act, gifting maintains a reciprocity in our dealings, even with non-human beings and things. While the above example is attached to ceremony, it is understood that these ceremonial procedures serve as a pedagogical tool that influences our legal norms.

Corporate Separateness and the Alienation of Good Relations

Even in the modest and speculative manner of this chapter, the application of wâhkôtowin principles (like those displayed in the creation story of Buffalo Lake) to the humanitarian and ecological challenges exacerbated by the principle of corporate separateness provides viable avenues toward environmental and social justice. The long-standing principle that a corporation, as a separate entity from its shareholders, carries on as its own agent, shields shareholders and parent companies from its liabilities. The use of corporate separateness as a tool to avoid humane obligations to human and non-human agents is fundamentally contrary to the principle of wâhkôtowin; corporate separateness ensures *unrelatedness*, the opposite of wâhkôtowin's precondition that everything is related. Other corporate law principles ensure this abstraction. While corporate personhood and the attendant human faculties ascribed to corporations (for example, giving the corporation the ability to enter into contracts and take steps toward their enforcement) can be viewed as practices of *relatedness*, the protections they provide to the operating hands of the corporation — the corporate veil — work against

---

26   Shalene Jobin, *Cree Economic Relationships, Governance, and Critical Indigenous Political Economy in Resistance to Settler Colonial Logics* (PhD Dissertation, University of Alberta, 2014) [unpublished] at 150.

27   *Ibid* at 172.

28   *Ibid* at 174. Also consider the story that was shared with me by Métis teacher Richard Letendre in March 2009, which highlights how non-human agents play a large wâhkôtowin in giveaways. In his âcimowin, he talked about being a young boy, watching his *kokom* (grandmother) bead an outfit for a whole year. When it came time for a tea dance (which includes a giveaway), he saw his kokom gift the outfit she had been working on for a whole year to strangers at the gathering, who had travelled a long distance to take part. He then recounts how the strangers were so touched to receive the gift that they went back to where they were camped and returned with a shotgun, and gifted that over in return. He said both his kokom and the strangers approached the fire at the centre of the ceremony with their gifts, and put them both in the fire, to give what they had received to the creator. Letendre shared this story for its pedagogy: he was teaching that gifting is not a human social relation, but relies upon *all of our relations*. My own experiences of gifting have worked my understandings of giveaways beyond human-to-human relations to include non-human beings, things and spirits as well. I have experienced strangers gifting moccasins, medallions and part of their bundles on first meeting. I have done this myself as well. Understanding the protocols of this, there is an implicit understanding that our exchange is not an individual-to-individual relationship, but ties into a wider societal gifting.

relationality. The corporate veil disavows the operating hands of the corporation from the bounds of humane obligation — any penalty will be felt by the corporation itself, while the human minds that operate it can flee its corporality. As this abstraction from humane obligation has become normalized through centuries of practice, coupled with transnational corporate practices, the effects of a corporation's degrading, inhumane, illegal or violent practices are often not understood by individuals who support corporate practice in one way or another. Or, to put it another way, abstract practices and principles within corporate law unwittingly allow good people to contribute to terrible actions and practices.

As the creation story of Buffalo Lake shows, the operation of wâhkôtowin, pastahowin, pastamowin and ohcinêmowin in our oral narrative traditions informs our obligations to good relations. Foundational principles within corporate law, like that of corporate separateness, provide a significant challenge to nêhiyaw laws of relationality. While these conflicts have not arisen explicitly in formal legal proceedings in Canada (where a principle such as wâhkôtowin has directly challenged a principle such as corporate separateness), these challenges are not merely philosophical, as they have significant and often devastating effects on Indigenous lifeworlds. While the structuring of corporations as human-like entities within legislation effuses a corresponding human-to-human relationality, they remain elusively alien and abstract. This is especially evident in situations where redress is sought for corporate harms in other jurisdictions. Further, as Indigenous nations and societies continue to have close relationships with landscapes and waterscapes that are resource-rich, this challenge disproportionately affects Indigenous peoples and societies.

Consider the operation of corporate separateness in *Yaiguaje v Chevron Corporation*.[29] In the court's decision, corporate separateness barred the appellants, Indigenous peoples from the Oriente region of Ecuador, from executing on a US$9.5 billion Ecuadorian judgment within Canada.[30] With no assets in Ecuador, the Chevron Corporation has been able to escape execution of the Ecuadorian judgment against it. The appellants were seeking the assets of Chevron Canada, the Canadian subsidiary of the Chevron Corporation. Often invoked as a safeguard to protect individuals who engage in entrepreneurial pursuits, corporate separateness may be employed to protect corporations from their own actions by moving assets to related corporate entities; *Yaiguaje v Chevron Corporation* is an example of how this is done. Of course, the employment of multinational webs of related corporations to effectively move assets away from the threat of execution of judgments is common.[31] The decision affirms the standing of the Chingola residents in the UK courts, citing the "high level of control and direction" of Vedanta on its subsidiaries' activities.[32] In Canada, corporate separateness has been invoked to bar claims of human rights abuses against Indigenous peoples in Guatemala,[33] claims of liability arising out of violence done by private security personnel to Guatemalan protestors,[34] and claims from

---

29   2018 ONCA 472.

30   *Ibid* at para 3.

31   The 2019 decision in *Vedanta Resources PLC and another (Appellants) v Lungowe and others (Respondents)* ([2019] UKSC 20) in the UK Supreme Court, where residents of Chingola, Zambia, sued Vedanta Resources for the ecological and human harms caused by its subsidiary, Konkola Copper Mines Plc in Zambia, opens the door a crack further toward retribution, in spite of corporate separateness.

32   *Ibid* at para 3.

33   See *Choc v Hudbay Minerals Inc*, 2013 ONSC 1414.

34   See *Garcia v Tahoe Resources Inc*, 2017 BCCA 39.

Eritrean refugees of working conditions that violate fundamental human rights,[35] to protect Canadian corporations from potential liabilities of attached corporations.

The doctrine of corporate separateness is founded upon principles that are opposite to wâhkôtowin's relational ethos — that non-human beings and things are merely property and commodity.[36] This oppositional ethos is a product of what Noble calls "coloniality." He states the gift-obligation orientation of treaty ecologies "is very different from the norm of action in deeply entrenched liberal settler-Indigenous political, social, cultural, and economic lives."[37] He contends that "coloniality can be thought of as the tendency of a 'self' in an encounter to impose boundary coordinates — such as those of territory, knowledges, categories, normative practices — on the domains of land, knowledge, [and] ways of life of an other who has had prior principal relations with those lands."[38]

Coloniality is behind western property law's tendency to orient itself opposite of wâhkôtowin's relational ethos. Neoliberal logics that view non-human beings and things simply as property and commodity displace our notions of relationality with non-human beings and things. This replaces real relationships within our lifeworlds with an alienating legal relationship that Brenna Bhandar calls a "commodity logic of abstraction."[39] She notes, "[T]he commodity logic of abstraction obliterates pre-existing relations to the land, and pre-existing conceptualizations of land as something other than a commodity. The legal form renders invisible (and severely constrains) the ways in which people live, act, (re)-produce the conditions of their existence, and relate to one another in ways not confined to commodity relations of ownership and exchange."[40]

This process of abstraction erases the "social bond" that is "presupposed" between an owner and their private property.[41] Thus it has allowed landscapes[42] and even waterscapes[43] to be enclosed, privatized and marketized, while requiring very little relationship between those who own and benefit from such commoditizations to what they are commoditizing. A result of this abstraction is a loss of humanity in our relationships with the non-human things that we rely upon for ease of living, and the human beings whose labour is exploited to provide these things. Returning to the appellants in *Yaiguaje v Chevron Corporation*, the commodity logic of abstraction serves as another mediating barrier for the consumer to overcome in order to fully empathize with the devastations to the appellants' Ecuadorian lifeworld. When abstraction logic is crystallized and embedded within legal principles — as it certainly is within the principle of corporate separateness — the obligation to relate is seemingly evaporated. Adherence to formal legal

---

35   See *Araya v Nevsun Resources Ltd*, 2017 BCCA 401.

36   Noble, *supra* note 25 at 319.

37   *Ibid* at 322.

38   *Ibid* at 323.

39   Brenna Bhandar, "Title by Registration: Instituting Modern Property Law and Creating Racial Value in the Settler Colony" (2015) 42:2 JL & Soc'y 253 [Bhandar, "Title by Registration"].

40   Brenna Bhandar, *Colonial Lives of Property: Law, Land, and Racial Regimes of Ownership* (Durham, NC: Duke University Press, 2018) at 98–99.

41   See David Harvey, *Seventeen Contradictions and the End of Capitalism* (Oxford: Oxford University Press, 2014) at 39.

42   Inspired by the idea of commoditization of shipping goods, or the original stocks, Robert Torrens (after whom the system of land registration is named) thought land was a better fit for such a scheme because it could be even more "indivisible" than shipping stock. See Bhandar, "Title by Registration", *supra* note 39 at 258–59.

43   Practices of enclosure that were originally thought limited to lands have been adapted to commoditize oceans as well. See Fiona McCormack, *Private Oceans: The Enclosure and Marketisation of the Seas* (London, UK: Pluto Press, 2017).

processes replaces internal moral obligations to right relations or good citizenry. Or, as Zygmunt Bauman contends, a "human morality" is replaced with "organizational morality."[44]

Our wâhkôtowin stories are integral in a corporate-logic world, as they recover the visibility of our shared existence with other peoples, animals, land and waterscapes, and other non-living things. Beyond giving moral or ethical guidance, our wâhkôtowin stories maintain the obligation to see kinship with others, and to walk in a lawful manner toward them.

The United Nations Declaration on the Rights of Indigenous Peoples, and the Potentials for Nêhiyaw Laws

In an implicit manner, the story shared at the beginning of this chapter tells us much about nêhiyaw futures, and potentials for adaptations of principles such as that of corporate separateness. The maintenance of understandings of the inspirited nature of non-human beings and things ensures relational thinking, even in the midst of legal norm creation and transformation. The reality is that, both domestically and internationally, Indigenous peoples are far too often the primary recipients of the harm and violence that come from environmental degradations done through corporate entities. The cover that corporate separateness provides to corporations remains a huge challenge for attaining environmental justice and human rights for Indigenous peoples. An accountability toward Indigenous legal traditions is a viable avenue to move toward such justice. In a broader sense, Indigenous legal principles, often with enriched obligations toward lands, waters, animals, other living things and non-living entities, offer touchstones for Canadian-state law to refer to in its legal relationships to the ecological world.

Coloniality has interrupted meaningful tools to practice nêhiyaw kinship with the ecological world and with our unmet human relations. This has resulted in a silence about the sovereignty and autonomy of the ecological world in Canadian treaty implementation, resulting in violations of nêhiyaw law. While still practised, nêhiyaw legal concepts such as pastahowin, ohcinêwin and ohcinêmowin have had little influence on how the Canadian state recognizes its obligations under the numbered treaties it signed generations ago with Indigenous peoples. However, there is hope in a collective revitalization of relationships to the ecological world, as we are starting to see the constitutive journeys of other nations influenced by Indigenous relationships to the environment. In 2010, Bolivia enshrined inherent rights for "mother earth" within its constitution.[45] Through centuries-old negotiation, the Māori peoples in New Zealand were recently successful in providing the Whanganui River with the same legal rights as a living entity.[46] In 2008, Ecuador granted essential rights to the environment within its written constitution, allowing citizens to raise legal challenges on behalf of the environment.[47] The voices of Indigenous peoples were integral in many of those movements. Within many Indigenous

---

44   Zygmunt Bauman, *Modernity and the Holocaust* (Ithaca, NY: Cornell University Press, 1989) at 12.

45   See David Humphreys, "Rights of Pachamama: The emergence of an earth jurisprudence in the Americas" (2017) 20:3 J Intl Relations & Development 459.

46   Eleanor Ainge Roy, "New Zealand river granted same legal rights as human being", *The Guardian* (16 March 2017), online: <www.theguardian.com/world/2017/mar/16/new-zealand-river-granted-same-legal-rights-as-human-being>.

47   Clare Kendall, "A new law of nature", *The Guardian* (24 September 2008), online: <www.theguardian.com/environment/2008/sep/24/equador.conservation>.

societies and nations in North America there lie broader methods of constituting societies that involve the ecological world. North American indigeneity offers thousands of avenues through which to give our plant, animal, stone and water relations (to name a few) a constitutional voice.

The respective steps taken by Bolivia, New Zealand and Ecuador have in common a reimagining of nation-state constitutional orders. Canada can take account of Indigenous legal orders, and the multiple forms of relationality that are operationalized within them, through similar constitutional changes. There is ample room within Canadian constitutionalism to operationalize Indigenous legal orders. Just as nêhiyaw constitutionalism is rooted in normative practices — like our narrative traditions — so is Canadian constitutionalism. John Borrows notes that the Canadian constitution is "open ended — a perpetual work in progress, a living tree. It is comprised of various written texts, an assortment of established conventions, and a diverse array of oral traditions. It is an open-ended marriage, polyandrous in many ways, allowing for multiple partners. It even has rules that contemplate divorce. In many respects, Canada's constitution is a fluid arrangement, and many people seem to like it that way."[48]

Borrowing largely from UK constitutional traditions of parliamentary structuralism and unwritten norms,[49] Canadian constitutionalism is tangle-rooted. Reimagining Canadian constitutionalism with substantive influences from Indigenous legal orders will make it more so. The diverse potentials of constitutional pluralism in Canada, through further recognition of Indigenous constitutional orders, challenges "the conventional court-centric view of early constitution-making in Canada [that] has concentrated on formal British Imperial instruments."[50] The reality is that Indigenous constitutions and the legal ordering they root have been continuously practised within Canada, despite the imposition of Canadian constitutionalism upon Indigenous lands and territories. Aaron Mills provides a helpful parallel for the relationship between a constitution and law. Mills states that while Canadian constitutionalism is moored by law and policy developed upon a liberal rights lifeworld, Anishinaabe constitutionalism is given life through a rooted lifeworld.[51]

The roots of a society are its lifeworld: the story it tells of creation, which reveals what there is in the world and how we can know. Creation stories disclose what a person is, what a community is, and what freedom looks like. The trunk is a constitutional order: the structure generated by the roots, which organizes and manifests these understandings as political community. The branches are our legal traditions, the set of processes and institutions we engage to create, sustain and unmake law. The trunk conditions the branches: it does not determine what they look like, but it powerfully shapes them.[52]

I contend that nêhiyaw constitutionalism shares a similar "rooted" nature. Wâhkôtowin serves as the ties that bind together nêhiyaw legal traditions, constitutional orders and lifeworld.

A second approach to raising up relational principles within Indigenous legal orders is through international treaties and agreements. The United Nations Declaration on the Rights

---

48   John Borrows, *Freedom and Indigenous Constitutionalism* (Toronto: University of Toronto Press, 2016) at 105.
49   *Ibid* at 105–6.
50   *Ibid* at 106.
51   Aaron Mills, "The Lifeworlds of Law: On Revitalizing Indigenous Legal Orders Today" (2016) 61:4 McGill LJ 847.
52   *Ibid* at 862.

of Indigenous Peoples (UNDRIP)[53] offers perhaps the most significant movement toward acknowledging Indigenous law and legal processes. UNDRIP articles 3, 4 and 5 provide Indigenous peoples with self-determining rights regarding economic development, governance and legal ordering. Implicit in article 25's assurance that distinctive spiritual relationships to landscapes and waterscapes are to be maintained is a right to the legal ordering that upholds these relationships. Although these articles ensure the ability for nêhiyaw societies to practise wâhkôtowin outwardly, they provide no standard for nation-states to take on wâhkôtowin obligations. Article 27 provides more grist for the recognition of wâhkôtowin norms. It declares: "States shall establish and implement, in conjunction with indigenous peoples concerned, a fair, independent, impartial, open and transparent process, giving due recognition to indigenous peoples' laws, traditions, customs and land tenure systems, to recognize and adjudicate the rights of indigenous peoples pertaining to their lands, territories and resources, including those which were traditionally owned or otherwise occupied or used. Indigenous people shall have the right to participate in this process."[54]

As a process-focused imperative, article 27 provides an avenue for wâhkôtowin obligations to be presented (or other, similar relational principles from other Indigenous legal traditions) in land conflicts. There is ample room in the wording of this article for states to implement an alternate process, aside from civil litigation, to address the types of harms experienced by Indigenous communities, such as occurred in Ecuador, that could sidestep barriers such as corporate separateness.

For the pragmatist, using article 27 of UNDRIP to provide alternatives to sidestep corporate law doctrines toward humane obligations may seem like a difficult road to travel. Indeed, there are two significant hurdles to utilizing article 27 in such a manner in Canada. The first is the implementation of UNDRIP within domestic law. As I complete this writing, Canadian senators have let Bill C-262, a private member's bill that would have required federal law to be aligned with the obligations of UNDRIP,[55] die on the order paper, citing concerns that UNDRIP provides Indigenous nations with vetoes over proposed projects within their territories.

The death of Bill C-262 in the Senate is also emblematic of the second challenge in invoking article 27 to use Indigenous legal principles to counteract long-standing corporate principles that cause Indigenous and/or ecological harms. This argument requires state processes to validate, and thus interpret, the articles. As Bill C-262 would have reiterated the influence of international law on domestic law in Canada, its passing would still have required interpretation. Whether Canada would implement the processes set out in UNDRIP in a manner that resets the corporation-Indigenous society relationship (void of the protections of corporate separateness) is a vast speculation at this point.

These two challenges return us to domestic constitutionalism. Instrumentalizing international law would require a similar reimagining of Canada's constitutional arrangements domestically. Normative movement (among the Canadian citizenry) and political action (among Canada's

---

53   *United Nations Declaration on the Rights of Indigenous Peoples*, GA Res 295, UNGAOR, 61st Sess, Supp No 49, UN Doc A/Res/61/295, 46 ILM 1013 (2007).

54   *Ibid*, art 27.

55   Bill C-262, *An Act to ensure that the laws of Canada are in harmony with the United Nations Declaration on the Rights of Indigenous Peoples*, 1st Sess, 42nd Parl, 2016 (as passed by the House of Commons 30 May 2018).

representative bodies) toward the recognition of Indigenous legal processes must occur before their formal legal instrumentation. Despite these challenges, I have faith that such imaginative experimentation (such as that engaged in this chapter) can result in real change. Returning to the story of the creation of Buffalo Lake, there is a hidden lesson on committing to such visioning. When I think of the story, I often wonder what it was like to travel for such a long time based on nothing but a dream; to come despairingly close to what nourishes you, only to see it flee away; to commit to follow it even more; and, finally, to be gifted something that is so much more than you asked for. I take this as a significant lesson in our pursuit of humaneness, wâhkôtowin and new legal landscapes upon which it could operate. We can reimagine our constitutive ordering and, if committed, we can make such journeys. *Ekosi.*[56]

---

56   Nêhiyawewin for "it is complete."

III.
CORPORATE CONDUCT REFLECTING VALUES

9

VESTING TRANSNATIONAL CORPORATE RESPONSIBILITY IN *NATURAL PERSONS V LEGAL PERSONS*

What Matters Today?

Malcolm Rogge

Introduction

Today's demands for corporate responsibility are often joined with the call for multinational enterprises to be accountable for their human rights impacts around the world. Most prominently, the United Nations Guiding Principles on Business and Human Rights state that respecting human rights is a "corporate responsibility."[1] Rather than asking what it means for a legal entity "to respect" human rights, the chapter examines closely the sense of the term "corporate responsibility" and considers its ethical significance for the corporate decision maker and the human rights victim alike. The chapter describes how today's transnational legal order does not adequately capture human rights in legal terms as an aspect of corporate responsibility; indeed, the legal order tends very often to leave the human rights victim facing

---

1   *Report of the Special Representative of the Secretary-General on the Issue of Human Rights and Transnational Corporations and Other Business Enterprises: Guiding Principles on Business and Human Rights: Implementing the United Nations "Protect, Respect and Remedy" Framework*, UNHRC, 17th Sess, UN Doc A/HRC/17/31 (2011) (the corporate responsibility to respect human rights is "a global standard of expected conduct for all businesses" at 13) [UN Guiding Principles on Business and Human Rights].

an accountability void.[2] The global governance "gap," as this void is often called today, is shown here to be constitutive of the global legal order, rather than something absent from it.[3] Given the persistence of this lamentable state of affairs, it is argued that primacy be given to natural persons over legal persons in how we conceptualize corporate responsibility today. As ethical responsibility, the corporate responsibility for human rights is vested in the natural persons who govern the corporate entity, rather than in the abstract corporate entity. This conclusion does not detract from multipronged efforts by victims and their advocates to hold multinational corporations legally accountable for violations of human rights; as a complement to such efforts, it provides reasons for reflective corporate decision makers to choose to govern the legal entities that they control in ways that uphold human rights rather than circumvent them.

The starting point for this examination is to fracture the familiar compound term "corporate responsibility" into its component parts: "corporate" and "responsibility." The contrast between these unique terms could not be more absolute: the former has a precise legal meaning, while the latter's meaning is truly amorphous. While the corporation is a well-defined legal construct, the notion of responsibility has broad legal and ethical meanings, neither of which dominates completely our ordinary understanding of the term. In a world of multinational enterprises, the nominally autonomous corporation takes its place within complex corporate group structures that transcend national boundaries — it is in this sense that the loosely used term "transnational corporation" has gained traction around the world. But what of "responsibility"? In a world of multinational enterprises, are the contours of corporate responsibility jurisdictionally bound, or do they expand with the extensive reach of responsibility as understood in its ethical sense? This chapter traces a route to understanding the transnational dimension of corporate responsibility as the ethical responsibility of natural persons, in particular as it relates to concerns that fall within the ambit of human rights.

The route begins by reflecting on a question: what *entity* or what *person* ought to be regarded as responsible for human rights violations that a multinational enterprise is alleged to have caused or contributed to?[4] From whom should the victims seek justice? The usual answers given, as we shall see, depend on one's position in relation to the matter at hand. Let us consider three very loosely stylized points of view and how they diverge and overlap: the value-maximizing welfare economist; the corporate counsel; and the human rights victim (often referred to as the rights-holder).

---

2   Writing in 2001, I observed, "While the global economy has evolved very rapidly to support business investment in developing countries, it remains virtually impossible to trace moral and legal accountability for industrial harms back to home-country courts. A perplexing and at times alarming divide is evolving in law and ethics in the new economy." Malcolm Rogge, "Towards Transnational Corporate Accountability in the Global Economy: Challenging the Doctrine of *Forum Non Conveniens* in *In Re:* Union Carbide, Alfaro, Sequihua, and Aguinda" (2001) 36 Tex Intl LJ 36 299 at 317 [Rogge, "Towards Transnational Corporate Accountability"].

3   As I noted in 2001 (*ibid*), "Any effort to make transnational corporations more accountable in domestic law for harms caused by their operations abroad will benefit from an understanding of how elements of the common law do precisely the opposite" (at 314).

4   I adopt the language of "cause or contribute" from the UN Guiding Principles on Business and Human Rights, *supra* note 1, Principle 17.

The Value-maximizing Welfare Economist

The welfare economist who gives priority to shareholder value begins by examining whether the impugned outcomes are correctly characterized as negative externalities (i.e., pollution, lower property values, habitat loss and so on) and, if so, the appropriate brake on the harm is thought to lie in state regulation. Here, the socially responsible corporation might be regarded as one that duly follows the rules of the game (including state regulations and local ethical customs) while seeking to maximize profit.[5] By this familiar credo, overall social welfare is thought to increase as profit increases,[6] while those who might be left worse off (the human rights victims) are potentially compensated through redistributive tax and transfer policies as well as other compensation mechanisms, such as tort law.

The Corporate Counsel

The technically minded corporate counsel might opine that corporate responsibility and accountability are synonymous with positive legal liability. From this perspective, a legal entity's responsibility generally arises in three ways: by the demands of state regulation (including criminal, environmental and labour laws); by the expectations created in the duty of care in tort;[7] or by obligations that arise from the company's contracts. By this view, the question of whether a business is responsible for something or not can be resolved deductively (more or less). Where doubts remain, the conflicting parties might call upon courts or arbitrators to settle the matter. But, as we shall see, when it comes to human rights, focusing narrowly on avoiding liability misses the forest for the trees. In today's multinational enterprise, legal counsel plays a critical role in shaping the organization's ethical culture, including its disposition toward the vexing question of human rights responsibility.[8]

The Human Rights Victim

The aggrieved human rights victim's perspective on corporate responsibility is much broader than either of those considered above. While the economist is concerned with valuing negative or positive externalities, one would be hard pressed to fix a market price for the injustice that the human rights victim is forced to bear.[9] For the victim, the matter of a corporation's liability is

---

5   See generally Milton Friedman, "The Social Responsibility of Business is to Increase its Profits", *The New York Times Magazine* (13 September 1970) 32.

6   See e.g. Reinier Kraakman et al, *The Anatomy of Corporate Law: A Comparative and Functional Approach*, 3rd ed (Oxford: Oxford University Press, 2017) (the "most appropriate" interpretation of the shareholder value maximization norm reflects the view that "focusing principally on the maximization of shareholder returns is, in general, the best means by which corporate law can serve the broader goal of advancing overall social welfare" at 23).

7   See John CP Goldberg, "Tort Law and Responsibility" in John Oberdiek, ed, *Philosophical Foundations of the Law of Torts* (Oxford: Oxford University Press, 2014) (tort law is "a law of responsibility….It allows for persons to be held responsible (or accountable) for having wrongfully injured others" at 17).

8   See e.g. Ben Heineman, "Implementing Human Rights in Global Business — High Performance with High Integrity" in Dorothée Baumann-Pauly & Justine Nolan, eds, *Business and Human Rights: From Principles to Practice* (London, UK: Routledge, 2016) 98. See also John F Sherman III, *Rights-Respecting Corporate Culture: Cultural Norms & Values that Underpin Business Respect for Human Rights* (Shift Project, 2019).

9   Human rights are "non-tradeable" goods. See Lewis A Kornhauser, "Wealth Maximization" in Peter Newman, ed, *The New Palgrave Dictionary of Economics and the Law*, 3rd ed (London, UK: Palgrave Macmillan, 1998) 679 ("many goods, such as environmental goods and rights to bodily integrity, do not trade on well-developed markets if they trade at all" at 680).

just one of many aspects of corporate responsibility. Pursuing justice, the victim may attempt to seek an injunction or constitutional *ámparo* to stop the offending activity altogether; failing that, the cause could be taken to the court of public opinion by organizing vigorous protests on the ground.[10] The problem here is that the human rights victim so often discovers that the search for the vindication of rights leads to a dead end — the age-old problem of limited "access to justice." At scale, we find that this common enigma is a global one. Together, many victims stand at the edge of what some have come to call the "global governance gap."[11] A novel way to visualize how this "gap" represents the presence of law, rather than its absence, will be introduced below.

The Disjointed Relationship of Liability to Corporate Responsibility

Corporate liability and corporate responsibility are sometimes viewed synonymously, yet it is critical to understand the ways that they diverge. The separation is most apparent when differentiating the view within the corporation from the view of the wider world. As much as a firm's decision makers seek to grow value, they seek also to avoid liability. In the extremely rare instance where it is necessary to defend a multinational company against allegations of human rights violations in court, the lawyer will draw on a familiar line of defences, including the common law doctrine of *forum non conveniens* (sending the case to what is regarded as the more appropriate court) and separate legal personality.[12] In the more proactive mode, a lawyer might advise corporate decision makers about how to operationalize a human rights policy across a firm's global operations. The proactive mode is concerned with both avoiding liability and growing value over the long run by reducing human rights risks to the business and generating goodwill. Yet this is no straightforward tick-the-box exercise. In describing efforts to implement a global human rights policy at a major extractive industry firm, Sybil Veenman, then general counsel of Barrick Gold, acknowledged: "The issues you face are unpredictable."[13] One of the reasons that some issues are unpredictable is that in the wider world (i.e., beyond the immediate concern of the corporate counsel or manager), corporate legal liability is just one aspect of the broader ethical and political demands for corporate responsibility and accountability. In this wider, expanded sense, the public's demand for redress is expressed in often unforeseeable

---

10   See generally Malcolm Rogge, "Ecuador's Oil Region: Developing Community Legal Resources in a National Security Zone" (1997) 14 Third World Legal Stud 233 (describing community lawyering efforts within a growing social movement in Ecuador that is putting pressure on the government and transnational oil corporations to respect human rights and protect the environment); Malcolm Rogge, "How to Make Them Hear: Challenging International Oil Interests in Ecuador's Amazon Region" (1997) 16:3 Refuge 32 (describing how environmental and human rights organizations work with local communities to counter threats to human rights and the environment that are linked to the operations of national and transnational oil corporations).

11   See Penelope Simons & Audrey Macklin, *The Governance Gap: Extractive Industries, Human Rights, and the Home State Advantage* (London, UK: Routledge, 2014). See also Georgette Gagnon, Audrey Macklin & Penelope C Simons, "Deconstructing Engagement" (2004) University of Toronto, Public Law Research Paper No 04-07. The term first appeared in John Ruggie's scholarly writing with reference to the UN Global Compact. John G Ruggie, "global_governance.net: The Global Compact as Learning Network" (2001) 7:4 Global Governance 371 at 377.

12   See Ashton Phillips, "Transnational Business, the Right to Safe Working Conditions, and the Rana Plaza Building Collapse" in Jena Martin & Karen E Bravo, eds, *The Business and Human Rights Landscape: Moving Forward, Looking Back* (Cambridge, UK: Cambridge University Press, 2016) (on "*forum non conveniens* as a hurdle to transnational tort claims" at 488; see also Rogge, "Towards Transnational Corporate Accountability", *supra* note 2.

13   See Nien-hê Hsieh & Rebecca Henderson, "Putting the Guiding Principles into Action: Human Rights at Barrick Gold (A) and (B)" (2016) Harvard Business School Teaching Note 317-015 at 5.

ways.[14] Take, for example, the case of farmers who face irregular and potentially violent removal from their land to make way for a mining project. For the aggrieved human rights victims, the search for justice may demand that the government and the company abandon their plans to evict and resettle the entire village.[15] It might demand that the company respect the results of a community-led plebiscite over whether to permit mining in the region,[16] even while the government and the company contest the legality of the referendum itself.[17] For the lawyers and managers concerned with a firm's corporate responsibility in the face of these calls for justice, fixating on legal liability is myopic. Many business leaders themselves are critical of such shortsightedness. For instance, Newmont Mining Corporation Chief Executive Officer Gary J. Goldberg warns against taking overly legalistic approaches in addressing conflicts with communities. "Don't depend on the law," he counsels, "…get down and listen to the people and understand what their concerns are — that's critical."[18] The business decision maker's concern with liability is primarily about minimizing roughly estimable legal risks to the business. The wider world is concerned about natural persons taking responsibility, and about people being accountable for the propriety and consequences of judgments made and decisions taken.

As seen from within the corporation, responsibility has both internally oriented and externally oriented aspects. Traditionally, corporate law is concerned with regulating internally oriented responsibility. By imposing a fiduciary duty on natural persons who hold positions of power within the business organization, corporate law seeks to inculcate within them the values of good faith and loyalty in their dealings with other corporate constituents.[19] These duties are not owed at all to persons who have no formal connection to the firm, such as people who live in the surrounding community who may be impacted negatively or positively by its activities.[20] In showing their fidelity to the corporation and its shareholders, corporate decision makers may assume a highly adversarial stance toward anyone who makes claims about the company's allegedly harmful external impacts. This tendency was cited by John Sherman, former deputy general counsel of National Grid and legal adviser to the United Nations Special Representative on Business and Human Rights John Ruggie, who regretted that, all too often, "[i]n community

---

14 See Matthew Murphy & Jordi Vives, "Perceptions of Justice and the Human Rights Protect, Respect, and Remedy Framework" (2013) 116:4 J Business Ethics 781 (in their case study from Guatemala, the authors describe the "wide gulf" that separates the community members' perception of justice from that of the company, at 792).

15 See e.g. Cecilia Jamasmie, "Community opposition forces Newmont to abandon Conga project in Peru" (18 April 2016), online: *Mining.com* <www.mining.com/community-opposition-forces-newmont-abandon-conga-project-peru/>.

16 See Mariana Walter & Leire Urkidi, "Community mining consultations in Latin America (2002–2012): The contested emergence of a hybrid institution for participation" (2017) 84 Geoforum 265 (over a 10-year period, the authors tracked 68 community referenda).

17 For example, a local judge in Ecuador suspended a pending municipal referendum on whether to prohibit mining; days later, the National Elections Council overruled the decision and the referendum was reinstated. See "Judge stops local mining referendum", *CuencaHighLife* (14 March 2019); "Mining referendum reinstated in Girón", *CuencaHighLife* (17 March 2019).

18 Gary J Goldberg, speech delivered at the UN Forum on Business and Human Rights, Opening Plenary (New York, 26 November 2018).

19 See generally David Kershaw, *The Foundations of Anglo-American Corporate Fiduciary Law* (Cambridge, UK: Cambridge University Press, 2018).

20 It remains a matter of debate whether the corporate fiduciary duty ought to be extended to allow fiduciaries to consider the interests of outside "constituencies." On the rise and fall of anti-takeover "constituency statutes" in the United States, see Nathan E Standley, "Lessons learned from the capitulation of the constituency statute" (2011) 4 Elon L Rev 209. In the United Kingdom, under the reformed Companies Act, directors may "have regard" to other constituencies, including "the community and the environment," insofar as doing so promotes the "success of the company." *Companies Act 2006* (UK), c 46, s 172(1) (duty to promote the success of the company).

conflict, lawyers show up and communicate to the other side that they regard the community as a legal liability."[21]

Quite apart from the internally oriented demands of fidelity that are placed on natural persons within the corporation, tort law creates externally oriented duties to people outside the corporation. These externally oriented duties fall on both legal and natural persons, although in practice, liability tends to fall on the corporation itself. Every corporation owes a duty of care to proximate third parties where certain harms are foreseeable.[22] To avoid liability, it is not enough for companies to comply with regulations; decision makers must also take steps to foresee potential risks of harm to third parties, and they must take reasonable steps to mitigate or prevent such risks to people.[23] Tort law has shown some promise for mending the accountability gaps mentioned earlier, but it has serious limitations, especially with regard to multinational enterprises. Such limitations will be considered further below.

So how do the demands of internally oriented fiduciary duties interact with the externally oriented demands of the duty of care in tort law?[24] The nature of such interactions depends, in part, on how the fiduciary duty of loyalty is construed. On this point, opinions often collide between the proponents of shareholder and stakeholder capitalism.[25] Consider the perspective of the hypothetical value-maximizing economist. In a strict shareholder-centric interpretation of the duty of loyalty, characterized by some as calling for "shareholder primacy" or "value maximization," management's role is to take steps to prevent or mitigate harm to third parties, insofar as the value of the company (and, by extension, shareholder value) may be adversely impacted by rebound effects. By this view, the foreseeable risk of harm to people outside the corporation is regarded instrumentally inasmuch as it may converge with a risk to the business.[26] Such strictly instrumentalist interpretations create a moral hazard — after all, preventing harm to third parties is not the sole means by which management can reduce material risk.[27] The company might choose to move operations into jurisdictions where there is less likelihood of facing a tort claim.[28] Litigation avoidance is never likely to be the sole reason for moving operations; nonetheless, in some sectors, concerns over liability are seen to play an important

---

21   John F Sherman III, remarks at the Inaugural Business and Human Rights Symposium panel discussion on "Developments in Business and Human Rights Governance" (Harvard Law School, 13 April 2018) (notes on file with the author).

22   See e.g. *Donoghue v Stevenson* [1932] UKHL 100.

23   In technical literature on human rights risk management, the uncertainty of outcomes for "rights holders" is given the term "risk to people." See e.g. Deanna Kemp, Sandy Worden & John R Owen, "Differentiated social risk: Rebound dynamics and sustainability performance in mining" (2016) 50 Resources Policy 19 at 24.

24   The duty of care in tort law is distinct from the corporate duty of care; however, they have common origins. See Robert J Rhee, "The Tort Foundation of Duty of Care and Business Judgment" (2012) 88 Notre Dame L Rev 1139.

25   On debates over the corporate fiduciary duty as construed within the "property" or "social entity" theory of the corporation, see William T Allen, "Our Schizophrenic Conception of the Business Corporation" (1992) 14 Cardozo L Rev 281; see also Lynn A Stout, "Why we should stop teaching Dodge v. Ford" (2008) 3 Va L & Bus Rev 163. I review the shareholder versus stakeholder debate in Malcolm Rogge, "Bringing Corporate Governance Down to Earth: From *Culmination* Outcomes to *Comprehensive* Outcomes in Shareholder and Stakeholder Capitalism" (2020) Harvard Kennedy School, Corporate Responsibility Initiative Working Paper No 72.

26   For an insightful discussion about such convergence, see John F Sherman III & Amy K Lehr, "Human Rights Due Diligence: Is It Too Risky?" (2010) CSR J.

27   See Björn Fasterling, "Human Rights Due Diligence as Risk Management: Social Risk Versus Human Rights Risk" (2017) 2:2 Business & Human Rights J 225 (suggesting that companies that "excel in social risk management could — *in extremis* — increase risks to right-holders" at 243).

28   See Peter Muchlinski, *Multinational Enterprises and the Law* (Oxford: Oxford University Press, 2007) (arguing that the multinational enterprise is structured to minimize "regulatory burdens" and "maximize operational flexibility" at 52).

role.[29] The first point to be taken here is that the broad notion of corporate responsibility has asymmetrical internal and external dimensions,[30] and that these dimensions are, at times, in tension with one another. The second point is that the corporate fiduciary duty concerns solely the responsibility of natural persons, while the duty of care in tort law concerns the responsibility of both legal persons (corporations) and natural ones.

The Global Governance Gap as a Constitutive Element of the Legal Order

Consider now the very significant limitations of tort law for addressing today's much lamented global governance gap. The history of transnational tort litigation over human rights violations involving parent companies in Canada, the Netherlands, the United Kingdom and the United States has been well documented by others and will not be repeated here.[31] There have been some qualified successes for human rights victims, and yet a sober assessment of the global jurisprudence shows that transnational tort lawsuits are extremely difficult to bring to a satisfactory conclusion and take a heavy toll on the victims and their advocates. Significant advances are often followed by retreats.[32] Long odds aside, the victim may nonetheless decide to bring a lawsuit against a parent company in the home state as part of a wider campaign for corporate accountability.[33] The evident shortcomings of tort law as a human rights remedy provide further motivation for the wider world's call for corporate responsibility to extend beyond what the law actually requires. And yet, from the perspective of our hypothetical corporate counsel, who considers that value seeking goes hand in hand with liability avoidance, the overwhelming difficulties faced by the tort claimants might be regarded as evidence of legal "success" for the enterprises involved.

---

29 As Henry Hansmann and Reinier Kraakman noted almost two decades ago: "Already, strong empirical evidence indicates that increasing exposure to tort liability has led to the widespread reorganization of business firms to exploit limited liability to evade damage claims." Henry Hansmann & Reinier Kraakman, "Toward Unlimited Shareholder Liability for Corporate Torts" (1991) Yale LJ 1879 at 1881.

30 Using similar language, Tara Van Ho calls for an "externalised locus" (i.e., a focus on the interests of people who are external to the corporation) in human rights due diligence. Tara Van Ho, "'Due Diligence' in 'Transitional Justice States': An Obligation for Greater Transparency?" in Jernej Letnar Cernic & Tara Van Ho, eds, *Human Rights and Business: Direct Corporate Accountability for Human Rights* (Wolf Legal, 2013) at 232.

31 For excellent surveys of transnational tort cases and the great challenges that litigants face, see Gwynne Skinner, Robert McCorquodale & Oliver De Schutter (with case studies by Andie Lambe), *The Third Pillar: Access to Judicial Remedies for Human Rights Violations by Transnational Business* (Brussels & London, UK: International Corporate Accountability Roundtable, CORE & European Coalition for Corporate Justice, 2013); Michael D Goldhaber, "Corporate Human Rights Litigation in Non-US Courts: A Comparative Scorecard" (2013) 3 UC Irvine L Rev 127; François Larocque, "Recent Developments in Transnational Human Rights Litigation: A Postscript to Torture as Tort" (2008) 46:3 Osgoode Hall LJ 6; Judith Schrempf-Stirling & Florian Wettstein, "Beyond Guilty Verdicts: Human Rights Litigation and its Impact on Corporations' Human Rights Policies" (2017) 145:3 J Business Ethics 545; Audrey Mocle & Yousuf Aftab, *Business and Human Rights as Law: Towards Justiciability of Rights, Involvement and Remedy* (Toronto: LexisNexis Canada, 2019). A substantial database of current cases is produced by the Business and Human Rights Resource Centre.

32 In a February 2020 decision widely heralded as a significant advance, the Supreme Court of Canada held that customary international law's prohibitions against slavery, forced labour, crimes against humanity and cruel, inhuman and degrading treatment are automatically adopted into Canadian law and "potentially apply" to the defendant corporation. See *Nevsun Resources Ltd v Araya*, 2020 SCC 5 at para 116. Nonetheless, the court's decision pertained to a preliminary motion only, leaving much uncertainty for all parties as the various points of law will be worked out in continuing litigation.

33 For two notable cases from Canada, see *Choc v Hudbay Minerals Inc* 2013 ONSC 1414 [*Choc v Hudbay*] (allegations of violent attacks by company security); *Garcia v Tahoe Resources Inc*, 2017 BCCA 39 (settled in 2019) (allegations of violent repression of protesters by company security).

For the human rights victims and their advocates, the formidable barriers to obtaining remedy are seen as prime instances of the global governance gap;[34] for defending enterprises, such barriers represent the legal order functioning precisely as it should. Using the basic building blocks of corporate law to shield one related entity from another, the corporation, with the help of its lawyers, is able to erect robust architectural defences against liability. The use of such defensive structures is scaled across the global corporate system.[35] The champions of today's corporate law regard its "entity shielding" function as economically and socially efficient.[36] Its critics argue that existing law increasingly gives licence to corporate irresponsibility.[37] The two positions seem irreconcilable. Yet there is another way to depict this impasse that accommodates both points of view. This picture is drawn by the impartial spectator[38] who characterizes the global governance gap as the void in a toroid (for example, the hole in a lifebuoy as shown in Figure 1), rather than a missing piece in a puzzle.

In this characterization, the unbroken grid that runs along the toroidal surface of the lifebuoy represents the seamless and rational legal order: limited liability, separate legal personality and the doctrine of *forum non conveniens* are just a few of its well-oiled components.[39] For the lawyer who represents a multinational enterprise, the grid represents a coherent, intact and predictable system of law that may be used creatively to shield the parent entity from its subsidiary's liabilities, but not to commit a fraud or merely as a sham.[40] This reasonably stable and predictable legal order has been replicated around the globe to undergird the development of market economies. The system lends distinct advantages and disadvantages to different actors depending on where they are situated: the corporations and their shareholders are firmly fixed to the toroid's grid, while the human rights victims drift in the void that runs through it. Politically speaking, reforming the legal order is not so easily achieved, if it means creating more litigation risk and legal uncertainty for businesses and shareholders. This is because truly transformative initiatives will be met with resistance from those players who find advantage in maintaining the status quo.[41] Recognizing this challenge does not mean that efforts to reshape the legal order

---

34   See Penelope Simons, "International law's invisible hand and the future of corporate accountability for violations of human rights" (2012) 3:1 J Human Rights & Environment 5 at 32. See also Simons & Macklin, *supra* note 11 at 8.

35   In 1932, Adolf Berle and Gardiner Means observed the emergence of a "corporate system" in America: "The corporation has, in fact, become both a method of property tenure and a *means of organizing economic life*. Grown to tremendous proportions, there may be said to have evolved a 'corporate system' — as there was once a feudal system — which has attracted to itself a combination of attributes and powers, and has attained a degree of prominence entitling it to be dealt with as a major social institution." Adolf A Berle & Gardiner C Means, *The Modern Corporation and Private Property* (New York: MacMillan, 1932) at 10.

36   On the essential role of "entity shielding" in corporate law, see Henry Hansmann, Reinier Kraakman & Richard Squire, "Law and the Rise of the Firm" (2005) 119:5 Harv L Rev 1333 at 1335; see also Henry Hansmann & Reinier Kraakman, "The End of History for Corporate Law" (2000) 89 Geo LJ 439 (arguing that a global convergence toward the efficient shareholder primacy model is observable and will persist).

37   On how corporate law rules are increasingly used for liability avoidance, see Lynn M LoPucki, "The Death of Liability" (1996) 106:1 Yale LJ 1.

38   I borrow the term "impartial spectator" from Adam Smith's *Theory of Moral Sentiments* (1759).

39   On Max Weber's (much contested) notion of a logical rational legal order as complete system of law, see Duncan Kennedy, "The Disenchantment of Logically Formal Legal Rationality, or: Max Weber's Sociology in the Genealogy of the Contemporary Mode of Western Legal Thought" (2003) 55:5 Hastings LJ 1031.

40   LoPucki, *supra* note 37, argues that such efforts have led to the "death of liability."

41   For example, Simons describes how lobbyists worked against legal reform efforts in Canada aimed at increasing corporate accountability for extraterritorial harms. See Simons, *supra* note 34 at 31. See also Simons & Macklin, *supra* note 11 at 260–70 (on failed legislative initiatives in Canada, the United States, Australia and the United Kingdom).

Figure 1: The Governance "Gap"

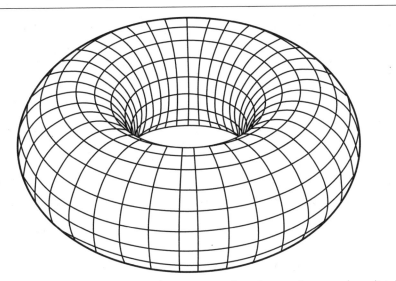

The unbroken lines of the grid trace the contours of a coherent, intact and predictable "Weberian" logical rational legal order. The global governance gap is shown as the void that runs through the centre of the lifebuoy. The gap is not a missing piece in the grid; rather, it is a constitutive element of the legal order itself. The global governance gap is instantiated by the presence of law rather than its absence.

Image source: YassineMrabet (Wikimedia Commons, CC BY-SA).

so that human rights victims are brought out of the void should be abandoned.[42] Inventive and bold proposals and actions for transformation are needed today. The purpose of this chapter is not to spell out a defined program for reform; rather, it is to contribute to our growing understanding of the transnational, global, structural and systemic character of the barriers that human rights victims face.[43] The following section considers the corporate law dimensions of such barriers in more detail.

Corporate Responsibility in a Poly-corporate System

Today's corporate system is comprised of vast constellations of separately incorporated entities that are organized into poly-corporate groups.[44] The answer to the question of whether

---

42   One proposed reform is that courts recognize "a common law duty of care of business to exercise human rights due diligence." See Douglass Cassel, "Outlining the case for a common law duty of care of business to exercise human rights due diligence" (2016) 1:2 Business & Human Rights J 179 (in presenting his case for the responsibility to conduct human rights due diligence, the author argues that "parent companies should exercise [human rights] due diligence with regard to all entities in the 'enterprise' or 'enterprise group,' including their subsidiaries" at 186).

43   In a related vein, Simons concludes that "one of the most significant impediments to corporate human rights accountability is the structure of the international legal system itself" (*supra* note 34 at 11–12). On "systemic" approaches to addressing the governance gap, see Simons & Macklin, *supra* note 11 at 13–15.

44   José Engrácia Antunes distinguishes today's poly-corporate group enterprises from the mono-corporate entities that existed prior to legal reforms of the late nineteenth century. José Engrácia Antunes, *Liability of Corporate Groups: Autonomy and Control in Parent-Subsidiary Relationships in US, German and EU Law: An International and Comparative Perspective* (New York: Springer, 1994).

corporate responsibility vests in natural or legal persons within this complex system is muddled by the coexistence of parent control and subsidiary autonomy with respect to each of the legally separate corporate entities within a corporate group. What does it mean to say that control and autonomy coexist in related entities? In their 1972 study on multinational enterprises, John Stopford and L. T. Wells concluded that the need "for control over decisions in foreign subsidiaries is the common element that has led certain kinds of firms to prefer to conduct their overseas operations through wholly owned entities."[45] Typically, the parent company in the home country (the domicile of the parent company) will be shielded from liability by several layers of intermediary subsidiaries that are domiciled in yet another jurisdiction (often in tax havens such as Bermuda or the Cayman Islands). The precise structures vary almost infinitely in their details.[46] Each limited liability company in the group plays a function within the larger whole. To the outsider, it may seem paradoxical that the law treats the subsidiary corporations within the group as autonomous entities, but for corporate counsel and management, this picture is very natural. The parent company exerts central control over the enterprise as an economic entity, while the subsidiaries retain legal and operational autonomy within the bounds of the policies and strategies that are set from above. While every firm's structure is unique, some degree of central control is essential for fulfilling its economic function as a vehicle for investment. In a multinational enterprise, the economic gain structure must be protected against threats that occur within and across national jurisdictions; the firm addresses such problems through its enterprise risk management strategy.[47] The troubling effects of the wholly controlled yet autonomous subsidiary come to light when people entirely outside the corporation are harmed by one or more of the entities within the corporate group. This is because a degree of legal autonomy may be given to each subsidiary entity by the controlling parent — a strategic and defensive separation of powers and liabilities among legal persons occurs. The outsiders who are harmed soon find that the subsidiary's seemingly paradoxical wholly controlled autonomy is just one more cryptogram to be solved in their quest for corporate responsibility.[48]

Today, the human rights victims who clamour for corporate accountability strive to hold the multinational enterprise responsible as a unified whole, as a unified brand. Facing such clamour, firms frequently use the defensive strategy of keeping the conflict geographically and legally local. In practice, this means that decision makers in the parent company and in the intermediary subsidiaries avoid becoming directly involved in the local dramas as they unfold — they are

---

45   John M Stopford & LT Wells Jr, *Managing the Multinational Enterprise: Organization of the Firm and Ownership of the Subsidiary* (New York: Basic Books, 1972) at 123.

46   For example, in 2007, the Boeing Company had 282 subsidiaries incorporated in dozens of jurisdictions, including the British West Indies, China, Delaware, Manitoba and the Netherlands. In 2009, Deutsche Bank AG operated in 56 countries, with 1,954 subsidiaries. In 2011, Newmont Mining Corporation had 206 subsidiaries incorporated in more than 30 jurisdictions, including Bermuda, Delaware, Guinea, Honduras, Jersey, Papua New Guinea and Peru.

47   See Latin American Companies Circle, *Corporate Governance Recommendations for Company Groups—Based on Experiences from the Latin American Companies Circle* (Latin American Companies Circle, with the Organisation for Economic Co-operation and Development, IFC World Bank & Swiss Confederation, 2014) (containing the following recommendations regarding group-wide (enterprise) risk management: "Based on best practice, for a conglomerate-wide risk oversight a Board of Directors of a holding company should at least (*i*) conduct ongoing mapping and monitoring of risks across all group companies; (*ii*) establish risk appetite for the entire corporate group; and (*iii*) ensure an effective risk management system has been implemented across the conglomerate. Should a Board deem it convenient, it could delegate these functions in a Board-level risk management committee" at 6).

48   On the issue of control and autonomy with regard to harms alleged to have been caused by Royal Dutch Shell's subsidiaries operating in Nigeria, see Sheldon Leader et al, "Corporate Liability in a New Setting: Shell & the Changing Legal Landscape for the Multinational Oil Industry in the Niger Delta" (2011) Essex Business and Human Rights Project, University of Essex.

counselled to focus on policy matters while delegating decision making about operational matters to managers who are working "on the ground."[49] Such delegation serves to maintain the formal separateness of the many related legal entities that comprise the corporate group. The advantage in keeping a dispute legally local is one among many reasons why the parent grants the wholly owned subsidiary such autonomy. But there may be unintended consequences to this formalistic division of labour in decision making. The victims may begin to see the enterprise as an organization that thrives in contradiction. Unimpressed by the local subsidiary's status as a separate legal entity, the outsiders demand accountability from the parent company and its shareholders, regardless of where they are based. The formalities of legal separateness have little salience for the human rights victim who demands ethical and political accountability from the natural person or persons whom they regard as responsible for the harm.

So, what changed? How is corporate responsibility in today's poly-corporate system different from the way it used to be? The difference lies in the changed relationship of the legal person — the corporate entity — to the natural persons who were traditionally responsible for it. The storied joint-stock charter companies of the pre-modern era were mono-corporate entities (the East India Company and the Hudson's Bay Company were sole entities); in contrast, today's multinational enterprises are poly-corporate structures.[50] The modern poly-corporate structures were introduced in the late 1800s when the State of New Jersey became the first jurisdiction in the world to allow a corporation to own shares in another corporation.[51] In short order, "parent" corporations became the sole or controlling shareholders of their "daughter" and "granddaughter" corporations (what we now refer to as subsidiaries). New Jersey lawyers set out to devise complex "holding company" structures. This legal innovation was quickly adopted in neighbouring US states and eventually worldwide, giving rise to the multinational enterprises that are now ubiquitous.

The shift from the mono-corporate system to the poly-corporate system transformed the nature of the shareholder's governance responsibility. In the pre-modern era, the flesh-and-blood shareholder (a natural person) was given the governance responsibility to cast votes in fundamental corporate decisions, such as electing board members, approving a merger, or changing the corporation's bylaws. In the poly-corporate regime, share voting was transformed into a function that could be carried out by the corporation itself (by the legal person). This, of course, was a highly formalistic innovation. Practically speaking, some natural person had to cause the corporation to cast its votes, so the board of directors took on this role. In today's poly-corporate groups, each operating and intermediary subsidiary corporation might have a sole board member who acts as the entity's legal representative. It is not uncommon that the sole board member of each intermediary subsidiary in a group is the same natural person, who, as it happens, also sits on the board of the ultimate parent company.[52] To maintain the legal separateness of the many subsidiary companies that are combined in this manner, it is essential that administrative formalities such as voting at annual meetings be attended to assiduously.[53]

---

49   See Martin Lipton, Sabastian V Niles & Marshall L Miller, "Risk Management and the Board of Directors", Harvard Law School Forum on Corporate Governance (28 July 2015).

50   See Antunes, *supra* note 44.

51   See Ralph Nader, Mark J Green & Joel Seligman, *Taming the Giant Corporation* (New York: Norton, 2007) at 43–46.

52   In some jurisdictions, this individual is known as the subsidiary's "administrator."

53   On this requirement in Delaware law, see *Sea-Land Services, Inc v The Pepper Source*, 941 F (2d) 519 (7th Cir 1911).

The traditionally human responsibility to vote shares is exercised in poly-corporate groups by what are essentially a series of clerical manoeuvres that cause the many layers of subsidiaries to act in predictable ways.[54] Such manoeuvres are regarded as perfectly normal by the economist, the general counsel and management. But for the human rights victim, a very troubling aspect arises from this regime: while the victim may have a clear sense of the person who ought to be held responsible for a wrongful act, legal liability for that wrongful act may be transferred or assigned through corporate reorganization, mergers and acquisitions. Moreover, by such transactions, the ultimate responsibility for governing the firm is shifted from one group of shareholders to another. In poly-corporate groups, these shareholders might be legal entities rather than natural persons. From an ethical point of view, such transfers of responsibility might well be regarded as arbitrary.

When it comes to governance responsibility, a world of difference lies between the human share-voter and the share-voting corporate entity. According to Adolf Berle and Gardiner Means, "The typical business unit of the 19th century…was owned by individuals or small groups; was managed by them or their appointees; and was, in the main, limited by the personal wealth of the individuals in control."[55] In becoming shareholders, these individuals took on the personal responsibility for governing the corporation; they could be held ethically accountable, albeit not legally accountable, for any harms caused by the corporation they governed.[56] While their liability for the corporation's debts was limited, they were nonetheless accountable in the sense that they were participants in the local community and in political life.[57] This marriage of personal and corporate responsibility was short lived, as the corporation underwent a dramatic transformation in scale beginning in the mid-nineteenth century. As the number of shareholders grew into the hundreds and then thousands, any sense of personal responsibility and accountability for the corporation's activities was diluted. In many of today's multinational corporate groups, the number of shareholders has expanded by orders of magnitude.

In both public and privately held corporate groups today, one finds multiple intermediary parent-subsidiary relationships — each parent takes on governance responsibility for its subsidiary companies, and so on down the chain. The share-voting parent or intermediary corporation can, in turn, be bought and sold, merged into or out of another firm, or transferred in an almost infinite number of ways. By such transactions, the governance responsibility for a single corporate entity can be shifted in almost any direction. Responsibility *qua* liability can

---

54   We might call this a form of digitalized responsibility, in contrast to the traditionally analogue function of voting shares by raising one's hand. By clerical manoeuvres, the digitalized vote propagates through the system of separate entities within a corporate group.

55   See Berle & Means, *supra* note 35 at 2. For the English history of the same period, see Ron Harris, *Industrializing English Law: Entrepreneurship and Business Organization, 1720–1844* (Cambridge, UK: Cambridge University Press, 2000). See also Faith Stevelman, "Global Finance, Multinationals and Human Rights: With Commentary on Backer's Critique of the 2008 Report by John Ruggie" (2011) 9:1 Santa Clara J Intl L 101 ("The hydra-like structure of holding companies owning subsidiaries, and subsidiaries of subsidiaries-creating compounding layers of bureaucracy and plausible deniability was an organizational impossibility in the first few decades of the twentieth century" at 129).

56   I refer to civil matters rather than criminal ones, which may attract personal liability. By drawing this distinction between old and new, I do not mean to imply that the sole-entity corporations of the eighteenth and nineteenth centuries were inherently more virtuous than businesses today. They were not.

57   Berle and Means give the example of the "first important manufacturing enterprise" in the United States that was organized as a corporation: the Boston Manufacturing Company. This company was incorporated in 1813 with 11 shareholders. The number of stockholders increased to 76 by 1830 and to 123 by 1850. In 1842, stock in the Merrimack Corporation (also in Massachusetts), was held by 390 people, including 80 administrators or trustees; 68 females; 52 retired businessmen; 46 merchants; 45 manufacturers and mechanics; 40 clerks, students and unspecified; 23 lawyers; 18 physicians; 15 farmers; and three institutions. See Berle & Means, *supra* note 35 at 11–12.

also be transferred or assigned as needed. The point to be taken here is that in a corporation many aspects of responsibility are depersonalized; they rest in the abstract legal entity, rather than in the specific natural persons who make specific decisions on its behalf. Again, this is all very natural from the corporate perspective. In deals involving "sophisticated" parties, be they lenders, suppliers, clients, investors or joint venture partners, shifting responsibility in this way poses little worry. The contracting parties will ensure *ex ante* that appropriate pathways to responsibility *qua* liability are present; such efforts fall within their governance responsibility to conduct due diligence. In a merger or acquisition, the parties to the transaction may stipulate which entity inherits the liability for pending litigation or other specified risk, such as latent environmental liability. By such rules, it is possible that an acquiring firm may find itself defending a contentious and politically damaging lawsuit for actions that were taken by the predecessor company.[58] While it's perfectly normal to transfer governance responsibility and responsibility *qua* liability among corporate entities this way, the decision maker's ethical responsibility for the choices they make is not normally regarded as transferable or assignable in this sense.[59] One has to live with the decisions one makes, even if one is not, strictly speaking, liable for them.

For consenting parties in a corporate transaction, attributing responsibility *qua* liability is a technical matter; it is a problem that can be solved deductively (more or less). The situation is very different for the non-consenting human rights victim who stands outside such transactions altogether. From the victim's perspective, the attribution of corporate responsibility is not a "merely technical" matter.[60] When it comes to the firm's responsibility to the outside world for human rights violations, the ethical and political accountability of decision makers cannot be avoided by technical legal fixes that aim to shift responsibility from one entity to another.

Conclusion

This brings us back to the original question: what natural person or legal entity in a corporate group ought to be held responsible for human rights violations? The foregoing analysis suggests that the answer depends very much on one's positional point of view: the economist, manager and general counsel will tend to vest corporate responsibility in the legal entity itself, while the human rights victim will tend to regard natural persons who control such entities as ultimately responsible for the injuries they endure. The translation of the demands of responsibility from one positional point of view to the other is not so straightforward; indeed, we might ask whether it is even possible.[61]

What does all of this mean in practice? One hypothesis that can be drawn from the foregoing analysis is that the relative ease of shifting both responsibility *qua* liability and governance responsibility from one person (legal or natural) to another comprises an aggravating factor when human rights are at stake in localized conflicts. For instance, such aggravation may occur when

---

58   In *Choc v Hudbay* (*supra* note 33), the allegations brought by the plaintiffs refer to the harmful acts of a predecessor company, Skye Resources. After the lawsuit began, the defendant, Hudbay Minerals Inc., sold the mine site in question (the Fenix mine) to Solway Investment Group, a Swiss company, while retaining liability in the lawsuit.

59   The point is made clear by analogizing to criminal law — the criminal law does not permit an accused person to transfer potential criminal liability or a conviction to another person.

60   I adapt the term "merely technical" from Duncan Kennedy's analysis of the "politics of contract technicality." Duncan Kennedy, "The Political Stakes in 'Merely Technical' Issues of Contract Law" (2002) 10 Eur Rev Priv L 7 at 7.

61   On "regime collisions" and the fragmentation of global law, see Andreas Fischer-Lescano & Gunther Teubner, "Regime-Collisions: The Vain Search for Legal Unity in the Fragmentation of Global Law" (2004) 25:4 Mich J Intl L 999.

a business that is thought to be responsible for causing or contributing to some human rights harm suddenly changes hands. In a multinational enterprise, the decision to sell is likely made by the parent company or intermediary company, which might be based in another country. For the companies involved, this is an entirely normal business transaction. Yet here the enterprise might appear to the human rights-holder as double-faced. How so? At the same time that the legally separate parent company disavows external responsibility (*qua* liability) for any harms that are allegedly caused by the local subsidiary's activities, it fully embraces the internal governance responsibility to direct and control the sale of that subsidiary. This seemingly paradoxical stance arises from the coexistence of control and autonomy discussed earlier. For the human rights victim, the situation may give rise to great uncertainty and serious concern about being left worse off and without any remedy. After all, the acquiring firm might have a less generous view of its social responsibility; it may have little regard for the "corporate responsibility to respect human rights," or for the requirement to conduct human rights due diligence under the UN Guiding Principles on Business and Human Rights.[62] Rightly or wrongly, the human rights-holders may interpret such actions as calculated avoidance of corporate responsibility.

Consider another example: in the course of a delicate and lengthy negotiation between community representatives and mining company representatives, the company involved is well within its legal right to sell its interest in the project without consulting the affected community.[63] Needless to say, we can see how community trust is difficult to earn when, without notice, the foreign parent company simply sells the project and exits the problem altogether. For this reason, some community representatives might refuse to engage in dialogue with the company at all, preferring instead to meet with high government officials — after all, the state is unable to transfer or assign its political responsibility to some other party.[64] At the local level, the rights-holders might be told to take their grievances to a "communities team" or a corporate social responsibility (CSR) committee that operates out of the local subsidiary.[65] But determined local leaders may not be satisfied by these low-level contacts. And this might help to explain why community representatives from host countries such as Ecuador, Guatemala and Papua New Guinea have made the long journey to shareholder meetings in other countries. They travel abroad to demand corporate accountability from the very natural persons they believe are ultimately responsible for the abuses on the ground.

Today's globalized poly-corporate law makes the human rights victim's quest for corporate responsibility exceedingly difficult. This chapter has argued that the global governance "gap" is not a missing piece in the puzzle, but a constitutive element of the legal order itself. Just

---

62   In its 2019 report, the Corporate Human Rights Benchmark found it "particularly alarming" that "nearly half of the companies assessed (49%) score 0 across all indicators related to the process of human rights due diligence." Corporate Human Rights Benchmark, "Key Findings, 2019", online: <corporatebenchmark.org>.

63   For example, in the middle of a long-standing company-community conflict in Guatemala between Xinka Indigenous people and Tahoe Minerals (a Canadian mining company), the parent company sold the mine to another firm, Pan American Silver. See Justice and Corporate Accountability Project, "Request to Investigate Failure to Disclose Material Information", Osgoode Hall Law School (3 January 2019).

64   For example, in the decades-long company-community conflict that was the subject of the *Copper Mesa Mining Corp v Ecuador* investment arbitration case (PCA 2012-2, UNCITRAL), many community leaders refused to dialogue directly with the Ecuadorean mining exploration company (a local subsidiary held by a Canadian parent), demanding instead to speak with government officials.

65   It should be noted that a company's local-level CSR *operations* might be transferable to another firm in similar fashion. The role that freely transferable CSR operations may play in aggravating or potentially alleviating company-community conflicts deserves further scrutiny.

how to neutralize this detrimental feature of the legal order is a matter of vigorous ongoing debate between those who call for an overarching international treaty on human rights and business,[66] and those who push for greater "policy coherence" through the implementation of the UN Guiding Principles on Business and Human Rights by governments and businesses alike.[67] It is far beyond the scope of this chapter to state exactly how to resolve this ongoing debate. Its purpose has been to clarify how the global and transnational dimension of corporate responsibility stands in relation to the legal accountability void that is constitutive of the transnational legal order. Today, corporate responsibility, as the ethical responsibility of flesh-and-blood decision makers, runs all the way from the lowest-level subsidiary to the apex of the multinational corporate group. When all is said and done, it implicates the very people who assert a legal claim to the residual value generated by the enterprise, the flesh-and-blood shareholders and the ultimate investors.

---

66   See Human Rights Council, Open-ended Intergovernmental Working Group on Transnational Corporations and Other Business Enterprises with Respect to Human Rights (OEIGWG), *Legally Binding Instrument to Regulate, in International Human Rights Law, the Activities of Transnational Corporations and Other Business Enterprises*, OEIGWG Chairmanship Revised Draft (16 July 2019).

67   "Access to Remedy" comprises the third pillar of the UN Guiding Principles on Business and Human Rights (*supra* note 1, Principles 25–31).

10

CORPORATE CAPTURE AND INSTITUTIONAL WORK

Lessons for the Canadian Ombudsperson for Responsible Enterprise

Daniela Chimisso dos Santos

Introduction

When the United Nations Human Rights Council unanimously endorsed the United Nations Guiding Principles on Business and Human Rights (UNGPs),[1] the business and human rights pillars took centre stage in the discussion of corporate accountability and the "governance gap."[2] Arguably, the human rights discourse has replaced the corporate social responsibility (CSR) discussion, as evidenced by initiatives undertaken by the Organisation for Economic Co-operation and Development (OECD), Denmark, Norway, the United Kingdom and other countries that are home to extractive industry corporations.[3] However, as home and host states

---

1   *Guiding Principles on Business and Human Rights: Implementing the United Nations "Protect, Respect and Remedy" Framework: Report of the Special Representative of the Secretary-General on the Issue of Human Rights and Transnational Corporations and Other Business Enterprise*, UNHRC, 17th Sess, UN Doc A/HRC/17/31 (2011) [UNGPs].

2   For an account of the governance gap and corporate accountability issues in Canada, see Penelope Simons & Audrey Macklin, *The Governance Gap: Extractive Industries, Human Rights, and the Home State Advantage* (New York: Routledge, 2014).

3   See e.g. Daniela Chimisso dos Santos & Sara L Seck, "Human Rights Due Diligence and Extractive Industries" in Surya Deva, ed, *Research Handbook on Human Rights and Business* (Edward Elgar, forthcoming 2020).

create and reform institutions to manage, monitor and administer the tool kit of the business and human rights agenda, concern about corporate capture is significant.

In 2018, after calls by the Inter-American Commission on Human Rights[4] and the United Nations Human Rights Commission[5] to take action against Canadian companies in the extractive sectors,[6] the Canadian government created a new institution called the Canadian Ombudsperson for Responsible Enterprise (CORE) and its multi-stakeholder advisory council, known as the Advisory Body on Responsible Business Conduct.[7] Designed to be a home-state grievance mechanism institution that encapsulates principles of the UNGPs, the creation of the CORE and its advisory council constitutes a significant measure in response to corporate malfeasance.[8] However, as the Canadian government details the role and responsibilities of the CORE, special attention should be given to its institutional design so that it is not unnecessarily exposed to corporate capture.[9]

To undertake a diagnostic of the CORE's inherent vulnerability to corporate capture, this chapter reviews two discrete areas of knowledge that focus on the influence of corporations on public institutions. The first is research on the corporate capture of human rights institutions. The second is institutional approaches to international business (IAIB), where the relationship between institutions and corporations, and the creation, maintenance and disruption of institutions by corporations is termed institutional work. It is feasible to apply the lessons from IAIB's institutional work to the corporate capture of human rights institutions.

This chapter is structured as follows. First, I explore what is meant by corporate capture and how it has affected human rights institutions. This section also highlights how corporate capture can be analyzed as three separate principles: a concept, a set of actions and a set of outcomes, which can be either proximate or final. Second, I explore how the literature on institutional work can inform the discussion on corporate capture of human rights institutions. In this section, I examine institutional enablers of institutional work and why they are essential to understanding corporate capture. Third, I turn to the CORE and its institutional design. By applying the

---

4   Daniela Chimisso dos Santos, "Canadian Mining Companies and the Inter-American Commission on Human Rights" (2004) 7:2 Rights Rev 10.

5   See Mike Blanchfield, "Ottawa Clashes with UN Human Rights Panel over Mining Complaints", *The Globe and Mail* (8 July 2015).

6   UN Human Rights Commission, Office of the High Commissioner, *Statement at the end of visit to Canada by the United Nations Working Group on Business and Human Rights* (1 June 2017) [UNHRC, *Statement*].

7   Global Affairs Canada, "Responsible Business Conduct Abroad", online: <www.international.gc.ca/trade-agreements-accords-commerciaux/topics-domaines/other-autre/csr-rse.aspx?lang=eng>; Global Affairs Canada, "Canadian Ombudsperson for Responsible Enterprise", online: <https://core-ombuds.canada.ca/core_ombuds-ocre_ombuds/index.aspx?lang=eng>; *Canadian Ombudsperson for Responsible Enterprise*, PC 2019-1323, annexed schedule replaces schedule to Order in Council PC 2019-299 [*CORE*].

8   Charis Kamphuis, "Advocating for a Home-State Grievance Mechanism: Law Reform Strategies in the Canadian Resource Justice Movement" in Isabel Feichtner & Markus Krajewski, eds, *Human Rights in the Extractive Industries: Transparency, Participation, Resistance* (New York: Springer, 2018).

9   The Canadian government has replaced the schedule to Order in Council PC 2019-299 of April 8, 2019, with Order in Council PC 2019-1323 of September 6, 2019. Further details on the role of the CORE are necessary to ensure its functionality, especially after all civil society and labour union representatives appointed to the advisory council quit en masse on July 11, 2019, because of the lack of clarity as to whether the CORE will have the ability to independently investigate allegations of human rights breaches. The replaced schedule has not assuaged the fears of civil society and labour unions; at the time of writing, they are not part of the advisory council of the CORE. As such, I have considered that the Canadian government is still in the process of implementing the CORE. See Alastair Sharp, "Advisors quit, accusing Trudeau government of dithering on corporate watchdog", *National Observer* (11 July 2019), online: <www.nationalobserver.com/2019/07/11/news/advisors-storm-out-and-accuse-trudeau-government-dithering-corporate-watchdog>.

lessons set out in the two overlapping literatures, I analyze the structure of the CORE. The CORE's vulnerability to corporate capture, due to current institutional ambiguity and the way in which the CORE is designed to interact with other institutions within the Canadian institutional matrix, will be highlighted. There is a risk that the institution will be the frustrated, as has already occurred with the previous Canadian Corporate Social Responsibility Counsellor role. The chapter ends with a few cautionary words.

Corporate Capture

Corporate capture originates from the term regulatory capture. As Richard A. Posner states, "The phenomenon of regulatory capture so understood must be as old as regulation itself."[10] Regulatory capture is when a regulation, in law or application, is geared away from the public interest and toward the interests of the industry the regulation was intended to regulate, by the purposeful action of the industry itself.[11]

However, corporate capture has gained a broader purview than regulatory capture, as it refers not only to intra-regional and national regulatory agencies but to all forms of intra-regional, national, inter-regional and transnational political and administrative decision making. It is also sometimes defined as political capture[12] and state capture.[13] Furthermore, corporate capture can be the result of corruption and illegal activities.[14] This chapter will focus only on legal forms of corporate capture, and not on unlawful, criminal corruption.[15]

Corporate capture is indiscriminate and has claimed institutions in the Global North as well as the Global South. Whether it is in national arenas, such as the judiciary[16] and the financial industry[17] in the United States, the public health system in the United Kingdom,[18] or

---

10   Richard A Posner, "The Concept of Regulatory Capture: A Short, Inglorious History" in Daniel Carpenter & David A Moss, eds, *Preventing Regulatory Capture: Special Interest Influence and How to Limit It* (Cambridge, UK: Cambridge University Press, 2014) at 49.

11   See Daniel Carpenter & David A Moss, "Introduction" in Carpenter & Moss, *ibid* at 13; see also Nolan McCarty, "Complexity, Capacity and Capture" in Carpenter & Moss, *ibid*; Jason MacLean, "Striking at the Root Problem of Canadian Environmental Law: Identifying and Escaping Regulatory Capture" (2016) 29 J Envtl L & Prac 111 [MacLean, "Striking at the Root"].

12   Francisco Durand, *Extractive Industries and Political Capture: Effects on Institutions, Equality and the Environment* (Lima: Oxfam, 2016).

13   Joel S Hellman, Geraint Jones & Daniel Kaufmann, "'Seize the State, Seize the Day': State Capture, Corruption and Influence in Transition" (2000) World Bank Policy Research Working Paper 2444.

14   Daniel Kaufmann & Pedro C Vicente, "Legal Corruption" (2011) 23:2 Economics & Politics 195.

15   For a discussion of legal and illegal forms of corruption, see *ibid*.

16   Senator Elizabeth Warren, Address (21st Annual Joseph L Rauh Jr Lecture, University of the District of Columbia David A Clarke School of Law, 5 October 2013, regarding the corporate capture of the federal courts).

17   Robert Monks, "The Corporate Capture of the United States", Harvard Law School Forum on Corporate Governance and Financial Regulation (5 January 2012), online: <https://corpgov.law.harvard.edu/2012/01/05/the-corporate-capture-of-the-united-states/>.

18   Jennifer S Mindell, "All in this together: the corporate capture of public health" (2012) BMJ 345.

in transnational agendas (for example, in the discourses of sustainable development,[19] climate change[20] and human rights),[21] corporate capture is ubiquitous.

Human rights institutions, whether national or transnational, are not immune to corporate capture.[22] Even though there is no precise definition of a national human rights institution (NHRI), it is understood to be a government-sponsored institution whose function is to promote and protect human rights.[23] The Paris Principles, endorsed by the United Nations General Assembly in 1993, defined NHRIs as meeting six main criteria: a broad mandate, based on universal human rights, norms and standards; autonomy from government; independence; pluralism; adequate resources; and adequate powers of investigation.[24] In most countries' institutional frameworks, there is an ombudsman institution; however, its mandate, function and role differ significantly from one country to another.[25] Almost 60 percent of ombudsman institutions worldwide have a directive related to the protection of human rights.[26]

Regardless of their institutional design, ombudsman organs are, like other public institutions, vulnerable to corporate capture. And, through corporate capture, such institutions lose their independence, transparency and legitimacy. Arguably one of the most comprehensive reviews of corporate capture in the human rights arena is led by the International Network for Economic, Social and Cultural Rights, known as ESCR-Net, a collaboration of more than 230 organizations and 50 individuals across more than 75 countries.[27] ESCR-Net has the objective of securing economic and social justice through human rights, and through its corporate capture project it has identified several actions that demonstrate how corporate capture manifests.[28]

As corporate capture is a complex term, it can be defined not only as a concept, but as a set of actions (as defined by ESCR-Net) and a set of outcomes that are both proximate and final. I will define corporate capture as a concept and as a set of actions. As a concept, I define corporate capture as the apprehension of the national, regional and transnational public realm by an elite corporate minority for both the protection of and the further gain of benefits, to the detriment of the social welfare of the majority. As a set of actions or manifestations, then, corporate capture includes:

---

19   David Miller & William Dinan, "Resisting meaningful action on climate change: think tanks, 'merchants of doubts' and the 'corporate capture' of sustainable development" in Anders Hansen & Robert Cox, *The Routledge Handbook of Environment and Communication* (London, UK: Routledge, 2015).

20   Susan George, "Committing Geocide: climate change and corporate capture" (22 September 2016), online: *Transnational Institute* <www.tni.org/en/article/committing-geocide-climate-change-and-corporate-capture>.

21   ESCR-Net, "Corporate Capture", online: <www.escr-net.org/corporateaccountability/corporatecapture/>.

22   Jens Martens, "Corporate Influence on the Business and Human Rights Agenda of the United Nations" (2014), online: *International Baby Food Action Network* <www.gifa.org/wp-content/uploads/2014/06/Corporate_Influence_on_the_Business_and_Human_Rights_Agenda.pdf>.

23   Jeong-Woo Koo & Francisco O Ramirez, "National Incorporation of Global Human Rights: Worldwide Expansion of National Human Rights Institutions, 1966-2004" (2009) 87:3 Social Forces 1321.

24   *National institutions for the promotion and protection of human rights*, UNGAOR, 85th Plen Mtg, UN Doc A/RES/48/134 (1993).

25   *Ibid.*

26   OECD, "The Role of Ombudsman Institutions in Open Government" (2018) OECD Working Paper on Public Governance No 29.

27   ESCR-Net, *supra* note 21.

28   *Ibid.*

- community manipulation, which consists of strategies used to influence community leaders, including economic incentives, but also intimidation, to accept projects that may be detrimental to the community;

- economic diplomacy, that is, the use of home country diplomatic channels to protect and defend home transnational corporate interests in host countries and international arenas;

- judicial interference, which ranges from influencing the proceedings and rulings of courts to influencing judges personally, as well as the use of international arbitration for the protection of the interests of transnational corporations (TNCs);

- legislative and policy interference, which is the pressure exerted by corporations to both remove and create laws and policies that are beneficial to their interests;

- privatizing public security services, resulting in the privatization of law enforcement, to the benefit of corporate interests and to the detriment of the public good and local communities;

- revolving door mechanisms, that is, the transfer of public sector employees to private sector roles and vice versa, leading to cronyism;

- manipulating the media through shaping and spreading dominant narratives about progress and development; and

- the capture of academic institutions through the financing of research, which determines research agendas and results in the capture of knowledge creation, formation and dissemination.[29]

Corporate capture is thus defined by the consequences that it produces, which can be divided into proximate and final outcomes. Proximate outcomes include the dismantling of laws, regulatory inaction, regulatory softening, institutional bypasses created by corporate interests, biased knowledge creation and institutional substitution. Final outcomes include irresponsible investments, human rights abuses, climate change inaction, increased inequality and environmental degradation. A summary of corporate capture and three possible definitions is set out in Figure 1.

---

29   ESCR-Net, "Corporate Capture Manifestations", online: <www.escr-net.org/corporateaccountability/corporatecapture/manifestations>.

Figure 1: Defining Corporate Capture

Concept	Set of Actions	Set of Outcomes	
		Proximate Outcomes	**Final Outcomes**
It is the apprehension of the national, regional and transnational public realm by an elite corporate minority for both the protection of as well as the further gain of benefits, to the detriment of the social welfare of the majority.	• Community manipulation • Economic diplomacy • Judicial interference • Legislative and policy interference • Regulatory interference • Privatization of public security • Revolving door mechanisms • Discourse creation	• Dismantling of laws • Regulatory inaction • Regulatory softening • Institutional bypass • Biased knowledge creation • Institutional substitution	• Irresponsible investments • Human rights abuses • Climate change inaction • Increased inequality • Environmental degradation

Source: Author.

As shown above, corporate capture is an agglomeration of corporate strategies, which result in public institutions being hijacked by corporate goals, to the detriment of the welfare of the majority. Ultimately, corporate capture is an evaluative term that describes the interaction between firms and public institutions from the perspective of public institutions and social welfare. A second, parallel area of research that explores the relationship between firms and institutions is IAIB. In contrast to the previously cited literature, IAIB concentrates on the strategies undertaken by firms, and whether they are successful from the firm's perspective. I now turn to IAIB.

Institutional Work

The traditional view of the relationship between TNCs and institutions was based on the understanding that institutions are exogenous constraints, where TNCs had only two choices: to avoid an institutional environment or adapt to such an environment.[30] Such a proposition was based on the premise that agents were passive, habitual and rule-abiding.[31] However, in the late 1980s and early 1990s, institutionalism took an "agentic turn," wherein the importance of the role of agents in institutional change was highlighted.[32] As a consequence, IAIB's understanding of the relationship between TNCs and institutions became more nuanced, and the proposition arose that this relationship is not static, but dynamic, where TNCs and institutions co-evolve.[33]

---

30   Julie Battilana & Thomas D'aunno, "Institutional Work and the Paradox of Embedded Agency" in Thomas B Lawrence, Roy Suddaby & Bernard Leca, eds, *Institutional Work: Actors and Agency in Institutional Studies of Organization* (Cambridge, UK: Cambridge University Press, 2009).

31   Samer Abdelnour, Hans Hasselbladh & Jannis Kallinikos, "Agency and Institutions in Organization Studies" (2017) 38:12 Organization Studies 1775.

32   Paul Dimaggio, "Interest and agency in institutional theory" in Lynne G Zucker, ed, *Research on Institutional Patterns: Environment and Culture* (Cambridge, UK: Balinger, 1988).

33   John Cantwell, John H Dunning & Sarianna M Lundan, "An Evolutionary Approach to Understanding International Business Activity: The Co-Evolution of MNEs and the Institutional Environment" (2010) 41:4 J Intl Business Studies 567.

In this case, the actions undertaken by TNCs in this dynamic relationship are referred to as institutional work (which includes the disruption, maintenance and creation of institutions),[34] institutional entrepreneurship[35] or merely as activities undertaken by change agents.[36] The consequence of the agentic turn is that TNCs' range of actions expanded from avoidance and adaptation to include the ability to transform its institutional environment.

Due to the complexity of TNCs, and the fact that by their nature they straddle various institutional environments, TNCs' institutional work is not limited to the host country where they operate but also includes activities in their home country, where they originate. Therefore, these dynamic relationships — Relationship A between the Parent Company (ParentCo) and the Home Country, and Relationship B between the Subsidiary Company (SubCo) and the Host Country — exist in tandem as the TNC goes about its business. Furthermore, two other relationships exist that influence TNCs. The first is extra-territorial legislation, which is when the home country enacts legislation that aims to constrain both ParentCo and SubCo, referred to here as Relationship A2. The second is the internal relationship between ParentCo and SubCo, where corporate culture and transfer practices are continuously engaged, referred to here as relationship Y. Figure 2 illustrates how such relationships interact. The feedback loop reflects the success and failure of SubCo's strategies in the host country, and how that is then incorporated by ParentCo, if at all, in its corporate practices.

The question then turns to: at what point does Relationship A and B result in TNCs engaging in institutional work? In other words, what are the enabling factors in Relationship A and B that make institutional work more likely? The literature identifies two main categories of factors that enable institutional work: intra-firm variables and institutional characteristics.[37] Intra-firm variables that are significant include the financial and relational resources of the TNC, as well as its corporate culture. This chapter will focus on institutional enablers.

Institutional enablers are factors that create a propensity for institutional work, which arise from the characteristics of the institutional environment where the targeted institution is located. In other words, the literature converges on the proposition that certain characteristics of national institutional environments are more likely to allow institutional work by TNCs.[38] One factor is the robustness of the institutional environment of the home or host country,[39] that is, whether the institutional matrix of a nation has a high degree of institutionalization and is uniformly consistent throughout the constellations of institutions in a country.[40] For example, countries in the Global North are deemed to have strong, robust institutional environments, while countries in the Global South have institutional environments that are fragile and contain institutional voids (i.e., institutional environments where there is an absence or underdevelopment of

---

34   *Ibid.*

35   Dimaggio, *supra* note 32.

36   Kathleen Thelen, "A Theory of Gradual Institutional Change" in James Mahoney & Kathleen Thelen, eds, *Explaining Institutional Change: Ambiguity, Agency, and Power* (Cambridge, UK: Cambridge University Press, 2009).

37   See e.g. Julie Battilana, Bernard Leca & Eva Boxenbaum, "How Actors Change Institutions: Towards a Theory of Institutional Entrepreneurship" (2009) 3:1 Academy Management Annals 65; Battilana & D'aunno, *supra* note 30.

38   Battilana, Leca & Boxenbaum, *supra* note 37.

39   *Ibid.*

40   Silvia Dorado, "Institutional Entrepreneurship, Partaking and Convening" (2005) 26:3 Organization Studies 385.

Figure 2: Dynamic Relationships between TNCs and Institutions

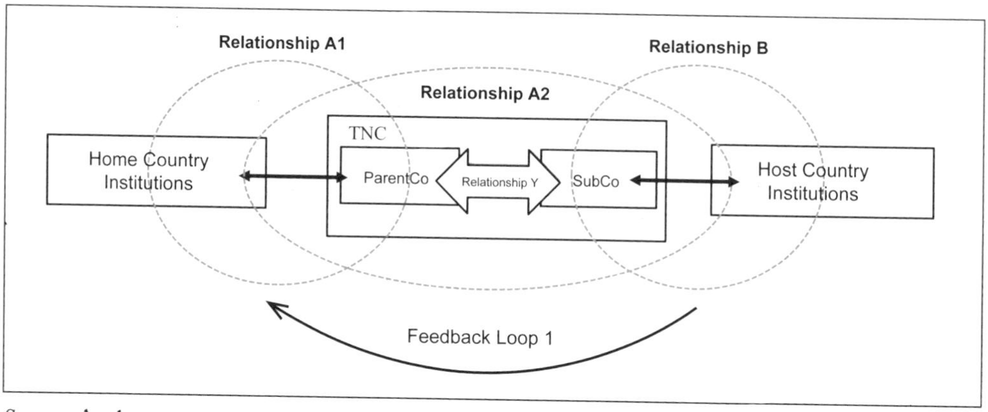

Source: Author.

institutions that enable and support market activity).[41] The consensus in the literature is that institutional work is more prevalent in the Global South due to the fragility of institutional environments.[42] The reasons for this are multifold: the differences in power between the TNC and the host country;[43] lack of institutional consistency throughout the institutional matrix of a country;[44] and/or the immaturity of institutions that regulate market participants.[45] Nevertheless, examples of institutional work in the Global North have also been documented.[46]

Two other institutional work enablers are institutional ambiguity[47] and institutional uncertainty.[48] Institutional ambiguity occurs when there is a lack of clarity about how the institutional environment is ordered (i.e., the roles, responsibilities and mandates for each institution within the institutional constellation of a country). Institutional uncertainty exists when actors do not know the outcome of their interactions with institutions. Therefore, as the very purpose of institutions is to diminish uncertainty for actors, once there is institutional ambiguity and/or institutional uncertainty, then firms are more prone to undertake creative measures to mould institutional outcomes to their benefit.[49] Thus, the existence of institutional

41   Battilana, Leca & Boxenbaum, *supra* note 37.

42   SL McGaughey, "Institutions, entrepreneurship and co-evolution in international business" (2016) 51 J World Business 871.

43   John Child, Suzana B Rodrigues & Kenneth K-T Tse, "The Dynamics of Influence in Corporate Co-Evolution" (2012) 49:7 J Management Studies 1246.

44   Battilana, Leca & Boxenbaum, *supra* note 37 at 74.

45   Jonathan Doh et al, "International business responses to institutional voids" (2017) 48:3 J Intl Business Studies 293.

46   See e.g. Bas Koene & Shahzad Ansari, "Institutional Change and the Multinational Change Agent: A Study of the Temporary Staffing Industry in Spain" (2011) 24:4 J Organizational Change Management 511; Juan J Durán-Herrera & Antonia M Garcia-Cabrera, "Crisis and MNEs as Institutional Entrepreneurs: An Analysis from a Co-Evolutionary Perspective", online: <www3.eeg.uminho.pt/economia/nipe/iibc2013/4.1.pdf>.

47   See e.g. Patrick Regné & Jesper Edman, "MNE Institutional advantage: How subunits shape, transpose and evade host country institutions" (2014) 45 J Intl Business Studies 275.

48   See e.g. Guido Möllering & Gordon Müller-Seitz, "Direction, not destination: Institutional work practices in the face of field-level uncertainty" (2018) 36 European Management J 28.

49   Thomas B Lawrence, Roy Suddaby & Bernard Leca, "Introduction: Theorizing and Studying Institutional Work" in Lawrence, Suddaby & Leca, *supra* note 30.

gaps (the conjunction of institutional ambiguity and uncertainty), creates an institutional environment that can enable and foster institutional work.[50]

Within institutional environments that enable institutional work, the following are some of the strategies undertaken by firms that can be found in the literature on institutional work:

- relational strategies are networking efforts to foster and manage dependency relationships with the government and key stakeholder groups;[51]

- infrastructure-building strategies address missing or inadequate regulatory, technological and physical infrastructure that support business activities;[52]

- socio-cultural bridging strategies tackle socio-cultural and demographic issues that can hinder economic development and trade, such as political and social unrest, illiteracy, poverty and ethnic or religious conflict;[53]

- institutional borrowing, that is, using institutions outside of the host country;[54]

- institutional substitution, that is, when the firm's internal resources are used to bridge institutionalized gaps;[55]

- internalization, that is, when the firm internalizes activities within the firm that may be undertaken by institutions of host countries;[56] and

- signalling, that is, when the firm uses its internal processes, such as CSR processes, to convey legitimacy and/or credibility to the investments of the TNC in relation to the negative vision of the host country's institutional environment.[57]

A summary of institutional work is set out in Figure 3.

50   Regné & Edman, *supra* note 47; Möllering & Müller-Seitz, *supra* note 48.

51   Chris Marqui & Mia Raynard, "Institutional Strategies in Emerging Markets" (2015) 9:1 Academy Management Annals.

52   *Ibid.*

53   *Ibid.*

54   Mike W Peng & Brian C Pinkham, "Overcoming institutional voids via arbitration" (2017) 48:3 J Intl Business Studies 344.

55   Graham AT Benjamin & Allison F Kingsley, "The effects of information voids on capital flows in emerging markets" (2017) 48:3 J Intl Business Studies 324.

56   Hyejun Kim & Jaeyong Song, "Filling institutional voids in emerging economies: The impact of capital market development and business groups on M&A deal abandonment" (2017) 48:3 J Intl Business Studies 344.

57   Jonathan Doh et al, "International business responses to institutional voids" (2017) 48:3 J Intl Business Studies 293.

Figure 3: Defining Institutional Work

Concept	Set of Actions	Set of Outcomes	
		Proximate Outcomes	**Final Outcomes**
Institutional work is the dynamic relationship between TNCs and institutions, which can result in institutional maintenance, disruption or creation.	• Relational strategies • Infrastructure-building strategies • Social-cultural bridging strategies • Institutional borrowing • Institutional substitution • Internalization • Signalling	• Economic return for firms • Regulatory changes • Regulatory softening • Institutional bypass • Knowledge creation • Institutional substitution	• Improved economic activity • Successful project implementation • Improved GDP

Source: Author.

Corporate Capture versus Institutional Work

The literature on corporate capture and IAIB's institutional work both seek to describe the dynamic relationship between TNCs and public institutions, which is complex, and both areas of knowledge attempt to break down what those strategies are. With nomenclatures that depict the ideology on which each area is premised, the strategies listed are both complementary and overlapping. For example, social-cultural bridging strategy, as well as relational strategy, fall nicely under community manipulation and economic diplomacy.

As can be expected, the outcomes of the two paths are vastly different. Neither literature explores its opposite. Thus, on one hand, the literature on corporate capture does not search for examples where corporate capture can result in positive changes to local institutions. On the other hand, the IAIB literature does not study the consequences of the firm's actions on the target institution and whether such change or disruption is positive for the greater social welfare of the country. Arguably, IAIB has the embedded assumption that positive economic results for firms will automatically result in positive economic outcomes for countries.

Where the literatures contribute to each other is in the further understanding of the institutional characteristics that enable firm action. The literature on corporate capture is clear that it is not a phenomenon that exists only in the Global South: it is ubiquitous also in the Global North and within transnational agendas. As such, the expansion of research in the area of institutional work in the Global North may be a beneficial path for IAIB. Furthermore, the fact that institutional gaps create opportunities for firm action is a significant lesson to contribute to the corporate capture literature.

Turning to the CORE and its advisory council, it is now possible to analyze how the two areas of literature described above highlight fragilities in the institutional design of the new institution. Such fragilities may result in the corporate capture of the institution, and its loss of independence, accountability and legitimacy.

The CORE and Its Advisory Council

It is undeniable that Canada and its provinces have failed to monitor the human rights conduct of Canadian extractive companies abroad. In 2013, the Inter-American Commission on Human Rights held a public hearing on the responsibility of home states for the activities of mining companies in the Americas, which focused on Canada as a mining powerhouse.[58] In 2015, the United Nations Human Rights Committee formally asked the Government of Canada what it was doing to regulate corporate citizens and to provide victims of corporate-related human rights violations with access to legal remedies.[59] In 2017, in a statement by the United Nations Working Group on Business and Human Rights, made at the end of its visit to Canada, the cases of alleged human rights abuse by Canadian companies abroad were highlighted, and Canada was encouraged "to broaden and deepen its emphasis on business and human rights in its CSR strategy."[60] Indeed, much has been written about the failure of the Canadian system to take action against its mining corporations, and this has been extensively documented by Sara Seck[61] and others, including Audrey Macklin and Penelope Simons in *The Governance Gap: Human Rights, Extractive Industries, and the Home State Advantage.*[62]

In 2006, as a result of recommendations from the June 2005 Standing Committee on Foreign Affairs and International Trade report, *Mining in Developing Countries — Corporate Social Responsibility*,[63] the Canadian government organized a series of consultations with industry, civil society and other stakeholders. The national round tables on CSR and the Canadian extractive industry in developing countries was a one-year process, which resulted in the 2009 Canadian CSR Strategy, *Building the Canadian Advantage: A Corporate Social Responsibility Strategy for the Canadian International Extractive Sector.*[64]

As part of the 2009 CSR Strategy, two institutions were created. The first was the CSR Centre of Excellence, which would develop best-in-class information and tool kits for clients in government and industry. The second institution was the Office of the Extractive Sector CSR Counsellor. The purpose of the CSR counsellor's office was to create a mechanism that would allow for CSR disputes related to Canadian extractive companies and their activities abroad to be undertaken in a timely and transparent manner. The counsellor would report directly to the Minister of International Trade, and had the mandate to review CSR practices of Canadian extractive sector companies operating outside of Canada, and to advise stakeholders on the implementation of endorsed CSR performance guidelines. The counsellor would be able to review cases only where all involved parties consented. Furthermore, it was determined that the counsellor could not review cases on their own initiative, make any binding recommendations

---

58   Dos Santos, *supra* note 4.

59   Blanchfield, *supra* note 5.

60   UNHRC, *Statement*, *supra* note 6.

61   Sara L Seck, "Canadian Mining Internationally and the UN Guiding Principles for Business and Human Rights" (2011) Can YB Intl L 53.

62   See Simons & Macklin, *supra* note 2.

63   Canada, Department of Foreign Affairs and International Trade, *Mining in Developing Countries — Corporate Social Responsibility* (2005).

64   Global Affairs Canada, *Building the Canadian Advantage: A Corporate Social Responsibility (CSR) Strategy for the Canadian International Extractive Sector* (2009).

or policy or legislative recommendations, create new performance standards or formally mediate between parties.[65]

After four years in the position, from 2009 to 2013, the first CSR Counsellor, Marketa Evans, resigned. No cases had been mediated during her tenure.[66] Her resignation was deemed a failure of the design of the CSR Counsellor position, due to its lack of investigative powers and its inability to penalize TNCs. In 2014, with its enhanced CSR guidelines, the Office of the Extractive Sector CSR Counsellor was given new powers to sanction companies that stray from the CSR guidelines by withdrawing support from government agencies, such as Export Development Canada, as well as from embassies abroad.[67] The enhanced CSR guidelines included benchmark guidelines that had been released by other institutions since 2009, such as the UNGPs and the OECD Due Diligence Guidance for Responsible Supply Chains of Minerals from Conflict-Affected and High-Risk Areas.[68] Yet even after the introduction of the enhanced CSR guidelines, progress continued to be elusive, as documented by correspondence from the United Nations Human Rights Committee,[69] as well as the United Nations Working Group on Business and Human Rights.[70]

In 2018, the Canadian government once again took action and created the CORE and its advisory council. In April 2019, an Order in Council was enacted and the CORE's role and mandate detailed; it was then promptly replaced in September 2019.[71] The new institution absorbed the role of the CSR Counsellor. The CORE has a multi-sector scope that includes the mining, oil and gas, and garment sectors. The Order in Council states that the CORE will have the power to independently investigate, report, recommend remedies and monitor the implementation of solutions related to allegations of human rights abuses linked to Canadian corporate activities abroad.[72] The Advisory Body on Responsible Business Conduct was created to advise the government and the CORE on responsible business conduct abroad.[73] It is intended to bring diverse perspectives to the institution, as it is comprised of politicians, civil servants, human rights experts and representatives from industry, labour and civil society.

The mandate of the CORE consists of three main activities. The first is to promote and provide advice to Canadian corporations on the implementation of the UNGPs and the OECD's 2011

---

65   *Ibid.*

66   Catherine Coumans, "The Federal CSR Counsellor has left the building — Can we now have an effective ombudsman mechanism for the extractive sector?" (1 November 2013), online (blog): *Mining Watch Canada* <https://miningwatch.ca/blog/2013/11/1/federal-csr-counsellor-has-left-building-can-we-now-have-effective-ombudsman>.

67   Global Affairs Canada, *2014 CSR Strategy — Doing Business the Canadian Way: A Strategy to Advance Corporate Social Responsibility in Canada's Extractive Sector Abroad*, online: <www.international.gc.ca/trade-agreements-accords-commerciaux/topics-domaines/other-autre/csr-strat-rse.aspx?lang=eng>; see also Seck, *supra* note 61. Although the Canadian government has touted the CORE as being the first institution of its kind, Latin American countries have a history of human rights ombudsman positions (which go by the name of *defensor del pueblo, procurador de derechos humanos,* or *comisionado nacional de derechos humanos*). See Erika Moreno & Richard Witmer, "The Power of the Pen: Human Rights Ombudsmen and Personal Integrity Violations in Latin America, 1982–2006" (2016) 17:2 Human Rights Rev 143.

68   OECD, *OECD Due Diligence Guidance for Responsible Supply Chains of Minerals from Conflict-Affected and High-Risk Areas,* online: <www.oecd.org/corporate/mne/mining.htm>.

69   Blanchfield, *supra* note 5.

70   UNHRC, *Statement, supra* note 6.

71   *CORE, supra* note 7.

72   *Ibid.*

73   *Ibid.*

Guidelines for Multinational Enterprises.[74] The second is to offer informal mediation services.[75] The third element of the mandate is the ability to review and investigate complaints. Under this function, the CORE has the ability to review complaints in one of the following categories: those submitted by third parties against a company; those submitted by a company that believes it is the subject of unfounded human rights abuse allegations; and those initiated by the CORE itself.[76] All three review provisions are limited by a time frame: complaints must be of events that occurred after the appointment of the first ombudsperson, or that are still ongoing at the time of review.[77]

In a recent call for action, the CORE's ability to investigate has been touted as the biggest concern of the CORE's structure.[78] Through the Inquiries Act, the Canadian government can give the CORE the powers to investigate, including, for example, the ability to enforce the attendance of witnesses and to compel the giving of evidence.[79] From the language of the Order in Council, it is unclear whether the CORE will have the ability to subpoena witnesses, as per the provisions of the Inquiries Act. Such lack of clarity as to whether the CORE will have the ability to independently investigate allegations of human rights violations became a critical issue, and on July 11, 2019, all civil society and labour union representatives appointed to the advisory council quit en masse.[80] Although the Order in Council was replaced in September 2019, as of the time of writing, civil society and labour union representatives have not returned as members of the council.

An analysis of the CORE's institutional design reveals its functions and institutional fragilities.

The CORE and Its Dynamic Relationships with TNCs

The CORE is an institution created by the home country (Canada) where ParentCos are located. The proposition is that the CORE will investigate and review the actions of ParentCos and their SubCos in various host countries. Its purpose is to provide a grievance mechanism for victims of human rights abuses. The UNGPs' third pillar, which is based on the principle that victims must have adequate and effective remedies when their rights have been breached, includes effectiveness criteria. Principle 31 of the UNGPs sets out criteria for non-judicial grievance mechanisms, whether state-based or non-state-based. These mechanisms must be legitimate, accessible, predictable, equitable, transparent, rights compatible, a source of continuous learning, and based on engagement and dialogue.[81]

---

74   *CORE, supra* note 7, ss 4(a), (b). See also OECD, *OECD Guidelines for Multinational Enterprises* (2011), online: <www.oecd.org/daf/inv/mne/48004323.pdf>.

75   CORE, *supra* note 7, s 4(f).

76   *Ibid*, ss 4(c)–(e).

77   *Ibid*.

78   See e.g. Amnesty International, "Ombudsperson for Responsible Enterprise Announced Today: Ombudsperson announced, but government fails to make good on promises" (8 April 2019), online (blog): *Human Rights Now* <www.amnesty.ca/blog/ombudsperson-responsible-enterprise-announced-today>; Penelope Simons, "Trudeau Government's global reputation at risk due to poor corporate accountability", *The Globe and Mail* (5 June 2019), online: <www.theglobeandmail.com/business/commentary/article-trudeau-governments-global-reputation-at-risk-due-to-poor-corporate/>.

79   *Inquiries Act*, RSC 1985, cI-11, ss 4, 5.

80   Sharp, *supra* note 9.

81   UNGPs, *supra* note 1, Principle 31.

Furthermore, the CORE is a public institution that is intended to curb corporate malfeasance. When the CORE functions as intended, it will interact with firms and such interaction will fall within the dynamic relationships with TNCs shown above in Figure 2. Using that diagram to analyze how the CORE and firms will interact, the following can be surmised.

The CORE and Relationship A1 and Relationship A2

The CORE will affect ParentCos, but also SubCos, due to its extraterritorial intent. Even though the CORE is aimed at Canadian companies in their home country, any malfeasance is usually undertaken by corporate subsidiaries, and it is those subsidiary actors that the CORE also wants to restrain. Therefore, two distinct constraining actions are envisioned. The first is to afford redress for victims of corporate wrongs, such as human rights violations and environmental damage. The ultimate goal is corporate accountability, and it can be understood as either the substitution of the host country's institutions (perhaps due to the host countries' lack of capacity or lack of will) or what has been termed the home-state advantage (i.e., the home state's ability to compel corporate accountability).

The second effect that the CORE's mandate will bring about is the creation of corporate preferences, practices and procedures that are created at the ParentCo level, and then disseminated to SubCos. The result of the second goal is for the TNC to act as an "evangelizing" institutional entrepreneur by championing the adoption or influence of specific practices in local institutions.[82] Thus, the second goal's purpose is to bring organizational change within the TNC that will be experienced first by the ParentCo and subsequently by the SubCo. In sum, the first purpose is to enforce the sanctions set out in the rules of the game (consequence driven), while the latter goal is to act as a coercive constraint, modifying the TNC institution through the force of the state and the provision of regulatory oversight and control, and thereby resulting in the TNC adapting to pressure to conform to institutionalized standards.[83]

The CORE and Relationship Y

As noted, the CORE's mandate and actions may constrain ParentCos, and thus will affect the transfer practices between ParentCos and their SubCos. As most TNCs produce subsidiaries that are ParentCo clones, such clones have limited "subversion" ability.[84] Thus, SubCos that operate in institutional environments that are diverse and lack corporate constraints should nevertheless mirror the practices of their ParentCo, perhaps leading to less deviant and harmful behaviour.

The CORE and Relationship B

As a SubCo seeks to follow its ParentCo practices, which are informed by the CORE's mandate, the SubCo will engage with local host country institutions in a manner that is consistent with the possible restraints and constraints imposed by the CORE.

A question remains as to how the CORE will interact with other Canadian institutions.

---

82   Walter W Powell, "The New Institutionalism" in Stewart R Clegg & James R Bailey, eds, *The International Encyclopedia of Organization Studies* (London, UK: Sage, 2008).

83   John L Campbell, *Institutional Change and Globalization* (Princeton: Princeton University Press, 2004) at 22; see also John H Dunning & Sarianna M Lundan, *Multinational Enterprises and the Global Economy*, 2nd ed (Cheltenham, UK: Edward Elgar, 2008) at 127.

84   Glen Morgan & Peer Hull Kristensen, "The Contested Space of Multinationals: Varieties of Institutionalism, Varieties of Capitalism" (2006) 59:11 Human Relations 1467.

The CORE and Canada's Institutional Matrix

From the IAIB literature, three institutional characteristics are significant in determining when corporate capture is enabled: institutional fragility, institutional uncertainty and institutional ambiguity. Institutional fragility is usually associated with developing countries, and thus it is assumed that institutional work is more prevalent in the Global South. The literature on corporate capture debunks this assumption, as it clearly shows that Global North institutions have been subject to capture by corporations in all ambits of institutional action.[85] Therefore, the mere fact that the CORE is in Canada, a robust and Global North jurisdiction, does not shield it from corporate capture.

Furthermore, the present iteration of the CORE stands within a bed of institutional uncertainty and institutional ambiguities. Institutional uncertainty has arisen as the CORE is operationalized. The most prominent uncertainty relates to the CORE's ability to independently investigate allegations of human rights breaches. As already noted, such lack of clarity has resulted in the labour unions and civil society representatives resigning from the advisory council. In one early crisis, because of institutional uncertainty, the CORE lost crucial legitimacy.

In addition, excessive discretion may produce uncertainty, and this can be seen in the ombudsperson's tool kit of recommendations, which fall into two categories. The first are sanctions related to trade measures, which include the withdrawal of trade advocacy reports and the refusal of Export Development Canada to provide future financial support.[86] The former sanctions can be recommended if the company has not acted in good faith during the review or in the follow-up period of the review process, but it is uncertain whether they are available as recommendations as a result of the review. The second grouping of sanctions are broad and vague, including financial compensation, a formal apology and changes to a Canadian company's policies. The Order in Council grants complete discretion to the ombudsperson on how such recommendations will be implemented and how they will be followed up.

Moreover, the ombudsperson has the ability to recommend that matters be referred to the Minister of International Trade if criminal offences or regulatory offences have been committed.[87] However, it remains unclear in what circumstances civil court action will ensue from the CORE's investigations, if at all. The CORE has the ability to allow for review processes to be confidential; will they also be permitted to be without prejudice? Will monetary reparations recommended by CORE be subject to litigation? If so, when and how will this be determined? Moreover, how and when will Crown prosecutors be expected to act when the alleged violations are criminal? For example, will the CORE have the standing of an investigative agency?[88]

As it now stands, companies do not know the full consequences of not adhering to recommendations made by the CORE. Similar to the previous CSR Counsellor iterations, the CORE has the ability to deny access to the trade commissioners' advisory and accessory

---

85   On corporate capture in Canada, see e.g. MacLean, "Striking at the Root", *supra* note 11; Jason MacLean, "Regulatory Capture and the Role of Academics in Public Policymaking: Lessons from Canada's Environmental Regulatory Review Process" (2019) 52:2 UBC L Rev 479.

86   *CORE*, *supra* note 7, ss 10, 11.

87   *Ibid*, s 7.

88   Public Prosecution Service of Canada Deskbook, Guideline of the Director Issues under Section 3.3(c) of the *Director of Public Prosecutions Act*, SC 2006, c 9, s 121.

services. The CORE has been given the additional measure that it can recommend that Canada's export credit agency, Export Development Canada, refuse to provide future financial support to companies.[89] The human rights policy of Export Development Canada requires it to cooperate with the CORE in this regard.[90] However, it is unclear whether debarment is an option, as the language in the policy of Export Development Canada speaks to transactional investment and divestment decisions, and not to absolute corporate debarment.[91] In other words, whether the CORE actually has "teeth" remains unclear.

Institutional ambiguities also plague the CORE. The CORE does not stand in a vacuum; it is part of several initiatives that the Canadian government has implemented on corporate accountability. Even though there is wording that suggests cooperation between institutions, from an institutional perspective who does what and when remains unclear, resulting in institutional disorder. If there is functional clarity for each institution,[92] so that the rules of the games are clear, then the role of each participant itself is also clear, and there is institutional order.

In the case of the CORE, overlapping institutional orders can cause ambiguity. For example, how will the CORE investigations interact with those under the Extractive Sector Transparency Measures Act[93] and the Corruption of Foreign Public Officials Act?[94] The Order in Council allows for cooperation and referrals, but it does not clarify how these institutions will work together. For example, will there be data sharing between the CORE, the RCMP and Natural Resources Canada, and, if so, how would this work when the CORE investigations are under the wrap of confidentiality? Moreover, how will the CORE interact with the National Contact Point created under the OECD Guidelines,[95] when the OECD Guidelines also have provisions regarding allegations of human rights violations? Again, the wording allows for referrals but does not clarify roles and responsibilities. Imprecise and vague terminology that calls for a fluid concept of cooperation results in a nebulous relationship between these initiatives that can result in institutional ambiguity and disorder.

In sum, the institutional gap that may be created by the institutional ambiguities and the institutional uncertainty of the CORE can create an environment that will allow for corporate actors to take action and engage in corporate capture. As the gaps allow for creative action, consideration should be given to the further articulation of the CORE's mandate, through policy guidance and potentially through legislation, to clarify how the CORE will interact with other Canadian institutions.

---

89   *CORE, supra* note 7, s 10(c).

90   Export Development Canada, *Human Rights Policy* (Ottawa: Export Development Canada, 2019), s 2.3, online: <www.edc.ca/content/dam/edc/en/corporate/corporate-social-responsibility/environment-people/human-rights-policy.pdf>.

91   *Ibid.*

92   See W Richard Scott, *Institutions and Organizations: Ideas, Interests and Identities* (London, UK: Sage, 2013).

93   *Extractive Sector Transparency Measures Act*, SC 2014, c 39.

94   *Corruption of Foreign Public Officials Act*, SC 1998, c 34.

95   Global Affairs Canada, *Canada's National Contact Point for the Organisation for Economic Co-operation and Development Guidelines for Multinational Enterprises*, online: <www.international.gc.ca/trade-agreements-accords-commerciaux/ncp-pcn/index.aspx?lang=eng>. See also *OECD Guidelines for Multinational Enterprises, supra* note 74.

Arguably, legislative ambiguity is a technique used by legislators in their attempt to compromise differing value propositions.[96] Constructive ambiguity, which is the indefinite language used to resolve disparate points of view, may also bring about positive outcomes where conciliation is necessary.[97] However, it is in this space of contestation, ambiguity and institutional uncertainty that corporate actors can capture institutions and work to undermine their original purpose.

Conclusion

The third initiative by the Canadian government to counteract corporate malfeasance is a step in the right direction. The CORE and its advisory council mirror other ombudsman institutions that have flourished worldwide, with the unique proposition that it counters corporate action and not state action. Although it is focused only on the extractive and textile sectors, the CORE and its advisory council are intended to act as a home-state grievance mechanism that fosters corporate accountability and allows victims their right to redress. However, like any other public institution, the CORE may be vulnerable to corporate capture.

To explore the CORE's vulnerability, this chapter used two overlapping and complementary areas of knowledge. The first is the literature on corporate capture, and specifically of corporate capture of the human rights agenda. The second is the literature on institutional work in IAIB. The two areas of literature are in separate silos, yet they are similar and account for the overlapping understanding of purposeful corporate action.

A significant contribution to the literature on institutional work (from the literature on corporate capture) is the fact that institutional work can be (and is) undertaken in institutional environments at all levels of development. Thus, institutional work can and does occur in the Global North. Furthermore, two institutional characteristics that enable institutional work are noteworthy: institutional ambiguity and institutional uncertainty.

This chapter argues that the CORE, as presently mandated, lies within a bed of institutional gaps. Institutional ambiguity arises from the lack of clarity about how the institution and its dynamic relationship with TNCs will occur in practice. The consequences of the reviews and the teeth of the CORE are still hazy at present. Institutional ambiguities arise because the institutional relationship between the CORE, other institutions and legislative actions within the constellation of Canada's institutional matrix is fluid. Hosted within a framework of cooperation, such relationships stand outside of certainty and exactitude. It is here, within institutional gaps, that corporate capture is enabled and facilitated.

As the Canadian government continues with the practicalities of the implementation of the CORE, it is critical that it brings greater clarity to its investigative powers, but also to the consequences to firms of such investigations. In the case of the CORE, ambiguities and uncertainties are detrimental to its operations and may make the CORE a target of corporate capture. Civil society and labour unions have already expressed their negative opinion on this new

---

96   Adam C Pritchard & Joseph A Grundfest, "Statutes with Multiple Personality Disorders: The Value of Ambiguity in Statutory Design and Interpretation" (2002) 54:4 Stan L Rev 627.

97   Valerie Oosterveld, "Constructive Ambiguity and the Meaning of 'Gender' for the International Criminal Court" (2014) 16:4 Intl Feminist J Politics 563.

institution and its legitimacy has already been placed into question.[98] The new Order in Council, as amended in September 2019, is not sufficient. To ensure the independence, transparency and legitimacy of the CORE, the government needs to bolster this new institution with a clear mandate and concomitant legal authority.

---

98   See e.g. Charis Khampuis, "Why does Justin Trudeau succumb to corporate pressure?", *The Conversation* (5 May 2019).

11

MINING FOR EQUALITY

Soft Targets and Hard Floors for Boards of Directors?

Keith MacMaster and Sara Seck

Introduction

Gender equality and the empowerment of women and girls are central to achieving the United Nations 2030 Sustainable Development Goals (SDGs).[1] An indicator of women's equality and empowerment is the number of women on boards of directors and in senior management of firms. The Canada Business Corporations Act (CBCA) was amended in 2018 to mandate disclosure of the number of designated persons, the percentage of the board that they comprise, whether the firm has a written policy in respect of diversity and whether there are targets

---

1   UN General Assembly, *Transforming our world: the 2030 Agenda for Sustainable Development*, UNGAOR, 70th Sess, UN Doc A/RES/70/1 (2015) [*2030 Agenda*], online: <www.un.org/ga/search/view_doc.asp?symbol=A/RES/70/1&Lang=E>.

for representation.[2] The changes include gender diversity and disclosure of representation of minority groups, Aboriginal peoples and people with disabilities.[3]

In this chapter, we consider the CBCA amendments in light of broader concerns associated with Canadian-based mining companies operating within and outside of Canada, including violations of rights of women and girls.[4] The industrial mining sector is male dominated, and has faced accusations and lawsuits over gender bias, violence (including sexual violence) against women and children, health and safety problems, and environmental harms.[5] The 2019 report of the National Inquiry into Missing and Murdered Indigenous Women and Girls (MMIWG) explicitly linked resource extraction with violence against Indigenous women and girls.[6] Among the calls to justice in the report are five aimed at "Extractive and Development Industries," including that industries consider "safety and security of Indigenous women and girls" at "all stages of project planning, assessment, implementation, management, and monitoring."[7]

This chapter aims to contribute to the literature on international law, women and mining from a Canadian perspective, focusing on legal developments related to corporate board diversity. We first examine the importance of women's equality and empowerment in sources of international human rights and sustainable development law, and then consider Canadian initiatives aimed at the extractive sector. Second, we review the data on female representation on Canadian corporate boards and in senior management, with particular attention to the mining sector. Third, we consider insights and limitations of current literature on corporate board diversity, with attention to the definition of "firm performance," arguing that it must account for respect for the rights of women and girls. A broader understanding of firm performance is essential in light of Canada's promotion of business responsibilities to respect international human rights law at home and overseas.[8] We conclude by considering different approaches to board

---

2   Bill C-25, *An Act to amend the Canada Business Corporations Act, the Canada Cooperatives Act, the Canada Not-for-profit Corporations Act and the Competition Act*, 1st Sess, 42nd Parl, 2015 (assented to 1 May 2018), SC 2018, c 8; *Regulations Amending the Canada Business Corporations Regulations*, 2001, SOR/2019-258 [*Regulations Amending*]; Laura Levine, "Increased Diversity Disclosure for CBCA Corporations Coming in 2020" (9 August 2019), online: *Stikeman Elliot LLP* <www.stikeman.com/en-ca/kh/canadian-securities-law/Increased-Diversity-Disclosure-for-CBCA-Corporations-Coming-in-2020>.

3   *Regulations Amending*, *supra* note 2, Part 8.2. Designated groups will be the same as under the *Employment Equity Act*, SC 1995, c 44, s 3; Corporations Canada, "Explanatory note on proposed regulatory amendments" (19 January 2018), online: <www.ic.gc.ca/eic/site/cd-dgc.nsf/eng/cs07274.html>.

4   Sara L Seck & Penelope Simons, "Resource Extraction and the Human Rights of Women and Girls" (2019) 31:1 CJWL 1 [Seck & Simons, "Resource Extraction"]; Sara L Seck & Penelope Simons, "Sustainable Mining, Environmental Justice, and the Human Rights of Women and Girls: Canada as Home and Host State" in S Atapattu, C Gonzalez & S Seck, eds, *The Cambridge Handbook on Environmental Justice and Sustainable Development* (Cambridge, UK: Cambridge University Press, forthcoming 2020) [Seck & Simons, "Sustainable Mining"]; Katy Jenkins, "Review Article: Women, mining and development: An emerging research agenda" (2014) 1:2 Extractive Industries & Society 329; Penelope Simons, "Unsustainable International Law: Transnational Resource Extraction and Violence against Women" (2017) 26:2 Transnat'l L & Contemp Probs 415; Raywat Deonandan, Kalowatie Deonandan & Brennan Field, "Mining the Gap: Aboriginal Women and the Mining Industry" (2016).

5   Seck & Simons, "Resource Extraction", *supra* note 4; Seck & Simons, "Sustainable Mining", *supra* note 4; Jenkins, *supra* note 4; Simons, *supra* note 4; Deonandan, Deonandan & Field, *supra* note 4; UN Women, *Promoting Women's Participation in the Extractive Industries Sector: Examples of Emerging Good Practices* (2016) at 10.

6   National Inquiry into Missing and Murdered Indigenous Women and Girls, *Reclaiming Power and Place: The Final Report of the National Inquiry into Missing and Murdered Indigenous Women and Girls*, vol 1A (2019) at 584–94 [MMIWG Report], online: <www.mmiwg-ffada.ca/wp-content/uploads/2019/06/Final_Report_Vol_1a.pdf>.

7   *Ibid* at 196 ("Calls to Justice: Calls for Extractive and Development Industries 13.1–13.5"). The report includes the rights of "2SLGBTQQIA people."

8   Sara L Seck, "Business, Human Rights, and Canadian Mining Lawyers" (2015) 56 Can Bus LJ 208 [Seck, "Business, Human Rights"]; Sara L Seck, "Canadian Mining Internationally and the UN Guiding Principles for Business and Human Rights" (2011) 49 Can YB Intl L 51 [Seck, "Canadian Mining Internationally"].

and management diversity in light of the recent amendments to the CBCA,[9] and offering recommendations for law and policy reforms as well as future research.

International and Canadian Law and Policy

Canada plays a prominent role in the global mining and natural resources industries.[10] Canada is the pre-eminent leader in mining finance, with more than 59 percent of the world's extractive financing taking place through the Toronto Stock Exchange (TSX) or TSX-Venture (TSX-V).[11] Canada is home to more than 214 TSX-listed companies, and 945 listed on the "junior" TSX-V.[12] The Canadian mining industry has been implicated in human rights violations within Canada and internationally, including violations of the rights of women and girls.[13] The most notorious international examples include those involving sexual violence, such as at Barrick Gold's Porgera Mine in Papua New Guinea,[14] or the allegations of gang rape in Guatemala that are the subject of the *Hudbay* litigation.[15] Within Canada, concerns have been raised about increased violence against Indigenous women from mining activities, most recently in the MMIWG report.[16] Gendered human rights violations also include environment-related violations of rights to health and food,[17] intersectional violations of Indigenous rights,[18] and employment-related dimensions of violations of a woman's right to mine.[19]

Paragraph 46 of the Plan of Implementation of the 2002 World Summit on Sustainable Development in Johannesburg states that active participation of women and Indigenous communities is essential for sustainable mining development.[20] Yet globally, women continue to be under-represented, especially in positions of power.[21] Indeed, women's under-representation

---

9   Bill C-25, *supra* note 2.

10   Natural Resources Canada, "10 Key Facts on Canada's Minerals Sector", online: <www.nrcan.gc.ca/sites/www.nrcan. gc.ca/files/emmc/pdf/2019/10-Key-Facts-on-Canada_s-Mineral-Sector-EN-access-1.pdf>; Natural Resources Canada, "Minerals and Metals Facts", online: <www.nrcan.gc.ca/our-natural-resources/minerals-mining/minerals-metals-facts/20507>.

11   TMX, "TMX TSX | TSXV — Mining", online: <www.tsx.com/listings/listing-with-us/sector-and-product-profiles/mining>.

12   *Ibid.*

13   Seck & Simons, *Resource Extraction*, *supra* note 4; Seck & Simons, "Sustainable Mining", *supra* note 4. See also Kalowatie Deonandan & Colleen Bell, "Discipline and Punish: Gendered Dimensions of Violence in Extractive Development" (2019) 31:1 CJWL 24.

14   Columbia Law School Human Rights Clinic & Harvard Law School International Human Rights Clinic, "Righting Wrongs? Barrick Gold's Remedy Mechanism for Sexual Violence in Papua New Guinea: Key Concerns and Lessons Learned" (2015).

15   *Choc v HudBay Minerals Inc*, 2013 ONSC 1414.

16   MMIWG Report, *supra* note 6.

17   Seck & Simons, "Sustainable Mining", *supra* note 4.

18   Sarah Morales, "Digging for Rights: How Can International Human Rights Law Better Protect Indigenous Women from Extractive Industries?" (2019) 31:1 CJWL 58.

19   See especially Kuntala Lahiri-Dutt, "Do Women Have a Right to Mine?" (2019) 31:1 CJWL 1.

20   *Report of the World Summit on Sustainable Development*, UNGAOR, UN Doc A/CONF.199/20 (2002) at 6 ("Resolution 2: Plan of Implementation of the World Summit on Sustainable Development") ["Plan of Implementation of the World Summit"]. For an assessment of the contested nature of this statement, see Sara L Seck, "Transnational Corporations and Extractive Industries" in Shawkat Alam et al, eds, *International Environmental Law and the Global South* (New York: Cambridge University Press, 2015) 380.

21   Linda Doku, "Why the Mining Industry Needs More Women", *Forbes* (24 May 2019).

in leadership positions in Canada's private sector was described as problematic by the UN Human Rights Committee in 2015.[22]

The most recent global consensus on sustainable development, women's empowerment and human rights is found in *Transforming Our World: The 2030 Agenda for Sustainable Development*, which was endorsed by 170 world leaders in September 2015.[23] Described as an action plan for "people, planet and prosperity," the SDGs consist of 17 goals and 169 targets. According to the preamble, the SDGs should be implemented by every country and "all stakeholders, acting in a collaborative partnership" to urgently "shift the world on to a sustainable and resilient path."[24] The preamble explicitly states that the SDGs "seek to realize the human rights of all and to achieve gender equality and the empowerment of all women and girls."[25] SDG 16 promotes "peaceful and inclusive societies," as well as "access to justice for all" and the building of "effective, accountable and inclusive institutions at all levels."[26]

SDG 5 is of particular relevance to corporate board diversity. SDG target 5.5 is to "[e]nsure women's full and effective participation and equal opportunities for leadership at all levels of decision-making in political, economic and public life." Indicator 5.5.2 is the "[p]roportion of women in managerial positions," while target 5.c is to "[a]dopt and strengthen sound policies and enforceable legislation for the promotion of gender equality and the empowerment of all women and girls at all levels."[27] Therefore, to meet the SDGs, private sector actors must promote and enable women to take on leadership roles, and government regulation should advance this action.

With regard to the extractive sector, the 2030 Agenda's overarching vision is described as sustainable production and consumption, including sustainable use of natural resources.[28] Paragraph 67 of the 2030 Agenda calls upon "all businesses to apply their creativity and innovation to solving sustainable development challenges," while protecting rights "in accordance with relevant international standards and agreements and other on-going initiatives…such as the Guiding Principles on Business and Human Rights"[29] [UNGPs]. The UNGPs date from 2011, and are comprised of three pillars: the state duty to protect human rights, the business responsibility to respect human rights and the need for access to remedy. The Government of Canada has promoted the UNGPs to Canada's mining sector operating internationally.[30] If women held equal power at the board level, they would be better positioned to contribute

---

22   Human Rights Committee, *Concluding observations on the sixth periodic report of Canada*, UNESCOR, UN Doc CCPR/C/CAN/CO/6 (2015) at para 7.

23   *2030 Agenda, supra* note 1; Office of the High Commissioner on Human Rights, *Human Rights and the 2030 Agenda for Sustainable Development*, online: <www.ohchr.org/en/issues/SDGS/pages/the2030agenda.aspx>; United Nations, "Sustainable Development Knowledge Platform", online: <https://sustainabledevelopment.un.org/post2015/summit>.

24   *2030 Agenda, supra* note 1 at Preamble.

25   *Ibid.*

26   *Ibid* at Goal 16.

27   *Ibid* at Goal 5.

28   *Ibid* at para 9.

29   *Ibid* at para 67; Human Rights Council, *Report of the Special Representative of the Secretary-General on the Issue of Human Rights and Transnational Corporations and Other Business Enterprises, John Ruggie: Guiding Principles on Business and Human Rights: Implementing the United Nations "Protect, Respect and Remedy" Framework*, UNGAOR, 17th Sess, UN Doc A/HRC/17/31 (2011) [UNGPs].

30   UNGPs, *supra* note 29. On Canada's endorsement of the UNGPs and promotion of them to the mining sector, see Seck, "Business, Human Rights", *supra* note 8; Seck, "Canadian Mining Internationally", *supra* note 8.

to ensuring business respect for human rights in sustainable mining, including respect for the human rights of women and girls.

Other international initiatives support corporate board diversity as well. The Women's Empowerment Principles (WEP) are a joint initiative of UN Women and the UN Global Compact.[31] Subtitled "Equality Means Business," the principles seek to emphasize the "business case for corporate action."[32] Principle 1 of the WEP is "[e]stablish high-level corporate leadership for gender equality," while Principle 2 is "[t]reat all women and men fairly at work — respect and support human rights and nondiscrimination."[33] Chief executive officers (CEOs) should issue a "statement of support" that "encourages business leaders to use the seven Principles as guide posts for actions that advance and empower women in the workplace, marketplace and community."[34] Yet, implementation of the WEP has been critiqued.[35]

The relationship between the business responsibility to respect rights and implementation of the SDGs has received increasing attention,[36] and international instruments have actively aligned their guidance with the SDGs.[37] From a human rights perspective, the 1979 Convention on the Elimination of All Forms of Discrimination Against Women is the key widely ratified foundational human rights instrument.[38] A March 2019 report by the Working Group on Business and Human Rights (WGBHR) on the gender dimensions of the UNGPs notes that while "women's human rights are an inalienable, integral and indivisible part of universal human rights," and businesses and states "should take concrete steps to identify, prevent and remedy gender-based discrimination and inequalities in all areas of life," in reality, neither "have paid adequate attention to gender equality" in meeting their respective human rights responsibilities and obligations.[39]

The annex to the WGBHR report contains a set of 31 guiding principles on gender that align with the "protect, respect, and remedy" framework of the UNGPs. Principle 1 highlights the

---

31   UN Women & UN Global Compact, "Women's Empowerment Principles", online: <www.empowerwomen.org/en/weps/about>; UN Global Compact, "Endorse the Women's Empowerment Principles", online: <www.unglobalcompact.org/take-action/action/womens-principles> [UNGC, "WEP"].

32   UNGC, "WEP", *supra* note 31.

33   *Ibid.* The other principles are: "Principle 3: Ensure the health, safety and well-being of all women and men workers; Principle 4: Promote education, training and professional development for women; Principle 5: Implement enterprise development, supply chain and marketing practices that empower women; and Principle 7: Measure and publicly report on progress to achieve gender equality."

34   *Ibid.*

35   *Gender dimensions of the Guiding Principles on Business and Human Rights: Report of the Working Group on the issue of human rights and transnational enterprises*, 42nd Sess, UN Doc A/HRC/41/43 (2019) at 7, para 28 [WGBHR, *Gender dimensions*].

36   Shift & Business and Sustainable Development Commission, *Business, Human Rights and the Sustainable Development Goals: Forging a Coherent Vision and Strategy* (2016) at 34–35, online: <http://s3.amazonaws.com/aws-bsdc/BSDC-Biz-HumanRights-SDGs.pdf>; Office of the High Commissioner for Human Rights, *The business and human rights dimension of sustainable development: Embedding 'Protect, Respect and Remedy' in SDGs implementation* (30 June 2017), online: <www.ohchr.org/Documents/Issues/Business/Session18/InfoNoteWGBHR_SDGRecommendations.pdf>.

37   UN Global Compact, "Advancing Sustainable Development", online: <www.unglobalcompact.org/what-is-gc/our-work/sustainable-development>; GRI, "GRI and the Sustainable Development Goals", online: <www.globalreporting.org/information/SDGs/Pages/SDGs.aspx>; Organisation for Economic Co-operation and Development (OECD), *OECD and the Sustainable Development Goals: Delivering on universal goals and targets*, online: <www.oecd.org/dac/sustainable-development-goals.htm>.

38   *Convention on the Elimination of All Forms of Discrimination against Women*, 18 December 1979, Can TS 1982 No 31 (entered into force 3 September 1981; entered into force for Canada 9 January 1982).

39   WGBHR, *Gender dimensions, supra* note 35 at para 3; *ibid* ("gender refers to socially constructed roles of and power relations among men, women and gender non-binary persons" at para 9).

duty of states to ensure respect of women's human rights by business enterprises, including through implementation of legislation.[40] States should "encourage business enterprises to appoint a certain percentage of women to their boards" and report "on the gender pay gap throughout their operations."[41] State-owned and controlled enterprises should "lead by example in achieving substantive gender equality" and use "leverage to require their business partners to do the same."[42] These enterprises should "appoint a certain percentage of women to their boards and annually disclose data on progress made in achieving gender parity in employment."[43]

Principle 11 concerns the responsibility of businesses to avoid infringing the human rights of women, including by reproducing existing discrimination in their own operations, and to "address adverse human rights impacts with which they are involved."[44] Illustrative actions include "affirmative action and professional development support" and to ensure "equal representation of women in the workforce at all levels, including on boards."[45] Principle 19 recommends implementation of "gender-transformative measures to prevent and mitigate adverse impacts" identified through impact assessment processes.[46] Illustrative actions include revising policies and management processes to address systemic concerns for women, and adopting "affirmative action policies to overcome underrepresentation of women in managerial positions and on boards."[47]

Despite international consensus in 2002 on the importance of the active participation of women and Indigenous communities for sustainable mining development,[48] to date, few international guidance tools promoted to the mining sector have explicitly embedded respect for the human rights of women and girls.[49] Human rights due diligence is an expectation for all businesses, and must receive attention in guidance tools for mining companies.[50] Yet while the 2017 OECD Due Diligence Guidance for Meaningful Stakeholder Engagement in the Extractive Sector dedicates an annex to gender, it does not adopt a human rights approach.[51] In 2019, the Prospectors and Developers Association of Canada adopted its own guidance document for gender diversity and inclusion.[52]

---

40   *Ibid* at Annex ("Gender guidance for the Guiding Principles on Business and Human Rights"), Guiding Principle 1.

41   *Ibid* at para 4(b).

42   *Ibid* at Guiding Principle 4.

43   *Ibid* at para 8(d).

44   *Ibid* at Guiding Principle 11.

45   *Ibid* at para 22(g).

46   *Ibid* at Guiding Principle 19.

47   *Ibid* at para 38(a)(i), (iii), (iv).

48   See "Plan of Implementation of the World Summit", *supra* note 20 at para 46.

49   Seck & Simons, "Sustainable Mining", *supra* note 4; Global Affairs Canada, "Canada's Enhanced Corporate Social Responsibility Strategy to Strengthen Canada's Extractive Sector Abroad: Doing Business the Canadian Way: A Strategy to Advance Corporate Social Responsibility in Canada's Extractive Sector Abroad" (14 November 2014), online: <www.international.gc.ca/trade-agreements-accords-commerciaux/topics-domaines/other-autre/csr-strat-rse.aspx?lang=eng>; Global Affairs Canada, "Responsible Business Conduct Abroad", online: <www.international.gc.ca/trade-agreements-accords-commerciaux/topics-domaines/other-autre/csr-rse.aspx?lang=eng#RBCGuidelines>.

50   Daniela Chimisso dos Santos & Sara L Seck, "Human Rights Due Diligence and Extractive Industries" in Surya Deva, ed, *Research Handbook on Human Rights and Business* (Edward Elgar, forthcoming 2020).

51   OECD, "OECD Due Diligence Guidance for Meaningful Stakeholder Engagement in the Extractive Sector" (2017) at Annex C ("Engaging with Women"), online: <http://mneguidelines.oecd.org/stakeholder-engagement-extractive-industries.htm>.

52   Prospectors and Developers Association of Canada, "Gender Diversity and Inclusion Guidance Document", online: <www.pdac.ca/priorities/responsible-exploration/gender/gender-diversity-and-inclusion-guidance-document>.

While gender inclusive rights-respecting guidance is essential to ensure businesses are able to implement their independent responsibility to respect human rights, states also have international human rights obligations. Additional opportunities exist to ensure that Canadian domestic law guarantees respect for the rights of women and girls in resource extraction, in particular Indigenous women as noted by the MMIWG report.[53] A recent domestic law reform initiative has integrated Gender-Based Analysis Plus (GBA+) into federal impact assessment legislation.[54] A second recently adopted domestic law reform initiative is legislation promoting corporate board diversity. The next section will examine the current state of Canadian board diversity, with particular attention on the mining sector.

Canadian Board and Management Diversity Data

Canada has low female representation on corporate boards compared to the percentage of women in the general population.[55] The TSX, and its more than 800 companies, has a female representation rate of 16.4 percent.[56] The rate of female representation on corporate boards jumps to 28.4 percent for the S&P/TSX 60 index, where only the large companies are included.[57] This percentage is comparable to the Australian S&P/ASX 100 at 31 percent, and the UK Financial Times Stock Exchange (FTSE) 100 index at 30 percent.[58] Examining a broader cross-section of stock exchanges, women comprise only 10.3 percent of directorships, with the lowest rates occurring in Chile, Japan and Morocco, and the highest occurring in France, Norway and Sweden.[59] Significant changes can occur in relatively short time periods, with France doubling female representation in five years, whereas Norway has fallen in the same time period.[60] There are no longer any all-male boards among the S&P/TSX 60 companies.[61]

Large companies (greater than CDN$10 billion of market capitalization) have higher rates of female representation than smaller firms.[62] The percentage of boards without women has declined to 31.3 percent, while the percentage of boards with at least two women has increased to

53   MMIWG Report, *supra* note 6.

54   *Impact Assessment Act*, SC 2019, c 28, s 2(2.1). GBA+ is used to analyze sex and gender as factors underlying and intersecting with other identity factors that may be disproportionately impacted by proposed activities. See Impact Assessment Agency of Canada, *Practitioner's Guide to Federal Impact Assessments Under the Impact Assessment Act*, s 2(2.1), "Guidance: Gender-Based Analysis Plus in Impact Assessment", online: <www.canada.ca/en/impact-assessment-agency/services/policy-guidance/practitioners-guide-impact-assessment-act/gender-based-analysis.html>.

55   Andrew MacDougall & John Valley, *2017 Diversity Disclosure Practices: Women in leadership roles at TSX-listed companies* (Toronto: Osler, 2017) at 10 [MacDougall & Valley, *2017 Diversity Disclosure Practices*].

56   Andrew MacDougall & John Valley, *2018 Diversity Disclosure Practices: Women in leadership roles at TSX-listed companies* (Toronto: Osler, 2018) at 3, 16 [MacDougall & Valley, *2018 Diversity Disclosure Practices*].

57   *Ibid.*

58   Hampton-Alexander Review, *FTSE Women Leaders Improving gender balance in FTSE Leadership* (2018) at 9, 34 [*FTSE Women*].

59   *Ibid* at 35.

60   Data for 2018 from *ibid* at 35; data for 2013 from Siri Terjesen, Ruth Aguilera & Ruth Lorenz, "Legislating a Woman's Seat on the Board: Institutional Factors Driving Gender Quotas for Boards of Directors" (2015) 128 J Business Ethics 233 at 234.

61   MacDougall & Valley, *2018 Diversity Disclosure Practices*, *supra* note 56 at 23.

62   Companies less than CDN$1 billion in market capitalization have 10 percent female participation. Approximately 65 percent of TSX-listed companies fall under CDN$1 billion in market capitalization. Canadian Securities Administration (CSA), "Roundtable Discussion — Third Review of Women on Boards and in Executive Officer Positions" (24 October 2017) at 13 [CSA, "Roundtable Discussion"], online: <www.osc.gov.on.ca/documents/en/Securities-Category5/sn_20171103_transcript-wob-roundtable.pdf>; CSA, "Staff Review of Women on Boards and in Executive Officer Positions Compliance with NI 58-101 Disclosure of Corporate Governance Practices", CSA Staff Notice 58-309 (5 October 2017) at Figures 3.1, 4.2.

33.7 percent.[63] This statistic is important, as research indicates that a critical mass of representation is required to be effective.[64] Strides are being made but have not yet been embraced by one important industry — the mining industry.

Canada has a concentrated stock market with approximately one-third being extractives companies, which lag in female board representation, with mining having 11 percent representation.[65] Yet direct comparisons with other stock markets are difficult. The US markets are comprised of a broad range of companies, and mining firms are less important than in Canada.[66] Australia and South Africa are similar to the Canadian market, as approximately 33 percent of firms listed are financial services and 15.5 percent are extractives.[67] Historically, these two industries are divergent, with the former having among the highest female representation rate and the latter having the lowest.[68] Policies in Australia and South Africa have assisted in pushing higher numbers of female participation, with South Africa having the largest percentage of women on mining boards.[69]

Mining suffers from a glaring lack of gender diversity at all levels, from entry-level positions up to the corporate and board levels.[70] Globally, women comprise only 10 percent of the industrial mining workforce, while in Canada it is 17 percent.[71] Internationally, a 2013 study noted a severe shortage of women on boards of mining companies, and by 2015 the pipeline of female talent in the industry was actually falling.[72] Yet the study observed: "there is no shortage of women in the talent pool; there is simply a perception of a lack of available female talent."[73] In 2009, Women in Mining Canada formed in order to better enable empowerment of women in

63   *Ibid* at 22.

64   Hisham Farag & Chris Mallin, "Board diversity and financial fragility: Evidence from European banks" (2017) 49 Intl Rev Financial Analysis 98; Carolyn Wiley & Mireia Monllor-Tormos, "Board Gender Diversity in the STEM&F Sectors: The Critical Mass Required to Drive Firm Performance" (2018) 25:3 J Leadership & Organizational Studies 290. This is explained by signalling theories.

65   TMX, "TSX Market Statistics, The MiG Report", online: <www.tsx.com/resource/en/2014/mig-report.pdf>; MacDougall & Valley, *2018 Diversity Disclosure Practices*, *supra* note 56 at 19, 25.

66   NYSE is the oldest stock exchange and a traditional auction market, while the NASDAQ is a dealer market. Thus, they differ in both size and types of listings, but also in fundamental operational methods.

67   Canaccord Genuity, "Overview of the Australian Share Market", online: <www.psl.com.au/Wealth-Management/News-Insights/Article-Library/Overview-of-the-Australian-Share-Market>; ASX List, "ASX 100 List", online: <www.asx100list.com/>.

68   MacDougall & Valley, *2018 Diversity Disclosure Practices*, *supra* note 56; CSA, "Report on Fourth Staff Review of Disclosure Regarding Women on Boards and in Executive Officer Positions", CSA Multilateral Staff Notice 58-310 (27 September 2018) [CSA, "Report on Fourth Staff Review"]; CSA, "Roundtable Discussion", *supra* note 62 at 11.

69   International Women in Mining & PwC, *Mining for talent: A study of women on boards in the mining industry* (London, UK: PwC, 2016) at 2, 11, 14.

70   Women in Mining Canada, *Welcoming to Women: An Action Plan for Canada's Mining Employers* (2016) at 5, online: <https://wimcanada.org/wp-content/uploads/2017/01/WIM-NAP-book-full.pdf>.

71   Mining Industry Human Resources Council, *Strengthening Mining's Talent Alloy: Exploring Gender Inclusion* (2016) online: <www.mihr.ca/pdf/publications/MiHR_Gender_Report_EN_WEB.pdf>. On women's experiences in the male-dominated occupations, see e.g. Phiona Marin & Antoni Barnard, "The experience of women in male-dominated occupations: A constructivist grounded theory inquiry" (2013) 39:2 South African J Industrial Psychology.

72   International Women in Mining & PwC, *supra* note 69 at 2; Women in Mining (UK) & PwC, *Mining for talent 2015: A review of women on boards in the mining industry 2012–2014* (London, UK: PwC, 2015) at 13. In 2013, globally, women occupied eight percent of board seats in the top 100 mining companies, and there were four female executive directors.

73   International Women in Mining & PwC, *supra* note 69 at 25.

the sector.[74] During the same period, the UK market had the most significant increase in female representation, likely due to increased regulatory scrutiny.[75]

The number of junior mining companies may also be relevant to the challenge of female representation. Junior mining companies tend to be small, and they may have only a few employees.[76] Many have little to no profit (many operate at a loss) and often have no revenue.[77] The TSX's approximately 815 listed companies include significant numbers that have market capitalizations of less than CDN\$100 million.[78]

Educational background is relevant to board membership and senior management service. Bias over educational requirements may be a factor, with 100 percent of female board members in the mining sector having undergraduate degrees and 69 percent having completed postgraduate study; 97 percent of male directors hold an undergraduate degree and 54 percent hold postgraduate degrees.[79] The most common degrees for female directors are finance/economics, whereas male directors are more likely to hold mining and engineering degrees.[80] Some argue that this is one reason why greater numbers of female engineers and mining science graduates are so desperately needed. While Canada now advocates STEM (science, technology, engineering and math) careers for women, there is a long way to go,[81] as only 16 percent of Canadian mining/mineral engineers are female.[82] This, together with the small number of women in junior positions, suggests change will be slow. Graduates of MBAs and engineering programs take time to work their way up the corporate ladder. In 2015, Engineers Canada launched its "30 by 30" program to increase the number of newly licensed female engineers to 30 percent by 2030.[83]

74 Women in Mining Canada, "Who we are", online: <https://wimcanada.org/who-are-we/>.

75 Women in Mining (UK) & PwC, *supra* note 72 at 17.

76 TSX-V, *Market Insight 7* (30 September 2016); TSX, "Current Market Statistics", online: <www.tsx.com/listings/current-market-statistics>.

77 TMX Money, "S&P/TSX Venture Composite Index", online: <https://web.tmxmoney.com/index_constituents.php?qm_symbol=^JX>.

78 TSX, "Current Market Statistics", online: <www.tsx.com/listings/current-market-statistics>.

79 Women in Mining (UK) & PwC, *supra* note 72 at 18.

80 *Ibid.*

81 Government of Canada, "The Government of Canada and STEM", online: <www.ic.gc.ca/eic/site/013.nsf/eng/00014.html>.

82 Engineers Canada, "Canadian Engineers for Tomorrow", online: <https://engineerscanada.ca/reports/canadian-engineers-for-tomorrow>; Engineers Canada, "Women in Engineering", online: <https://engineerscanada.ca/diversity/women-in-engineering>.

83 Engineers Canada, "2018 National Membership Information", online: <https://engineerscanada.ca/reports/national-membership-report/2018-report>.

Board Diversity and Firm Performance: Gender and Mining

International instruments are pushing for corporate board and senior management diversity as part of a movement toward implementation of international human rights and sustainable development law. Yet the rationale for increased numbers of women on corporate boards differs depending on whether the focus is on women's empowerment or on the protection of the human rights of women who may be adversely impacted by industrial mining yet are not part of the enterprise.

The UN Global Compact claims there is a business case for corporate action on gender equality and women's empowerment, as well as a gender equality justification.[84] Research shows that having more women on boards leads to lower volatility in share prices, and higher return on equity.[85] There is clear and concrete evidence showing gender diversity and equality means greater profit and lower risk for companies. Increased gender diversity and younger average board age are shown to have strong associations with improved share price performance. These findings are mainly attributed to human capital and signalling theories.[86] Women directors have a stronger quantitative impact on conditionally high-performance firms compared to low-performance firms.[87] While one study did not find that returns were materially different for companies with greater gender representation,[88] the same study showed that additional women were found to lead to lower financial risk.[89] Another study found a statistically significant positive relationship between a diverse board and company performance.[90] Other research has found that, over the long term, firms with lower risk should be able to survive market-shocking events such as corrections, contractions and bubbles. Whether it is higher returns or lower risk, the result is the same: more women lead to financial improvement.

More importantly, in our view, an increased number of women on boards of directors is associated with greater firm commitment to corporate social responsibility (CSR), environmental

---

84   UN Global Compact, "Gender equality" ("Companies that focus on women's empowerment experience greater business success. Research shows investing in women and girls can lead to increases in productivity, organizational effectiveness, return on investment and higher consumer satisfaction"), online: <www.unglobalcompact.org/what-is-gc/our-work/social/gender-equality>.

85   Bank of America, Merrill Lynch, "Women the X-Factor" (7 March 2018) at 1, online: <https://mlaem.fs.ml.com/content/dam/ML/bulletin/PDFs/ml_women-the-X-factor-BAML-Report.pdf>; Daniel Low, Helen Roberts & Rosalind Whiting, "Board gender diversity and firm performance: Empirical evidence from Hong Kong, South Korea, Malaysia and Singapore" (2015) 35 Pacific-Basin Finance J 381; Martin Conyon & Lerong He, "Firm performance and boardroom gender diversity: A quantile regression approach" (2017) 79 J Business Research 198; Shams Pathan & Robert Faff, "Does board structure in banks really affect their performance?" (2013) 37:5 J Banking & Finance 1573; Emma García-Meca, Isabel-María García-Sánchez & Jennifer Martínez-Ferrero, "Board diversity and its effects on bank performance: An international analysis" (2015) 53 J Banking & Finance 202.

86   Cobus CH Taljaard, Michael JD Ward & Chris J Muller, "Board Diversity and Financial Performance: A Graphical Time-Series Approach" (2015) 18:3 South African J Economic & Management Sciences 425.

87   Conyon & He, *supra* note 85.

88   Bank of America, Merrill Lynch, *supra* note 85 at 5.

89   *Ibid* at 6; Victoria Geyfman, Wade A Cooper & Laura M Davis, "Board Gender Diversity and Bank Performance" (2018) 18:1 J Business Diversity 51.

90   Vivian Hunt et al, *Delivering through Diversity* (2018), online: *McKinsey & Company* <www.mckinsey.com/~/media/McKinsey/Business%20Functions/Organization/Our%20Insights/Delivering%20through%20diversity/Delivering-through-diversity_full-report.ashx>.

sustainability and improved decision making more generally.[91] Gender diversity also leads to innovation and respect for different viewpoints, both of which prepare businesses for inclusivity and sustainability.[92] These would seem essential for tackling the challenges facing mining companies.

Others critique this justification for addressing inequitable board/management diversity, raising concerns that it reinforces unverifiable assumptions about human behaviour, with causation unprovable.[93] According to this view, companies with effective gender diversity programs are already run more efficiently, so gender diversity "is only one result and a correlation not a cause."[94] The outcome of this debate remains to be seen.

This brief overview of studies examining justifications for increased gender diversity on corporate boards and in senior management suggests that while arguments could be made that increased gender diversity leads to better financial, social and environmental results for businesses, at best there is evidence of a correlation. The WGBHR proposes a different justification for states taking action to address the problems of the mining industry: to encourage business enterprises "to contribute to achieving substantive gender equality" would "enable the enterprises to discharge their responsibility to respect women's human rights."[95] This broader understanding is consistent with Canada's commitment to respect international human rights law in operations both at home and overseas.

Approaches to Board Diversity: "Comply or Explain" and Quotas

Two types of interventions are believed to be most effective to increase the number of women on boards and senior management: comply or explain (CoE), and quotas.

CoE

CoE requires companies to disclose how many women are on boards and/or in executive officer positions, and whether there is a policy for diversity.[96] If they do not have targets or goals, then the company needs to publicly explain why it does not, with a goal of applying pressure on

---

91   Dolors Setó-Pamies, "The Relationship between Women Directors and Corporate Social Responsibility" (2015) 22:6 Corporate Social Responsibility & Environmental Management 334; Corinne Post, Noushi Rahman & Cathleen McQuillen, "From Board Composition to Corporate Environmental Performance Through Sustainability-Themed Alliances" (2014) 130 J Business Ethics 423; Lin Liao, Le Luo & Qingliang Tang, "Gender diversity, board independence, environmental committee and greenhouse gas disclosure" (2015) 47:4 British Accounting Rev 409; Aaron A Dhir, *Challenging Boardroom Homogeneity: Corporate Law, Governance & Diversity* (Cambridge, UK: Cambridge University Press, 2015) at 118–29 (noting improvements in decision-making processes and risk mitigation with increased gender diversity).

92   Irene Lynch Fannon, "'A Toad We Have to Swallow': Perceptions and Participation of Women in Business and the Implications for Sustainability" in Irene Fannon & Beate Sjafell, eds, *Creating Corporate Sustainability: Gender as an Agent for Change* (Cambridge, UK: Cambridge University Press, 2018) 114 at 129.

93   *Ibid* at 123–24.

94   Kim Willey, "Bringing Canadian Women on Board: A Behavioural Economics Perspective on Whether Public Reporting of Gender Diversity Will Alter the Male-Dominated Composition of Canadian Public Company Boards and Senior Management" (2017) 29:1 CJWL 182 at 183, 191.

95   WGBHR, *Gender dimensions, supra* note 35, Annex at para 2(c).

96   Walid Ben-Amar, Millicent Chang & Philip McIlkenny, "Board Gender Diversity and Corporate Response to Sustainability Initiatives: Evidence from the Carbon Disclosure Project" (2017) 142 J Business Ethics 369.

public companies through mandatory transparency.[97] CoE is preferred in Canada, Australia and the United Kingdom, because its goal is to increase transparency and disclosure to widely dispersed shareholders.[98] These soft law measures, allowing parties to disclose their strategies and activities, are considered the preferred regulatory tool to gradually, but steadily, increase diversity through various market practices and mutual understanding of needs.[99] Companies remain able to not comply. The only obligation is to explain the non-compliance in order to convince the outside world that being non-compliant is as appropriate as complying.[100] CoE, problematically, often follows this one-size-fits-all approach.[101] This contributes to a lack of dialogue between management and shareholders about diversity: "shareholders and investors are predominantly focused on short-term prospects and are diverted from evaluating the potential positive long-term effects."[102]

Securities law is predicated on disclosure of material information.[103] Investors can make informed decisions if they possess all material information about a company.[104] Materiality, to which disclosure obligations are oriented, is subject to a great deal of academic debate and is traditionally viewed as information that a reasonable investor would view as relevant to making an investment decision.[105] Companies are confronting a "disclosure dilemma," in that too much information can be as bad as too little.[106]

Regulatory authorities are attempting to balance the requirements of disclosure of board composition. The Ontario Securities Commission (OSC), Canada's largest provincial regulator, adopted its CoE disclosure model in 2014, which was subsequently adopted by most (but not all) other provinces.[107] In order to improve the relationship between firms and shareholders, the Canadian CoE model requires public disclosure documents to address compliance with a range of diversity initiatives or explain non-compliance.[108] NI 58-101 focuses on five disclosure areas, including targets and policies of identifying, nominating and selecting women on boards and as executive officers, term limits or other mechanisms of board renewal.[109]

97   Jean-Christophe Duhamel, "'Comply or Explain' Approach as a Pascalian Wager" (2015) 5:3 Accounting, Economics & L 289 at 290.

98   Konstantinos Sergakis, "Deconstruction and Reconstruction of the 'Comply or Explain' Principle in EU Capital Markets" (2015) 5:3 Accounting, Economics & L 233.

99   *Ibid* at 236.

100   Duhamel, *supra* note 97 at 290.

101   Sergakis, *supra* note 98 at 255.

102   Duhamel, *supra* note 97 at 291.

103   Kurt Schulzke & Gerlinde Berger-Walliser, "Towards a Unified Theory of Materiality in Securities Law" (2017) 56 Colum J Transnat'l L 6 at 8.

104   Alison Miller, "Navigating the Disclosure Dilemma: Corporate Illegality and the Federal Securities Laws" (2014) 102 Georgetown L Rev 1647 at 1652.

105   Schulzke & Berger-Walliser, *supra* note 103 at 8, 9.

106   Miller, *supra* note 104 at 1649, 1653.

107   Ontario Securities Commission (OSC), *Amendment Instrument for National Instrument 58-101, Disclosure of Corporate Governance Practices 1* (11 December 2014).

108   OSC, *National Instrument 58-101, Corporate Governance Disclosure* (17 November 2015), ss 11–15; Sir Adrian Cadbury, *Report of the Committee on the Financial Aspects of Corporate Governance* (London, UK: Gee, 1992) [Cadbury Report] at 2.8; Maria Elisabeth Sturm, "Corporate Governance in the EU and U.S.: Comply-or-Explain Versus Rule" (2016) European Union Law Working Papers No 16, Stanford-Vienna Transatlantic Technology Law Forum at 9.

109   *Ibid*; see also CSA, "Report on Fourth Staff Review", *supra* note 68 at 11.

Despite the implementation of CoE in Canadian securities law, the federal government determined that variations on this approach should be implemented in federal corporate law.[110] Bill C-25 received royal assent on May 1, 2018, and includes new diversity disclosure requirements, consistent with CoE.[111] Federally incorporated "prescribed corporations" (defined as distributing corporations under the CBCA,[112] these are reporting issuers, or publicly traded companies, and have filed a prospectus with a provincial securities commission)[113] must disclose the number of designated persons, percentage of board, whether there is a written policy in respect of diversity, and whether there are targets for representation.[114] The changes in Bill C-25 include the requirement to disclose the board's gender diversity, as well as board members with visible minority, Aboriginal or disability status.[115] The amendments do not mandate a change in policies or adopting specific targets ("comply"), but if the corporation does not have policies, it needs to state why ("explain").

Unfortunately, only prescribed corporations are required to comply.[116] Thus, only publicly traded companies registered under the CBCA will be subject to these new disclosure requirements.[117]

Many are unsatisfied with the updates.[118] The New Democratic Party voted against Bill C-25 on the grounds that the bill did not go far enough in advancing diversity rights.[119] The new CBCA regulations indicate that the information respecting gender diversity required by NI 58-101 needs to be disclosed at every annual shareholder meeting, which basically means that the CoE model is duplicated. The scope of diversity is broader than in NI 58-101,[120] however, and appears more consistent with a human rights approach and justification.

CoE is the standard of corporate governance in Australia and the United Kingdom.[121] Introduced in 1992 by the Cadbury Report,[122] and implemented in the Stewardship Code,[123] CoE has been

---

110   Bill C-25, *supra* note 2; Nova Scotia, *Companies Act*, RSNS, c 81; Ontario, *Business Corporations Act*, RSO 1990, c B16. For considerations when selecting a jurisdiction, see McInnes Cooper, "5 Key Considerations When Deciding Between Federal & Provincial Incorporation", online: <www.mcinnescooper.com/publications/weighing-the-options-5-key-considerations-when-deciding-between-federal-provincial-incorporations/>.

111   Bill C-25, *supra* note 2; OSC, *supra* note 108; Lawson Lundell, "Bill C-25: A Catalyst for Corporate Diversity in Canada?" (14 May 2018), online: <www.lawsonlundell.com/the-business-law-blog/bill-c-25-a-catalyst-for-corporate-diversity-in-canada>.

112   *Canada Business Corporations Act*, RSC 1985, c C-44, s 2.

113   *Regulations Amending*, *supra* note 2, s 2(1).

114   *Ibid*, s 172.1; Steven E Salterio, Joan ED Conrod & Regan N Schmidt, "Canadian Evidence of Adherence to 'Comply or Explain' Corporate Governance Codes: An International Comparison" (2013) 12:1 Accounting Perspectives 23; Yan Luo & Steven E Salterio, "Governance Quality in a 'Comply or Explain' Governance Disclosure Regime" (2014) 22:6 Corporate Governance 460.

115   *Employment Equity Act*, *supra* note 3.

116   Bill C-25, *supra* note 2, s 172.1.

117   Venture issuers are not exempt. See Rima Ramchandani & Glen Johnson, Torys LLP, News Release, "CBCA Reforms Receive Royal Assent" (3 May 2018); *Regulations Amending*, *supra* note 2, s 2.

118   "Vote #348 on June 21st, 2017" re Bill C-25 ["Vote #348"], online: *Open Parliament* <https://openparliament.ca/votes/42-1/348/>; Parliament of Canada, "Bill C-25", online: <https://openparliament.ca/bills/42-1/C-25/>.

119   "Vote #348", *supra* note 118; Parliament of Canada, *supra* note 118.

120   Caroline Moreau, "Women on boards and the 'comply or explain' rule", *Canadian Lawyer* (27 February 2017), online: <www.canadianlawyermag.com/article/women-on-boards-and-the-comply-or-explain-rule-3542/>.

121   Andrew Keay, "Comply or explain in corporate governance codes: in need of greater regulatory oversight?" (2014) 34:2 LS 279; Willey, *supra* note 94 at 193.

122   Cadbury Report, *supra* note 108 at 4.2, 4.7.

123   Financial Reporting Council, *The UK Stewardship Code* (2012), online: <www.frc.org.uk/getattachment/d67933f9-ca38-4233-b603-3d24b2f62c5f/UK-Stewardship-Code-(September-2012).pdf>; Keay, *supra* note 121 at 282.

partly responsible for increasing board representation of women on the FTSE.[124] Unfortunately, some UK firms neither comply nor explain their non-compliance, and the regulations do not give any regulatory power to induce action.[125] Australia has slightly more onerous provisions.[126] Yet, in essence, authorities regulate on whether a statement was made, not on the statement's substantive merit.[127] Securities regulators, in general, do not opine on the adequacy or merits of an investment or solution, only whether the broad public interest is considered.[128]

Quota Systems

Countries that have instituted mandatory quotas have higher levels of female board representation, and have achieved these levels more rapidly, than countries that have opted for CoE.[129] Belgium, France, Germany, Iceland, Italy and Spain have all implemented stringent quotas, while India has implemented a weak quota system.[130] Germany requires 50 percent female representation, which was set in 2018, and also requires 3,500 medium-sized businesses to set their own targets to increase the number of women.[131] Quotas do work, at least in the short term, and can help legitimize female representation in the long term.[132]

There are drawbacks with quotas, including companies de-listing, going private or registering in another country.[133] There have been accusations of the promotion of "golden skirts" — women who hold a number of directorships, or figurehead directors promoted due to their celebrity status.[134] The cascading effect also has not materialized, as had been promised.[135] Quotas may result in "tokenism," which is based on a suspicion that a woman is only appointed for legal purposes rather than for merit, causing a host of problems, including alienation and assimilation of the female director (that is, the director is not seen as an individual, but rather as a stereotype). The CSA Roundtable noted that "even when you have quotas in place and the numbers have risen quickly at the board level, there actually hasn't been the knock on effect, the cascading effect, into the executive teams that they had hoped for. Now it's possible that because Norway, for instance, kind of had to hollow out the female executives to move them up to the board that we have not seen the next generation of women come up, so maybe we need to give it more time."[136]

---

124 Catalyst, *Gender Diversity on Boards in Canada: Recommendations for Accelerating Progress* (Ontario: Catalyst & Province of Ontario, 2016) at 25; *FTSE Women*, *supra* note 58 at 25, 30.

125 Keay, *supra* note 121 at 282; Sridhar Arcot, Valentina Bruno & Antoine Faure-Grimaud, "Corporate Governance in the UK: Is the Comply-or-Explain Approach Working?" (2010) 30:2 Intl Rev L & Econ 193 at 194.

126 Catalyst, *supra* note 124 at 26, 30.

127 Keay, *supra* note 121 at 285.

128 *In the Matter of 3IQ Corp and the Bitcoin Fund*, 3iQ Corp (Re), 2019 ONSEC 37.

129 *Ibid*.

130 Willey, *supra* note 94 at 191.

131 *Ibid* at 192.

132 Cathrine Seierstad, "Beyond the Business Case: The Need for Both Utility and Justice Rationales for Increasing the Share of Women on Boards" (2016) 24:4 Corporate Governance 390.

133 Terjesen, Aguilera & Lorenz, *supra* note 60 at 248.

134 *Ibid*.

135 CSA, "Roundtable Discussion", *supra* note 62 at 35.

136 *Ibid* at 35.

Norway, in 2004, implemented a quota system.[137] The Norwegian stock market is small, with approximately 190 companies.[138] They do not have a large mining sector, so comparisons to Canada and Australia are difficult. Four of the largest six companies, representing 46.1 percent of the Norsk Index, are significantly owned by the government.[139] Canada's stock market is widely held, such that "investors are not likely to have the same influence on those companies."[140] This is also true for the United Kingdom, where "the dispersed ownership structure that exists in the UK can create hindrances to effective organization of shareholders so as to hold directors accountable."[141]

Making comparisons between countries is likely to overlook the myriad of complexities and nuances that cannot be fully assessed in a cursory analysis. No two countries share identical legislative or governance frameworks, board structures or initiatives to help drive female representation on listed company boards. The varying size of a country's index makes comparisons difficult. One can simply observe that CoE and quotas recognize the need for gender-balanced boards, and many firms are now implementing processes to achieve greater numbers of women on boards and in executive positions.[142]

Conclusions and Recommendations for Future Law and Policy Reform

The problem of a lack of diversity, and in particular gender diversity, on Canadian corporate mining boards is multi-faceted. First, the problem represents a failure of women's empowerment and equality, and a failure to respect the equal rights of women to participate in economic activity in the mining industry. Solutions to the problem conceptualized in this way might include implementing quotas in university engineering programs to ensure that sufficient women are educated and ready to enter the mining industry, work their way up to senior management and eventually join a corporate board. However, a second way to view the problem is from the perspective of women and girls who are subject to gender-based human rights violations as a result of industrial mining practices. This perspective might suggest that replicating the educational backgrounds of those already in positions of power within the mining industry would not serve to help management and boards to understand the problems facing women, whether as employees or as members of communities affected by mining. Could it be that part of the problem is with the kinds of educational expectations that exist for corporate board members?

---

137 Dhir, *supra* note 91; Amanda K Packel, "Government Intervention into Board Composition: Gender quotas in Norway and Diversity Disclosures in the United States", Book Review of *Challenging Boardroom Homogeneity: Corporate Law, Governance & Diversity* by Aaron A Dhir (2016) 21 Stan JL Bus & Fin 192 at 205; Margarethe Wiersema & Marie Louise Mors, "What Board Directors Really Think of Gender Quotas" (14 November 2016), online (blog): *Harvard Business Review* <hbr.org/2016/11/what-board-directors-really-think-of-gender-quotas>.

138 Oslo Børs, "Facts and figures May 2018", online: <www.oslobors.no/ob_eng/Oslo-Boers/Statistics/Facts-and-figures/2018-Facts-and-figures-May-2018>.

139 Oslo Børs, "Benchmark Index Market Capitalization", online: <www.oslobors.no/ob_eng/markedsaktivitet/#/details/OSEBX.OSE/overview>; Telenor, "About Us", online: <www.telenor.com/about-us/our-history/>.

140 CSA, "Roundtable Discussion", *supra* note 62 at 39.

141 Keay, *supra* note 121 at 287.

142 CSA, "Roundtable Discussion", *supra* note 62 at 30.

The excuses for a lack of women in boardrooms point to many factors, ranging from the sublime to the ridiculous.[143] In Canada, the top reasons include that more women would compromise the principles of meritocracy; that more women may not result in the best candidates being selected; that corporations frequently have a small number of directors, with low turnover; and that existing policies are ineffective or arbitrary.[144] It must be acknowledged that in the mining sector, there may be differences between junior mining companies and senior producing companies, differences that require further study.

The idea that it is important to encourage more women in business[145] and engineering[146] is well accepted. Universities might consider following Engineers Canada's lead by mandating at least 30 percent of all types of engineering and computer science classes be female by no later than 2030. To date, there are no quotas in Canadian universities, but some people, such as the Institution of Engineering and Technology's first female president, Naomi Climer, have called on the engineering sector to bring in quotas.[147] Yet humans exhibit boundedly rational behaviour in decision making (that is, we often make poor, but predictable, decision-making errors).[148] This bias results in better treatment of "in"-group members (males) than members of stigmatized or "out" groups (women). This may also result in the use of heuristics, or mental shortcuts, pursuant to which certain attributes (in this case, being male) are seen as better suited to board and senior management positions, creating a conjunction fallacy that white males with experience (in law or business) make good candidates. The negative effect of such bias creates what behavioural economists term a "blind spot problem."[149] This suggests that the solution may not be as simple as having more women in STEM programs, but also that men with power need to value expertise from other disciplines that better support the human rights-respecting and environmentally conscious decision making that is essential for mining sustainability. This is particularly so once intersectional dimensions are considered, and the value of Indigenous knowledge, including gendered dimensions of such knowledge, is recognized.[150]

Women have a positive effect on the bottom line, and increasing the number of women on boards is correlated with increased attention to environmental and social responsibility, and better decision making. Thus, a second recommendation is for more active institutional and retail investor involvement.[151] State Street Global Advisors will engage in active dialogues with companies and board leadership on gender diversity, and if companies fail to take action to increase the

---

143   Kevin Rawlinson, "FTSE firms' excuses for lack of women in boardrooms pitiful and patronising", *The Guardian* (31 May 2018), online: <www.theguardian.com/business/2018/may/31/pitiful-views-on-women-in-boardrooms-permeate-ftse-firms.

144   MacDougall & Valley, *2017 Diversity Disclosure Practices*, *supra* note 55 at 22; MacDougall & Valley, *2018 Diversity Disclosure Practices*, *supra* note 56 at 28.

145   Ryan Derousseau, "The MBA degree and the astronomical rise in CEO pay", *Fortune* (18 December 2014), online: <http://fortune.com/2014/12/18/mba-ceo-pay-connection/>.

146   Stefano Hatfield, "Where are all the female engineers?", *The Independent* (29 June 2015), online: <www.independent.co.uk/voices/comment/where-are-all-the-female-engineers-9571044.html>.

147   Edd Gent, "Would quotas bring more women into engineering?" *Engineering & Technology* (9 November 2015), online: <https://eandt.theiet.org/content/articles/2015/11/would-quotas-bring-more-women-into-engineering/>; Harriet Minter, "Want a plan for how to get more women into engineering? It's easy", *The Guardian* (9 October 2015), online: <www.theguardian.com/women-in-leadership/2015/oct/09/want-a-plan-for-how-to-get-more-women-into-engineering-its-easy>.

148   Willey, *supra* note 94 at 200.

149   *Ibid* at 195.

150   Morales, *supra* note 18.

151   Sergakis, *supra* note 98 at 236.

number of women on their boards, they will vote against the chairs of the boards' nominating and/or governance committees.[152] Bank of Montreal, a large financial institution, launched the BMO Women in Leadership Fund to invest in companies promoting "gender diverse leadership environments."[153] RBC Royal Bank, Canada's largest financial institution, launched the RBC Vision Women's Leadership MSCI Canada Index ETF, focusing on companies that demonstrate commitment to gender diversity as part of their CSR strategy.[154] The Pax Ellevate Global Women's Leadership Fund allows investors to close the gender gap by investing in companies that value women as leaders.[155] This is the first mutual fund that invests in the highest-rated companies in the world for advancing women through gender diversity.[156] And in 2020, Goldman Sachs announced it would no longer take companies public if they have an all-white, all-male board, and will force an increase to two diverse directors in 2021.[157] If Canadian financial institutions follow suit, as arguably they should, this will have a major positive impact on the mining sector. Thus, it will be the financial institutions themselves that implement a quota system, rather than waiting for a government to bring in regulation. It also sends the signal that a single change in board diversity membership is not enough to have a meaningful impact.

Another issue is the lack of vacancies. Implementing term limits and mandating at least one female candidate for all board and CEO vacancies is recommended.[158] If a woman is not selected by the end of this process, the board must be satisfied that there is an objective reason to support this outcome. The board should also have a diversity and/or inclusion committee.[159] While the Goldman Sachs initiative currently applies to initial public offerings, a similar policy for follow-on offerings (secondary stock sales, debt issuances and others) will put pressure on firms to enact term limits, as the only options for the company are to increase the board size or to rotate board vacancies.

A fourth recommendation is to create a new model with soft targets, stretch goals and hard floors. The 30 by 30 program is an example. It is a soft target, but as soon as it is reached, it becomes a mandatory floor. More work is required for several industry sectors, especially mining, and the work on gender parity on boards must go much further than publicly traded corporations and include privately held and state-owned enterprises.[160] The CBCA amendments do not go far

152 Amy Whyte, "State Street to Turn Up the Heat on All-Male Boards", *Institutional Investor* (27 September 2018), online: <www.institutionalinvestor.com/article/b1b4fh28ys3mr9/State-Street-to-Turn-Up-the-Heat-on-All-Male-Boards>; Rob Kozlowski, "SSGA plans on increasing efforts to get women on company boards", *Pensions & Investments* (27 September 2018), online: <www.pionline.com/article/20180927/ONLINE/180929890/ssga-plans-on-increasing-efforts-to-get-women-on-company-boards>.

153 BMO Asset Management Inc, "BMO Women in Leadership Fund, Fund Facts" (2018); Morningstar, "BMO Women in Leadership Fund", online: <http://quote.morningstar.ca/quicktakes/fund/f_ca.aspx?t=0P00017TVN&region=CAN&culture=en-CA>.

154 RBC Asset Management Inc, "RBC Vision Women's Leadership MSCI Canada Index ETF", online: <http://etfinfo.rbcgam.com/exchange-traded-funds/fund-pages/rldr.fs>.

155 Pax World Funds, "Pax Ellevate Global Women's Leadership Fund", online: <https://paxworld.com/funds/pax-ellevate-global-womens-leadership-fund/>.

156 *Ibid.*

157 Jeff Green, "Goldman to refuse IPOs if all directors are white, straight men", *BNN Bloomberg* (23 January 2020), online: <www.bnnbloomberg.ca/goldman-to-refuse-ipos-if-all-directors-are-white-straight-men-1.1379006>.

158 Catalyst, *supra* note 124 at 35.

159 *Ibid* at 38.

160 Not all private companies are small, and solutions are equally applicable to medium and large-scale enterprises. Statscan, "Study: Representation of Women on Boards of Directors, 2016", *The Daily* (7 May 2019), online: <www150.statcan.gc.ca/n1/daily-quotidien/190507/dq190507a-eng.htm>; Industry Canada, "Key Small Business Statistics — January 2019 — SME research and statistics", online: <www.ic.gc.ca/eic/site/061.nsf/eng/h_03090.html>.

enough. Private company directors reported similar proportions of women on their boards as public company directors.[161] The WGBHR highlights the need for state-owned enterprises to play a leading role in gender diversity.[162] The Canada Pension Plan Investment Board created a Global Gender Diversity Voting Practice, to vote against the chair responsible for director nominations if the board has no women directors.[163] Internationally, the International Organization of Securities Commissions as well as Principles for Responsible Investment created guides for diversity in 2016 and 2017, respectively, yet no concrete actions have yet been taken.[164]

Future amendments must take a tougher stance in setting normative standards (for example, 30 percent of boards should be filled with women by 2020) and require compliance (or detailed reasons and penalties for non-compliance). Canadian securities commissions must communicate results and educate issuers on the very existence of an unconscious bias. Quotas may have merit, and this method of "debiasing law" should be effectively communicated to the market, if voluntary measures are ineffective.[165]

Finally, Patricia Devine's studies in the context of racial bias show that stereotypes can be activated regardless of a person's beliefs.[166] Having more women on nominating committees and represented as idealized board imagery could actually undermine the unconscious gender bias prevalent in the industry.[167] While mandatory disclosures seem like a valid solution to implicit bias, there are many shortcomings of mandatory disclosure, such as raising trust levels.[168]

In conclusion, there are many possible avenues to pursue in order to address the lack of gender diversity in Canada's mining sector. Among these are arguments for and against educational requirements due to conscious and unconscious bias. Women who do make it to board levels tend to have more advanced levels of education than their male counterparts, yet women have low enrolment in the kinds of degree programs (specifically engineering and master of business administration [MBA] programs) that are seen as most important to get them onto boards. But is this a cause or an effect? That is, is part of the problem that MBAs and STEM backgrounds are seen as important for boards? Is education needed to change the perception of what is valuable on boards? Further research is required on this subject.

Canadian law has yet to take seriously Canada's international law obligations to prevent and remedy violations of the human rights of women and girls arising from resource extraction. Women's empowerment through board and management diversity initiatives may be a crucial piece of the solution.

---

161   Catalyst, *supra* note 124 at 15.

162   WGBHR, *Gender dimensions, supra* note 35, Guiding Principle 4.

163   Canada Pension Plan Investment Board (CPPIB), News Release, "Canada Pension Plan Investment Board to Increase Board Diversity Advocacy" (21 December 2018), online: <www.cppib.com/en/public-media/headlines/2018/cppib-increase-board-diversity-advocacy/>; CPPIB, News Release, "How CPPIB is advocating for more women on boards" (25 October 2018), online: <www.cppib.com/en/public-media/headlines/2018/how-cppib-advocating-more-women-boards/>.

164   Principles for Responsible Investment, *Engaging on Director Nominations: An Investor Guide* (2017) at 11; International Organization of Securities Commissions, *Report on Corporate Governance* (2016) FR10/16 at 19.

165   Willey, *supra* note 94 at 210.

166   *Ibid* at 197.

167   *Ibid* at 203.

168   *Ibid*.

12

VOLUNTARY CODES OF CORPORATE GOVERNANCE
Evolution and Implications

Cally Jordan

Introduction

As a tool of modern corporate governance, there is nothing as ubiquitous as the corporate governance code. In the 1990s, corporate governance codes, voluntary for the most part, popped up like mushrooms everywhere, from Albania to Zimbabwe. To understand the significance of this phenomenon, it is useful to consider the reasons for this explosive proliferation that began nearly 30 years ago, and how the codes have evolved in the intervening years.

The proliferation of voluntary codes of corporate governance marked the internationalization of corporate governance. At the epicentre was the United Kingdom's Cadbury Report,[1] which in turn informed a set of international standards, the Organisation for Economic Co-operation and Development (OECD) Principles of Corporate Governance, which first appeared in 1999. A complex dynamic between domestic initiatives, rooted in local circumstances, and international standards, was thus created.

---

1   Sir Adrian Cadbury, *Report of the Committee on the Financial Aspects of Corporate Governance* (London, UK: Gee, 1992) [Cadbury Report].

Since neither Albania nor Zimbabwe would appear to have been in desperate need of a corporate governance code, the rapid spread of the codes, at least initially, was likely driven by supply rather than demand. Voluntary codes of corporate governance were adopted in different places for different reasons. Despite their superficial similarities, the codes have not produced the predicted convergence to one global set of best practices. Over time, they have evolved differently in various places in the world, producing, not surprisingly, varying results. This chapter looks at the evolution of voluntary codes of corporate governance and their internationalization, before considering some of the implications.

Evolution of the Voluntary Code of Corporate Governance

It all started innocuously enough: an industry committee struck in the wake of a spate of corporate scandals. But even before the final report appeared, it had captured public attention in the United Kingdom, much to the astonishment of its authors. The modern debate on corporate governance had begun.

The Cadbury Report

A committee of the London Stock Exchange, the UK Financial Reporting Council and the UK accountancy profession published their report, *The Financial Aspects of Corporate Governance*, on December 1, 1992. The report quickly became known by the name of the committee's chairman, Sir Adrian Cadbury.

The committee had begun as a modest exercise in response to several high-profile cases of corporate fraud and director malfeasance. In particular, the dramatic disappearance of Jan Ludvik Hoch off his yacht in the Canary Islands on November 5, 1991, had captured headlines and fuelled public anger in the United Kingdom. He had simply vanished, as well as funds from the employee pension plans of the companies he operated. Born in the former Czechoslovakia, he was known in the United Kingdom as Robert Maxwell and held sway over a newspaper empire. At the time of his disappearance, there was much speculation as to what had occurred. Did he slip? Did he commit suicide? Was he pushed? Or, perhaps, in a James Bond moment, spirited away by helicopter to a new life in an unknown location?[2] This was the stuff of tabloid news and caught the imagination of the public in the United Kingdom.

To the surprise of Sir Adrian Cadbury and his colleagues, the Cadbury Report was an unlikely bestseller: "When our Committee was formed...neither our title nor our work programme seemed framed to catch the headlines. In the event, the Committee has become the focus of far more attention than I ever envisaged....The harsh economic climate is partly responsible, since it has exposed company reports and accounts to unusually close scrutiny. It is, however, the

---

2   According to Wikipedia, this was quite literally a James Bond moment. The disappearance of Robert Maxwell inspired the end of the eighteenth Bond film, *Tomorrow Never Dies*, in which the villain, a newspaper magnate who tried to take over the world, is said to disappear off his yacht. "Tomorrow Never Dies", online: *Wikipedia* <en.wikipedia.org/wiki/Tomorrow_Never_Dies>. On a more serious note, the BBC reported that Maxwell's body was recovered from "the sea off the Canary Islands after he had been reported missing from his private yacht." See "Robert Maxwell: A Profile", *BBC News World Edition* (29 March 2001). Likewise, *The Guardian* published a report that Maxwell's body was found after being missing for (at most) one day. See Ben Laurance et al, "Maxwell's body found in sea", *The Guardian* (6 November 1991).

zeal. The OECD Principles 1999 appeared just as the Financial Stability Forum (FSF, the predecessor to the current Financial Stability Board) was established and as the Financial Sector Assessment Program (FSAP) was launched by the IMF and the World Bank. The IMF had been caught flat-footed by the Asian financial crisis and much criticized. The FSAP exercises, whereby the financial systems of countries were benchmarked and rated, country by country, against sets of international financial standards, were designed to act as both prophylactic and early warning system.[21] The FSF formally adopted 12 sets of international financial standards for this purpose, the OECD Principles 1999 among them. The book of international financial standards in hand, small armies of international bureaucrats fanned out across the globe to spread the word.[22]

The exercise was a textbook demonstration of the "transplant effect," highlighting the difficulties associated with dropping assumption-ridden "international" standards into non-native legal environments. The OECD Principles 1999, being inspired by the Cadbury Report and the US Revised Model Business Corporations Act, were not easily adapted to many of the countries in which they were introduced. For one thing, corporate law and governance structures were based on different principles, such as internal audit functions and dual board structures. Voluntary codes implemented through stock exchange listing rules would be of limited effectiveness because very few countries possessed a stock exchange with the heft and persuasiveness of the London Stock Exchange. Despite these shortcomings, the benchmarking exercises continued apace. The authority and influence of the international organizations justified the transplantation — or more coercively, the imposition — of handy Anglo-American legal concepts and models around the world, irrespective of their appropriateness or likely effectiveness. In the end, Cadbury-esque corporate governance codes appeared nearly everywhere.[23]

Corporate Governance Codes in the Wake of Cadbury

It is important not to lose sight of the ostensible purpose of corporate governance codes: deterrence of corporate managerial malfeasance. It is not at all obvious that voluntary codes of corporate governance served this purpose, either in the United Kingdom or elsewhere, but the momentum to create a set of global best practices in the interests of convergence and harmonization proved irresistible, irrespective of outcome. In the immediate wake of Cadbury and the OECD Principles, the best practices they put forward manifested themselves in a variety of ways, and with dubious outcomes.

---

21 See Cally E Jordan, "The Dangerous Illusion of International Financial Standards and the Legacy of the Financial Stability Forum" (2011) 12 San Diego Intl LJ 333.

22 In January 1999, as a newly engaged World Bank staff member, I was sent, OECD Principles 1999 in hand, to Indonesia to promote the adoption of the principles as part of the crisis resolution team. A classic confrontation of legal cultures ensued in meetings with leading legal practitioners in Jakarta. What did the OECD Principles 1999 mean when referring to "directors," since Indonesia had a European-style dual board structure? Why would you need independent directors (and on what board) in a dual board structure? What is the role of an audit committee (and what is it a committee of) where there is an internal audit board? How do these principles apply to state-owned enterprises or majority-controlled listed corporations?

23 By one count, and not an exhaustive one at that, there are nearly 100 countries, regions and organizations that have adopted corporate governance codes. For a list of national corporate governance codes and reports, see European Corporate Governance Institute (ECGI), "Codes", online: <https://ecgi.global/content/codes>.

China: Corporate Governance with Chinese Characteristics

China was an early adopter. Its Code of Corporate Governance for Listed Companies[24] appeared in 2001. The Code of Corporate Governance adopted "commonly accepted standards in international corporate governance" and followed the structure of the OECD Principles 1999. There the similarities ended for the most part. This code was hardly voluntary, taking the form of a regulatory decree. Despite the superficial similarity in organization to the OECD Principles 1999, the content of the code was quite different. It contained statements such as: "assets of a listed company belong to the company." The company as a legal institution was brand new in China, the first modern companies act having come into effect only six years previously. The major purpose to be served by that legislation was "corporatization" of state-owned enterprises so as to permit partial flotation on domestic and foreign stock exchanges (but with the state remaining firmly in control). Again, despite superficial (and quite deliberate) resemblances to English and European companies, these Chinese companies were very different beasts under the surface.

Rapid change is the norm in modern China, and by 2006 there was a new, more sophisticated companies law in place, adapted to a wider set of purposes. The new legislation included a specific corporate governance section, entitled "Special Provisions for the Organizational Structure of Listed Companies," which contained some of the international best practices then in vogue.

The inappropriateness of dropping into China, in 2001, the OECD Principles 1999 and Cadbury-style corporate governance code developed for the commercial environment in the modern City of London is pretty obvious. Equally, by 2006, serious questions were arising as to some of the so-called international best practices. It appears that China was deliberately adopting at least the semblance of the prevailing international corporate governance orthodoxy to suggest that the domestic market had become aware of and taken up the corporate governance debate. China was "signalling" to international capital markets, especially US institutional investors. The existence of a corporate governance code purporting to be in accordance with "commonly accepted standards in international corporate governance" would raise a little red flag attracting the momentary attention of the international capital markets. However, as an effective mechanism of promoting better governance in the corporate sector domestically, the measures were irrelevant.

In addition to invoking the signalling effect, there may also have been a certain amount of gaming of the corporate governance ratings exercises. In the context of the FSAPs conducted by the IMF and the World Bank, and in various privately conducted corporate governance rating exercises, the OECD Principles 1999 (and subsequent revisions) figure prominently. Curtis Milhaupt and Katharina Pistor recount an anecdote about Chinese companies law reforms designed to score points and improve ratings in these exercises.[25]

---

24   China Securities Regulatory Commission, *Code of Corporate Governance for Listed Companies* (7 January 2001), online: <www.Csrc.Gov.Cn/Pub/Csrc_En/Newsfacts/Release/200708/t20070810_69223.htm>.

25   Curtis J Milhaupt & Katharina Pistor, *Law and Capitalism: What Corporate Crises Reveal about Legal Systems and Economic Development around the World* (Chicago: University of Chicago Press, 2008) ("We were amused by a scholar from Beijing who began a presentation about China's new Company Law by highlighting the fact that it scores significantly higher on the investor protection index of the La Porta et al than the law it replaced. But he noted a bit wistfully that the index had been recently updated and that the new law would no longer score as high" at 248, n 18).

Germany: Corporate Governance as Political Gesture

Some corporate governance mechanisms, voluntary codes among them, may in fact be designed to be ineffective, a strategy not restricted to developing economies. Deliberately introducing an ineffective but internationally recognized corporate governance delivery mechanism, such as a voluntary code, may permit political interests to divert attention from approaches that could be more effective but also more disruptive to the cosy corporate and political status quo.

The German corporate governance code introduced in 2002 provides an example. Justice Minister Herta Daubler-Gmelin "argued that while the code contained no sanctions for non-compliance, 'the capital market will provide very effective sanctions' for those that chose to ignore it."[26] A voluntary code, introduced not by industry but by government initiative, was dropped into one of the leading European codal countries. The *Financial Times* editorial writer was skeptical at the time of the voluntary code's introduction, stating flatly that it would do "little to nudge German corporate governance towards a more investor-friendly model."[27] This skepticism was borne out by subsequent events: three years later, the voluntary code was considered "a failure" and plans were afoot to replace it with written legislation.[28]

It is likely that in introducing a voluntary code of corporate governance, at the time that it did, Germany too was signalling, not to the international capital markets, but rather to its neighbours in the European Union, that it would engage in the corporate governance dialogue. German interests in protecting Volkswagen from unwanted takeover attempts had been credited with the defeat of the proposed Takeover Directive in the European Parliament. It had taken nearly 13 years for the proposed directive to make it as far as the Parliament, where its approval had been more or less taken for granted. The wasted time and effort were a source of much criticism directed toward Germany. It may well be that the subsequent speedy introduction of this voluntary corporate governance code was an attempt to make amends. That the voluntary code would likely change little in the political and commercial status quo may have been a collateral advantage.

Italy: Inadvertent Chaos

There is certainly reason to believe that, for different reasons, both China and Germany were advertently making use of the implementation of various internationally recognized corporate governance mechanisms in a calculated manner. Italy, on the other hand, was engaging in a somewhat uncoordinated flurry of legislative and other activity, in response to the debates raging internationally on corporate governance. Alternative models of corporate governance were being created under Italian law. According to Federico Ghezzi and Marco Ventoruzzo

---

26 Sven Clausen & Hugh Williamson, "Berlin Announces Voluntary Business Code", *Financial Times* (27 February 2002) at 7.

27 "German Takeover", *Financial Times* (27 February 2002) ("Common rules for corporate takeovers have become a test for Europe's capacity to reform itself. Thanks to the conservatism of German business and the refusal of the Berlin government to look beyond narrow political interests, is one that Europe is likely to fail. Despite the eye-catching call for greater disclosure of executive pay, Germany's new voluntary code, published yesterday, does little to nudge German corporate governance towards a more investor-friendly model" at 12).

28 See Patrick Jenkins & Hugh Williamson, "Executives Under Pressure on Pay", *Financial Times* (19 January 2005) ("A group of 21 Social Democrat members of the German parliament will today table a draft bill to force company executives to disclose details of their remuneration and bring to an end a deep-rooted culture of secrecy in the country's boardrooms. The bill, drafted in consultation with corporate governance expert Theodor Baums, comes in response to what the legislators see as the failure of a three-year-old voluntary code to prompt disclosure" at 16).

at Bocconi University in Milan, by 2006 Italy was experiencing both "the good and evil of the 'globalization' of corporate governance."[29] The result, according to Ghezzi and Ventoruzzo, was a "Tower of Babel."

Italy presented a striking illustration of the collision of Anglo-American corporate governance mechanisms with a continental European legal system, and the potentially deleterious results of indiscriminate mixing and matching of legal concepts drawn from very different systems in an attempt to demonstrate adherence to international best practice. According to Ghezzi and Ventoruzzo, duplicative and conflicting rules in certain areas generated uncertainty. The agency problem addressed by Anglo-American corporate governance mechanisms was different in Italy, as it is different in many other places in the world. Because of the predominance of majority-controlled (often family-controlled) businesses, the problematic relationship was between majority and minority shareholders, not managers and widely dispersed shareholders. There was a culture of weak institutional investors. The legislative and other corporate governance initiatives in Italy were producing neither top-down harmonization nor effective regulatory competition. All in all, Ghezzi and Ventoruzzo wondered whether it was "a recipe for disaster."

Thus, in the early days of the post-Cadbury era, despite widespread adoption of international best practices, there was little evidence that these corporate governance measures were, in fact, addressing problems of managerial malfeasance.

Cadbury: Going on 30 Years

The Cadbury Report is going on 30. The first set of OECD principles, which internalized and internationalized the Cadbury Report, appeared more than 20 years ago. The debate on corporate governance struggles on, somewhat overshadowed by the 2008 global financial crisis, but relatively undiminished. The "legal origins" literature,[30] which had bolstered the practice of dropping Anglo-American legal concepts and approaches into unfamiliar terrain, has fallen into disrepute among legal scholars.[31]

Nevertheless, the Cadbury Report spawned more than 100 codes of corporate governance in countries around the world.[32] Its CoE implementation methodology pops up everywhere. Many of these codes are easy, show pieces of no practical import.[33] But rather than convergence and

---

29   Federico Ghezzi & Marco Ventoruzzo, "Boards of Directors and Audit Committees in Italian Listed Corporations", Presentation to the World Bank, February 2006 (on file with the author).

30   See Rafael La Porta et al, "Law and Finance" (1998) 106:6 J Political Economy 1113.

31   Holger Spamann, "'Law and Finance' Revisited" (2008) Harvard Law School, John M Olin Center Discussion Paper No 12 ("While follow-up papers recently appeared that use more refined indices to support the link from legal origins to investor protection postulated in LLSV [the legal origins literature]…the collapse of the results that inspired this entire line of research is at least remarkable" at 3).

32   See ECGI, *supra* note 23.

33   However, in other places, the corporate governance debate spurred real innovation and change, for example, in Brazil with the Novo Mercado, or Corporate Governance Listing Board. The introduction of the Novo Mercado premium listing board in 2001, with its novel investor protection mechanisms, appears to have had a direct impact in stimulating Brazil's then moribund capital markets. Between 1996 and 2000, there had been only three initial public offerings on the BOVESPA. In 2007, there were 64, and between 2004 and 2011, the great majority of them occurred on the Novo Mercado. The average capital raised by offerings in the three years prior to 2007 was BRL764 million, compared to BRL3.15 *billion* between 2008 and 2009. See Patrícia Pellini, "Stock exchanges as an engine for corporate governance improvements: Reaching out to non-listed companies" (Presentation delivered at the Latin American Roundtable on Corporate Governance, Peru, 30 November 2011) [unpublished], online: <www.oecd.org/dataoecd/61/17/49287485.pdf>.

conformity to international best practices, major economies such as Germany, the European Union, the United Kingdom and the United States have gone their own ways on issues of corporate governance. The OECD Principles of Corporate Governance have, arguably, lost their way.

United States

In the United States, despite a lively transatlantic dialogue on corporate governance, there was no single phenomenon comparable to the Cadbury Report. In part, this was attributable to the complexity of the corporate and legislative environment and the multitude of competing voices. Listing rules, industry practices and organizations, a heavy federal regulatory apparatus overlaying state incorporation statutes and judiciaries, the presence of vocal and powerful institutional investors such as the California Public Employees' Retirement System (known as CalPERS), and iconic personalities such as Warren Buffet ("the Sage of Omaha"), all played a part in the cacophony on corporate governance. And in 2002, the Sarbanes-Oxley Act,[34] the first major piece of federal corporate governance legislation in decades, eclipsed other efforts.

Voluntary codes of corporate governance are not of much interest in the United States. Unlike other jurisdictions in the world where voluntary codes and CoE models of corporate governance flourish, the corporate governance rules in the United States tend to be mandatory in nature and disclosure-based. The debate on corporate governance and how best to promote it grinds along nevertheless, with shareholders persistently pushing and straining for purchase on a sometimes barren and rocky landscape.

In 2010, the New York Stock Exchange commissioned yet another report on corporate governance.[35] From the introductory comments, it is obvious that it did so reluctantly, seeing no compelling need to reopen issues that had already been quite exhaustively explored in the previous decade. The global financial crisis, however, had prompted reconsideration of a wide variety of issues, corporate governance among them. The conclusion was that the "current governance system generally works well."[36] In a nod to more modern sensibilities regarding stakeholders, though, it did state that the fundamental objective of corporate governance was to promote "long term sustainable growth in value for shareholders and by extension other stakeholders."[37] This was an explicit acknowledgement by a powerful institution that shareholder wealth maximization was not the only benchmark against which to assess corporate decision making.

Most recently, in January 2019, the council of the ALI voted to launch a new project, "The Restatement of the Law on Corporate Governance," led by Edward Rock. The ALI first canvassed the subject more than 25 years ago, culminating in the 1994 publication of *Principles of the Law, Corporate Governance: Analysis and Recommendations*. These principles offered guidance for best practices in what was then a new and unfamiliar area of law. The ALI is now elevating

---

34   *Sarbanes-Oxley Act of 2002*, Pub L No 107-204, [2002] USCCAN 116 Stat 745.

35   ECGI, *Report of the New York Stock Exchange Commission on Corporate Governance* (2010), online: <https://ecgi.global/sites/default/files//codes/documents/nyse_cgreport_23sep2010_en.pdf>.

36   *Ibid* at 32.

37   *Ibid.*

the principles to a "restatement" to reflect the current emphasis on corporate governance in US law, taking into account developments over the intervening decades.[38]

Rock explained that the ALI's motivation in launching the project was a result of key changes in the marketplace, one of which is the increasingly important role that non-controlling shareholders, such as hedge funds and large institutional shareholders, have on the governance of corporations. These types of shareholders were not considered significant in the 1994 Principles.[39] Corporate social responsibility and environmental, social and governance issues are now on the radar. Hot button issues such as sustainability and board diversity are examples of topics that may be freshly analyzed in the restatement.[40] The 1994 Principles were contentious in their time and taxed the reporters' ability to achieve consensus; the proposed restatement will likely do the same. In some respects, the ALI is playing catch-up on issues well-canvassed elsewhere (in Europe, for example), but there is no doubt that the outcomes will be decidedly American and focused on legislative action. Voluntary codes, CoE and adherence to international standards will not be the driving forces.

Germany

After its initial, failed, experiment with a voluntary code, Germany has produced a succession of corporate governance codes over the last dozen or more years. Interestingly, corporate governance remains an alien concept in Germany; the English phrase "corporate governance" appears to have no German equivalent, the phrase appearing in English in the German language code. Unlike Cadbury, these German codes are largely a restatement of existing statutory law, indicative of the German conviction that corporate governance is, for the most part, adequately dealt with in existing legislation. The codes apply only to German incorporated public, listed companies, thus avoiding the extraterritorial reach of the US Sarbanes-Oxley Act 2002. The codes reaffirm the iconic German dual board structure and principle of co-determination, with worker representation on the supervisory board.

The Cadbury Report nonetheless leaves its traces in the "supplementary" recommendation provisions, indicated by "shall" terminology. In these cases, the CoE methodology of Cadbury is invoked and companies deviating from the recommendations must disclose and explain their reasons. Additionally, there are some provisions that are suggestions only, thrown in for good measure. Departures from these suggestions do not have to be explained.

The newest version of the German Code, adopted on May 2019 by the German Government Commission on the German Corporate Governance Code, will enter into force at a later date.[41] The streamlined German Code 2019 has as its worthy goal the strengthening of trust in corporate governance by, *inter alia*, restating management board remuneration rules and specifying independence requirements for shareholder representatives on the supervisory board. In addition, one of the objectives of the code is to make the German dual board structure

---

38   American Law Institute, Press Release, "Four Restatement Projects Launch" (28 January 2019), online: <www.ali.org/news/articles/four-restatement-projects-launch/>.

39   "Laying Down the Law: Edward Rock will oversee drafting of the first ALI Restatement on corporate governance", *NYU Law News* (5 April 2019), online: <www.law.nyu.edu/news/ideas/edward-rock-ALI-corporate-governance-restatement>.

40   *Ibid.*

41   German Corporate Governance Code 2019, online: *Regierungskommission Deutscher Corporate Governance Kodex* <www.dcgk.de/en/code//foreword.html>.

unimaginatively called "The Combined Code."[48] However, in 2010 there was a break in this process with the appearance of two new voluntary codes, the UK Code of Corporate Governance 2010 and the brand new UK Stewardship Code 2010, applicable to institutional investors.

The lineage of the UK Code of Corporate Governance 2010 can be traced straight back to the Cadbury Report, referring to that well-known definition of corporate governance, but it was a much different creature. Gone was the two-page Code of Best Practice, replaced by a detailed and differentiated approach to corporate governance structured along the lines of the OECD Principles 2004.

A great deal had changed in the United Kingdom since Cadbury first appeared, most notably a new Companies Act 2006 (UK), which at its introduction was touted as the first major rethinking of UK companies law in 140 years.[49] The statutory statement of directors' duty of care in section 172, enumerating the factors that directors must consider in decision making, was a breakthrough.[50] For example, the list of considerations includes the interests of employees and creditors, demonstrating the impact of stakeholder theory (and likely continental European perspectives) and captures many of the considerations detailed by Kenneth Scott in his definition of corporate governance a decade earlier.

In addition to the new Companies Act 2006, by 2010 more EU-level legislative instruments had appeared; the European Union had been churning out directive after directive affecting public and listed companies, increasingly using directly applicable regulations. The result in the United Kingdom was much greater interaction of older-style British approaches, informed by centuries of self-regulation and industry practices, with "hard law" emanating in various forms from Brussels.

But the CoE methodology of the voluntary codes remained unscathed. In a 2011 update, the Financial Reporting Council, the monitoring agency for the new codes, took a poke at the more European and American approaches to corporate governance. It noted the "advantages

---

48   The reports that culminated in the Combined Code were as follows: UK, Study Group on Directors' Remuneration, *Directors' Remuneration: Report of a Study Group Chaired by Sir Richard Greenbury* (1995) (Greenbury Report); UK, Committee on Corporate Governance, *Final Report* (1998) (Hampel Report); Derek Higgs, "Review of the role and effectiveness of non-executive directors: Consultation Paper" (London, UK: Department of Trade and Industry, 2002).

49   See remarks by the Rt Hon Patricia Hewitt, MP, then Secretary of State for Trade and Industry, made in the foreword of the 2005 UK White Paper on company law reform: UK, Department of Trade and Industry, *Company Law Reform* (2005) ("Britain was among the first nations to establish rules for the operation of companies, and our law remains a model for many nations overseas....[O]ver time the law can become outdated, and risks presenting obstacles to the ways companies want and need to do business in today's world. We are determined to avoid this. That is why we established the Company Law Review" at 3).

50   *Companies Act 2006* (UK), *supra* note 10, s 172: "Duty to promote the success of the company:
   (1) A director of a company must act in the way he considers, in good faith, would be most likely to promote the success of the company for the benefit of its members as a whole, and in doing so have regard (amongst other matters) to—
      (a) the likely consequences of any decision in the long term,
      (b) the interests of the company's employees,
      (c) the need to foster the company's business relationships with suppliers, customers and others,
      (d) the impact of the company's operations on the community and the environment,
      (e) the desirability of the company maintaining a reputation for high standards of business conduct, and
      (f) the need to act fairly as between members of the company.
   (2) Where or to the extent that the purposes of the company consist of or include purposes other than the benefit of its members, subsection (1) has effect as if the reference to promoting the success of the company for the benefit of its members were to achieving those purposes.
   (3) The duty imposed by this section has effect subject to any enactment or rule of law requiring directors, in certain circumstances, to consider or act in the interests of creditors of the company."

this [UK code-based approach] has over slower-changing law-based systems," in particular, its responsiveness to a rapidly changing business environment.[51]

The UK Code 2010 continues to be a work in progress, subject to continuous tinkering and fine tuning. The efficacy of the voluntary code and CoE implementation, however, has been subject to criticism over the years in the United Kingdom. There were questions about the substantive nature of the principles as well as the implementation methodology. As rates of compliance rose, criticism shifted to the standardized and unhelpful nature of the corporate disclosure provided by the explainers. Critics have suggested the "flexibility" rationale behind the voluntary code concept is "overstated."[52] The fact the codes have been in a continuous state of flux, revised almost yearly, may suggest the codes are simply not getting it right.

According to Iain MacNeil and Xiao Li, much of what is addressed in the voluntary codes could, and should, have been moved to mainstream companies legislation[53] or, according to Andrew Keay, subjected to regulatory oversight of some kind.[54] To some extent, this has come to pass, with the voluntary codes being revised in connection with enactment of the Companies Act 2006 and the guidance to its interpretation and application. The voluntary code provides a tempting alternative to grappling with and resolving the more contentious issues of corporate governance. The latest iteration of the code, released in 2018 and effective January 2019, was the result of yet another comprehensive review started in 2017. The most recent code was accompanied by the release of the Companies (Miscellaneous Reporting) Regulations 2018, thus forming part of a broader set of corporate governance reforms. The new code continues to retain its CoE methodology, recognizing its supporting role, but still taking a swipe at rigid rules.

The aspirational nature of the code on long-debated issues such as executive compensation (noted in the original Cadbury Report), diversity of representation on corporate boards and meaningful engagement with employees continues to thwart resolution and momentum. There is smoke, but little fire.[55] Several European countries have already moved on in these areas.[56]

---

51   Financial Reporting Council, *Developments in Corporate Governance and Stewardship 2011: The impact and implementation of the UK Corporate Governance and Stewardship Codes* (2011).

52   Iain MacNeil & Xiao Li, "'Comply or Explain': Market Discipline and Non-compliance with the Combined Code" (2006) 14:5 Corporate Governance: Intl Rev 476.

53   *Ibid.*

54   Andrew Keay, "The Public Enforcement of Directors' Duties: A Normative Inquiry" (2014) 43:2 Comm L World Rev 89.

55   The rhetoric is there in the UK Code 2018. The code speaks of greater emphasis on the importance of the relationships between companies, shareholders and stakeholders; managing the expectations of various stakeholders of a company, and not just its shareholders being conducive to good corporate governance; fostering a corporate culture that aligns with the company's purpose and strategy, and that promotes integrity and diversity; more meaningful engagement with the company's workforce and other stakeholders as part of board members' fulfilment of their section 172 duties; guidance on succession planning with a focus on diversity; and considerations on proportionality and greater transparency in executive remuneration.

56   More aggressive responses are demonstrated in Europe: 18 percent of countries, worldwide, surveyed in the *OECD Corporate Governance Factbook 2019*, have adopted mandatory legislative quotas requiring a certain percentage of board seats to be filled by women. Leading the way in this regard are Denmark, France, Iceland, Norway and Spain, which all require at least 40 percent female representation or, alternatively, the least represented gender on company boards.

OECD Principles of Corporate Governance

By definition "soft law," the OECD Principles of Corporate Governance represent an international manifestation of a voluntary code. The OECD learned from experiences with the OECD Principles 1999. Five years on, the Revised OECD Principles of Corporate Governance (2004) appeared. They were more nuanced and balanced, reflecting the lessons learned through their implementation in the course of the IMF and World Bank FSAP exercises and the OECD's own regional corporate governance round tables. The Revised Principles 2004 were more attuned to the reality and variety of corporate experience around the world. One of the realities that implementation of the original OECD Principles had encountered was the diversity of dominant corporate ownership patterns, which raised issues of accountability unlike those associated with the Berle and Means agency paradigm. In Asia especially, the state often controlled listed and publicly traded companies — a fact so striking that in 2005, the OECD prepared a separate set of corporate governance principles for state-owned enterprises.[57] The Revised Principles 2004 proved to be remarkably enduring, lasting more than a decade without revision. As with other contemporaneous financial standards, such as the Objectives and Principles of Securities Regulation released by the International Organization of Securities Commissions (IOSCO),[58] the Revised Principles 2004 gained widespread international recognition and currency through the IMF and World Bank FSAP exercises. Thus was created a complex dynamic between hard and soft law, with rules moving back and forth along a continuum of normativity — practices, voluntary codes, contract, listing rules and legislation.[59]

However, the 2008 global financial crisis raised tangential issues of corporate governance failures. The corporate landscape in Asia had changed dramatically with the rise of public markets, and the OECD became interested in the linkages between corporate governance and capital markets development, an interest foreshadowed in its original 1998 report. The next update was conducted against the backdrop of a purported inclusive process whereby non-OECD G20 countries were invited to participate in the review on equal footing, along with experts from the usual key international organizations, including the Basel Committee on Banking Supervision, the Financial Stability Board and the World Bank. Significant inputs were also received from the OECD's regional corporate governance round tables, the OECD's official advisory bodies, through stakeholder consultations and from comments solicited from an online public consultation. From a select group of academics, practitioners and businesspeople, the participants in the OECD standard-setting process broadened to include various hegemonic national regulators and international institutions. As such, the standard-setting process became more complex and politically driven.

The third iteration of the OECD Principles of Corporate Governance is unabashedly political. They are now the G20/OECD Principles of Corporate Governance 2015, endorsed at the G20 Leaders Summit in November 2015. The OECD justified the joint review with the G20 as

---

57   Apparently without the participation of the United States, which purportedly objected in principle to considering state-owned enterprises.

58   IOSCO, *Objectives and Principles of Securities Regulation* (Madrid: IOSCO, 2017), online: <www.iosco.org/library/pubdocs/pdf/IOSCOPD561.pdf>.

59   See Cally Jordan, "The Conundrum of Corporate Governance" (2005) 30 Brook J Intl L 983.

an effort to broaden the global reach of the principles.[60] A further justification was the desire that the principles reflect "experiences and ambitions in a wide variety of countries at different stages of development and with varying legal systems" and, accordingly, be formulated to accommodate the different corporate governance frameworks that exist around the world.[61] The G20/OECD Principles of Corporate Governance 2015 are a riot of diverse views. The illusion of one set of international best practices has been abandoned in the collision with economic, legal and political realities, thus fundamentally changing the original unifying purpose of the principles.

Implications for Voluntary Codes of Corporate Governance and the OECD Principles

The Cadbury Report — and the charming Sir Adrian Cadbury — provided the inspiration for the first set of OECD Principles of Corporate Governance. In turn, the OECD Principles popularized CoE voluntary codes of corporate governance around the world. The Principles were picked up early on by the FSF as one of the sets of international financial standards to be used in the FSAP exercises conducted by the IMF and the World Bank. The OECD contributed to the dissemination of its principles through OECD regional round tables and, more recently, the yearly *OECD Corporate Governance Factbook*. Indeed, according to the 2019 Factbook, of 49 jurisdictions considered, 83 percent follow a CoE model in their corporate governance codes.[62] Indicative of the influence exercised internationally by the OECD, nearly half of these 49 jurisdictions have amended their national corporate governance codes since the release of the latest OECD Principles.[63]

But does ubiquity represent success? Could the implementation of voluntary codes of corporate governance and showy adherence to OECD Principles be driven by the "ratings game" for which the FSAP exercises are responsible? Voluntary "national" codes may serve little purpose domestically, but signal to the international investment community that there has been engagement in the corporate governance dialogue (while not disrupting the status quo at home).[64] Any expectation of compliance may have disappeared. CoE may have become simply "explain," an approach consistent with US disclosure-based regulatory regimes.

The politicization of the OECD Principles has transformed them. The agenda of the standard setter is now dictated from above, by political imperatives that may be disconnected from commercial or economic realities. There are several implications. Ideological differences have

---

60   This justification sounds somewhat hollow, as the various iterations of the OECD Principles of Corporate Governance had already attained a wide global reach through the FSAP process.

61   *G20/OECD Principles of Corporate Governance 2015, supra* note 11.

62   OECD, *OECD Corporate Governance Factbook 2019* (Paris: OECD, 2019).

63   *G20/OECD Principles of Corporate Governance 2015, supra* note 11.

64   As two commentators explain, the G20/OECD Principles 2015 may be unfit for economies traditionally characterized by ineffective formal institutions, corruption, weak rule of law, and where non-transparency and avoidance of accountability are characteristic of the local business environment. The principles may also not be able to achieve their intended effects where family-owned businesses or similar concentrated corporate ownership structures dominate the business landscape. The international G20/OECD Principles were created with the assumption that these negative environmental features are not present. Mathias Siems & Oscar Salvador Alvarez-Macotela, "The G20/OECD Principles of Corporate Governance 2015: A Critical Assessment of Their Operation and Impact" (2017) J Bus L 31 at 14.

undermined the coherence of the latest iteration of the OECD Principles. The principles are not moving toward convergence or a unified international best practice, which was the aspiration of the drafters of the original principles.

More troubling is that important issues at the forefront of corporate governance, such as board diversity, may be buried due to the disproportionate influence of a hegemonic power such as the United States. Other major economies, especially in Europe, are simply walking away from the principles, which to them appear retrograde. Issues of board diversity, especially gender diversity, are glossed over in the latest OECD Principles, whereas Germany, following the lead of France, Italy, the Netherlands, Norway and Spain, among others, has imposed mandatory quotas (usually set at 40 percent) for gender diversity on the boards of large corporations. The disengagement of major economies from well-known international standards and methodologies such as voluntary codes can only undermine their credibility.

Nonetheless, the legacy of the Cadbury Report lives on in the United Kingdom and elsewhere. Proponents continue to laud the flexibility and opportunity for easy, rapid adjustments of the voluntary code approach. Critics, on the other hand, contend that the nearly annual tinkering and revisions to the UK Code of Corporate Governance demonstrate a failure to engage firmly with hard issues through legislation.

Despite the global reach of the OECD Principles and the ubiquity of CoE voluntary codes of corporate governance, there are unmistakable signs that the discourse on corporate governance has already moved elsewhere. Brian Cheffins postulates that traditional "internal" corporate governance mechanisms, focusing on board composition and formal shareholder rights, for example, have reached the limits of effectiveness. The influential factors are now "external" ones: governmental regulation, market competition and pressures from organized labour.[65] The OECD Principles and the voluntary code may be in the process of being left behind.

Author's Note

The author would like to thank Elgin Taing, Faculty of Law, McGill University, for his able assistance in the preparation of this chapter. The usual disclaimers apply. Parts of this chapter have appeared in Cally Jordan, "Cadbury Twenty Years On" (2013) 58 Vill L Rev 1 and Cally Jordan, "International Financial Standards: An Argument for Discernment" CIGI Policy Brief No 135, 30 August 2018.

---

65   Brian R Cheffins, "Corporate Governance and Countervailing Power" (2019) European Corporate Governance Institute, Law Research Working Paper No 448/2019.

IV.
INVESTOR OBLIGATIONS DRAWING FOCUS

13

REMEDIES IN THE CONTEXT OF INVESTOR RESPONSIBILITIES

Hugo Perezcano Díaz and Ksenia Polonskaya

Introduction

Growing discomfort with international investment agreements (IIAs) and investor-state arbitration (ISA) has prompted states to consider broad areas of reform.[1] IIAs contain obligations that states undertake vis-à-vis each other with regard to the treatment of foreign investors and their investments. However, in general, IIAs grant only foreign investors a right to bring a claim against one of the signatory states — the one where they have made an investment — for non-compliance with the provisions of the applicable IIA.

---

1   See e.g. Michael Waibel, ed, *The Backlash Against Investment Arbitration: Perceptions and Reality* (The Hague: Kluwer Law International, 2010). Note that certain IIAs, such as the ICSID Convention (*Convention on the Settlement of Investment Disputes between States and Nationals of Other States*, 18 March 1965 [entered into force 14 October 1966]), may also allow for contractual claims between a foreign investor and a state to be submitted to arbitration, and in such cases the state may be able to bring a claim against the investor. However, this chapter focuses on breach of treaty claims, which presently constitute the vast majority of cases brought to ISA.

Most IIAs do not impose obligations on investors. Only recently have some newly negotiated agreements begun to incorporate references to investor responsibilities.[2] For instance, the Comprehensive Economic and Trade Agreement (CETA)[3] and the Comprehensive and Progressive Agreement for Trans-Pacific Partnership (CPTPP)[4] include only timid references in hortatory provisions that encourage voluntary compliance with certain non-binding international standards of corporate social responsibility (CSR).[5] Since 2018, some states have shown sympathy to the inclusion of investor responsibilities that could be enforced through the dispute settlement mechanisms of IIAs. For example, the Group of 77 countries (G77) and China have issued a special statement addressed to the United Nations Commission on International Trade Law (UNCITRAL) Working Group III on ISA reform that emphasizes: "*any dispute settlement regime* should *appropriately* address the rights and *responsibilities* of foreign investors."[6]

There is ample scholarly commentary on the potential inclusion of investor responsibilities in IIAs and ISA.[7] Such soul searching in the context of international investment law is well placed within a broader intellectual movement that seeks to conceptualize the scope and limitations of

---

2   "Investor responsibilities," as used in this chapter, refers to provisions in IIAs related to investor conduct that are meant to enhance their accountability to the host state, and to the legal consequences that could arise in the context of ISA from an investor's non-compliance with such provisions. To our best knowledge, the United Nations Conference on Trade and Development (UNCTAD) was the first to coin this term in the context of international investment law. UNCTAD, *Investment Policy Framework for Sustainable Development* (2015), s 7, online: <https://unctad.org/en/PublicationsLibrary/diaepcb2015d5_en.pdf>. See also Peter Muchlinski, "Negotiating New Generation International Investment Agreements: New Sustainable Development Oriented Initiatives" in Steffen Hindelang & Markus Krajewski, eds, *Shifting Paradigms in International Investment Law: More Balanced, Less Isolated, Increasingly Diversified* (Oxford: Oxford University Press, 2016) 41 at 57–59.

3   *Comprehensive Economic and Trade Agreement between Canada, of the one part, and the European Union [and its Member States...]*, 30 October 2016 (provisionally entered into force 21 September 2017) [*CETA*].

4   *Comprehensive and Progressive Agreement for Trans-Pacific Partnership*, 8 March 2018 (entered into force with Vietnam 14 January 2019) [*CPTPP*].

5   *CPTPP, ibid*, provides in its investment chapter:
    Article 9.17: Corporate Social Responsibility
        The Parties reaffirm the importance of each Party encouraging enterprises operating within its territory or subject to its jurisdiction to voluntarily incorporate into their internal policies those internationally recognised standards, guidelines and principles of corporate social responsibility that have been endorsed or are supported by that Party.
    CETA, *supra* note 3, Preamble, states:
        The parties resolve to...
        ENCOURAGE enterprises operating within their territory or subject to their jurisdiction to respect internationally recognized standards and principles of corporate social responsibility, notably the OECD Guidelines for multinational enterprises and to pursue best practices of responsible business conduct.

6   *Statement on Behalf of the Group of 77 and China by H.E. Mr Mohamed Edrees, Permanent Representative of Egypt to the United Nations, at UNCITRAL Working Group III Meeting on the Investor-State Dispute Settlement Reform* (2018) [emphasis added], online: <www.g77.org/statement/getstatement.php?id=180423>.

7   By no means, however, is there agreement on how to proceed. Commentators offer divergent views. See e.g. Stephan Schill, "Reforming Investor-State Dispute Settlement (ISDS): Conceptual Framework and Options for the Way Forward" (2015) E15 Initiative, International Centre for Trade and Sustainable Development & World Economic Forum, online: <https://pure.uva.nl/ws/files/2512304/163092_E15_Investment_Schill_FINAL.pdf> ("Many problems of the current regime, such as those concerning vagueness and ambiguity of substantive standards of treatment, the lack of clarity of the rights of states vis-à-vis foreign investors, and the inexistence of enforceable investor obligations under international law, can only be tackled through a reform of substantive standards" at 10); Gus Van Harten, "Reforming the System of International Investment Dispute Settlement" in CL Lim, ed, *Alternative Visions of the International Law on Foreign Investment* (Cambridge, UK: Cambridge University Press, 2016) at 115–18; Lise Johnson, Lisa Sachs & Jesse Coleman, "International Investment Agreements 2014: A Review of Trends and New Approaches" in Andrea Bjorklund, ed, *Yearbook on International Investment Law and Policy 2014–2015* (Oxford: Oxford University Press, 2016) at 50–60.

performance.[40] In *Chevron v Ecuador*, the tribunal fashioned a remedy in such a way as to "'wipe out all the consequences' of the Respondent's internationally wrongful acts, so as to re-establish the situation which would have existed if those internationally wrongful acts had not been committed by the Respondent."[41] To achieve this, the tribunal specified that Ecuador must "immediately" suspend "the enforceability of the Lago Agrio Judgment."[42]

In *Enron v Argentina*, the tribunal stated that, "in addition to declaratory powers, *it has the power to order measures involving performance or injunction of certain acts.*"[43] Gisele Stephens-Chu confirms that "it appears uncontroversial that, subject to the provisions of the applicable investment treaty(ies), investment tribunals have the power under international law to order restitution and specific performance."[44] However, the tribunals "have diverged on the circumstances in which the award of restitution or specific performance is 'materially possible' and 'proportionate.'"[45] A possible non-enforceability of the award, nonetheless, does not preclude tribunals from granting the remedy. In *Micula v Romania*, the tribunal noted that "the fact that such a remedy might not be enforceable pursuant to Article 54 of the ICSID Convention should not preclude a tribunal from ordering it. Remedies and enforcement are two distinct concepts."[46] Some arbitral tribunals, however, hesitate to "grant non-pecuniary remedies" because of the concern that the implementation of such awards would be "materially impossible."[47] In summary, while the ILC Articles and *Chorzów* recognize restitution as the preferred form of reparation, it is safe to say that compensatory damages remain the most frequently used remedy in ISA.

Investor Responsibilities in the Context of Remedies: Current Approaches in IIAs and Arbitral Practice

In recent years, attention has begun to shift from investment protection to investor responsibilities, both in scholarly circles and in international negotiations between states. There appears to be an emerging trend in that direction at various fora.[48] However, little attention (if any) has been afforded to remedies. It appears to be no more than an afterthought, at best, rather

---

40   See e.g. *Antoine Goetz et consorts c République du Burundi*, Award, ICSID Case No ARB/95/3 (1999), as discussed in Sivard Jarvin, "Non-Pecuniary Remedies: The Practices of Declaratory Relief and Specific Performance in International Commercial Arbitration" in Arthur Rovine, ed, *Contemporary Issues in International Arbitration and Mediation: The Fordham Papers* (The Hague: Brill, 2008) at 172–73.

41   *Chevron v Ecuador, supra* note 17, Second Partial Award on Track II at para 9.17 (Arbitrators: Horacio A Grigera Naón, Vaughan Lowe, VV Veeder).

42   *Ibid.*

43   *Enron Corp and Ponderosa Assets, LP v Argentine Republic* (2004), Decision on Jurisdiction, ICSID Case No ARB/01/3 at para 81 (Arbitrators: Francisco Orrego Vicuña, Héctor Gros Espiell, Pierre-Yves Tschanz) [emphasis added].

44   Gisele Stephens-Chu, "Is It Always All About the Money? The Appropriateness of Non-Pecuniary Remedies in Investment Treaty Arbitration" (2014) 30:4 Arb Intl 661 at 667.

45   *Ibid* at 668; see also Bradfield & Thomas, *supra* note 23 at 635–64 (identified total of 24 awards where the issue of non-pecuniary remedies was discussed).

46   *Micula v Romania* (2008), Decision on Jurisdiction and Admissibility, ICSID Case No ARB/05/20 at para 166 (Arbitrators: Laurent Lévy, Stanimir Alexandrov, Claus-Dieter Ehlermann).

47   Bradfield & Thomas, *supra* note 23 at 656.

48   See e.g. UNCTAD, *World Investment Report: Special Economic Zones* (2019) at 100–01 (discussing Guiding Principles for Investment Policymaking developed by various international organizations, including UNCTAD, the Organization of Islamic Cooperation, and the G20 Guiding Principles for Global Investment Policymaking).

than an integral element of any conceptual approach. Assuming that states eventually agree to impose obligations on foreign investors through IIAs and allow states to submit claims to ISA against investors, what will it mean for the states and investors from the perspective of available relief? For example, what if a foreign investor that operates in the host state is responsible for a significant oil spill, in violation of potential IIA obligations to exercise responsible environmental management? Does it mean that IIAs should allow host states to seek damages, (which is, in practice, the remedy that IIAs currently grant investors), or should they provide for alternative relief? Should ISA tribunals be allowed, for example, to order the responsible investor to clean up and remediate the affected zone? Would such a remedy fall under the notion of restitution?

Furthermore, could ISA tribunals order that the persons affected by the spill, rather than the state, be compensated for the injuries or losses suffered? Should IIAs contemplate penalties, either by allowing ISA tribunals to determine the penalties to be imposed or by validating penalties imposed by the state or, as a result of the arbitration, validate the state's ability to impose penalties? What would be the appropriate remedy under an IIA in cases involving corruption or human rights violations? Would investment tribunals be granted jurisdiction to make findings and determinations that pertain to the realm of criminal law, and would they be the appropriate adjudicators — or even the appropriate triers of fact — in such cases? It thus appears that awarding damages to the host state could be quite an inadequate remedy in many, if not most, cases. This raises a further and no less complex question of how such alternative remedies can be enforced and under what terms.

Jurisdiction

In some circumstances, tribunals have rejected jurisdiction over claims submitted to ISA by investors, where the underlying investment had been involved in or linked to illegal acts in the host state. This approach appears to be most prominent in investor-state cases where the investor engaged in corruption in relation to the investment project subject of the dispute.[49] For example, the tribunal took this approach in *Duty Free v Kenya*, where Kenya raised corruption as a defence.[50] The tribunal upheld Kenya's defence and ruled that "bribery is contrary to the international public policy of most, if not all, states or, to use another formula, to transnational public policy."[51] The tribunal explained that "the claimant is not legally entitled to maintain any of its pleaded claims in these proceedings as a matter of *ordre public international* and public policy under the contract's applicable laws."[52] Accordingly, the tribunal dismissed all claims for lack of jurisdiction.

Other investment tribunals have taken a similar approach to illegality by refusing to establish jurisdiction when the investor deliberately acted in contradiction to the host state's law. For example, in *Fraport v Philippines*, the host state also raised illegality as the defence in the investment proceedings.[53] The tribunal observed that "the Claimant's own internal documents show that Fraport was consciously, intentionally and covertly structuring its investment in a way

---

49   See e.g. Mavluda Sattorova, *The Impact of Investment Treaty Law on Host States: Enabling Good Governance?* (London, UK: Bloomsbury, 2018).

50   *World Duty Free v Kenya* (2006), Award, ICSID Case No ARB/00/7 at para 157 (Arbitrators: Gilbert Guillaume, Andrew Rogers, VV Veeder).

51   *Ibid.*

52   *Ibid* at para 188 [emphasis in original].

53   *Fraport AG Frankfurt Airport Services Worldwide v the Philippines* (2007), Award, ICSID Case No ARB/03/25 at para 5 (Arbitrators: L Yves Fortier, Bernardo M Cremades, W Michael Reisman).

environmental pollution, provoked human rights violations or engaged in other acts that are illegal under domestic or international law.

Compensation and satisfaction may not provide effective redress. On this point, Chester Brown has observed: "Although there is a large measure of acceptance of the availability of restitution, compensation and declaratory judgments in international adjudication, this does not mean that *each form of reparation will be appropriate or even available as remedies in individual cases. The appropriateness of different remedies will depend on the nature of the court, the type of dispute, the identity of the parties, and, of course, the particular relief sought by the claimant in the proceedings.* In addition, the express terms of the constitutive instrument of each international court may prescribe the remedies that are available."[75]

Brown's logic is particularly relevant to remedies in the context of investor responsibilities. It is useful to briefly consider how such "appropriateness" of particular remedies plays out in different scenarios. In the straightforward circumstances of an investment dispute where a state, for example, expropriates a foreign investor's investment, the investor is likely to seek restitution or monetary compensation.[76] Investors and states are likely to agree that restitution and compensation are, in principle, appropriate remedies, even if in a particular case the claimant investor and the respondent state disagree on the measure of damages.

However, in the context of investment disputes that engage investor responsibilities, the three forms of reparation that are traditionally available under international law may not constitute an effective form of redress. For example, consider the factual circumstances of the *Chevron v Ecuador* arbitration.[77] In this case, the investor submitted a claim against Ecuador with respect to rights under an oil concession. Ecuador argued that the investor's activities resulted in significant environmental damage that impacted the region and affected the health of local residents.

Depending on the scale and type of environmental damage, it may be materially impossible to re-establish the situation that existed prior to the illegal act. Christine Gray observes, "The doctrine that restitution is not available in cases of material impossibility is well accepted and relatively uncontroversial....Restitution will not be possible in the event of the disappearance or fundamental alteration of the property whose return is requested."[78]

Turning to compensation, according to John Barker, it "is commonly employed where the loss or injury can be quantified in money terms, but can also include recognized non-pecuniary injuries, such as emotional trauma associated with violations of human rights."[79] However,

---

75   Chester Brown, *A Common Law of International Adjudication* (Oxford: Oxford University Press, 2007) at 192 [emphasis added].

76   John Barker, "The Different Forms of Reparation: Compensation" in James Crawford, Alain Pellet & Simon Olleson, eds, *The Law of International Responsibility* (Oxford: Oxford University Press, 2010) at 599.

77   *Chevron v Ecuador, supra* note 17, First Partial Award on Track I. For commentary, see Gabriel Bottini & Elisa Méndez Bräutigam, "Investment Claims Against Latin American States: Environmental Protection and the Applicable Law" in Kate Miles, ed, *Research Handbook on Environment and Investment Law* (Cheltenham, UK: Edward Elgar, 2019) at 416–17.

78   Christine Gray, "The Different Forms of Reparation: Restitution" in Crawford, Pellet & Olleson, *supra* note 76 (noting there could be substantial disagreements as to the meaning of the term "material impossibility" at 596).

79   Barker, *supra* note 76 at 599.

where investment activities affect human, animal or plant life or health, it may be impossible to quantify the damage and order compensation.

This may be the case as well with investment projects that occur within the territories that belong to Indigenous communities, in particular when such projects impact an aspect of traditional heritage that has cultural, religious or historical value that, quite simply, cannot be quantified.[80] For instance, it may be impossible to quantify the damage if the investors' activities resulted in the destruction of sacred heritage sites, which effectively limits the value of compensation as a remedy. Accordingly, with respect to remedies in the context of investor responsibilities, three basic questions arise: whether compensation is an appropriate remedy in every case; whether other remedies should be available; and who should obtain relief.

Satisfaction has played an important role in the context of international law. Eric Wyler and Alain Papaux explain that "according to the classic approach, satisfaction was intended to redress the injuries caused to the honor, dignity or reputation of the State, in other words an injury characterized as 'moral and political.'"[81] They suggest that satisfaction can take the form of, for example, "apologies and statements of regret, punishment of responsible persons, declaration of wrongfulness, the establishment of special missions charged with expressing the regret of the responsible State or commissions of enquiry, the creation of a fund assigned to a humanitarian goal."[82] In *Rainbow Warrior*, for instance, the UN Secretary-General ruled that France had to issue "a formal and unqualified apology for the attack, contrary to international law."[83] In *Certain Questions of Mutual Assistance in Criminal Matters*, the ICJ required France to issue a declaration of wrongfulness.[84]

In the context of investment arbitration, Patrick Dumberry has analyzed investment disputes to determine whether satisfaction would be an appropriate remedy in the context of international investment law. Among other cases, Dumberry examined the *Europe Cement v Turkey* and *Cementownia v Turkey* cases, where "Turkey sought an award of monetary compensation for moral damages it allegedly suffered with regards to its 'reputation and international standing' as a result of baseless claims filed by the foreign investors."[85] Dumberry concluded, "The reasoning of the tribunals in the recent ICSID cases of *Europe Cement* and *Cementownia* rightly suggests that satisfaction, in the form of a declaration of wrongfulness, would be the most appropriate form of reparation to remedy any moral damage suffered by a respondent State."[86]

The existing international law framework on reparations provides a useful starting point for thinking about remedies in the context of investor responsibilities. Yet it is hardly more than that.

---

80   Valentina Vadi, "When Cultures Collide: Foreign Direct Investment, Natural Resources and Indigenous Heritage in International Investment Law" (2011) 42 Colum HRLR 797.

81   Eric Wyler & Alain Papaux, "The Different Forms of Reparation: Satisfaction" in Crawford, Pellet & Olleson, *supra* note 76 at 625.

82   *Ibid.*

83   *Rainbow Warrior (New Zealand v France)* (1990) 82 ILR 500. For commentary on apology as a form of satisfaction, see Richard Bilder, "The Role of Apology in International Law and Diplomacy" (2006) 46:3 Va J Intl L 433.

84   *Certain Questions of Mutual Assistance in Criminal Matters (Djibouti v France)*, [2008] ICJ Reports 2008 at para 18.

85   Patrick Dumberry, "Satisfaction as a Form of Reparation for Moral Damages Suffered by Investors and Respondent States in Investor-State Arbitration Disputes" (2012) 3:1 J Intl Dispute Settlement 205.

86   *Ibid* at 242.

Step Two: Integrating the "Protect, Respect and Remedy" Framework in International Investment Law

Overview

John Ruggie was appointed in 2005 as the Special Representative of the Secretary-General on Business and Human Rights to identify a potential scope of accountability for transnational companies under international law.[87] Ruggie has developed a conceptual CSR framework that includes the duty to protect, respect and remedy as three core pillars of corporate accountability for human rights violations.[88] The framework particularly emphasizes, among other issues, the importance of access to remedy to ensure corporate accountability.

The framework highlights what it deems *limitations* of domestic judicial mechanisms in guaranteeing effective access to remedy. These limitations include a lack of a "basis in domestic law on which to found a claim," as well as various "political, economic or legal considerations [that] may hamper enforcement."[89] Particular concern is expressed about different procedural obstacles that prevent successful enforcement of the claims in the domestic courts. According to the framework: "Some complainants have sought remedy outside the State where the harm occurred, particularly through home State courts, but have faced extensive obstacles....In common law countries, the court may dismiss the case based on *forum non conveniens* grounds — essentially, that there is a more appropriate forum for it. Even the most independent judiciaries may be influenced by governments arguing for dismissal based on various 'matters of State.' These obstacles may deter claims or leave the victim with a remedy that is difficult to enforce."[90]

The framework also emphasizes "gaps in access" to remedy due to "intended and unintended limitations in the competence and coverage of existing mechanisms."[91] The framework emphasizes, therefore, that domestic law and domestic judicial remedies may not suffice to advance access to remedy in the transnational context where corporations operate in multiple jurisdictions. With respect to investor responsibilities in international investment law, it is necessary to think strategically and contextually about access to remedy if international investment law is to provide remedies against investors where the latter have breached obligations imposed on them by IIAs.

The framework resulted in the Guiding Principles on Business and Human Rights: Implementing the United Nations "Protect, Respect and Remedy" Framework.[92] According to Principle 25: "As part of their duty to protect against business-related human rights abuse, States must take appropriate steps to ensure, through judicial, administrative, legislative or other appropriate means, that when such abuses occur within their territory and/or jurisdiction *those affected have access to effective remedy*."[93]

---

87   Christian Tomuschat, *Human Rights: Between Idealism and Realism* (Oxford: Oxford University Press, 2014) at 135.

88   *Protect, Respect and Remedy Framework, supra* note 16.

89   *Ibid.*

90   *Ibid* at para 89. For a detailed discussion on the *forum non conveniens* doctrine in the context of access to remedies, see Erika George & Lisa Laplante, "Access to Remedy: Treaty Talks and the Terms of a New Accountability Accord" in Surya Deva & David Bilchitz, *Building a Treaty on Business and Human Rights: Context and Contours* (Cambridge, UK: Cambridge University Press, 2017) 383.

91   *Protect, Respect and Remedy Framework, supra* note 16 at para 103.

92   *Implementing the "Protect, Respect and Remedy" Framework, supra* note 9.

93   *Ibid*, Principle 25 [emphasis added].

Principles 27 and 31 provide that states should establish "effective and appropriate non-judicial grievance mechanisms" that should be legitimate, accessible, predictable, equitable and transparent.[94] More recently, the drafting team of the Draft Rules on Business and Human Rights Arbitration (known as the Draft Hague Rules)[95] emphasized that it is necessary to explore ways in which ISA, as a non-judicial grievance mechanism, could fill gaps in access to remedy.

Filling the Gaps: Investment Arbitration and Access to Remedy

Arguably, ISA could become a valuable platform to advance access to remedy (as envisaged by the framework) in the transnational context. Investment arbitration remains a popular avenue for resolving disputes, in part due to its perceived neutrality. Certain structural features of ISA could serve as valuable reference points to advance access to remedy. For instance, ISA arbitrators are appointed by investors and states, or by neutral appointing authorities, including arbitration institutions. This model of arbitral appointments can remove foreign investors' concerns over allegedly biased domestic courts in adjudicating matters that relate to corporate responsibility.

Types of Remedies

The Draft Hague Rules offer a path forward by offering a more flexible approach to the types of remedies that ISA tribunals can employ. According to the Draft Hague Rules, the tribunals "may order monetary compensation and non-monetary relief, including restitution, rehabilitation, satisfaction, specific performance and the provision of guarantees of non-repetition. An award may also contain recommendations for other measures that may assist in resolving the underlying dispute and preventing future disputes or the repetition of harm, which shall be binding only if agreed by the parties. The arbitral tribunal shall take into account the proportionality and cultural appropriateness of its awards."[96] This approach is based on the commentary to Principle 25 of the UN Guiding Principles and it suggests that the tribunals "should seek to appropriately tailor remedies to the needs of the case."[97]

Conclusion

Various stakeholders seek to reimagine the system of international investment protection by recalibrating IIAs, taking investor responsibilities into account. Such recalibration should contemplate the development of a framework on remedies for breach of investor obligations. ISA can provide an important forum for access to remedy, without the limitations that exist in domestic fora. Yet the issue of remedies in the ISA context poses multiple complexities. A potentially fruitful approach might be for ISA reformers to recalibrate their approach to remedies in the context of investor responsibilities in the spirit of the "Protect, Respect and Remedy" Framework.

---

94   *Ibid*, Principles 27, 31.

95   Centre for International Legal Cooperation, "Draft Rules on Business and Human Rights Arbitration", online: <www.cilc.nl/project/the-hague-rules-on-business-and-human-rights-arbitration/>.

96   *Ibid*, art 40.

97   *Ibid*, art 40, commentary.

14

PIERCING THE CORPORATE VEIL IN INTERNATIONAL INVESTMENT LAW
Problems with the Denial of Benefits Clause

Charles-Emmanuel Côté

Introduction

The abolition of investor-state dispute settlement (ISDS) between Canada and the United States in the Canada-United States-Mexico Agreement (CUSMA)[1] is likely to renew the interest for corporate strategies aiming to take advantage of the protection of investment agreements concluded with third countries.[2] Treaty shopping and the problem of free-riding by third-country investors are certainly not new features of foreign investment. This problem is specifically addressed by denial of benefits (DoB) clauses in many investment agreements. DoB clauses allow a host state to "pierce the corporate veil" in order to deny treaty protection to foreign investors that have no economic connection to the state of incorporation.[3]

---

1   *Canada–United States–Mexico Agreement*, 30 November 2018 (not yet in force) [*CUSMA*].

2   See Charles-Emmanuel Côté, "Investissement" (2018) 55 Can YB Intl L 424 at 441.

3   Rudolf Dolzer & Christoph Schreuer, *Principles of International Investment Law*, 2nd ed (Oxford: Oxford University Press, 2012) at 55.

The corporate separateness from shareholders affirmed by the International Court of Justice in the *Barcelona Traction* case[4] remains the bedrock principle applicable in general international law.[5] The state of incorporation determines the nationality of a corporation, despite the fact that it might be owned or controlled by third-country shareholders. International investment agreements reaffirm this principle in their definition of an investor of a state party.[6] Except for the DoB clause, all the exceptions to this principle allowing the piercing of the corporate veil under general international law or international investment law are designed in favour of the corporation.

A first exception under general international law allows the state of nationality of the shareholders to exercise diplomatic protection for the injury caused to the corporation if it ceased to exist in the country of incorporation, for reasons unrelated to the injury.[7] A second exception concerns "Calvo corporations," when incorporation in the host state is a condition for doing business there. The state of nationality of shareholders can exercise diplomatic protection in such cases.[8] The Convention on the Settlement of Investment Disputes between States and Nationals of Other States[9] (ICSID Convention) also allows the disputing parties to agree to pierce the corporate veil in those circumstances, in order to give to the foreign shareholders access to arbitration against the host state. As noted in *Tokios Tokelės v Ukraine*,[10] this provision aims to extend the jurisdiction of the International Centre for Settlement of Investment Disputes (ICSID) in favour of the corporation, not to reduce it. The International Law Commission proposes a third exception, as a progressive development of international law, already alluded to in *Barcelona Traction*, in order to allow the real state of management *and* financial control of a corporation to exercise diplomatic protection, instead of the state of incorporation, when the corporation has no substantial business activities in that state.[11] Finally, international investment law typically allows the piercing of the corporate veil in order to allow indirect ownership of an investment by the corporation of a state party through a third-country corporation.[12]

Consequently, international law allows and even encourages treaty shopping through corporate structuring or restructuring. While the law remains largely unsettled on the issue, a possible limit to this is corporate restructuring after a dispute has arisen or is foreseeable, which may constitute an abuse of right that makes the claim inadmissible or deprives the arbitral tribunal of

---

4   *Barcelona Traction, Light and Power Company, Ltd (Belgium v Spain)*, [1970] ICJ Rep 3, 33–37 at paras 38, 41, 44–50; 42 at para 70; 46 at para 88 [*Barcelona Traction*].

5   See "Draft Articles on Diplomatic Protection with Commentaries" in *Yearbook of the International Law Commission 2006*, vol 2, part 2 (New York: UN, 2006) at 26, art 9; 37 at para 3 (UN Doc A/61/10).

6   See e.g. *North American Free Trade Agreement Between the Government of Canada, the Government of Mexico and the Government of the United States*, 17 December 1992, Can TS 1994 No 2 art 1139, *sub verbo* "enterprise of a Party" (entered into force 1 January 1994) [*NAFTA*]; *Energy Charter Treaty*, 17 December 1994, 2080 UNTS 95, 34 ILM 360 art 1:7(a)(ii) (entered into force 16 April 1998) [*ECT*].

7   *Barcelona Traction, supra* note 4, 40–41 at paras 65–68; "Draft Articles on Diplomatic Protection", *supra* note 5, art 11(a); 39–40 at paras 5–7.

8   "Draft Articles on Diplomatic Protection", *supra* note 5, art 11(b); 39, 41–42 at paras 9–12. See *Barcelona Traction, supra* note 4, 48 at para 92.

9   *Convention on the Settlement of Investment Disputes Between States and Nationals of Other States*, 18 March 1965, 575 UNTS 159, 17 UST 1270, TIAS 6090 art 25:2(b) (entered into force 14 October 1966).

10   *Tokios Tokelės v Ukraine* (2004), Decision on Jurisdiction, ICSID Case No ARB/02/18 at para 46 [*Tokios*].

11   "Draft Articles on Diplomatic Protection", *supra* note 5, art 9; 37 at paras 3–6. See *Barcelona Traction, supra* note 4 at 42–44, paras 70–76.

12   See e.g. *NAFTA, supra* note 6, art 1139, *sub verbo* "investment of an investor of a Party"; *ECT, supra* note 6, art 1(6); *Waste Management v Mexico (II)*, (2004) Award, ICSID Case No ARB(AF)/00/3 at paras 77–85.

its jurisdiction.[13] Otherwise, it is normally legitimate for a foreign investor to adopt a corporate structure to benefit from the protection of a third-country investment agreement.[14] The general principle of good faith has had no significant impact in defeating this corporate strategy, arbitral tribunals preferring textual interpretation of investment agreements.[15]

DoB clauses are precisely designed to address this corporate strategy. The United States first introduced them in its post-war treaties of friendship, commerce and navigation (FCN), in order to prevent free-riding by third-country corporations.[16] Given the broad protection offered to corporations, and the compulsory jurisdiction of the International Court of Justice, DoB clauses were deemed necessary to rebalance the respective interests of the host state and the state of incorporation. DoB clauses were reproduced in US bilateral investment treaties (BITs) and free trade agreements and spread to other countries' treaty practice. They remain relatively rare, since less than 10 percent of all investment agreements include a DoB clause.[17] They continue to pursue important policy objectives in modern investment agreements.[18] They aim to prevent third-country investors from having a free ride on bilateral investment agreements, in a field of law characterized by the absence of a multilateral agreement imposing identical obligations on all states. They help states to preserve reciprocity in their obligations, as well as preserving their ability to negotiate future agreements with third countries. In addition to third-country investors, the clause may also prevent host-state nationals from taking advantage of an agreement to invest in their own country and evade the jurisdiction of domestic courts.[19]

---

13   See e.g. *Philip Morris Asia v Australia*, Award on Jurisdiction and Admissibility, PCA Case No 2012-12 (2015) at paras 585–88; Tania Voon, Andrew Mitchell & James Munro, "Legal Responses to Corporate Manoeuvring in International Investment Arbitration" (2014) 5 J Intl Disp Settlement 41 at 43, 62–65; Jean-François Hébert, "Issues of Corporate Nationality in Investment Arbitration" in Armand LC de Mestral & Céline Lévesque, eds, *Improving International Investment Agreements* (Abingdon, UK: Routledge, 2013) 230 at 233–35; Mark Feldman, "Setting Limits on Corporate Nationality Planning in Investment Treaty Arbitration" (2012) 27 ICSID Rev 281 at 282, 293.

14   See *Gold Reserve v Venezuela*, Award, ICSID Case No ARB(AF)/09/1 (2014) at paras 252, 255; *Tokios, supra* note 10 at para 36; Hébert, *supra* note 13 at 233.

15   M Sornarajah, "Good Faith, Corporate Nationality, and Denial of Benefits" in Andrew D Mitchell, M Sornarajah & Tania Voon, eds, *Good Faith and International Economic Law* (Oxford: Oxford University Press, 2015) 117 at 118.

16   Kenneth J Vandevelde, *The First Bilateral Investment Treaties: U.S. Postwar Friendship, Commerce, and Navigation Treaties* (Oxford: Oxford University Press, 2017) at 393–94. See Herman Walker Jr, "Provisions on Companies in United States Commercial Treaties" (1956) 50 AJIL 373 at 388.

17   UNCTAD, "International Investment Agreements Navigator", online: Investment Policy Hub <https://investmentpolicy.unctad.org/international-investment-agreements/iia-mapping> (221 out of 2,577 mapped treaties). See Rachel Thorn & Jennifer Doucleff, "Disregarding the Corporate Veil and Denial of Benefits Clauses: Testing Treaty Language and the Concept of 'Investor'" in Michael Waibel, ed, *The Backlash against Investment Arbitration: Perceptions and Reality* (Austin, TX: Wolters Kluwer Law & Business, 2010) at 9; Stephen Jagusch & Anthony Sinclair, "Denial of Advantage under Article 17(1)" in Graham Coop & Clarisse Ribeiro, eds, *Investment Protection and the Energy Charter* (Huntington, NY: Juris, 2008) 17 at 23.

18   See Anne K Hoffmann, "Denial of Benefits" in Marc Bungenberg et al, eds, *International Investment Law* (Munich: Beck, 2015) 598 at 601.

19   Thorn & Doucleff, *supra* note 17 at 4. See e.g. *2004 Model BIT*, United States, art 17; *Treaty concerning the Reciprocal Encouragement and Protection of Investment*, United States and Argentina, 14 November 1991, 31 ILM 124 art I:2 (entered into force 20 October 1994).

Four types of DoB clauses can be identified in treaty practice, requiring either a positive action in order to produce their effects, or producing them automatically:

- The "unlimited clause" is activated by the host state at its discretion, regarding corporations owned or controlled by third-country nationals.[20]

- The "conditional clause" is activated by the host state at its discretion, regarding corporations owned or controlled by third-country nationals, on the alternative condition that it lacks substantial business activities in the host state, that diplomatic relations do not exist between the host state and the third country, or that economic sanctions imposed by the host state against the third country are circumvented.[21]

- The "consensual clause" is activated by joint decision of the host state and the state of incorporation, regarding corporations owned or controlled by third-country nationals.[22]

- The "automatic clause" excludes at the outset from the definition of "investor" any corporations owned or controlled by third-country nationals, or corporations not having substantial business activities in the host state.[23]

The most common type of DoB clause in treaty practice is by far the conditional clause. It was invoked or considered in nearly 30 reported cases, all involving the Energy Charter Treaty[24] (ECT) or US investment agreements. Many problems stem from the conflicting arbitral decisions, and strict interpretation of the clauses has severely restricted their applicability, especially under the ECT. The invocation of the clause was successful in only three cases, none of which dealt with the ECT, in *Pac Rim Cayman v El Salvador*,[25] *Guaracachi America v Bolivia*[26] and *St. Marys VCNA v Canada*.[27] The rest of this chapter will explore the problems of form and substance of the DoB clause raised in arbitral decisions, with some concluding remarks.

---

20   See e.g. *Treaty between the United States of America and the Republic of Panama concerning the Treatment and Protection of Investment*, 27 October 1982, TIAS 91-530 art I(c), sub verbo "company of a Party" (entered into force 30 May 1991) [*US-Panama BIT*]; *1955 Standard Draft US FCN Treaty*, reproduced in Vandevelde, *supra* note 16 at 547, art XXI:1(e).

21   See e.g. *NAFTA*, *supra* note 6, art 1113; *ECT*, *supra* note 6, art 17.

22   See e.g. *Agreement between the Government of Australia and the Government of the Arab Republic of Egypt on the Promotion and Protection of Investments*, 3 May 2001, [2002] ATS 19 art 2:2 (entered into force 5 September 2002); *Agreement between Australia and the Socialist Republic of Vietnam on the Reciprocal Promotion and Protection of Investments*, 5 March 1991, [1991] ATS 36 art 2:2 (entered into force 11 September 1991; terminated 14 January 2019).

23   See e.g. *Comprehensive Economic and Trade Agreement between Canada, of the One Part, and the European Union and its Member States, of the Other Part*, 30 October 2016, art 8.1, sub verbo "investor" [*CETA*]; *Agreement on Encouragement and Reciprocal Protection of Investments*, Netherlands and Bangladesh, 1 November 1994, 1941 UNTS 97 art 1(b)(iii), sub verbo "national".

24   *ECT*, *supra* note 6.

25   Decision on the Respondent's Jurisdictional Objections, ICSID Case No ARB/09/12 (2012) at para 4.92 [*Pac Rim Cayman*].

26   Award, PCA Case No 2011-17 (2014) at para 384 [*Guaracachi*].

27   Consent Award, UNCITRAL (NAFTA, 12 April 2013) at para 3 [*St Marys VCNA*].

and the commencement of the arbitration.[57] Surprisingly, the tribunal disregarded the absence of disagreement between the state of incorporation and the host state after the consultations.[58] This interpretation seems to be contrary to the very purpose of the consultations, which is to allow the states to reach a mutually satisfactory solution on the invocation of the DoB clause.

Later treaties have replaced the obligation to hold consultations by providing only for compulsory notification of the invocation of the DoB clause, with state-to-state consultations only at the request of the state of incorporation. This softened version of consultations facilitates the exercise of the right to deny benefits. In *Pac Rim Cayman*, the host state duly notified the state of incorporation prior to invocation of the clause.[59] The denial of benefits was successful in this case, the state of incorporation not having requested consultations. The clause did not require specifically prior notification, but only notification "to the maximum extent possible."[60] The clause in NAFTA explicitly requires notification prior to the exercise of the right to deny benefits.[61] It has been invoked only in one case (*St. Marys VCNA*), by means of a notification to the state of incorporation of the intention to invoke the clause, supplemented by a letter setting out the reasons for doing so.[62] Again, the state of incorporation did not request consultations and the invocation of the clause was successful in leading to a settlement agreement in which the foreign investor acknowledged that it could not benefit from the rights of NAFTA.

The Burden of Proof in Applying the Clause

The issue of allocation of the burden of proof in the application of DoB clauses raises practical difficulties and may be decisive in the success (or not) of the denial of benefits. Arbitral tribunals have generally followed the principle of *actori incumbit probatio*, according to which the party that makes an allegation must bear the burden of proving it, i.e., the host state exercising its right to deny benefits.[63] However, the host state may not easily have access to information on third-country ownership or control of the foreign investor, and on the nature of the business activities that it conducts in the state of incorporation. The opacity of corporate structures and tax havens may raise insurmountable difficulties for the host state. Disclosure of relevant information by the investor is critical in this regard, otherwise the exercise of the right may be impracticable. That is probably why some arbitral tribunals have seemed to consider that the burden of proof rests instead on the investor.[64] One author suggested that these tribunals made a terminological confusion between the legal burden of proof of the host state, and the duty of the investor to

---

57 *Ibid* at 35, 160.

58 *Ibid* at 91.

59 *Pac Rim Cayman, supra* note 25 at para 4.84.

60 *CAFTA/DR, supra* note 52, arts 10.2.2, 18.1.3, 20.4.1.

61 *NAFTA, supra* note 6, arts 1113:2, 1803, 2006.

62 *St. Marys VCNA, supra* note 27 at 3, 5.

63 See *Pac Rim Cayman, supra* note 25 at para 4.60; *Ulysseas, supra* note 41 at para 166; *AMTO v Ukraine*, Award, SCC Case No 080/2005 (2008) at para 65 [*AMTO*].

64 *Pan American Energy v Argentina; BP America Production Company v Argentina*, Decision on Preliminary Objections, ICSID Cases No ARB/03/13 & ARB/04/8 (2006) at para 221; *Plama, supra* note 28 at paras 167–68. See Hoffmann, *supra* note 18 at 609.

disclose information and evidence in its possession.[65] Deciding otherwise would establish a rebuttable presumption that the corporation is not entitled to the benefits of the agreement.[66]

One possible solution could be to put the preliminary burden of proof on the host state, which would establish a rebuttable presumption of third-country ownership or control, and of lack of substantial business activities on its territory. The evidential burden would then shift to the foreign investor to rebut the presumption, based on its better knowledge of the relevant information.[67] This compromise approach has been followed explicitly in *Bridgestone Licensing Services v Panama*,[68] and in practice in *St. Marys VCNA*.[69] Disclosure of strategic information on business activities may also raise problems; a confidentiality agreement between the disputing parties could be a solution.[70]

Problems of Substance

The Legal Nature of the Clause

The issue of the legal nature of the DoB clause and of its consequences is controversial. Depending on the wording of the clause, arbitral tribunals have considered the exercise of the right to deny benefits to be a jurisdictional or an admissibility issue. The full implications of this qualification are generally not addressed in arbitral decisions, leaving the false impression that the issue is moot, since, in either case, the tribunal immediately rules on the exercise of its right by the host state.[71] Jan Paulsson underlined the critical difference between jurisdictional and admissibility issues in terms of reviewability of the decision.[72] If the exercise of the right is a jurisdictional issue, the disputing parties could challenge the decision of the tribunal on this point in accordance with the applicable annulment procedures.[73] Conversely, if it is an admissibility issue, the decision of the tribunal on this point should be final and not reviewable. According to Yas Banifatemi and Emmanuel Jacomy, however, review of decisions on admissibility could be possible under the ICSID Convention.[74]

Arbitral decisions under the ECT consistently consider that the invocation of the DoB clause is an issue of admissibility of the claim, going to the merits of the case.[75] This interpretation is

---

65   Elvira R Gadelshina, "Burden of Proof under the Denial-of-Benefits Clause of the Energy Charter Treaty: *Actori Incumbit Onus Probandi*" (2012) 29 J Intl Arb 269 at 284.

66   *Ibid.*

67   See Feldman, *supra* note 13 at 298.

68   Decision on Expedited Objections, ICSID Case No ARB/16/34 (2017) at para 289 [*Bridgestone*].

69   *St. Marys VCNA*, *supra* note 27 at 2.

70   See *St. Marys VCNA, ibid* at 6; *St. Marys VCNA v Canada (AG)* (2012), Toronto, FC T-668-12 (Notice of application) at para 22.

71   See Hoffmann, *supra* note 18 at 611.

72   Jan Paulsson, "Jurisdiction and Admissibility" in Gerald Asken et al, eds, *Global Reflections on International Law, Commerce and Dispute Resolution (Liber Amicorum in Honour of Robert Briner)* (Paris: ICC, 2005) 601 at 603, 605, 617.

73   Banifatemi, *supra* note 40 at 242, n 51.

74   Yas Banifatemi & Emmanuel Jacomy, "Compétence et recevabilité dans le droit de l'arbitrage en matière d'investissements" in Charles Leben, ed, *Droit international des investissements et de l'arbitrage transnational* (Paris: Pedone, 2015) 773 at 790–92.

75   See *Isolux*, *supra* note 34 at para 712; *Stati*, *supra* note 34 at para 745; *Khan Resources*, *supra* note 28 at para 412; *Yukos*, *supra* note 28 at paras 441, 443; *Veteran Petroleum*, *supra* note 28 at paras 497, 499; *Hulley Enterprises*, *supra* note 28 at paras 440, 442; *AMTO*, *supra* note 63 at para 60; *Petrobart*, *supra* note 33 at 151, 147–48; *Plama*, *supra* note 28 at paras 147–48, 151.

was adopted in *Masdar*, the tribunal finding that the key in the assessment of the nature of the activities is their materiality and not their magnitude.[106] Thus the examination of the business activities of the corporation should be more qualitative than quantitative.[107]

The nature of the activities of holding corporations — that is, corporations owning other corporations, but not producing goods or services — is more problematic, as its connection with the state of incorporation is less concrete. The arbitral tribunal in *9Ren Holdings* took the view that "the test of substantial business activities must take its colour from the nature of the business" conducted by the corporation.[108] A holding corporation is not characterized by bricks and mortar, but rather by paperwork, board meetings, bank accounts and chequebooks. The colourability of the condition according to the nature of the business is questionable and could lead to unfair results, defeating the very purpose of the DoB clause. By creating a two-tier test, instead of simply applying the same test to all corporations, it could be more difficult for host states to exercise their right to deny benefits to holding corporations, even if those corporations do not have a genuine link with the state of incorporation.

Another problem raised with the assessment of this condition is that of the focus of the analysis, when the corporation to which the host state wants to apply the DoB clause forms part of a larger corporate group. Some companies in that group may conduct more substantial business activities in the state of incorporation than others of the same group, which could colour the test and make it more difficult to satisfy for the denying host state. In *Pac Rim Cayman*, the arbitral tribunal faced this situation and ruled that the condition must be satisfied specifically by the corporation that brought the claim against the host state, and not collectively by the corporate group to which it belongs.[109]

A remaining problem with this substantive condition is that of the moment at which the assessment should be made. *EuroGas* raised the issue, but the arbitral tribunal did not need to make a ruling on it. The corporation argued that it was sufficient to demonstrate the existence of substantial business activities in the state of incorporation at only one point in the lifetime of the investment.[110] The host state replied that this demonstration must take place at the time of the notice of arbitration.[111] The latter argument would seem to be logical, since it is the moment at which the investor consents to the arbitration.

Conclusion

DoB clauses pursue important policy objectives, but remain rare in investment treaty practice, especially in first generation BITs. The United Nations Conference on Trade and Development (UNCTAD) recommends that states — and especially developing countries — include DoB clauses in their investment agreements, as a key tool for sustainable development.[112] All recent

---

106 *Masdar, supra* note 29 at paras 254–56.

107 Thorn & Doucleff, *supra* note 17 at 23.

108 *9Ren Holdings v Spain*, Award, ICSID Case No ARB/15/15 (2019) at para 182.

109 *Pac Rim Cayman, supra* note 25 at para 4.66.

110 *EuroGas, supra* note 31 at para 281.

111 *Ibid* at para 271.

112 UNCTAD, "Investment Policy Framework for Sustainable Development" (2015) at 94, online: Investment Policy Hub <https://investmentpolicy.unctad.org/investment-policy-framework>.

mega-regional agreements containing an investment chapter include a DoB clause, even the Draft Pan-African Investment Code, which will cover only developing countries if it enters into force.[113] It shows that DoB clauses are an essential feature of any progressive investment agreement. They offer greater legal predictability than relying on the unsettled law on abuse of right.[114]

One problem that dissemination of the clause in newer agreements may create is to give an impetus for foreign investors treaty shopping for older agreements to avoid a possible denial of their benefits. A problem also emerges regarding the interplay of the DoB clause with asymmetrical ISDS rules within multilateral agreements, as exemplified by CUSMA and the CPTPP. In face of the narrow interpretation given to conditional DoB clauses, M. Sornarajah suggests replacing the state of incorporation criterion with a more effective test of corporate nationality, akin to the automatic DoB clause used in *CETA*.[115] Before amending or replacing existing agreements, states parties could clarify the DoB clause by adopting, if possible under the agreement, an authoritative interpretation of its conditions of form and substance. Besides, the problem of consistency of retrospective application with the ICSID Convention is serious and requires further analysis. The proper function of state-to-state consultations in relation to the invocation of the DoB clause should also be clarified.

The result of the denial of benefits of an investment agreement is to prevent the corporation owned or controlled by third-country nationals to vindicate its rights, make its claim and possibly to obtain justice outside of municipal law. Given the lack of genuine linkage between the corporation and the state of incorporation, the latter is unlikely to be willing to exercise its diplomatic protection and pursue the matter any further on the international plane. It is fortunate that the International Law Commission proposed a progressive development of international law, in order to allow the state of management and financial control of the corporation to exercise the default mechanism of diplomatic protection, outside of the framework of an investment agreement. This possibility, already envisaged in *Barcelona Traction*, restores the minimal conditions in international law for justice to be served at the state-to-state level for third-country investors.

Author's Note

I would like to thank Cecilia Landi for her able research assistance. I would also like to thank all participants of the research workshop on the corporation organized by CIGI in Toronto on March 2, 2019.

---

113 African Union Commission, *Draft Pan-African Investment Code* (2016), art 10:4. See also *ASEAN Comprehensive Investment Agreement*, Association of Southeast Asian Nations, 26 February 2009, art 19 (entered into force 24 February 2012).

114 Feldman, *supra* note 13 at 282, 301–02.

115 Sornarajah, *supra* note 15 at 141.

15

RECONCEPTUALIZING INTERNATIONAL INVESTMENT GOVERNANCE

The Challenges of Establishing Foreign Investor Obligations

Enrique Boone Barrera

Introduction

At the behest of the UN Human Rights Council, the independent expert Alfred-Maurice de Zayas set out to test international investment agreements (IIAs) and investor-state arbitration "for conformity with the Charter of the United Nations."[1] The results were damning. His report concluded that "[a]mong the major threats to a democratic and equitable international order is the operation of arbitral tribunals that act as if they were above the international human rights regime."[2] The report also called for systemic reforms to the regime of foreign investment protection.[3] The risks posed by this regime have become more acute as international economic

---

1   *Report of the Independent Expert on the Promotion of a Democratic and Equitable International Order, Alfred-Maurice de Zayas*, UNGAOR, 30th Sess, Human Rights Council, UN Doc A/HRC/30/44 (2015) at 1.

2   *Ibid* at para 15.

3   *Ibid* at para 41.

agreements cover an ever-expanding range of "beyond the border" issues that directly interfere with the ability of states to respond to local demands without a financial penalty. [4]

IIAs can facilitate the operation of multinational corporations (MNCs) in developing countries, bringing both benefits and challenges.[5] Joseph Stiglitz, Nobel laureate in economics, has identified six main reasons why MNCs have become such a threat to international governance: they often have more resources than the countries where they operate; they join forces with home states to pressure less powerful nations to get preferential treatment; they take advantage of the lack of administrative capacity and technical expertise of less developed countries; in coordination with their home states, they take advantage of the lack of expertise during treaty negotiations; they use their multinational status to avoid accountability; and they use different standards abroad than in their home countries.[6]

The effects of this imbalance may be felt differently depending on the country. Some developing countries have deficient institutions and weak rule of law. When a wealthy MNC enters a market in these conditions, it creates incentives for corruption, and it exposes vulnerable populations to potential harm. Furthermore, the regime of investment protection could also create incentives for MNCs to form alliances with despotic regimes at the expense of the general population.[7]

One of the selling points of IIAs when they came to prominence in the 1990s, was that they were tools to improve the domestic governance of host states, [8] yet their typical dispute resolution mechanisms do not contain incentives for investors to behave appropriately. In this chapter, I will discuss how newer treaties, including model agreements, have responded to the challenges posed by MNCs in the international investment protection regime. I will argue that signed treaties lack sufficient provisions to hold foreign investors accountable, while model agreements could benefit from more clarity regarding how they would operate in practice. Next, I examine the few awards that have covered the issue of investor obligations. Finally, I make recommendations regarding how to approach the challenges posed by trying to hold foreign investors accountable. I will argue that without a reconceptualization of the purpose and ethos of the regime of foreign investment protection, these challenges will not disappear.

---

4   Joseph E Stiglitz, "On the Wrong Side of Globalization", *The New York Times* (15 March 2014).

5   Yannick Radi, "Introduction: Taking Stock of the Societal and Legal Interplay between Human Rights and Investment" in Yannick Radi, ed, *Research Handbook on Human Rights and Investment* (Cheltenham, UK: Edward Elgar, 2018) 1 at 5–6.

6   Joseph E Stiglitz, "Multinational Corporations: Balancing Rights and Responsibilities" (2007) 101 Proceedings of the ASIL Annual Meeting 3 at 16–18.

7   Soumyajit Mazumder, "Can I Stay a BIT Longer? The Effect of Bilateral Investment Treaties on Political Survival" (2016) 11:4 Rev Intl Organizations 477 at 515–16.

8   José A Alvarez, *The Public International Law Regime Governing International Investment* (The Hague: Hague Academy of International Law, 2011) 378–79.

The Challenges of Incorporating and Enforcing Investor Obligations

Signed Treaties and Model Agreements

Currently, there are very few obligations on foreign investors in IIAs. The ones that do exist usually ask only that the investor follow the laws of the host state and, increasingly, of international agreements. This section analyzes the signed and model agreements that have the strongest clauses to date in terms of investor obligations.

The 2016 Morocco-Nigeria bilateral investment treaty (BIT) is not yet in force, but it contains a series of innovations in this area.[9] The obligations in this treaty can be divided into three kinds: obligations to follow domestic law; obligations to follow international law; and obligations to follow international standards. In terms of environmental protection, for instance, the treaty contemplates obligations of both the first and third type. The treaty has both declarative and prescriptive provisions. In the declarative sections, the treaty reaffirms the intention of the parties to fulfill their international obligations regarding the environment.[10] While declaratory provisions can send a signal to tribunals to interpret the agreement having in mind that the signatory parties expected the investor to behave a certain way, their effectiveness is very limited.[11] In the more prescriptive section, the treaty establishes that the investor should follow domestic law and, secondly, requires that the investor incorporate the highest international environmental standards for sensitive industries.[12]

In terms of labour rights and human rights, the approach is similar. The BIT reaffirms the intent of the parties not to lower labour rights and to respect human rights,[13] while also directing the investor to follow the International Labour Organization (ILO) declaration.[14] In this regard, much will depend on how the tribunal would apply such provisions. It is here that the treaty proves to be less innovative, in particular when it comes to the minimum standard of treatment (MST).

Article 7 of the BIT deals with the MST, which encompasses the fair and equitable standard of treatment (FET). The description does not go much further than where the NAFTA Interpretative Note left it in 2001.[15] Newer treaties have more precise provisions regarding what the MST should encompass. Omitting FET clauses is a necessary step toward a more coherent regime of foreign investment protection, given that this standard of protection is the most

---

9   *Reciprocal Investment Promotion and Protection Agreement between the Government of the Kingdom of Morocco and the Government of the Federal Republic of Nigeria*, 3 December 2016 (not yet in force) [*Morocco–Nigeria BIT*], online: <https://investmentpolicy.unctad.org/international-investment-agreements/treaty-files/5409/download>.

10   There are references to environmental protection in both the preamble and in article 13. *Ibid.*

11   Alison Giest, "Interpreting Public Interest Provisions in International Investment Treaties" (2017) 18:1 Chicago J Intl L 321 at 337.

12   *Morocco–Nigeria BIT, supra* note 9, art 18.1.

13   *Ibid*, art 15.

14   *Ibid*, arts 18.2, 18.3.

15   NAFTA Free Trade Commission, *Notes of Interpretation of Certain NAFTA Chapter 11 Provisions* (31 July 2001), online: *Global Affairs Canada* <www.international.gc.ca/trade-agreements-accords-commerciaux/topics-domaines/disp-diff/ NAFTA-Interpr.aspx?lang=eng>.

likely to present a threat to the right to regulate.[16] That being said, the treaty does have some minor innovations such as clarifying what "like circumstances" means in the national treatment and most-favoured-nation clauses. In particular, the treaty establishes that in examining "like circumstances," the tribunal should consider the cumulative effects of all investments on the environment rather than just a particular investment in isolation.[17] In addition, the treaty clarifies that the right to regulate includes "the goals and principles of sustainable development," and it should be balanced with the rights and obligations of investors.[18]

The Belarus-India BIT, signed in 2018, has an even shorter chapter regarding investor obligations. The "chapter" is comprised of only a couple of articles that refer to compliance with the law and corporate social responsibility (CSR).[19] This is consistent with India's model BIT, which significantly reduced the chapter on investor obligations from its first model BIT draft.[20] That being said, it is interesting to note that the phrasing of the MST is novel in the sense that it replaces the "fair and equitable treatment standard" with a specific reference to customary international law that is defined in traditional terms ("general and consistent practice accepted as law").[21] As I have argued elsewhere, this is a better approach, since the FET clause brings much uncertainty to IIAs.[22]

The Morocco-Nigeria BIT is the most advanced in terms of investor obligations, even if it represents more of a gradual evolution than a revolution. Model agreements contain more sophisticated provisions in this regard. The Draft Pan-African Investment Code goes further than the BITs mentioned above in achieving a balance between protecting foreign investors and the state's right to regulate. In particular, the Pan-African Code goes further in imposing concrete obligations on foreign investors as well as making clear that human rights obligations are binding on foreign investors. The code lacks an FET clause, which, as mentioned above, should be considered best practice.[23] Similar to the Morocco-Nigeria BIT, the Pan-African Code is careful in determining what constitutes "like circumstances" when it comes to most-favoured-nation and national treatment clauses. Articles 7(3) and 9(3) clarify that "in like circumstances" requires a case-by-case examination that takes into account the rights of third persons and local communities and, most notably, "its effects on the local, regional or national environment, the health of the populations, or on the global commons."[24]

---

16   Michael Waibel, "Fair and Equitable Treatment as Boilerplate" (2019) University of Cambridge Faculty of Law Research Paper No 16/2019 at 3, online: <https://ssrn.com/abstract=3401770>.

17   *Morocco-Nigeria BIT*, *supra* note 9, art 6.3(b).

18   *Ibid*, art 23(1)(2).

19   *Treaty Between the Republic of Belarus and the Republic of India on Investments*, 24 September 2018, arts 11–12 (not yet in force) [*Belarus-India BIT*], online: <https://investmentpolicy.unctad.org/international-investment-agreements/treaty-files/5724/download>.

20   Jesse Coleman et al, "International Investment Agreements, 2015-2016: A Review of Trends and New Approaches" in Lisa Sachs & Lise J Johnson, eds, *Yearbook on International Investment Law & Policy* (Oxford: Oxford University Press, 2018) 42 at 48.

21   *Belarus-India BIT*, *supra* note 19, arts 1.2, 3.1.

22   Enrique Boone Barrera, "The Case for Removing the Fair and Equitable Treatment Standard from NAFTA" CIGI, CIGI Papers No 128, 27 April 2017 at 8, online: <www.cigionline.org/sites/default/files/documents/Paper%20no.128web_2.pdf>.

23   *Ibid* at 10.

24   African Union Commission, Economic Affairs Department, *Draft Pan-African Investment Code* (2016), art 7(3)a–b, [African Union Commission, *Draft Code*], online: <https://au.int/sites/default/files/documents/32844-doc-draft_pan-african_investment_code_december_2016_en.pdf>.

Another innovation is article 17, regarding performance requirements. Instead of prohibiting performance requirements, the Pan-African Code allows the parties "to promote domestic investments and local content."[25] The code also includes a chapter entirely devoted to investor obligations. Most of the obligations are related to abstaining from doing harm rather than requiring the performance of a particular duty or action. For instance, the code asks that investors refrain from interfering in political affairs, bribing public officials, interfering with the development objectives of states and exploiting natural resources to the detriment of the host state.[26]

Other innovations in the Pan-African Code are related to corporate governance. In this regard, the code requires that corporations meet "national and internationally accepted standards of corporate governance for the sector involved."[27] There is no specific standard mentioned; however, the code does mention certain goals that the investor should meet, such as ensuring equitable treatment of shareholders, encouraging cooperation between corporations and other stakeholders to maximize the positive spillovers of economic activity, and disclosing, in a timely manner, information about the company and its "human resource policies."[28] In addition, the code specifies a series of principles that should govern business ethics and human rights. These principles go from vague statements (i.e., "support and respect" human rights) to more specific obligations (i.e., eliminate labour discrimination).[29] Other provisions are too vaguely drafted to understand what exactly is intended by their drafters. For instance, article 24 requires that investors "ensure equitable sharing of wealth derived from investments,"[30] without any further clarification.

It is not entirely clear how these provisions would be enforced. As opposed to the Morocco-Nigeria BIT, the Pan-African Code does not have an organization in charge of overseeing its implementation. The code was intended to provide a blueprint regarding what to include in investment treaties, but it does not substitute or override other IIAs.[31] States can decide to make the code binding after some time, as determined by the states themselves.[32] The code specifies several methods of dispute resolution. It encourages states to resolve their disputes through consultation, negotiation or mediation. However, the code also contemplates submitting disputes to the African Court of Justice and to investor-state arbitration.[33] It is not clear, however, which is to be the default method of dispute resolution.

Other model treaties have tried to include investor obligations, with varying degrees of clarity. Top among these efforts is the Southern African Development Community (SADC) model BIT. While not as ambitious as the Pan-African Code, the SADC model BIT contains a

---

25   *Ibid*, art 17(2).

26   *Ibid*, arts 20.1(c), 21.1, 22.2, 23.1.

27   *Ibid*, art 19.1.

28   *Ibid*, art 19.3.

29   *Ibid*, art 24.

30   *Ibid*, art 24(e).

31   Amr Hedar, "The Legal Nature of the Draft Pan-African Investment Code and its Relationship with International Investment Agreements" (2017) South Centre Investment Policy Brief No 9 at 3, online: <www.southcentre.int/wp-content/uploads/2017/07/IPB9_The-Legal-Nature-of-the-Draft-Pan-African-Investment-Code-and-its-Relationship-with-International-Investment-Agreements_EN.pdf>.

32   African Union Commission, *Draft Code, supra* note 24, art 3.2.

33   *Ibid*, arts 41, 42.

chapter on investor obligations. Among these obligations are a prohibition against corruption, a legality clause, disclosure rules, compliance with environmental and social assessments, an obligation to maintain an environmental management system and incorporation of international environmental standards, compliance with labour laws and international agreements (including the ILO Declaration on Fundamental Principles and Rights of Work), and respect for internationally recognized corporate governance standards.[34]

The International Institute for Sustainable Development (IISD) Model International Agreement on Investment for Sustainable Development also has a chapter dedicated to investor obligations. Similar to the treaties discussed above, this model IIA includes provisions against bribery as well as a mandate to comply with international and domestic environmental and human rights standards.[35] The IISD model agreement requires investors in risky industries to obtain ISO 14001 certification or an equivalent environmental management system.[36] The specification of a particular environmental standard makes for easier interpretation in the event of a dispute.[37] It also suggests that the investor should "strive" to contribute to the sustainable development of the host state.[38] It is not clear how this provision will be interpreted and enforced by the state.

This model agreement is more specific in terms of the consequences for the investor if there is a breach of obligations. A violation of the agreement could deprive the foreign investor of bringing a claim against the state, or it could affect the merits of the claim or affect the damages to which it would be entitled otherwise.[39]

Some BITs have very vague references to investor obligations, but they are complemented by additional agreements. For instance, the investment chapter in the Canada-Colombia Free Trade Agreement relegates obligations for investors to a CSR clause. Article 816 states that the parties should encourage enterprises to "voluntarily incorporate internationally recognized standards of corporate social responsibility in their internal policies."[40] This clause is clearly insufficient, given Colombia's well-known problems with the persecution of union members.[41,] However, the same parties signed the Canada-Colombia Agreement on Labour Cooperation, which came into effect in 2011. That same year, Colombia and the United States also signed a "labour action plan" in which the Government of Colombia agreed to expand its program to

---

34   Southern African Development Community (SADC), *SADC Model Bilateral Investment Treaty Template with Commentary* (2012), arts 10–17, online: IISD <www.iisd.org/itn/wp-content/uploads/2012/10/sadc-model-bit-template-final.pdf>.

35   Howard Mann et al, *IISD Model International Agreement on Investment for Sustainable Development* (2005), arts 13, 14, online: <www.iisd.org/sites/default/files/publications/investment_model_int_handbook.pdf>.

36   *Ibid*, art 14(a).

37   Indeed, the model agreement stipulates that disputes should be resolved in accordance with the terms contained in said agreement. *Ibid*, art 48(A).

38   *Ibid*, art 16.

39   *Ibid*, art 18.

40   *Free Trade Agreement between Canada and Colombia*, 21 November 2008 (entered into force 15 August 2011), online: <www.international.gc.ca/trade-commerce/trade-agreements-accords-commerciaux/agr-acc/colombia-colombie/fta-ale/08.aspx?lang=eng>.

41   "Trade unions 'face global persecution'", *BBC News* (18 June 2002), online: <http://news.bbc.co.uk/2/hi/2050886.stm>.

protect labour union members and activists.[42] While these are steps in the right direction, the agreements fail to impose direct obligations on foreign investors.[43]

This is not to suggest that all these problems are caused by foreign investors or that including more specific obligations on foreign investors is the only solution available. However, if there is more that can be done to convey to foreign investors that they would be penalized if they move to a developing country solely to take advantage of lower labour standards (or, worse, to exacerbate these problems), then there is a moral responsibility to do so.

Cases Involving Investor Obligations

These agreements leave many questions regarding their implementation, adjudication and the sort of outcomes they may produce. Furthermore, there seems to be little appetite to include binding and enforceable obligations on foreign investors. However, even in these circumstances, arbitral tribunals have wrestled with whether to find investor obligations derived either from customary international law or from international treaties. The source of the obligation matters, as it affects how the obligation is interpreted and the kind of remedy available.

In terms of customary international law, we can also make a distinction between easy and hard cases. The easy cases are when the violation of a human rights norm is simultaneously considered an international criminal offence. That is, the human right in question exists as customary international law and is also contemplated in an international criminal law treaty. Some of these cases are related to business people engaging in war crimes as a result of their economic activities. Since the aftermath of World War II, there have been several cases in which individuals have been subject to international prosecution for grave violations of human rights, either by international tribunals or by states exercising extraterritorial jurisdiction.[44] These actions could potentially be expanded to include legal persons such as MNCs.[45]

The hard cases relate to violations of human rights that are not as clear-cut. These may be related to issues such as labour law violations or environmental degradation. In June 2019, a group of UN experts argued that "[f]ailing to protect biodiversity can constitute a violation of the right to a healthy environment, a right that is legally recognised by 155 States and should now be globally recognised as fundamental."[46] However, can this emerging human right be enforced against corporations? Is any oversight regarding the protection of biodiversity tantamount to

---

42   *Colombian Action Plan Related to Labor Rights*, United States and Colombia, 7 April 2011, online: Office of the United States Trade Representative <https://ustr.gov/sites/default/files/uploads/agreements/morocco/pdfs/Colombian%20 Action%20Plan%20Related%20to%20Labor%20Rights.pdf>.

43   In 2017, the Canadian National Administrative Office, established in the Agreement on Labour Cooperation, issued a series of recommendations after the Canadian Labour Congress and five Colombian labour organizations accused Colombia of failing to meet the standards established in the agreement. Employment and Social Development Canada, "Report Issued Pursuant to the Canada-Colombia Agreement on Labour Cooperation" (2017), online: <http://publications.gc.ca/collections/collection_2017/edsc-esdc/Em8-26-2017-eng.pdf>. The Colombian Action Plan Related to Labor Rights has also been criticized as insufficient to address the violence against labour in Colombia. See Lisa Haugaard, "A Plan Still on Paper: Three Years of the US-Colombia Labor Action Plan", *The Huffington Post* (blog) (9 June 2014), online: <www.huffpost.com/entry/labor-action-plan-colombia_b_5118210>.

44   Joanna Kyriakakis, "International criminal responsibilities for MNCs' violations of human rights" in Radi, *supra* note 5, 273 at 277–79.

45   *Ibid* at 280, 281.

46   United Nations, Human Rights, Office of the High Commissioner, News Release, "Failing to Protect Biodiversity can be a Human Rights Violation – UN Experts" (25 June 2019), online: <www.ohchr.org/EN/NewsEvents/Pages/ DisplayNews.aspx?NewsID=24738&LangID=E>.

a human rights violation? These are the types of questions that arbitrators may ask themselves when faced with a claim that a corporation violated the human right to biodiversity.

A further complication may be when a corporation acts in strict accordance with the domestic law of a despotic regime.[47] In other instances, local authorities may lack the capacity and appropriate regulations to address violations of human rights. In these cases, and in the absence of specific treaty provisions to deal with them, it may be hard for an arbitral tribunal to find fault with the corporation. In the *Bear Creek* case,[48] for example, which involved a Canadian mining company and the Government of Peru, the tribunal recognized that the behaviour of the corporation was not consistent with international standards, but it also noted that the government had not taken steps to correct the situation.

In the *Urbaser* award,[49] the tribunal determined that it could enforce investor obligations, based on international human rights treaties. In this case, Argentina presented a counterclaim against the investor, alleging that the failure to make the necessary investments affected the local population's access to water, which was a violation of a fundamental human right.[50] The tribunal admitted the counterclaim by finding, first, that the BIT gave jurisdiction to the tribunal on any dispute in connection with an investment covered by that agreement.[51] As a result, the tribunal proceeded to examine the counterclaim on the merits. The tribunal determined that the BIT's purpose of protecting foreign investment did not mean that the state would not have any rights under the treaty and the investor would have no obligations.[52]

The challenge for the tribunal was to find the precise source of such obligations. Even if true that the Spain-Argentina BIT did not explicitly state the investor would have no obligations, it also did not specify any obligations. The tribunal proceeded to adopt new understandings of international law and of the relation between IIAs and human rights. The first principle to tackle was whether a corporation could be considered a subject of international law. The tribunal recognized that, in the past, the answer had always been in the negative. Using the same rights afforded to investors as grounds to impose obligations, however, the tribunal reasoned that if the BIT was predicated on the idea that an investor was capable of holding rights under international law, that notion "would reject by necessity any idea that a foreign investor company could not be subject to international obligations."[53]

Having established that a foreign investor could have international obligations, the tribunal set out to find if any were imposed on Urbaser in particular. Here, it is important to differentiate between two separate steps: the identification of the international obligation (i.e., what is its

---

47   This was the case with Wang Xiaoning and Shi Tao, who were arrested and imprisoned by the Chinese authorities under what could be considered political charges. It is alleged that they may have been subjected to forced labour and torture. Both men were arrested with the help of a subsidiary of Yahoo in China. David Jason Karp, *Responsibility for Human Rights: Transnational Corporations in Imperfect States* (Cambridge, UK: Cambridge University Press, 2014) at 17.

48   *Bear Creek Mining Corporation v Republic of Peru*, Award, 30 November 2017, ICSID Case No ARB/14/21 [*Bear Creek*].

49   *Urbaser SA and Consorcio de Aguas Bilbao Bizkaia, Bilbao Biskaia Ur Partzuergoa v Argentina*, Award, 8 December 2016, ICSID Case No ARB/07/26.

50   *Ibid* at 1156–57.

51   *Ibid* at para 1143.

52   *Ibid* at paras 1182, 1187.

53   *Ibid* at para 1194.

source? Is it relevant to the case at hand?); and the individualization of the obligation (i.e., was Urbaser under such obligation once the obligation was identified as relevant?).

Consequently, the first task was to determine whether there was an international obligation to provide access to water. The tribunal identified the 1948 Universal Declaration of Human Rights, which could also be applied to corporations, as relevant, as well as the 1966 International Covenant on Economic, Social, and Cultural Rights and the International Labour Office's Tripartite Declaration of Principles concerning Multilateral Enterprises and Social Policy.[54] From these documents, the tribunal identified an obligation "on all parts, public and private parties, not to engage in activity aimed at *destroying* such rights."[55] Furthermore, the tribunal argued that "[t]he BIT has to be construed in harmony with other rules of international law of which it forms part, including those related to human rights."[56]

Thus, the first step identified a relevant obligation of international law that is applicable to both public and private actors. Roughly, that obligation is not to destroy the fundamental elements that guarantee an adequate standard of living, including access to water. Furthermore, the tribunal identified a human right to water and sanitation as well as "its corresponding obligation of States *to provide* all living persons under their jurisdiction with safe and clean drinking water and sewage services."[57] Consequently, there is a universal obligation not to interfere with the right to access water and an obligation upon states to provide such access.

As a result, the second step can only conclude by finding the investor not liable. That is, according to the tribunal, the obligation to provide access to water does exist in international law, but it applies only to states. Private actors' only obligation is not to destroy such access. Urbaser's obligation to provide access to water is only contractual and not based in international law.[58] The tribunal thus differentiated between the obligation to take proactive measures to uphold human rights, which is imposed only on states, and the obligation not to destroy or to abstain from interfering in the exercise of rights under international law, which is incumbent upon both public and private actors. On these grounds, Argentina's counterclaim failed.[59]

In *Bear Creek*, Peru argued that the investor had contributed to the resistance to the mining project because of its deficient outreach to the local communities.[60] The tribunal seemed to agree with this claim, but also determined that the government was aware of the actions of the investor and did not object.[61] The problem with this approach is that it further entrenches the notion that corporations have no responsibilities to the international community.[62] The implication of this case is that even if some MNCs have more resources than some developed

---

54   *Ibid* at paras 1196–98.

55   *Ibid* at para 1199 [emphasis added].

56   *Ibid* at para 1200.

57   *Ibid* at para 1205 [emphasis added].

58   *Ibid* at para 1210.

59   *Ibid* at para 1221.

60   *Bear Creek*, *supra* note 48 at paras 560–62.

61   *Ibid* at 412.

62   This in addition to the lack of responsibilities of foreign investors toward local communities. I will not cover this important topic here, but for more see Nicolas Perrone, "The 'Invisible' Local Communities: Foreign Investor Obligations, Inclusiveness, and the International Investment Regime" (2019) 16:21 AJIL Unbound 113.

countries,[63] international law still focuses on states' responsibility for enforcing human rights obligations, rather than the failures of MNCs to respect human rights.

Even though it was not a counterclaim, as in the *Urbaser* case, Peru further claimed that the investor had failed to comply with the Indigenous and Tribal Peoples Convention (ILO Convention 169).[64] The majority of the tribunal disagreed by pointing out that the convention imposed obligations only on states and not on corporations.[65] The dissenting opinion, however, considered that even if the convention did not impose obligations on corporations, it did set a standard that the investor should have been more sensible to, specifically by assuming the responsibility of obtaining the "social licence" to operate the mine.[66]

Thus, both the *Bear Creek* and the *Urbaser* tribunals were ultimately unable to hold foreign investors accountable in the absence of concrete obligations established in an IIA. It is also important to distinguish how the two tribunals approached the application of international agreements to MNCs. I described above how the *Urbaser* tribunal rejected the traditional notion that human rights instruments could apply only to states, considering this approach antiquated. The *Bear Creek* tribunal, however, took a different position.

Taken together, the *Urbaser* and *Bear Creek* cases expose the challenges of holding MNCs accountable. The cases reveal three main obstacles: outdated conceptions in international law that exempt the private sector from having any sort of responsibility toward the international community; the asymmetry of IIAs (i.e., the lack of clearly stated obligations for investors); and the lack of sufficient precedents holding MNCs accountable in the international arena.

An alternative to imposing and enforcing direct obligations is to look for principles of international law that could affect the strength of the claim of the investor before an arbitral tribunal or the amount of compensation that could be awarded. This is, of course, a limited response to the lack of accountability of MNCs, since it would apply only in the international investment regime. As mentioned above, the IISD model agreement would limit the benefits of an IIA if an investor breaches one or more of the obligations described in that agreement. In this case, however, instead of positive obligations, we are discussing principles of international law that do not have to be spelled out in a specific agreement in order to be binding on the parties.

The concept of social licence, which was relevant in the *Bear Creek* case, is one of those emerging principles that is starting to have effects in international law. Social licence has several objectives, among them: ensuring that the behaviour of corporations is legitimate; opening avenues for the communities (Indigenous groups in particular) affected by a corporation to influence economic projects; and diminishing the instances of social unrest because of the activities of a corporation.[67]

---

63   Fernando Belinchón & Ruqayyah Moynihan, "25 Giant Companies that are Bigger than Entire Countries", *Business Insider* (25 July 2018), online: <www.businessinsider.com/25-giant-companies-that-earn-more-than-entire-countries-2018-7#netflix-had-a-greater-revenue-in-2017-than-maltas-gdp-2>.

64   *Bear Creek*, *supra* note 48 at para 256; see International Labour Organization, C-169, *Indigenous and Tribal Peoples Convention, 1989*.

65   *Ibid* at para 664.

66   *Ibid*, dissenting opinion at para 37.

67   These are some of the goals identified by Domènec Melé and Jaume Armengou in their review of the different understandings of the concept of social licence to operate. Domènec Melé & Jaume Armengou, "Moral Legitimacy in Controversial Projects and its Relationship with Social License to Operate: A Case Study" (2016) 136:4 J Business Ethics 729 at 731–34.

The majority in the *Bear Creek* case diluted this principle to the point of making it meaningless by making the state responsible for the corporation obtaining the social licence to operate. However, the dissent shows that new understandings of the responsibilities of corporations are starting to reach even the fairly closed arbitral community.[68]

The second principle worth discussing is that of "clean hands," which was relevant in some arbitral proceedings, such as the *Yukos* and *Copper Mesa* cases.[69] The doctrine of clean hands in this context refers to the notion that wrongdoing on the part of a claimant diminishes the admissibility of a claim,[70] or the amount of compensation.[71] Some consider this doctrine a basic principle of justice,[72] while others deny that it has reached general applicability.[73]

In *Copper Mesa*, the tribunal considered that the alleged wrongdoings of the investor should have been known to the Government of Ecuador well before the arbitral proceedings. As a result, the tribunal refused Ecuador's request to decline jurisdiction.[74] In terms of the admissibility of the claims, the tribunal decided to interpret the doctrine of clean hands "under analogous doctrines of causation and contributory fault applying to the merits of the Claimant's claims."[75]

Ultimately, however, after considering other precedents, the tribunal determined that the doctrine of clean hands, the concept of contributory fault as described in article 39 of the International Law Commission's Articles on State Responsibility,[76] and the notion of causation were "materially the same."[77] However, perhaps because of the precise wording and the existence of clear precedents, the tribunal proceeded to rely exclusively on article 39 of the ILC articles. Using this legal approach, the tribunal found that Copper Mesa had contributed to its own injury, in the amount of 30 percent, for one of its claims.[78]

It is illuminating to analyze the different approaches taken by the *Copper Mesa* and *Bear Creek* tribunals. In both cases, the tribunals found that the states probably knew, or should have known, of the misconduct of the foreign investor. As discussed above, the *Copper Mesa* tribunal considered that omission to act in time was relevant to determine jurisdiction, but it later came back to analyze the misconduct of the investor under the doctrine of contributory fault. The majority in the *Bear Creek* tribunal did not follow a similar approach, in spite of

---

68   Moshe Hirsch, "The Sociology of International Investment Law" in Zachary Douglas, Joost Pauwelyn & Jorge E Viñuales, eds, *The Foundations of International Investment Law: Bringing Theory into Practice* (Oxford: Oxford University Press, 2014) 143 at 147.

69   *Yukos Universal Ltd (Isle of Man) v Russia*, Final Award, 18 July 2014, PCA Case No AA 227 [*Yukos*]; *Copper Mesa Mining Corp v Ecuador*, Award, 15 March 2016, PCA Case No 2012-2 [*Copper Mesa*].

70   Isuru C Devendra, "State Responsibility for Corruption in International Investment Arbitration" (2019) 10 J Intl Dispute Settlement 248 at 280.

71   Jun Zhao, "Human Rights Accountability of Transnational Corporations: A Potential Response from Bilateral Investment Treaties" (2015) 8:1 J East Asia & Intl L 47 at 68.

72   *Inceysa Vallisoletana, SL v El Salvador*, Award, 2 August 2006, ICSID Case No ARB/03/26 at para 244.

73   In the *Yukos* award, the tribunal did take into consideration the misconduct of the claimants that contributed to their injury, but questioned the general applicability of the doctrine of clean hands. *Yukos*, *supra* note 69 at paras 1358–59, 1362–63, 1633–37.

74   *Copper Mesa*, *supra* note 69 at paras 5.63–5.64.

75   *Ibid* at para 5.65.

76   International Law Commission, *Responsibility of States for Internationally Wrongful Acts*, UNGAOR, 56th Sess, UN Doc A/56/10 (2001).

77   *Copper Mesa*, *supra* note 69 at para 6.97.

78   *Ibid* at para 6.133.

finding that the investor could have done a better job communicating with the Indigenous communities opposing the mining project. Given this finding, it is puzzling that the majority stated, "Respondent has the burden of proof that its breaches of the FTA…were to some extent caused by Claimant. In view of the above cited conclusions of the Tribunal, Respondent has not met that burden."[79]

As the dissenting opinion stated, the fact that the investor did not properly reach out to communities was a contributing factor to losing the right to operate.[80] For the majority, the fact that the investor failed to reach out to Indigenous communities properly was also a failure of the state. If arbitral tribunals do not expect MNCs to take proactive steps to achieve higher standards of conduct in their operations, this will not encourage MNCs to become more responsible international actors.

As demonstrated above, tribunals have struggled to hold corporations accountable. The asymmetry of IIAs, antiquated notions of international law, the ambiguous legal framework in which MNCs operate, the weak rule of law and lack of rigorous standards in many developing countries, as well as the lack of precedents in holding MNCs accountable, are all contributing factors. The status quo represents real risks for vulnerable populations in both developed and developing countries. In what follows, I will address each of these issues.

Moving Forward: Reconceptualizing International Investment Law

The main purpose of the international regime of protection of foreign investment was to protect the economic interests of capital exporters in developing countries by providing a reliable international dispute settlement mechanism to deter disruptive actions by host states.[81] Developing countries might also have considered these treaties a means to attract foreign investment and spur development.[82] The insulation of the foreign investor from domestic conditions was the guiding ethos of the treaty-based regime of foreign protection and that has made incorporating investor obligations in IIAs more challenging. The assumption is that host states can promulgate and enforce their own laws to regulate the behaviour of foreign investors if they so wish.[83] However, examples provided earlier suggest that IIAs can empower MNCs to evade regulations and discourage states from enacting public policies for fear of litigation.[84] As a result, it is important to reconceptualize the purpose of this legal regime before we can make suggestions to reform it.

In this regard, a group of experts on international investment law put together a proposal to rethink how the international community should approach the regime of foreign investment

---

79   *Bear Creek, supra* note 48 at para 568.

80   *Ibid*, dissenting opinion at para 38.

81   Enrique Boone Barrera, "Property Rights as Human Rights in International Investment Arbitration: A Critical Approach" (2018) 59:8 Boston College L Rev 2635 at 2643.

82   Jonathan Bonnitcha, Lauge N Skovgaard Poulsen & Michael Waibel, *The Political Economy of the Investment Treaty Regime* (Oxford: Oxford University Press, 2017) at 46.

83   *Ibid* at 15.

84   *Ibid* at 241.

protection.[85] These experts considered the treaty-based regime of investment protection as part of a broader system of global governance that incorporates the "principles of transparency, participation, reciprocity, accountability, and subsidiarity."[86] International investment law, as part of global governance, implies that the regime should evolve from exclusively protecting the economic interests of foreign investors to become an instrument that improves international public policy.[87] In this regard, the authors argue that the focus should be on the real interests of states such as "the tax revenue, development, jobs, and the positive spillovers that foreign investment can — but does not necessarily — bring."[88] Furthermore, international investment law should "align with and support the goals of reducing host country poverty and inequality, maintaining and improving host country health and environmental needs, and assuring human dignity for all."[89]

For investor obligations to be meaningful, and for the regime of investment protection to become a positive factor in global governance, the regime must change its ethos. A piecemeal approach to reform would only lead to confusion, and would risk leaving some developing countries behind if they lack sufficient power to influence negotiations. Reconceptualizing the regime of investment protection as part of global governance is a necessary first step toward holding foreign investors accountable before the international community.

With this goal of reconceptualizing the regime of foreign investment, we can start exploring options for reform. There are two main ways of addressing the issue of investor obligations: by expanding the right to regulate and limiting the scope of investor rights; and by introducing concrete performance obligations in IIAs. The first option is the most used in newer treaties. The Comprehensive Economic and Trade Agreement[90] and the EU-Singapore Investment Agreement[91] have introduced stronger language regarding the state's right to regulate and have also limited the scope of the FET and the concept of legitimate expectations. This new phrasing, however, still falls short by not actually imposing obligations on investors and shifting the responsibility to states to legislate on the matter.

The problem with this approach is that it still assumes the host state has the capacity and willingness to address human rights violations or other negative externalities of foreign investments. The need to reduce asymmetry is important because there is a general awareness now that some MNCs have more resources than the localities where they invest. In this regard,

---

85   The group was convened by the Columbia Center on Sustainable Investment, at Columbia University. Emma Aisbett et al, *Rethinking International Investment Governance: Principles for the 21st Century* (German Federal Ministry for Economic Cooperation and Development, 2018) at 10.

86   *Ibid* at 20 [emphasis in original is omitted].

87   "Global governance" refers here to the fact that states, while still central actors on the global stage, lack the capacity to solve, on their own, the most significant global challenges of the twenty-first century, such as climate change, economic inequality and those issues identified in the UN's Sustainable Development Goals. Furthermore, the concept of global governance implies the need to coordinate the collective action of various state, international and transnational actors. Thomas G Weiss, "Governance, Good Governance and Global Governance: Conceptual and Actual Challenges" (2000) 21:5 Third World Q 795 at 808.

88   Aisbett et al, *supra* note 85 at 44.

89   *Ibid* at 133.

90   *Comprehensive Economic and Trade Agreement between Canada and the European Union*, 30 October 2016 (partially entered into force 21 September 2017), arts 8.9.1, 8.9.2, 8.10.2, online: Global Affairs Canada <www.international.gc.ca/trade-commerce/trade-agreements-accords-commerciaux/agr-acc/ceta-aecg/text-texte/toc-tdm.aspx?lang=eng>.

91   *European Union-Singapore Investment Protection Agreement*, 19 October 2018, arts 2.4.2, 2.4.4 (not yet in force), online: <https://trade.ec.europa.eu/doclib/press/index.cfm?id=961>.

investors sometimes have more capacity to address issues of human rights and sustainable development than the host state has. The second reason this approach is insufficient is that merely reducing the scope of investor rights in IIAs may communicate to foreign investors that they do not need to contribute proactively to the goals of the host state. Finally, this approach also fails to make IIAs effective tools for sustainable development.[92]

This leads us to the second option, which is imposing concrete obligations for investors in treaties. The draft Pan-African Investment Code, with all its limitations, is the best example. This approach, however, requires rethinking how the current system of investor-state arbitration should operate. This broad question can be broken down into several more precise ones: where can investor obligations to the state be formalized; what forum would be best to address these issues, and to what extent; and what would be the implications of this approach in the larger legal system?

The first question, as to how to formalize obligations for foreign investors, can be further divided into two others: where should obligations be placed in an IIA; and what sort of obligations belong in an IIA? Placing obligations in the preamble could be useful, as they may help in the interpretation of the treaty as a whole.[93] However, as the *Urbaser* case demonstrated, obligations of performance require precise wording. Therefore, it is recommended that investor obligations be as specific as possible to avoid confusion.[94]

There are two ways of achieving this goal: including the obligations in a specialized treaty dealing with the behaviour of MNCs; and including in each IIA a chapter dedicated to investor obligations. The first option would be to introduce obligations in an international agreement that applies to all MNCs in general. The treaty could be similar to the UN's Guiding Principles on Business and Human Rights (known as the Ruggie Principles),[95] but with greater enforceability.[96] These instruments could be taken into account by investor-state arbitration tribunals through the principle of systematic integration[97] or by expanding the concept of legitimate expectations to incorporate the expectations of the state regarding the conduct of

---

92   When IIAs are properly drafted, contributing to the development of the host country should not come at the expense of the investor, nor should prosperity for the investor come at the expense of the host country. United Nations Conference on Trade and Development, *International Investment Agreements: Flexibility for Development* (2000) UNCTAD Series on Issues in International Investment Agreements at 14, online: <https://unctad.org/en/Docs/psiteiitd18.en.pdf>.

93   Giest, *supra* note 11 at 338. See also IISD, "A Sustainability Toolkit for Trade Negotiators: Trade and Investment as Vehicles for Achieving the 2030 Sustainable Development Agenda" at 5.1, online: <www.iisd.org/toolkits/sustainability-toolkit-for-trade-negotiators/5-investment-provisions/1-why-is-sustainable-development-important-for-trade-and-investment-agreements/>; Max H Hulme, "Preambles In Treaty Interpretation" (2016) 164:5 U Pa L Rev 1281 at 1296.

94   As Patrick Dumberry and Gabrielle Dumas-Aubin argue, "Merely *encouraging* investors to do something has not worked in the past and is quite unlikely [to] be an effective remedy in the future. It is therefore paramount that a treaty provision creates mandatory legal obligations *forcing* corporations to adopt a certain behavior." Patrick Dumberry & Gabrielle Dumas-Aubin, "How to impose human rights obligations on corporations under investment treaties? Pragmatic guidelines for the amendment of BITs" in Karl P Sauvant, ed, *Yearbook on International Investment Law & Policy 2011–2012* (New York: Oxford University Press, 2013) 568 at 580 [emphasis in original].

95   *Report of the Special Representative of the Secretary-General on the Issue of Human Rights and Transnational Corporations and Other Business Enterprises: Guiding Principles on Business and Human Rights: Implementing the United Nations "Protect, Respect and Remedy" Framework*, UNHRC, 17th Sess, UN Doc A/HRC/17/31 (2011).

96   The United Nations Human Rights Council's "Open-Ended Intergovernmental Working Group on Transnational Corporations and Other Business Enterprises with Respect to Human Rights" seems to be getting closer to a final draft of such an agreement. Joe Zhang, "Business and Human Rights Treaty Negotiation Sees a Light at the End of the Tunnel" (2019) 10:5 IISD Investment Treaty News 8 at 9.

97   Campbell McLachlan, "The Principle of Systemic Integration and Article 31(3)(C) of the Vienna Convention" (2005) 54 Intl & Comp L Q 279 at 280–81.

the investor.[98] The main obstacle with this approach is the same that John Ruggie faced when coming up with the Guiding Principles in the first place: there is not much appetite among states to come up with an agreement along these lines.[99] Because it is not clear when states would agree on a multilateral agreement on MNCs, the recommended approach is to include the obligations in IIAs.

In considering the second option, of incorporating obligations directly in IIAs, the treaties examined earlier in this chapter show that they tend to cover: human rights; the environment; labour rights; contributions to the (sustainable) development of the host country; prohibition against bribery and corruption; and corporate governance. There is a problem of complexity of the issues, in that one must ask to what extent this type of agreement can be expected to cover so many topics with sufficient detail and efficacy. One option would be to leave these provisions at a higher level of abstraction, but this risks creating only fuzzy pledges to protect the public interest that are already present in many IIAs.

The model agreements analyzed here show a way to solve this problem. Most model agreements refer to existing international standards, in particular when it comes to human rights, labour rights, environmental standards and corporate governance. The second tool that can help move obligations from the general rule to the particular case is to ensure that the contracts states sign with investors have specific obligations relevant to the industry and investor in question.[100] Finally, it is important to make sure that IIAs protect only those investments that are properly vetted by environmental and human rights impact assessments.[101]

The second issue is that of forum. Who should settle these disputes? Three options are suggested here.

The most straightforward option is to leave enforcement to domestic courts and administrative bodies. As mentioned earlier, this approach is particularly dangerous for developing countries, which may not have the capacity or willingness to enforce such obligations. An alternative could be to empower home states to hold their investors accountable for misconduct abroad. The IISD model agreement has a provision in this regard.[102] The problem with this option is that there may be little incentive for home states to intervene when the host states themselves do nothing in the case of misconduct by a foreign investor. Furthermore, if they do intervene, they may do so to help the investors rather than to hold them accountable.[103] It is thus important that the IIA empower potential victims in host states as much as possible to bring claims in home states.

---

98 Karl P Sauvant & Güneş Ünüvar, "Can host countries have legitimate expectations?" (2016) Columbia FDI Perspectives: Perspectives on Topical Foreign Direct Investment Issues No 183.

99 John Gerard Ruggie, "Global Governance and 'New Governance Theory': Lessons from Business and Human Rights" (2014) 20 Global Governance 5 at 6–7.

100 For guidance on this topic, see Lise Johnson & Oleksandr Volkv, "Investor-State Contracts, Host-State 'Commitments' and the Myth of Stability in International Law" (2013) 24 Am Rev Intl Arb 361; Enrique Boone Barrera, "Human Rights Obligations in Investor-State Contracts: Reconciling the Investors' Legitimate Expectations with the Public Interest" in Clair Gammage & Tonia Novitz, eds, *Sustainable Trade, Investment, and Finance: Toward Responsible and Coherent Regulatory Frameworks* (Cheltenham, UK: Edward Elgar, 2019).

101 See e.g. SADC, *supra* note 34, art 13.

102 Mann et al, *supra* note 35, art 31.

103 Dumberry & Dumas-Aubin, *supra* note 94 at 575.

Another option is to have investor-state arbitration tribunals deciding these issues. If this is the case, the regime of protection of foreign investors would need an almost complete overhaul, since human rights issues cannot be filtered through the narrow aims of current IIAs. In this regard, it is important that before this becomes a feasible option, IIAs incorporate the reconceptualization discussed earlier. The second challenge here is also one of complexity; that is, what kind of tribunal would have enough expertise to address all issues related to the public interest? It is important that sensitive issues related to human rights, labour rights and environmental regulations be referred by investor-state arbitration tribunals to the proper domestic and international fora. In investor-state arbitration proceedings, however, breaches of investor obligations should lead to denial of benefits, reduction of compensation, or other financial penalties.[104] It is paramount that investment tribunals refrain from setting precedent in areas of international law such as human rights or environmental regulations, since they are not the proper forum to do so.

The third option is to have an international private judicial dispute resolution for human rights violations by MNCs. Researchers at the Center for International Legal Cooperation have launched the Hague Rules on Business and Human Rights Arbitration,[105] meant to complement the UN's Guiding Principles. It is important to note, however, that foreign investors would need to agree to be subject to these rules of arbitration.[106] Some countries may have the capacity to convince investors to agree to this forum, but this would probably not be the case for developing and least-developed countries.

Conclusion

There is no single policy that will resolve all the problems posed by the regime of foreign investment protection. It is up to states to decide what combination of policies works best for them. What is important at this moment is that states finally decide to move away from the old conception of the regime of foreign investment as an isolated legal framework to protect economic interests. Given the challenges of the twenty-first century, this is no longer acceptable. This chapter recommends reconceptualizing investment law as one more element of global governance.

Finally, there are outstanding issues that deserve more research. For instance, given that we already have established human rights courts, as well as domestic avenues with jurisdiction over labour rights, environmental laws and so on, what should be the relation between all these different fora? In terms of jurisdiction, should there be an established order of preference? What should be the role of precedents in this plurality of international courts, tribunals and domestic courts? And how should potential conflicts between all these different legal instruments and fora be resolved? These issues need more investigation in order to develop a comprehensive approach to regulating the conduct of MNCs.

---

104 *Ibid* at 594.

105 Center for International Legal Cooperation, "The Hague Rules on Business and Human Rights Arbitration" (2019), online: <www.cilc.nl/launch-of-the-hague-rules-on-business-and-human-rights-arbitration/>.

106 *Ibid*, art 1.

16

USING INTERNATIONAL INVESTMENT AGREEMENTS TO ADDRESS ACCESS TO JUSTICE FOR VICTIMS OF HUMAN RIGHTS VIOLATIONS ASSOCIATED WITH TRANSNATIONAL RESOURCE EXTRACTION

Penelope Simons and J. Anthony VanDuzer

Introduction

Access to justice for victims of corporate-related human rights violations, and in particular those associated with transnational business activity, remains an ongoing global concern. A 2018 study by the Office of the United Nations High Commissioner for Human Rights (OHCHR) notes that such victims "continue to struggle to achieve effective remedies for the harm they have suffered."[1] This is despite the development and widespread endorsement of the United Nations Guiding Principles on Business and Human Rights,[2] which reiterate and provide guidance on the international human rights law obligation of states to provide an effective remedy for victims of human rights violations associated with business activity.

---

1   *Report of the United Nations High Commissioner for Human Rights: Improving accountability and access to remedy for victims of business-related human rights abuse through State-based non-judicial mechanisms*, UNHRC, 38th Sess, UN Doc A/HRC/38/20 (2018) at para 4 [*UNHRC Report*].

2   *Report of the Special Representative of the Secretary-General on the Issue of Human Rights and Transnational Corporations and Other Business Enterprises, Guiding Principles on Business and Human Rights: Implementing the United Nations "Protect, Respect and Remedy" Framework*, UNHRC, 17th Sess, UN Doc A/HRC/17/31 (2011) [*UNGPs*].

Individuals and communities affected by transnational business activity have few mechanisms available to them to seek meaningful redress and to hold multinational enterprises (MNEs) accountable for human rights abuses.[3] There are many impediments to obtaining relief in the courts of the host state, where the harm occurred, or in the courts of the MNE's home state. Even where victims are able to bring a claim for redress in a home- or host-state court, efforts to obtain relief may be frustrated where MNEs seek to avoid or minimize liability by using complex business structures involving multiple entities. Corporate law principles of separate legal personality and limited liability often mean that only the operating subsidiary in the host state can be held responsible for any harm caused, and such entities may be undercapitalized and unable to pay any damages awarded in a successful civil suit. Parent corporations or other members of the MNE's corporate group with the resources to pay compensation can usually avoid civil liability in both home- and host-state courts or avoid the execution of judgments in such fora.[4]

It is widely accepted that a regulatory or governance gap exists with respect to transnational business activity that violates human rights.[5] International human rights law does not impose direct obligations on MNEs to respect human rights.[6] The scope of an MNE's home-state obligation to regulate the transnational MNE conduct remains contested,[7] and few states have enacted legislation governing such conduct.[8] International law recognizes the MNE not as a single enterprise, but rather as a disaggregation of separate entities, each of which is left to be governed by the domestic law of the states in which they are incorporated or operate. Many host states, in particular in the Global South, may be unwilling or unable to effectively regulate such entities and all states struggle to regulate MNE conduct.[9] These factors, along with other structural aspects of the international legal system, mean that MNEs are often able to operate with impunity for the human rights violations and other harm they have caused or to which they have contributed.[10]

International investment law is implicated in both MNE impunity and the problem of access to justice. International investment agreements (IIAs) provide an additional layer of protection

3   Penelope Simons & Audrey Macklin, *The Governance Gap: Extractive Industries, Human Rights, and the Home State Advantage* (London, UK: Routledge, 2014) at 246–47.

4   See e.g. Chloe A Snider, "The latest development in *Yaiguaje v. Chevron Corporation* — The Court of Appeal for Ontario refuses to pierce the corporate veil" (29 June 2018), online (blog): *Dentons Insights* <www.dentons.com/en/insights/alerts/2018/june/27/the-latest-development-in-yaiguaje-v-chevron-corporation>.

5   See e.g. *Report of the Special Representative of the Secretary-General on the issue of human rights and transnational corporations and other business enterprises, John Ruggie: "Protect, Respect and Remedy": A Framework for Business and Human Rights*, UNHRC, 8th Sess, UN Doc A/HRC/8/5 (2008) at para 3.

6   Except to the extent that, like individuals, legal persons are prohibited from committing international crimes.

7   See e.g. Olivier de Schutter, "Towards a New Treaty on Business and Human Rights" (2016) Business & Human Rights J 41 at 45; *cf* Clair Methven O'Brien, "The Home State Duty to Regulate the Human Rights Impacts of TNCs Abroad: A Rebuttal" (2018) 3 Business & Human Rights J 47.

8   See *Loi n° 924 du 21 février 2017 relative au devoir de vigilance des sociétés mères et des entreprises donneuses d'ordre*, JO, 21 February 2017 [*Loi n° 924*]; see also Modern Slavery Act 2015 (UK), s 54. The former requires large companies registered in France to develop and publish a due diligence plan for ensuring that the enterprise avoids human rights violations as well as environmental or other social harms. See further discussion in the final section below. The UK law is much narrower and more limited. It requires business enterprises to report on whether they have taken steps "to ensure that slavery and human trafficking is not taking place" within their operations or supply chains. No state has yet enacted a broader legal framework aimed at preventing transnational business-related human rights violations and providing redress to victims.

9   Susan Marks, "Empire's Law" (2003) 10 Ind J Global Leg Stud 449 at 461.

10 Penelope Simons, "International Law's Invisible Hand and the Future of Corporate Accountability for Violations of Human Rights" (2012) 3 J Human Rights & Environment 5 at 35.

for business actors. IIAs contain broad protections for foreign investors against host-state action. Typically, under these agreements, investors (often MNEs) have the right to bring host states to binding arbitration (referred to as investor-state dispute settlement or ISDS) to seek compensation for the impact on the investment of new public interest measures that violate treaty standards. Potential ISDS claims can have a constraining effect on states' willingness and capacity to address investors' human rights abuses. At the same time, the host state has no recourse against the members of the MNE under the treaty for the latter's failure to comply with domestic law, including for human rights violations caused by the investor's activities. Individuals and communities that may be affected by the investor's activities have no rights under these treaties to seek redress against the investor. Investors may even be able to obtain orders from ISDS tribunals that undermine attempts by individuals and/or communities to access justice and attain redress in the host state's courts.[11] Investor conduct, if considered at all in the context of the ISDS proceedings, is often only considered in the amount of damages awarded.[12] Affected individuals and communities have no role in such proceedings, except potentially in a limited way as *amicus curiae*, with no right to relief.[13]

While the ability of victims of alleged corporate-related human rights violations to seek redress against business actors in all industry sectors is a significant issue, transnational resource extraction provides a useful lens through which to consider the problem of access to effective remedies. There is a greater likelihood of extractive corporations becoming involved in human rights violations compared to other industries, and the violations associated with resource extraction are likely to be more severe. Extractive MNEs have also been the subject of a significant proportion of allegations of wrongdoing, as well as civil suits.[14] Additionally, a number of transnational extractive enterprises that have been implicated in human rights violations have used ISDS to obtain significant damages from host states.

IIAs are often bilateral or negotiated between a small number of states, providing opportunities to modify them in order to address some of their core shortcomings, including the problem of access to an effective remedy for individuals and communities in the host state that have suffered harm. The United Nations Conference on Trade and Development (UNCTAD), along with scholars and non-governmental organizations (NGOs), have proposed a variety of IIA reforms.[15] A number of states have made (or are in the process of making) changes to their bilateral and/or model investment agreements.[16] However, to date, there has been little focus,

---

11 See e.g. *Chevron Corporation and Texaco Petroleum Company v Ecuador,* Second Partial Award on Track II (2018), PCA Case No 2009-23 [*Chevron v Ecuador*].

12 See e.g. *Copper Mesa Mining Corporation v Republic of Ecuador*, Award, PCA Case No 2012-2 (2016) [*Copper Mesa*].

13 As *amicus curiae*, affected individuals are not parties to the case and have no rights to relief. They may be permitted to make submissions regarding the investor's liability that provide a perspective or information beyond what can be provided by the investor and the state. See J Anthony VanDuzer, "Enhancing the Procedural Legitimacy of Investor-State Arbitration Through Transparency and Amicus Curiae Participation" (2007) 52:4 McGill LJ 681.

14 See the discussion in the next section.

15 See UNCTAD, *UNCTAD's Reform Package for the International Investment Regime: 2018 Edition* (2018). See e.g. J Anthony VanDuzer, Penelope Simons & Graham Mayeda, *Integrating Sustainable Development into International Investment Agreements: A Guide for Developing Country Negotiators* (London, UK: Commonwealth Secretariat, 2013); see also IISD, "Investment Policy Best Practices Advisory Bulletins", online: <https://iisd.org/project/investment-policy-best-practices-advisory-bulletins>.

16 See e.g. Global Affairs Canada, News Release, "Minister Carr launches public consultation on foreign investment promotion and protection agreements" (14 August 2018); see also Prabhash Ranjan & Pushcar Anand, "The 2016 Model Indian Bilateral Investment Treaty: A Critical Deconstruction" (2017) 38:1 Nw J Intl L & Bus 10.

either in reform proposals or amended IIAs, on the problem of access to justice of host-state communities and individuals for human rights violations and other harms.

This chapter will explore these issues and consider some proposals to reform IIAs in a manner that would enable access to justice and redress for victims of human rights violations related to the activity of extractive MNEs. The second section of the chapter discusses human rights violations that are associated with transnational resource extraction and the significant number of allegations of human rights abuses against extractive corporations. The third section examines the key obstacles for victims of alleged business-related human rights abuses to gaining access to the courts and obtaining redress. The fourth section provides an overview of the problems with existing IIAs and their role in undermining access to an effective remedy for affected communities and individuals. The final section considers how IIAs can be modified to facilitate states' compliance with their international human rights obligations to provide an accessible, effective remedy to victims of alleged violations of human rights by transnational resource extraction enterprises. In this context, the chapter will also consider how to address the problem posed by the doctrines of separate legal personality and limited liability that contribute to MNE impunity and undermine access to justice.

Transnational Resource Extraction and Human Rights Violations

Transnational resource extraction can affect the full range of human rights. The types of human rights violations associated with resource extraction have been well documented in academic literature, reports of NGOs and intergovernmental organizations, and in domestic and international legal proceedings. Unlike many other industries, the decisions about foreign investment by extractive MNEs are primarily based on location of resources and are less likely to take into account other factors such as "macroeconomic stability, level of development, or institutional quality" of and within the host state.[17] Extractive MNEs are thus more likely than business actors from other sectors to invest in countries governed by repressive regimes, or that are conflict-affected, and to operate in remote areas that may not be subject to strong government oversight or where governance is otherwise weak. Because they invest in these contexts, extractive MNEs run a greater risk of being implicated in human rights violations and other allegations of wrongdoing. A recent study that compared extractive foreign direct investment (FDI), and in particular oil, petroleum, mining and minerals, with non-extractive FDI, found that extractive activity was associated with worse levels of respect for human rights by the host government. The authors concluded that this reflects "a worrisome global pattern across countries and time."[18]

Even where extractive enterprises invest in democratic states, or non-conflict affected areas, and/or may put in place well-intentioned policies and processes in order to mitigate the harmful impacts of their operations, the nature of extractive activity means it will have impacts (often

---

17   James P Walsh & Jiangyan Yu, "Determinants of Foreign Direct Investment: A Sectoral and Institutional Approach" (2010) IMF Working Paper WP/10/187 at 21.

18   Indra de Soysa, Nicole Janz & Krishna Chaitanya Vadlamannati, "US Multinationals and Human Rights: A Theoretical and Empirical Assessment of Extractive vs. Non-Extractive Sectors" (2019) University College Dublin Law Criminology & Socio-Legal Studies Working Paper No 9/2019 at 24.

negative) on land rights and resources of local communities, including those of Indigenous peoples. Extractive enterprises may win concessions to operate where there is pre-existing socio-political conflict over land,[19] or where such concessions have been granted in a manner that violates Indigenous peoples' rights to free, prior and informed consent. Extractive activity may therefore exacerbate existing local tensions or create new tensions or conflict where part of the local community opposes, or one or more local communities oppose the project, or where the project has or will have differentiated impacts on the variety of local communities.[20]

Resource extraction can implicate the full range of human rights, from the right to life to the rights to food, adequate housing and health, to the particular rights of Indigenous peoples with respect to their lands, culture and religion, and so on. Additionally, the human rights abuses associated with resource extraction often rank among the most egregious, and may include forced displacement,[21] inadequate reparation for involuntary or voluntary resettlement, criminalization of human rights and environmental land defenders,[22] and violence by public, private or hybrid security forces against individuals and communities. Security force violence may include extra-judicial murder, torture, forced labour,[23] gender-based violence (including rape and gang rape),[24]

---

19   In *Choc v HudBay Minerals Inc*, 2013 ONSC 1414, the Mayan Q'eqchi' plaintiffs alleged that they have valid title to their ancestral lands from which they had been displaced during Guatemala's civil war. This claim to the land was validated by a decision from the Constitutional Court of Guatemala. When the plaintiffs tried to reclaim their lands, including lands in the area of the Fenix mine, they were allegedly forcibly evicted by private and public security providers. See *ibid* at paras 11–13.

20   See Shin Imai, Ladan Mehranvar & Jennifer Sander, "Breaching Indigenous Law: Canadian Mining in Guatemala" (2007) 6:1 Indigenous LJ 101 at 114. The paper discusses attempts by a foreign mining corporation to prevent, undermine and then ignore an independently monitored referendum (*consulta*) by the various Indigenous communities in Sipacapa. The consulta went ahead and 98.5 percent of those voting rejected mining activity in the area. See also José de Echave C, *Guests at the Big Table? Growth of the Extractive Sector, Indigenous/Peasant Participation in Multi-Partite Processes, and the Canadian Presence in Peru* (Ottawa: North-South Institute, 2010; revised 2011) at 26. The report discusses Talisman's engagement with some organizations representing local communities, and its failure to consult with others (such as the organization that claimed to represent the largest number of Achuar communities), thereby creating divisions and tensions among different communities.

21   From the late 1990s to early 2000s, when the civil war was being fought in the oil fields of what is now South Sudan, the Government of Sudan forcibly displaced civilian populations from the villages located in and around the oil extraction and development areas, in order to protect the businesses from rebel attack. In doing so, they perpetrated or facilitated the perpetration of a variety of other grave violations of human rights, including rape, murder, abduction into slavery, and looting and burning of villages. See John Harker, *Human Security in Sudan: The Report of a Canadian Assessment Mission* (Ottawa: Minister of Foreign Affairs, 2000); Georgette Gagnon & John Ryle, *Report of an Investigation into Oil Development, Conflict and Displacement in Western Upper Nile Sudan* (Toronto: Canadian Auto Workers et al, 2001); Human Rights Watch, *Sudan, Oil, and Human Rights* (2003), online: <www.hrw.org/reports/2003/sudan1103/sudanprint.pdf>.

22   For a discussion of the tactics of criminalization against women human rights defenders, see e.g. Kalowatie Deonandan & Colleen Bell, "Discipline and Punish: Gendered Dimensions of Violence in Extractive Development" (2019) 31:1 CJWL 24.

23   See e.g. *Araya v Nevsun Resources Ltd*, 2016 BCSC 1856 [*Araya v Nevsun*]; confirmed 2017 BCCA 4011856; appeal dismissed 2020 SCC 5. The plaintiffs allege that they were subjected to forced labour, torture and slavery committed by the Eritrean military and two contractors engaged to develop the Bisha gold mine in Eritrea and with the complicity of the Canadian parent corporation, Nevsun Resources Inc.

24   For reports on the sexual and other violence perpetrated by Barrick Gold Corporation's security forces in Porgera, Papua New Guinea, see e.g. Human Rights Watch, *Gold's Costly Dividend: Human Rights Impacts of Papua New Guinea's Porgera Gold Mine* (2010), online: <www.hrw.org/sites/default/files/reports/png0211webwcover.pdf>; Human Rights Clinic (Columbia Law School) & International Human Rights Clinic (Harvard Law School), *Righting Wrongs? Barrick Gold's Remedy Mechanism for Sexual Violence in Papua New Guinea: Key Concerns and Lessons Learned* (2015) at 1, online: <http://hrp.law.harvard.edu/wp-content/uploads/2015/11/FINALBARRICK.pdf>. See also *Caal v HudBay Minerals Inc and HMI Nickel Inc* (2012), No CV-11-423077, Amended Statement of Claim at paras 63–64 (ON Sup Ct J) (in which 11 Mayan Q'eqchi' women plaintiffs allege they were gang-raped by security forces who forcibly evicted them and their families from their traditional lands in and around the formerly Canadian-owned Fenix mining project in Guatemala).

targeted violence against human rights and environmental land defenders,[25] repression of peaceful protest,[26] and the destruction of homes and livelihoods.[27]

Such abuses may be differentially and intersectionally experienced by Indigenous peoples, tribal peoples, and Afro-descendant, peasant and other marginalized rural communities.[28] The Inter-American Commission on Human Rights (IACHR), for example, has found that the adverse impacts of resource extraction on Indigenous peoples "are multiple, complex and intertwined with other situations of violations of rights, such as poverty and extreme poverty, in which many peoples and communities find themselves."[29] Similarly, women, including Indigenous women, may experience adverse impacts from resource extraction that are differentiated from, and disproportionate to, those experienced by men. Such impacts may be intersectional depending on a women's race, socio-economic class, religion, culture and sexuality, among other factors.[30]

Extractive MNEs have consistently been the subject of a considerable proportion of the allegations of wrongdoing made against business actors and of claims in both non-judicial mechanisms and domestic courts. One of the early reports of the United Nations Special Representative of the Secretary-General on human rights and transnational corporations and other business enterprises stated that, in 2008, the sector that was the subject of the largest number of allegations of business-related human rights abuses listed on the website of the

---

25   See *Report of the Special Rapporteur on the Situation of Human Rights Defenders, Michael Forst*, UNGAOR, 71st Sess, UN Doc A/71/281 (2016) (discussing the killings and other violence faced by environmental human rights defenders, at paras 26–30); *ibid* (noting "that most individuals and groups facing threats are those who oppose land grabbing, extractive industries, the industrial timber trade and large-scale development projects" at para 31).

26   Royal Dutch Shell was accused of complicity in the violent repression of Ogoni protesters by the Nigerian military in the Niger Delta, which ended with the execution of 10 Ogoni leaders (*Wiwa v Royal Dutch Petroleum Co*, 226 F.3d 88 (2nd Cir 2000)). See also the more recent case of *Garcia v Tahoe Resources Inc*, 2015 BCSC 2045; *Garcia v Tahoe Resources Inc*, 2017 BCCA 39 (reversed), in which the plaintiffs allege they were shot and injured by the security forces for the mine during a peaceful protest outside the Escobal mine site in Guatemala (settled).

27   The forced and violent eviction of the Mayan Q'eqchi' farmers from their lands in and around the Fenix mine site in El Estor, Guatemala, was recorded by Steven Schnoor, a documentary filmmaker. See *Schnoor v Canada (AG)*, (7 May 2010) Toronto SC-09-00080779-0000 (Ont Sm Cl Ct) (Amended Claim of the Plaintiff), online: <www.schnoor-versuscanada.ca/docs/statement-of-claim.pdf>; *Schnoor v Canada (AG)*, (16 June 2010) Ottawa SC-09-00080779-0000 (Ont Sm Cl Ct) (Order of the Court), online: <www.schnoorversuscanada.ca/docs/order-june162010.pdf>.

28   See e.g. IACHR, *Indigenous and Tribal Peoples' Rights over their Ancestral Lands and Natural Resources: Norms and jurisprudence of the Inter-American Human Rights System*, OEA/Ser.L/V/II (30 December 2009) (noting resource extraction, along with infrastructure and development mega-projects "may affect [I]ndigenous populations with particularly serious consequences, given that they imperil their territories and the ecosystems within, for which reason they represent a mortal danger for their survival as peoples" at para 205).

29   IACHR, *Indigenous Peoples, Afro-Descendent Communities, and Natural Resources: Human Rights Protection in the Context of Extraction and Development Activities*, OEA/Ser.L/V/IL Doc.47/15 (2015) at para 249.

30   See Katy Jenkins, "Women, Mining and Development: An Emerging Research Agenda" (2014) Extractive Industries & Society 329; Susan Manning et al, "A Literature Synthesis Report on the Impacts of Resource Extraction for Indigenous Women" (2018) Canadian Research Institute for the Advancement of Women. See also IACHR (2015), *supra* note 29 at paras 319–21. The report states that "largescale mining activities leave deep impacts on the lives and…the bodies of women." These impacts include increased work, where men go to work for the extractive companies and the women are left to care for other members of the community who have been affected by conflict with extractive companies, "such as orphaned children of murdered leaders," and children who are the offspring of women who have been raped. Other differentiated intersectional impacts include the trafficking of women and girls, and other gender-based violence, including sexual violence against women and girls by extractive workers or family members, and the "weakening of the communal and family life."

Business and Human Rights Resource Centre,[31] was resource extraction at 28 percent.[32] A more recent study by Menno Kamminga, published in 2016 and using data from the Business and Human Rights Resource Centre up to 2014, confirmed that the extractive industry remains the sector with the most allegations of human rights violations.[33]

Moreover, a substantial number of the transnational civil suits brought against MNEs over the past two decades have been against extractive MNEs. For example, of the 216 completed or ongoing lawsuits referenced on the Business and Human Rights Resource Centre website, 61 (or approximately 28 percent) were against mining, oil and gas corporations.[34] According to Jonathan Drimmer, of the lawsuits filed against business actors up to 2010 in the United States under the Alien Tort Statute, the extractive sector was the most targeted industry and suits against extractive corporations constituted approximately 25 percent of all cases.[35] A study of lawsuits filed in EU member states against corporations for business-related human rights violations found "a slight overrepresentation of companies in natural resources extraction (mining, forestry and petroleum)."[36] Of 35 cases, 16 (or approximately 45 percent) were filed against mining or oil and gas corporations.[37] The number of allegations and civil suits against extractive MNEs is particularly significant, given that only 10 percent of global FDI is from the extractive sector.[38]

---

31   The Business and Human Rights Resource Centre is widely considered to be the most comprehensive repository of business and human rights information. It currently tracks more than 8,000 companies.

32   The next highest number was 21 percent in retail and consumer products. See Report of the Special Representative of the Secretary-General on the Issue of Human Rights and Transnational Corporations and Other Business Enterprises, John Ruggie — Corporations and Human Rights: A Survey of the Scope and Patterns of Alleged Corporate-Related Human Rights Abuse, Addendum, UNHRC, 8th Sess, UN Doc A/HRC/8/5/Add.2 (2008) at 9, Figure 1.

33   Menno T Kamminga, "Company Responses to Human Rights Reports: An Empirical Analysis" (2016) 1:1 Business & Human Rights J 95 at 100. Of course, as Kamminga points out, "the number of reports [alleging human rights violations] is not in itself a reliable indicator of abusive corporate conduct [as there] may be all kinds of extraneous reasons unrelated to the severity of the alleged abuses why a report is or is not produced on a particular company" (at 103).

34   Business and Human Rights Resource Centre, "Case Profiles: Industry", online: <www.business-humanrights.org/en/corporate-legal-accountability/case-profiles/industry>.

35   Jonathan Drimmer, "Human Rights and the Extractive Industries: Litigation and Compliance Trends" (2010) 3:2 J World Energy L & Bus 121 at 123.

36   Directorate General for External Policies of the Union, "Access to Legal Remedies for Victims of Corporate Human Rights Abuses in Third Countries" (2019) at 18, online: *European Parliament* <www.europarl.europa.eu/RegData/etudes/STUD/2019/603475/EXPO_STU(2019)603475_EN.pdf>.

37   *Ibid* at 20–30.

38   In 2012, the global stock of inward FDI in the mining, quarrying and petroleum sectors was 6.14 percent. See UNCTAD, *World Investment Report 2014: Investing in the SDGs: an Action Plan* (2014), table 24.

Obstacles for Affected Communities and Individuals in Accessing and Obtaining Effective Remedies

Unlike foreign extractive enterprises that may have access to ISDS under an IIA (as discussed in the next section), communities and individuals face significant obstacles in accessing and obtaining effective remedies for harm they have suffered from transnational extractive activity.[39] The right to an effective remedy is a fundamental human right and is reflected in the United Nations Guiding Principles on Business and Human Rights (UNGPs).[40] The UNGPs were unanimously endorsed by the UN Human Rights Council in 2011,[41] and are considered an authoritative framework governing states' human rights obligations and businesses' responsibilities with respect to preventing and addressing business-related human rights violations.[42] However, almost a decade since their adoption and despite the widespread support of these principles by states and businesses alike,[43] there are few effective means through which victims of business-related violations can seek reparations for the harm they have suffered.[44]

The UNGPs emphasize that "[e]ffective judicial mechanisms are at the core of ensuring access to remedy."[45] Yet states have done little to ensure that victims of business-related human rights violations can seek and obtain justice in domestic courts. A study by the International Corporate Accountability Roundtable (ICAR) assessing the national action plans of states regarding their implementation of the UNGPs, found that, to date, the majority of such plans fail to address adequately the issue of effective remedies. Most lack "specificity in the commitments… to improve access to remedy" and ignore "domestic barriers to access to judicial remedy for business-related human rights abuses which occur at home or abroad, focusing instead on regional or international initiatives and non-judicial mechanisms."[46]

Civil Suits in Host States

Claimants who choose to bring suits in the host state may encounter a range of structural and other impediments, such as "fragmented, poorly designed or incomplete legal regimes;

---

39 For a full discussion of the range of challenges in bringing civil claims against extractive MNEs in home-state courts, see Simons & Macklin, *supra* note 3 at 246–59. For a discussion of transnational human rights litigation more broadly, see François Larocque, *Civil Actions for Uncivilized Acts: The Adjudicative Jurisdiction of Common Law Courts in Transnational Human Rights Litigation* (Toronto: Irwin Law, 2010) [Larocque, *Civil Actions*].

40 See *UNGPs*, *supra* note 2, Principles 1, 22, 25ff. See also *Report of the Working Group on the Issue of Human Rights and Transnational Corporations and Other Business Enterprises*, UNGAOR, 72nd Sess, UN Doc A/72/162 (2017) (the UNGPs are "'a coherent whole' [and] access to effective remedies should be regarded as a common thread running through all three interconnected and interdependent pillars" at para 57).

41 *Human Rights and Transnational Corporations and Other Business Enterprises*, UNHRC, 17th Sess, UN Doc A/HRC/RES/17/4 (2011). The UNGPs reflect binding human rights obligations and non-binding recommendations for states and they set out non-binding norms (responsibilities) for private sector actors.

42 *Business and Human Rights: Improving Accountability and Access to Remedy*, UNHRC, 32nd Sess, UN Doc A/HRC/RES/32/10 (2016), Preamble.

43 See e.g. the UNHRC resolution unanimously endorsing the UNGPs, *supra* note 41; *Human Rights and Transnational Corporations and Other Business Enterprises*, UNHRC, UN Doc A/HRC/RES/26/22 (2014).

44 *UNHRC Report, supra* note 1 at para 4.

45 *UNGPs, supra* note 2, Guiding Principle 26, Commentary.

46 International Corporate Accountability Roundtable, "Assessments of Existing National Action Plans (NAPs) on Business and Human Rights: August 2017 Update" (2017) at 5.

international law to the SCC. The SCC dismissed Nevsun's appeal on both issues. This decision was a significant step forward for the plaintiffs' case and may open the doors for more of these types of cases to be brought in Canadian courts. Having said that, the plaintiffs must still prove their case in the lower courts. Additionally, the other obstacles noted above persist, and both the doctrine of act of state and the constraints of tort law in providing an effective remedy remain significant hurdles in other common law jurisdictions. Defending against such motions and litigating a case on the merits against defendant corporations, often with abundant financial resources, continues to be onerous and expensive for victims.

These considerable obstacles mean that many of these cases may be dismissed at the pleadings stage and never be heard on the merits, and in those cases that proceed to the merits, the plaintiffs will often face an uphill battle in proving their claims.

The Implications of International Investment Law for Access to an Effective Remedy for Victims of Extractive-related Human Rights Violations

International investment law is implicated in both corporate impunity and the problem of access to justice. International investment treaty protections for corporations can impair host-state efforts to respect, protect and fulfill the human rights of individuals and groups affected by foreign investors' activities, while providing no process for those affected to seek relief for human rights violations. Worldwide, more than 3,000 bilateral investment treaties (BITs) and other IIAs protect investors from actions of the host states in which they operate.[68] In these treaties, ISDS allows an investor of one state party to bring a direct claim for financial compensation against another state party on the basis that the state breached an investor protection obligation in the treaty. Investors have used ISDS successfully to challenge a wide range of state actions, including those intended to advance important public policy goals, such as human rights protection.

But the pernicious effects of IIAs are far more wide-ranging than the direct costs of ISDS claims. Potential exposure to large awards and the substantial costs that states incur when forced to participate in ISDS, even when they win, means that IIAs can discourage states from regulating in ways that might become the subject of an investor-state claim. This regulatory chill can discourage host states from discharging their obligation to protect individuals and communities from human rights violations perpetrated by private actors. While more recent IIAs have been revised in modest ways to better protect states' right to regulate, all investment treaties reflect a binary conception of the investment relationship: only states' and investors' interests are relevant. Human rights and other rights and interests of individuals and groups in host states affected by the activities of treaty-protected investors are not adequately considered, if at all. In this part of the chapter, we explain the actual and potential impact of IIAs on human rights, focusing on the extractive sectors.

---

68   See UNCTAD, *Recent Developments in the International Investment Regime*, IIA Issues Note No 1 (2018) at 2.

Experience with ISDS and Regulatory Chill

A number of characteristics of IIAs and the awards rendered in ISDS contribute to regulatory chill. Investors have been encouraged to resort to ISDS to challenge a wide range of state actions by the very broad and ill-defined nature of IIA investor protection standards such as "fair and equitable treatment."[69] More and more investors are doing so.[70] Arbitral tribunals have interpreted these standards in surprising, inconsistent and even incoherent ways, making it hard for states to predict what their IIA obligations require.[71] As a consequence, the risk of state measures being challenged is both significant and hard to assess.

The consequences of facing ISDS claims are also significant. Awards in ISDS cases can be very large and the process very costly. The average amount claimed is US$454 million and the average amount awarded is US$125 million.[72] According to a 2012 report by the Organisation for Economic Co-operation and Development (OECD), "On average, costs, including legal fees and tribunal expenses, have exceeded $8 million per party per case."[73] High costs are a concern for all states, but especially for states in the Global South.[74] Even if the state ends up winning the case, a tribunal may decide not to order the claimant investor to pay the state's costs.[75] In fact, most investment tribunals have ordered parties to share the costs of the proceedings equally and to bear their own legal fees.[76]

Increasing resort by investors to ISDS, combined with the unpredictable risk of large awards being made against host states based on broadly worded IIA standards, and the high costs of defending an ISDS even where the state wins the case, all contribute to creating an environment in which states are susceptible to regulatory chill.[77] For example, New Zealand refrained from enacting new cigarette packaging requirements designed to discourage smoking, pending the resolution of a claim by a cigarette producer that had challenged similar requirements in Australia.[78] But it is not only the generalized threat of an investor-state claim that discourages state action. Foreign investors, using the threat of an ISDS claim, may directly pressure host

---

69   Marc Jacob & Stephan W Schill, "Fair and Equitable Treatment: Content, Practice, Method" in Marc Bungenberg et al, eds, *International Investment Law* (Baden-Baden, Munich & Oxford: CH BECK & Hart & Nomos, 2015) 701 at 754.

70   UNCTAD, *Fact Sheet on Investor-State Dispute Settlement Cases in 2018* (2019). The figure is limited to publicly available claims. Not all investor-state cases are made public.

71   For a recent survey of cases, the views of states and possible reforms, see UNCITRAL Working Group III (Investor-state Dispute Settlement Reform), *Possible reform of investor-State dispute settlement (ISDS): Consistency and related matters*, Note by the Secretariat, 28 August 2018, UN Doc A/CN.9/WGIII/WP/150/.

72   These statistics are set out in UNCTAD, *Investor-State Dispute Settlement: Review of Developments in 2017*, IIA Issues Note No 2 (2018) at 5.

73   David Gaukrodger & Katharine Gordon, "Investor-State Dispute Settlement: A Scoping Paper for the Investment Policy Community" (2012) OECD Working Papers on International Investment No 2012/3 at 19.

74   *Ibid* at 23.

75   UNCTAD, *Investor-State Dispute Settlement: A Sequel*, UNCTAD Series on Issues in International Investment Agreements II (2014) at 147.

76   *Ibid* at 149, referring to Susan Franck, "Rationalizing Costs in Investment Treaty Arbitration" (2011) 88:4 Washington UL Rev 769. There has been a trend in recent cases to shift at least some costs to the losing party (Gaukrodger & Gordon, *supra* note 73 at 22).

77   Gaukrodger & Gordon, *supra* note 73 at 23. See also Gus Van Harten & Dayna Scott, "Investment Treaties and the Internal Vetting of Regulatory Proposals: A Case Study from Canada" (2016) 7:1 J Intl Dispute Settlement 92. For a recent survey of the evidence, see Kyla Tienhaara, "Regulatory Chill in a Warming World: The Threat to Climate Policy Posed by Investor-State Dispute Settlement" (2018) 7 Transnational Environmental L 229 at 233–39.

78   Eric Crosbie & George Thomson, "Regulatory Chills: Tobacco Industry Legal Threats and the Politics of Tobacco Standardised Packaging in New Zealand" (2018) 131 NZ Medical J 25.

As well, Ecuador's failure to act promptly to protect the human rights of its citizens benefited the investor. Inaction or ineffective host-state action to address injuries to its citizens is not uncommon. It is not clear to what extent Ecuador's failure to act in this case was due to regulatory chill, incompetence, lack of resources or complicity in the investor's actions. Regardless of the motivation, the state's failure to act for a long time to protect the interests of its people demonstrates the need for improved mechanisms for affected individuals and groups to pursue relief directly. As well, because Ecuador did not raise human rights abuses before the investor filed its claim, Copper Mesa was successful in getting the tribunal to reject Ecuador's request to have its claim thrown out as inadmissible on the basis of the abuses, paving the way for its recovery of substantial damages.

In short, *Copper Mesa* shows that IIAs are not designed to protect and do not protect individuals and groups harmed by foreign investors, even through illegal activity that violates their human rights. Indeed, despite such conduct, investors may be able to successfully use ISDS to obtain substantial compensation. While there is some prospect for damages to be reduced to the extent that the investor's misconduct caused the state to act, this mitigating consideration will be attenuated in the common situation where the investor is an MNE acting through local subsidiaries. At the same time, state action to mitigate harms caused by investors is often delayed, if it comes at all, underscoring the crucial need for more effective civil remedies for victims.

Recent Reforms to International Investment Law

In recent years, there has been a wide variety of reforms introduced in IIAs, including the development of new treaty models used to negotiate IIAs, and amendments to existing treaties. The main goals of these reforms have been to clarify and rebalance the substantive investor protections to ensure that host states can regulate in the public interest without breaching their IIA obligations, and to improve the ISDS process. With rare exceptions, none of these reforms address the fundamental nature of IIAs as instruments obliging states to protect investors, or permit other affected parties to seek relief directly. In this section, we briefly discuss a few reforms that help to protect individuals and groups in the host state affected by investor behaviour.

A few treaties impose obligations in relation to investor conduct that may benefit individuals and groups in host states, such as to meet standards related to corporate social responsibility.[107] In most treaties, however, these provisions are not binding.[108] The BIT entered into by Morocco and Nigeria in December 2016 represents a radical departure from traditional IIAs by imposing binding obligations directly on investors.[109] In addition to provisions requiring investors to do social and environmental impact assessments, meet certain environmental standards and not engage in bribery, the Morocco-Nigeria BIT sets specific human rights standards in the following terms. Articles 18(2) and (3) state: "Investors and investments shall uphold human rights in the host state [and] act in accordance with core labour standards as required by the

---

107 See e.g. Southern African Development Community (SADC), *SADC Model Bilateral Investment Agreement Template and Commentary* (2012), online: <www.iisd.org/itn/wp-content/uploads/2012/10/sadc-model-bit-template-final.pdf>.

108 Yulia Levashova, "The Accountability and Corporate Social Responsibility of Multinational Corporations for Transgressions in Host States through International Investment Law" (2018) 14 Utrecht L Rev 40. See also VanDuzer, Simons & Mayeda, *supra* note 15 at 300–01.

109 *Reciprocal Promotion and Protection Agreement Between the Government of the Kingdom of Morocco and the Government of the Federal Republic of Nigeria*, 3 December 2016 (not yet in force) [*Morocco–Nigeria BIT*].

ILO Declaration on Fundamental Principles and Rights of Work 1998." Article 18(4) states: "Investors and investments shall not manage or operate the investments in a manner that circumvents international environmental, labour and human rights obligations to which the host state and/or home state are Parties."[110]

These kinds of provisions can be operationalized by host-state implementation. As well, they can be given effect in relation to ISDS in several ways. For example, where an investor makes a claim, a state may be able to counterclaim in circumstances in which the investor has failed to fulfill its human rights obligations in the treaty. Any resulting compensation to the state could be used to remediate harms caused by the investor within the host state. Alternatively, an investor in breach of its obligations could be barred from proceeding with an investor-state claim.[111] Finally, as in *Copper Mesa*, an investor's damages could be reduced where its failure to comply with the standard is causally connected with its loss.

None of these approaches, however, provides relief directly to individuals and groups whose human rights have been abused by investors. As the *Copper Mesa* example illustrates, state action cannot always be counted on to protect people harmed by the activities of foreign investors. The Morocco-Nigeria BIT does contemplate a mechanism for direct relief: investors' home states must provide for their investors to be held civilly liable in their courts. However, the scope of liability is limited to investor actions that "lead to significant damage, personal injuries or loss of life in the host state."[112]

This provision represents an important initial effort to ensure domestic civil liability for foreign investors in their home states for their actions in host states. In the next section, we revisit some of the challenges associated with providing relief directly to affected persons in home-state courts and how they can be addressed through reformed IIAs.

Using IIAs to Ensure Access to an Effective Remedy

Some scholars argue that, given the well-recognized problems with IIAs and the ISDS system, states should refrain from negotiating and ratifying IIAs,[113] or at least dispense with ISDS. Others suggest that the problems posed by the international investment regime, including corporate impunity, might be tackled most effectively at the grassroots level through multi-actor contracts between local communities, the state and extractive MNEs.[114] There is a strong argument that states should cease to negotiate IIAs and also that there may be other

---

110   *Ibid.* See also Dutch Ministry of Foreign Affairs, *Model Investment Agreement* (2019), art 6(6) [*Dutch Model Investment Agreement*].

111   Under the *Comprehensive Economic and Trade Agreement* (between Canada and the European Union), 5 August 2014 (partially entered into force 1 September 2017), an investor may not submit a claim where its investment was made through "fraudulent misrepresentation, concealment, corruption or conduct amounting to an abuse of process" (art 8.18(3)). Such a provision would appear to give a tribunal some scope to refuse to hear an investor's claim based on the investor's misconduct in some circumstances.

112   *Morocco-Nigeria BIT*, *supra* note 109, art 20.

113   David Schneiderman, "How to Make Investment Agreements More Progressive: Stop Signing Them", *The Globe and Mail* (26 October 2018).

114   Ibironke Odumosu-Ayanu, "Governments, Investors and Local Communities: Analysis of a Multi-Actor Investment Agreement Framework" (2014) 15 Melbourne J Intl Law 473 at 478–82. See also James Gathii & Ibironke Odumosu-Ayanu, "The Turn to Contractual Responsibility in the Global Extractive Industry" (2015) 1:1 Business & Human Rights J 69.

avenues to address the problem of access to justice for individuals and communities harmed by foreign investor activity. Nonetheless, to the extent that states continue to see IIAs as valuable instruments for the protection of their investors, and therefore continue to negotiate and sign them, these agreements present an opportunity for activists and experts to encourage states to modify them to ensure they are consistent with, and facilitative of, states' international human rights obligations to respect, protect and fulfill human rights in the context of transnational business activity. It is certainly arguable that the right to an effective remedy imposes an obligation on states, when negotiating an IIA, to ensure not only that the provisions of the IIA do not undermine the right to an effective remedy, but also that they operate so as to ensure an effective remedy for individuals and communities affected by investor conduct. The UN Human Rights Council has invited states in a number of resolutions to "work though relevant intergovernmental processes to enhance accountability and access to remedy for victims in cases of business involvement in human rights abuses."[115] The negotiation of IIAs is one such intergovernmental process.

All states have a legal obligation to provide an effective remedy through judicial, administrative, legislative or other mechanisms, as part of their international human rights obligation to protect individuals and groups from human rights violations perpetrated by, or with the complicity of, private actors.[116] This includes the obligation to provide an effective remedy where business activities take place in whole or in part within a state, but result in reasonably foreseeable violations of human rights in other countries.[117] As mentioned above, this obligation is reflected in the UN Guiding Principles on Business and Human Rights, which state: "Effective judicial remedies are at the core of ensuring access to [an effective] remedy."[118] This right is both procedural and substantive. As the Working Group on Business and Human Rights maintains in its interpretive guidance for the UNGPs on the right to an effective remedy, states must "ensure that they put in place effective remedial mechanisms that can deliver effective remedies," and that such "remedies should result in some form of corporate accountability."[119]

We have outlined above a range of obstacles to bringing civil claims against MNEs. It is beyond the scope of this chapter to consider how all of them could be addressed in an IIA. We therefore confine our comments to a few of the common legal hurdles, namely: establishing domestic liability in the host and home state; ensuring the courts have jurisdiction over the claim;

---

115 See e.g. *Business and Human Rights: Improving Accountability and Access to Remedy*, UNHRC, 32nd Sess, UN Doc A/HRC/RES/32/10 (2016) at para 7; *Business and Human Rights: Improving Accountability and Access to Remedy*, UNHRC, 38th Sess, UN Doc A/HRC/RES/38/13 (2018) at para 5.

116 General Comment No 31 [80], *The Nature of the General Legal Obligation Imposed on States Parties to the Covenant*, UNHRC, 80th Sess, UN Doc CCPR/C/21/Rev.1/Add.13 (2004) at paras 4, 8, 16.

117 See e.g. *International Covenant on Civil and Political Rights*, General Comment No 36, *Article 6: right to life*, UNHRC, UN Doc CCPR/C/GC/36 (2018) at para 22.

118 *UNGPs, supra* note 2 at 23. While it is clear that judicial remedies are central, the Working Group on Business and Human Rights states that in order to provide full redress to victims of a corporate-related human rights violation, the latter should have access to a full spectrum of remedies "depending upon varied circumstances, including the nature of the abuses and the personal preferences of the rights holders." See UN Working Group on Business and Human Rights, *Human Rights and Transnational Corporations and Other Business Enterprises*, UN Doc A/72/162 (2017) at para 38. States should take this into account in developing their laws and policies to prevent and redress business-related human rights violations.

119 UN Working Group on Business and Human Rights, *supra* note 118 at paras 15, 17. This obligation is incorporated in the new Dutch Model Investment Agreement, *supra* note 110 ("As part of their duty to protect against business-related human rights abuse, the Contracting Parties must take appropriate steps to ensure, through judicial, administrative, legislative or other appropriate means, that when such abuses occur within their territory and/or jurisdiction those affected have access to effective remedy", art 5(3)).

minimizing the available opportunities for the defendants to have the case dismissed before it is heard on the merits; and addressing the separate legal personality of entities in MNEs.

Jurisdictional Issues

The concern about remedies for business-related human rights violations is relatively recent and few, if any, states have laws in place that establish liability for violations of human rights and other harms that an MNE has perpetrated or caused, or to which it has contributed. For example, in common law jurisdictions, plaintiffs must ensure that their allegations are framed so as to "correspond to established categories of tortious liability, or else run the risk of having their claim struck for failing to raise a reasonable cause of action."[120] Traditional categories of tort, however, often fail to capture the nature of the harm, in particular where it relates to egregious violations of human rights. For example, François Larocque argues, "Torture is qualitatively different from these wrongs and its normative weight ought to be given full expression and not merely shoehorned into existing tort categories."[121] Torts such as trespass to the person and unlawful confinement do not represent "the indignity and indignation felt by torture survivors."[122] An IIA provision could require the state parties to establish appropriate legal liability for investors for the potential range of human rights abuses and ensure that any cause of action effectively reflects the harm. As noted by the OHCHR, "Depending on the laws, structures and legal traditions of the relevant jurisdiction, the cause of action could be based on a statutory provision, general principles of law, legal precedent or some other basis (e.g. custom)."[123] Additionally, a provision could be included in an IIA requiring state parties to allow the plaintiffs to choose whether to apply home- or host-state law in the civil claim, thereby ensuring that the plaintiffs can take advantage of potentially more generous home-state laws without the burden of having to prove that they fall within a public policy or other applicable exception.[124]

The IIA would also need to include an obligation on state parties to enact legislation requiring courts to assume jurisdiction over a claim by an individual or community allegedly harmed by an investor, even where the claim is brought in the home state. If states were to require their courts to assume jurisdiction in this way, it would eliminate the need to prove jurisdiction *simpliciter* and it would prevent defendants from seeking to have the home-state court dismiss the claim on the basis of *forum non conveniens*. Applications to have the case stayed on this latter basis remain common. The defendants argue that the host state in which the harm occurred is the most appropriate forum to hear the claim, with the goal of displacing the claim to the host state where the case may never be litigated (for the variety of reasons discussed earlier). Extractive MNEs often have significant resources to provide a robust case in support of a motion of *forum non conveniens*. Despite the rules in the Brussels Convention addressing jurisdiction, courts in EU states that are party to the convention may still refuse to exercise jurisdiction over claims where the acts occurred outside the European Union and/or the plaintiffs are non-nationals or non-residents

---

120 Larocque, "Tort of Torture", *supra* note 65 at 165.

121 *Ibid* at 169.

122 *Ibid*.

123 *Report of the United Nations High Commissioner for Human Rights: Improving accountability and access to remedy for victims of business-related human rights abuse: explanatory notes for guidance: Note by the Secretariat*, UNHRC, 32nd Sess, UN Doc A/HRC/32/19/Add.1 (2016) at 13.

124 See Larocque, *Civil Actions*, *supra* note 39 at 188–94.

of an EU state.[125] Additionally, even though there appears to be a growing trend of common law courts to dismiss such motions, it remains a major obstacle for plaintiffs.[126]

A provision requiring home-state courts to take jurisdiction would also remove the possibility of having the case dismissed for reasons of international comity. A motion to dismiss for international comity is a request that the court "decline jurisdiction out of deference to the laws and interests of the foreign state, insofar as such deference can be reconciled with the laws and interests of the forum."[127] Considerations of international comity are thus based on concerns about encroaching on the sovereignty of the host state by adjudicating on acts that occurred in the latter. Where both states have agreed in a treaty to permit their courts to assume jurisdiction over a case, these considerations would no longer be relevant.

The act of state doctrine is related to the customary international law rule of sovereign immunity. It is, however, a common law doctrine that limits the subject matter competence of a court on the basis that the claim before it will require adjudication of official and other governmental acts and therefore allegedly transgresses the sovereignty of the host state. In transnational human rights claims, the application of the act of state doctrine can effectively provide an extractive MNE with immunity from a suit where it is accused of complicity in violations of human rights perpetrated by, or legitimized by, the actions of a sovereign state.[128]

An IIA provision could deal with the common law doctrine of act of state (or its equivalent) by providing that the state parties agree that the courts of one state may hear claims relating to the contributory liability of an investor, even where the primary or co-perpetrator of the harmful acts or omissions is the other state. Again, if both states agree to this in the treaty, then the concern upon which the doctrine is based is removed. Providing a cause of action and removing the potential for the investor to bring expensive motions and potentially have the case stayed or dismissed would also address some but not all of the issues related to the cost of litigation. While states may be reluctant to agree to have their actions subject to foreign court scrutiny in this way, such a commitment would be consistent with the trend in trade and investment treaty-making toward holding states to their international obligations through effective dispute settlement procedures.[129]

---

125   See e.g. *Owusu v Jackson*, [2005] ECR 1-1383; see also *Group Josi Reinsurance Company SA v Universal General Insurance Company*, [2000] ECR I-5925. The full name of the Brussels Convention is the Convention on jurisdiction and the enforcement of judgments in civil and commercial matters, Council of the European Union, 27 September 1968.

126   See Sarah Joseph, *Corporations and Transnational Human Rights Litigation* (London, UK: Hart, 2004) at 98, discussing litigation in the United States. In all cases brought against extractive MNEs in Canada, to date, the defendants have brought motions for *forum non conveniens*. It is only in the most recent cases in British Columbia that such motions have been dismissed. See *Garcia v Tahoe*, *supra* note 26; *Araya v Nevsun*, *supra* note 23.

127   Larocque, *Civil Actions*, *supra* note 39 at 197.

128   *Araya v Nevsun*, *supra* note 23, Factum of Joint Interveners, Amnesty International Canada and the International Commission of Jurists, SCC File No 37919 at para 14.

129   States can be held accountable through treaty-based mechanisms if they violate international labour commitments under the *Agreement between Canada, the United States and the United Mexican States*, 20 November 2018 (not yet in force), art 4, and *Protocol of Amendment to the Agreement between Canada, the United States and the United Mexican States*, 10 December 2019 (not yet in force), Annex to Article 20.50, Annex 31-A, Annex 31-B.

Addressing Liability Challenges Resulting from the Principle of Separate Corporate Legal Personality

As noted earlier, one of the key challenges for individuals and groups who have suffered human rights abuses at the hands of MNE investors (or agents acting on their behalf) is MNEs' use of complex corporate structures involving numerous entities, combined with the almost universally accepted principle that each corporation has a separate legal personality. Separate corporate legal personality insulates shareholders from liability for corporate acts. It was adopted in the late nineteenth century to encourage individual entrepreneurs to carry on business through corporations by protecting them and their personal assets from claims by creditors of the business.[130] Where the shareholder is a corporation, however, this policy justification has little application, since individual assets are not at risk.[131] Rigidly applying the principle in the context of the global activities of MNEs constrains the ability of individuals and groups, who have suffered from the actions of MNEs, from obtaining relief in at least two ways. First, if the local subsidiary operating in the host state has insufficient assets to pay compensation awards in favour of local people, shielding the parent corporation and others in the MNE group from liability will prevent full recovery. Second, domestic courts may refuse to hold corporations in an MNE group liable on the basis that only the local subsidiary directly implicated in wrongdoing is responsible.[132]

Attempts to get domestic courts to push the boundaries of corporate law to disregard the separate personality of corporations in a corporate group have been largely unsuccessful.[133] Similarly, efforts to get domestic courts to attach direct liability to a parent corporation or its executives, based on their being a party to the subsidiary's actions or their failure to discharge a duty of care under domestic tort law to prevent a subsidiary from abusing the human rights of individuals and groups in the host state, have typically failed.[134] It would be wrong, however, to conclude that solutions cannot be found to the problem of attaching liability to corporations acting as a group. Legislators have addressed the problem in different ways in particular jurisdictions. The next section provides some examples of these strategies, with a view to identifying how IIA provisions could address the barriers to individuals and groups seeking relief from human rights abuses perpetrated by MNEs.

---

130   VanDuzer, *Law of Partnerships and Corporations, supra* note 99 at 138–42.

131   Indeed, both law and economics scholars and progressive corporate law scholars have argued that the principle should not apply in these circumstances. See Martin Petrin & Barnali Choudhury, "Group Company Liability" (2018) 19 European Business Organization L Rev 771 at 779-82.

132   There are other ways in which the principle may make it more difficult for people affected by actions of a subsidiary to successfully claim against other corporations in an MNE group, as discussed above.

133   Regarding the United Kingdom, see Petrin & Choudhury, *supra* note 131 at 774–75. For some other jurisdictions, see Siel Demeyere, "Liability of a Mother Company for Its Subsidiary in French, Belgian, and English Law" (2015) 3 European Rev Private L 385.

134   This kind of claim was made unsuccessfully by members of the local community affected by this investor in *Piedra v Copper Mesa, supra* note 61. Cases in the United Kingdom are surveyed by Nicolas Bueno, "Corporate liability for violations of the human right to just conditions of work in extraterritorial operations" (2017) 21 Intl JHR 565 at 575–78. For a discussion of the distinctive experience of the United States, see Ma Ji, "Multinational Enterprises' Liability for the Acts of their Offshore Subsidiaries: The Aftermath of *Kiobel* and *Daimler*" (2015) 23 Michigan State Intl L Rev 397.

Strategies to Address Liability of Corporate Groups

One approach to imposing liability on entities acting as a corporate group is illustrated by EU competition law. Multiple entities within a group can be held responsible if they are part of an "undertaking" that violates EU competition law obligations.[135] An undertaking includes every "entity engaged in an economic activity, regardless of the legal status of the entity and the way in which it is financed."[136] The criteria for being part of an undertaking are vague, although, in practice, liability for being part of an undertaking has been limited to parent corporations controlling subsidiaries infringing competition law. The key test to determine if a subsidiary is controlled, a test developed by the Court of Justice of the European Union, is whether the parent exercises "decisive influence" over the conduct of the subsidiary.[137] Where all or almost all of the shares of the subsidiary are held directly or indirectly by the parent and it can exercise the rights attached to those shares to control the subsidiary, there is a rebuttable presumption that the subsidiary and the parent are part of a single undertaking.[138] All legal entities within a single undertaking may be held jointly and severally liable for infringement by one entity in the undertaking.[139]

EU competition law's concept of undertaking incorporates two related ideas regarding a fundamental challenge for designing IIA provisions that impose human rights obligations on MNEs, that is, how to define the participants in a corporate group.

The first idea is that for a parent corporation to be part of an undertaking, it must have control over the corporation directly infringing competition law, where control is defined by the ability to have decisive influence over the infringer. Where a parent corporation has legal control through majority share ownership (direct or indirect), the control is presumed to exist. Relying exclusively on legal control, however, would create the risk that sophisticated investors will be able to avoid being part of an undertaking and so escape liability through the use of contracts and other non-ownership techniques of control. Undoubtedly, that is why decisive influence rather than legal control was adopted as the EU competition law test. In a similar way, in order to be effective, any provision in an IIA that imposes liability on a parent corporation should not limit liability to the actions of entities under its legal control. However, a presumption of control based on the existence of legal control is justifiable. Legal control is a clear and certain test that, in some cases, can be assessed by publicly available information regarding share ownership. Where such control apparently exists, it is reasonable to require the parent to show that it nevertheless does not have control, in fact, because evidence of limitations on control, such as a shareholder agreement limiting a majority shareholder's rights, may only be available to the parent.

---

135 *Consolidated Version of the Treaty on the Functioning of the European Union*, 2008 OJ C 115/47, arts 101, 102. The EU competition law rules are discussed in Caroline Cauffman, "Civil Liability of Parent Companies for Infringements of EU Competition Law by their Subsidiaries" (2019), online: <https://ssrn.com/abstract=3331083>.

136 Case C-41/90, *Klaus Höfner and Fritz Elser/Macrotron GmbH*, 1991 ECR I-1979 at 21.

137 Case 48/69, *Imperial Chemical Industries/Commission*, 1972 ECR 619.

138 Case C-97/08 P, *Akzo Nobel NV/Commission*, ECR 2009 I-8237.

139 Case C-440/11P, *Commission/Stichting Administratiekantoor Portielje*, ECLI:EU:C:2013:514. Recent academic proposals and some other reform efforts in this regard are discussed in Petrin & Choudhury, *supra* note 131 at 784–89.

The second idea is that for an entity to be part of an undertaking under EU competition law, it must be engaged in a common economic activity with the entity directly implicated in the competition law infringement. In the context of foreign investment in the extractive industries, there may be many entities engaged in an extraction business. It is common for the extraction activity itself to be carried out by a locally incorporated subsidiary, while many functions essential to that business, such as finance, marketing, personnel, research and development, and management, are carried out by other corporations or other kinds of entities in other jurisdictions, all ultimately under the control of a parent corporation. Entities performing functions complementary to the extraction business are engaged in a common economic activity.

Some entities connected to an MNE, however, may not be engaged in the extractive operation. In large MNEs, there will often be other corporations and entities linked by ties of ownership and contract, each carrying on distinct businesses.[140] In designing an IIA provision to impose liability on a corporate group, a key question is whether liability within a group of related entities under common control should extend only to those carrying on the extractive business.[141] Imposing liability only on entities involved in the business in relation to which a breach of human rights occured is a more readily justifiable allocation of liability because such entities are part of a group that together profit from the business.[142] On the other hand, imposing liability more broadly to include all those entities under common control, whether they are engaged in the business or not, would enhance the prospects for recovery by victims of human rights abuse. It would be much more difficult for MNEs to move assets into entities that would not be the subject of claims by victims of human rights abuse if all entities of an MNE under common control (through ownership or contract) were held responsible.

A recent initiative by France illuminates some other issues that could inform the design of an IIA provision attaching liability to corporate groups. In 2017, France introduced a requirement for all large corporations registered in France to comply with a duty of vigilance in relation to their global activities and supply chains.[143] The obligation extends not only to the operations of all corporations under the MNE's control, but also to subcontractors and suppliers with which it has an established business relationship.[144] The duty requires such MNEs to develop a plan to identify, analyze and regularly assess the risk of human rights abuse in connection with their operations, as well as to take actions to mitigate or prevent such risks. As originally enacted, specific civil penalties were to be imposed for failing to comply, but these were struck down by the French constitutional court.[145]

---

140 At the same time, as discussed below, some of the entities involved in carrying on aspects of the extraction business may not be controlled (directly or indirectly) by the parent in the MNE group, such as some subcontractors.

141 Another issue is whether the group carrying on the business should be limited to entities that are under common control for liability purposes.

142 Peter T Muchlinski, "Limited liability and multinational enterprises: a case for reform?" (2010) 34 Cambridge J Economics 915 at 923.

143 *Loi n° 924, supra* note 8. The law applies to French registered corporations with their headquarters in French territory and at least 5,000 employees worldwide (including through subsidiaries) or, regardless of the location of their headquarters, with at least 10,000 employees worldwide (*French Commercial Code*, art L 255-102.4-I).

144 *French Commercial Code, supra* note 143, art L 233-16 II, defines control by a person as directly or indirectly holding a majority of voting rights, appointing for a period of two consecutive years the majority of the members of the administration, management or supervisory bodies or over which it exercises a dominant influence by virtue of a contract. Article 442-6 I(5) addresses what constitutes an established business relationship.

145 This regime, as well as a similar regime proposed in Switzerland, are discussed in Petrin & Choudhury, *supra* note 131 at 784–85.

This approach provides another example of how to conceptualize an MNE for the purposes of human rights obligations. Its strength is that it imposes an obligation on MNEs to engage in human rights due diligence within the corporate group and supply chain. Its weakness is that it does not provide a direct mechanism for relief. At best, a possible failure to comply could support a claim for negligence against corporations in the MNE under the French civil law.[146] In contrast, the approach in EU competition law provides a more certain avenue for claims to relief by imposing direct liability on all entities that are part of an undertaking.[147] On the other hand, the French law extends to actions beyond those in a group of entities under common control to include those in other kinds of established relationships with a corporation: subcontractors and suppliers. In the context of investors' violations of human rights, there have been (and will continue to be) situations in which independent private security subcontractors and others acting at the request or otherwise in support of investors are implicated in wrongdoing. While these actors might be directly responsible, the question is whether their actions should trigger MNE group liability. Finding an appropriate answer to this question must take into account that there will be other situations in which suppliers and subcontractors have no involvement in human rights abuses. In part, this range of possibilities explains the French approach of imposing an obligation on the parent corporation to exercise due diligence to ensure that its suppliers and contractors are not implicated, rather than imposing liability on parent corporations for the actions of suppliers and subcontractors directly.[148]

The same approach could be adopted in an IIA provision.[149] Holding entities outside this controlled group responsible would likely need to be based on demonstrating that they are closely connected to the controlled group through some combination of financial and organizational ties, and benefit from the business in which the human rights abuse occurred.[150]

Summary of Considerations for Designing IIA Provisions to Impose Liability on Corporate Groups

Diversity in business structures and the likely use of strategic behaviour by MNEs to avoid liability create significant complications in designing IIA provisions to hold corporate groups responsible for human rights abuses. The discussion in the previous section discloses a number of critical design issues related to the development of IIA provisions to address the liability of multiple entities in an MNE group. The starting point, of course, is the existence of a legal obligation on private parties, in relation to the human rights of individuals and groups in the host state, that is backed up by a civil remedy. Such an obligation may exist under domestic law or be incorporated in an IIA or both.[151]

---

146 This criticism is made by Petrin & Choudhury, *supra* note 131, although they acknowledge that the law is intended to shift the burden onto the MNE to show it has been duly diligent.

147 In other contexts, the scope and content of such a duty of care has proven difficult. See Petrin & Choudhury, *supra* note 131, discussing the UK Court of Appeal decision in *Chandler v Cape*, [2010] 1 WLR 3111 (at 783–85).

148 French legislators might also have been concerned about imposing liability on foreign suppliers and subcontractors with no connection to France.

149 Petrin & Choudhury (*supra* note 131) suggest that liability of parent corporations in relation to actions of non-controlled entities in such "network" MNEs could be based on vicarious liability (at 792–93).

150 While the French law contemplates only suppliers and subcontractors in this regard, in some structures there will be entities (not just corporations) in other kinds of non-control relationships, such as joint venturers and partners.

151 Possible human rights obligations are discussed in VanDuzer, Simons & Mayeda, *supra* note 15 at 294–338. Strategies to impose civil liability are also discussed (at 387–403).

Direct civil liability for breaching such an obligation could be imposed on all entities within an MNE group without a requirement for an independent finding of fault against a particular entity within the group, so long as one entity in the group committed a breach. Doing so requires an IIA provision defining which links are sufficient to connect a particular entity to the group. Corporations or other entities that control (directly or indirectly through intermediary entities) (here called "controlling entities") the entity directly responsible for the human rights abuse should be held responsible on the basis that they are the ultimate beneficiaries as well as the controllers of the business in which the human rights abuse occurred. Ownership of equity sufficient to create a relationship of legal control should create a rebuttable presumption of control, but control should include contractual and other control mechanisms.

Apart from controlling entities themselves, entities they control that are engaged in carrying on the business in connection with which the human rights abuse occurred should also be responsible, on the basis that they, too, benefit from the business with respect to which the human rights abuse occurred. Liability could also be extended to: all entities linked by ties of control (here called a "controlled group") even if they do not participate in carrying on the business in which the human rights abuse occurred; and entities outside the controlled group, such as subcontractors and suppliers, who have some specified close relationship to the group and benefit from the business in which the human rights abuse occurred. With respect to entities in the first category, the main justification for liability is that the prospect for MNEs to locate assets beyond the reach of victims of human rights abuse would be minimized. With respect to entities in the second category, liability would have to be justified based on their close connection to the business in which the human rights abuse occurred and benefits they derive from that business. An alternative to imposing liability on all entities in the second category would be to hold responsible only controlling entities in the controlled group for the actions to entities in the second category, either strictly or where they could not establish that they had been duly diligent to prevent the human rights abuse.

Conclusion

International human rights law obliges states to provide an effective remedy for victims of alleged human rights violations associated with business activity. But ensuring business accountability and redress for victims of transnational human rights violations is a complex issue that requires a holistic response at all jurisdictional levels to address a wide range of practical, evidentiary and legal barriers.[152] IIAs provide an opportunity to address some of these barriers, but they are only part of a broader response. This chapter discussed only the inclusion in an IIA of civil liability for investors in the home- and host-state courts. It should be noted, however, that such an approach would not be sufficient to address fully the problem of access to an effective remedy. A range of changes are needed to address the imbalances of IIAs and the problems they pose for the protection of human rights and host-state regulatory capacity. We have considered and drafted detailed proposals for a more holistic reform to IIAs elsewhere.[153]

---

152 Simons & Macklin, *supra* note 3 at 271.

153 See VanDuzer, Simons & Mayeda, *supra* note 15. On investor obligations, see *ibid* at 292–345.

Nevertheless, IIAs can impose human rights obligations on investors that can be implemented by treaty parties. As well, treaties can require that both the host state where an investor operates and its home state create domestic civil liability regimes that provide effective access to relief for victims of actions by investors that breach those obligations. Some of the impediments currently faced by victims of human rights abuse seeking civil relief can be specifically addressed. State parties can agree that their courts will take jurisdiction over claims from host-state victims and will not permit investors to challenge jurisdiction on grounds of *forum non conveniens*, act of state or international comity. IIAs provide a context in which judicial reluctance to act when sovereign state interests are implicated in a case based on these doctrines can be addressed through the simple expedient of having the state agree that its interests, in the context of investor violations of human rights within their territory, do not need their protection.

How to define a corporate group for the purposes of assigning liability to the various entities within the group and how to assign liability within the group, however, cannot be so simply addressed. Conceptually, it is relatively easy to create a rule holding entities in an MNE that have control over a subsidiary in a host state responsible for abuses by the subsidiary of the human rights of locals. To the extent that control is not limited to legal control, however, defining control in IIA provisions becomes much more challenging and the evidentiary burden on victims to prove control much heavier. As well, the practical utility of such a rule can be readily undermined where the controlling entities transfer assets to other entities within the group. An IIA provision that holds responsible all entities linked by control would mitigate this risk. A final challenge is dealing with entities outside the control group, such as suppliers, subcontractors, joint venturers, partners and so on, that have some connection to the business in which the human rights abuse occurred. These non-controlled entities might be held directly responsible depending on the level of their involvement. The difficult issue is defining the circumstances in which the controlling entities in an MNE (or all entities in the control group) should be held responsible for the actions of these non-controlled entities, and the circumstances in which these non-controlled entities should be held liable just by virtue of their relationship to the controlled group and the business. Any liability regime involving such non-controlled entities must address daunting issues regarding how to define the nature of the relationship between the controlled group and the business in relation to which a human rights abuse occurs.

Authors' Note

The authors would like to thank Melissa Morton, Loai Eyadt, Anna Romaniszyn and Angela Lee for their excellent research assistance.

V.
INSTITUTIONS ARTICULATING TRANSNATIONAL JUSTICE

CONCLUSION

Oonagh E. Fitzgerald

This last chapter recaps the international, transnational and domestic law and governance challenges identified by the many contributors to this book. It reviews the international community's slow, incremental progress in finding legal and global governance solutions for the transnational corporation that justly reconcile economic, social and environmental interests. The recent decision of the Supreme Court of Canada (SCC) in *Nevsun Resources Ltd v Araya* (*Nevsun*)[1] is then examined to assess whether it might provide the judicial breakthrough needed to set a course forward to achieve transnational justice.

Challenges Identified

The chapters of this book highlight that the transnational corporation is exposing the limits of existing international, transnational and domestic law and governance. The authors paint a

---

1   *Nevsun Resources Ltd v Araya*, 2020 SCC 5 [*Nevsun*].

complex, multi-faceted and contradictory portrait of the transnational corporation at a moment that may prove to be the inflection point in globalization.[2]

In Part I, the authors depict the transnational corporation straining at the boundaries of existing legal frameworks. This strain has become apparent in the economic and political tensions that arise when national governments seek to address globally significant antitrust matters, in the governance implications of the new sophisticated activist shareholder, the inherent limits of the corporate form to satisfy socially responsible objectives, and the desire to imagine a better balance between the transnational corporation's legal rights and its obligations.

The chapters in Part II illustrate accountability frameworks taking shape. These frameworks include the use of Indigenous legal storytelling to understand and manage human relationships to the corporation, adapting Indigenous environmental principles for improved corporate accountability, new legal avenues that are developing to hold corporations accountable for managing the risks of climate change, and using artificial intelligence and the Internet of Things in global supply chains to manage social and environmental impacts and track fair trade practices.

In Part III, the authors reveal the limits of corporate conduct reflecting values, whether this be through the proliferation of toothless voluntary codes of corporate governance, the chasm between ethics and justice in the human rights zone of transnational corporate decision making, or corporate capture and institutional work subtly undermining the efficacy of watchdog institutions.

The authors in Part IV depict investor obligations drawing focus, ever so gradually, through efforts to reconceptualize international investment law and governance. These efforts include rebalancing investor rights and obligations, addressing corporate impunity for human rights and environmental harms, exploring what remedies might be feasible for breaches of investor obligations, and examining how denial of benefits clauses could be used to help promote sustainable development.

Incremental Progress

With the proliferation of international, regional and bilateral trade and investment agreements in the last decades of the twentieth century came globalized business. Globalization of supply chains brought to the fore new issues for multinational corporations, host states and home states, and provoked calls for better international law and governance from civil society groups concerned about a global race to the bottom in labour, environmental, human rights and ethical standards. Burgeoning public protests at international meetings and networked civil

---

2   As this book goes through production, the rules-based global trading system is under enormous stress from the conduct of powerful individual countries and the inability of the rest to negotiate a way forward to meet current needs. See Oonagh E. Fitzgerald, "Introduction", *Modernizing the World Trade Organization*, CIGI, Essay Series, 20 April 2020, online: <www.cigionline.org/articles/modernizing-world-trade-organization>. As well, the World Trade Organization predicts global trade will be crushed by the COVID-19 pandemic, with many nations closing borders to all but essential travel, adopting protectionist measures to secure necessary medical equipment, and abandoning factories and their workers in their global supply chains. Trade-dependent nations are being jolted into re-evaluating the human security risks of being so exposed. The pandemic is exposing the best and worst of national, corporate and human character. What the future holds for globalization is very much up in the air. See World Trade Organization, Press Release, "Trade set to plunge as COVID-19 pandemic upends global economy" (8 April 2020).

society action[3] helped to introduce labour and environmental side agreements into the North American Free Trade Agreement,[4] and to halt the negotiation of the Organisation for Economic Co-operation and Development (OECD) Multilateral Agreement on Investment.[5]

In response to these concerns, voluntary codes of corporate social responsibility proliferated, developed through multi-stakeholder processes.[6] The enthusiastic embrace of Klaus Schwab's notion of "global corporate citizenship"[7] helped elevate the multinational corporation to the status of key stakeholder in international affairs and global governance, justifying and legitimizing the rise of corporate influence, even as the power and importance of state-to-state diplomacy declined. As calls grew for more international coordination to address the growing corporate accountability and governance gap, this changing dynamic between state-to-state and corporate diplomacy may well have added to the complexity in finding solutions to the challenges that were emerging.

In 2003, the United Nations Commission on Human Rights oversaw the development of the Norms on the Responsibilities of Transnational Corporations and Other Business Enterprises with Regard to Human Rights.[8] The lengthy preamble to the Norms recognizes states' "primary responsibility to…secure the fulfilment of…and protect human rights," but asserts that "transnational corporations…are also responsible for promoting and securing…human rights" and "are also obligated to respect generally recognized responsibilities and norms contained in United Nations treaties and other international instruments." These statements are followed by a long list of humanitarian, human rights, labour and environmental treaties and declarations. Article 1, General Obligations, reiterates states' primary responsibility to promote human rights, but also proclaims: "Within their respective spheres of activity and influence," transnational corporations "have the obligation to promote…and protect human rights recognized in international as well as national law, including the rights and interests of indigenous peoples and other vulnerable groups."

Although the UN Commission on Human Rights was at the centre of the international human rights system, it lacked the legitimacy and capacity to lead such an important initiative, as its membership included human rights-abusing nations and it repeatedly failed to sanction human rights abuses around the world. The Norms would have provided a non-voluntary code

---

3   See e.g. Roland Bleiker, "Politics After Seattle: Dilemmas of the Anti-Globalisation Movement" (2002) Cultures et Conflits.

4   *North American Agreement on Labour Cooperation Between the Government of Canada, the Government of the United Mexican States and the Government of the United States of America* (final draft 13 September 1993), online: *Government of Canada* <www.canada.ca/en/employment-social-development/services/labour-relations/international/agreements/naalc.html>; *North American Agreement on Environmental Cooperation Between the Government of Canada, the Government of the United Mexican States and the Government of the United States of America* (1993), online: *Commission for Environmental Cooperation* <www.cec.org/about-us/NAAEC>.

5   OECD, *Multilateral Agreement on Investment* (draft negotiating text April 1998), online: <www.oecd.org/investment/internationalinvestmentagreements/multilateralagreementoninvestment.htm>.

6   Kernaghan Webb, ed, "Voluntary Codes: Private Governance, the Public Interest and Innovation" (2004) Carleton University Research Unit for Innovation, Science and Environment.

7   Klaus Schwab, "Global Corporate Citizenship: Working with Governments and Civil Society", *Foreign Affairs* (January/February 2008), online: <www.foreignaffairs.com/articles/2008-01-01/global-corporate-citizenship>; see also Klaus Schwab, "Global Corporate Citizenship" (Remarks delivered to the Foreign Policy Association, 17 April 2008), online (video): *Youtube* <www.youtube.com/watch?v=tmK0-3rrrIY>.

8   *Norms on the responsibilities of transnational corporations and other business enterprises with regard to human rights*, Sub-Commission on the Promotion and Protection of Human Rights, 55th Sess, UN Doc E/CN.4/Sub.2/2003/12/Rev.2 (2003).

of conduct for transnational corporations, but an exaggerated critique of the notion of applying international law standards to transnational corporations was launched by powerful states aligned with corporate interests. They successfully undermined and derailed the initiative.[9]

As controversies and legitimacy issues were rendering the UN human rights system impotent, pressure continued to grow to address the most problematic aspects of corporate globalization. There ensued a period of norm experimentation with voluntary and contractual approaches outside the UN human rights system in what might be considered "international institutional bypasses,"[10] three notable examples being the Kimberley Process for Conflict Diamonds,[11] the UN Global Compact[12] and the UN Guiding Principles on Business and Human Rights (UNGPs).[13] Global corporate citizens were key stakeholders and participants in each of these initiatives. Work on the three initiatives may have slowed or prevented the adoption of more decisive solutions to the issue of transnational corporate accountability. However, each contributed to finding different ways to tackle the issue and engage key stakeholders in the solutions, and produced useful frameworks, knowledge and experience that could be applied to future challenges requiring corporate and intergovernmental collaboration. The emphasis on voluntary approaches, however, may have tended to foster and entrench the notion that transnational businesses could not and should not be held legally responsible for their conduct.

After years of norm entrepreneurship outside the UN human rights system, exploring non-legal means of addressing corporate accountability,[14] the issue returned to the heart of the now reformed UN human rights system: in 2011, the UN Human Rights Council adopted the UNGPs and began work on their implementation. In 2014, with its adoption of Resolution 26/9, the Human Rights Council commenced work "to elaborate an international legally binding instrument to regulate, in international human rights law, the activities of transnational corporations and other business enterprises,"[15] a project that is ongoing.

Making progress on the question of corporate accountability at the international level has been complex and non-linear. It has not been much easier at the national or transnational level. Host states and home states, bound together by their mutual desire for economic growth and by investment agreements that provide rights of action for dissatisfied corporate investors, remain reticent to take firm action to sanction transnational corporations for human rights or

---

9   Discussed in more detail in Oonagh Fitzgerald, "Addressing the Human Rights Conduct of Transnational Corporations through International Institutional Bypasses" (2019) 10:3-4 Transnat'l Leg Theory 355 at 357–63 [Fitzgerald, "Addressing Human Rights Conduct"].

10   *Ibid.* These three initiatives are analyzed as international institutional bypasses as part of a collaborative research project. See Mariana Prado & Steven Hoffman, "The Concept of an International Institutional Bypass" (2017) 111 AJIL Unbound 231; Mariana Mota Prado & Steven J Hoffman, "The Promises and Perils of International Institutional Bypasses: Defining a New Concept and its Policy Implications for Global Governance" (2019) 10:3-4 Transnat'l Leg Theory 275.

11   Kimberley Process, online: <www.kimberleyprocess.com>.

12   UN Global Compact, online: <www.unglobalcompact.org/>.

13   *Report of the Special Representative of the Secretary-General on the Issue of Human Rights and Transnational Corporations and Other Business Enterprises: Guiding Principles on Business and Human Rights: Implementing the United Nations "Protect, Respect and Remedy" Framework*, UNHRC, 17th Sess, UN Doc A/HRC/17/31 (2011).

14   Fitzgerald, "Addressing Human Rights Conduct", *supra* note 9 at 30.

15   *Elaboration of an international legally binding instrument on transnational corporations and other business enterprises with respect to human rights*, Res 26/9, UNHRC, 26th Sess, UN Doc A/HRC/RES/26/9 (2014).

environmental harms they cause,[16] although we are now seeing a gradual dawning of interest in reform of international investment.[17] The lack of firm national legislative or policy action has left domestic courts to determine whether and how to craft remedies that achieve some measure of transnational justice. Recent judicial breakthroughs may indicate the potential for Canadian courts to help lead the way.

Judicial Breakthrough

Canadian courts have also struggled with the issue of transnational corporate accountability, participating in a Canadian chapter of the litigation against Chevron for environmental harms in Ecuador,[18] a saga that takes Charles Dickens's cautionary legal tale, *Bleak House*,[19] into the twenty-first century of globalized legal practice, but with none of the Victorian author's wry humour. The Ontario Court of Appeal recognized this was a "tragic case" in which "through no fault of their own, the appellants have suffered lasting damages to their lands, their health, and their way of life,"[20] that they were understandably frustrated in not being able to obtain justice, and had only brought their judgment enforcement request to Canada because they were not able to have the judgment enforced in the United States. However, the court rejected arguments that it was permissible to execute on shares of Chevron Canada under the applicable statute,[21] or that there were grounds to pierce the corporate veil to render the shares exigible, finding there was no legal basis "consistent with the common law as developed in our jurisprudence and the statutes enacted by our democratically elected legislatures,"[22] to rule in the appellants' favour. The case brought by Guatemalan villagers against Hudbay Minerals[23] is another lengthy legal saga with moments of disappointment, as well as glimmers of possibility, spanning more than a decade, but as yet without a final resolution.

With the benefit of time's perspective, the recent decision of the SCC in *Nevsun* may come to be seen as either a momentous breakthrough or another small step in articulating a theory of transnational corporate accountability. This depends, in part, on how the case proceeds at the next stages, how Canadian and foreign courts interpret the words of Madam Justice Rosalie Abella in writing the majority opinion,[24] and whether the dissenting opinions, in casting doubt on her analysis, will carry much weight and temper enthusiasm for her approach.[25]

---

16   For an excellent discussion of the issues, see Penelope Simons & Audrey Macklin, *The Governance Gap: Extractive Industries, Human Rights, and the Home State Advantage* (London, UK: Routledge, 2014).

17   This is examined in detail in the chapters in Part IV of this book.

18   *Yaiguaje v Chevron Corporation*, 2018 ONCA 472; leave to appeal refused 2019 CanLII 25908 (SCC) [*Yaiguaje*].

19   Published serially in 1852 and 1853, and then in book form in 1853.

20   *Yaiguaje*, *supra* note 18 at para 8, Hourigan JA.

21   *Ibid* at para 7, citing *Execution Act*, RSO 1990, c E.24.

22   *Ibid* at para 8.

23   *Choc v Hudbay Minerals Inc*, 2011 ONSC 4490; *Choc v Hudbay Minerals Inc*, 2013 ONSC 998; *Caal Caal v Hudbay Minerals Inc*, 2020 ONSC 415.

24   The judgment of Chief Justice Richard Wagner and Justices Abella, Karakatsanis, Gascon and Martin was delivered by Justice Abella.

25   Brown and Rowe JJ dissenting in part; Moldaver and Côté JJ dissenting.

Justice Abella heralds the significance of the judgment with dramatic opening words, hearkening back to the horrors of World War II, and the conviction and hope that emerged from those depths:[26]

> This appeal involves the application of modern international human rights law, the phoenix that rose from the ashes of World War II and declared global war on human rights abuses. Its mandate was to prevent breaches of internationally accepted norms. Those norms were not meant to be theoretical aspirations or legal luxuries, but moral imperatives and legal necessities. Conduct that undermined the norms was to be identified and addressed.

> The process of identifying and responsively addressing breaches of international human rights law involves a variety of actors. *Among them are courts, which can be asked to determine and develop the law's scope in a particular case. This is one of those cases.*[27]

In dismissing the appeal, Justice Abella first rejects Nevsun's argument that the foreign act of state doctrine precludes any claim against Nevsun that was based on its cooperation with the foreign state. She reviews UK jurisprudence and determines that the doctrine does not exist in Canada and its policy objectives are dealt with through conflict of laws and judicial restraint principles. She writes: "Our courts determine questions dealing with the enforcement of foreign laws according to ordinary private international law principles which generally call for deference, but allow for judicial discretion to decline to enforce foreign laws where such laws are contrary to public policy, including respect for public international law."[28]

The majority's analysis of how international customary law becomes part of Canadian domestic law is richly bolstered by citations to international law experts.[29] Justice Abella observes that, "Since '[i]nternational law not only percolates down from the international to the domestic sphere, but…also bubbles up,' there is no reason for Canadian courts to be shy about implementing and advancing international law."[30] She asserts that by "[u]nderstanding and embracing our role in implementing and advancing customary international law," Canadian courts can "meaningfully contribute…to the 'choir' of domestic court judgments around the world shaping the 'substance of international law.'"[31]

---

26   Justice Abella's public speaking sometimes draws on the theme of her family's war-time experience and how it helped shape her commitment to the law and human rights.

27   *Nevsun, supra* note 1 at paras 1, 2 [emphasis in original].

28   *Ibid* at para 45.

29   *Ibid* at paras 71–86. It is noted that some of the authors cited by the majority have been associated with the International Law Research Program of the Centre for International Governance Innovation.

30   *Nevsun, supra* note 1 at para 71. Citing Anthea Roberts, "Comparative International Law? The Role of National Courts in Creating and Enforcing International Law" (2011) 60 ICLQ 57 at 69; Jutta Brunnée & Stephen J Toope, "A Hesitant Embrace: The Application of International Law by Canadian Courts" (2002) 40 Can YB Intl L 3 at 4–6, 8, 56 [Brunnée & Toope, "A Hesitant Embrace"]; see also Hugh M Kindred, "The Use and Abuse of International Legal Sources by Canadian Courts: Searching for a Principled Approach" in Oonagh E Fitzgerald, ed, *The Globalized Rule of Law: Relationships between International and Domestic Law* (Toronto: Irwin Law, 2006) 5 at 7 [Fitzgerald, *Globalized Rule of Law*].

31   *Nevsun, supra* note 1 at para 72, citing Osnat Grady Schwartz, "International Law and National Courts: Between Mutual Empowerment and Mutual Weakening" (2015) 23 Cardozo J Intl & Comp L 587 at 616. See also René Provost, "Judging in Splendid Isolation" (2008) 56 Am J Comp L 125 at 171.

Noting that in some circumstances it is challenging to define elements of customary law, Justice Abella finds this is not such a case, since the norms the Eritrean workers claim Nevsun breached "emerged seamlessly from the origins of modern international law, which in turn emerged responsively and assertively after the brutality of World War II. It brought with it acceptance of new laws like prohibitions against genocide and crimes against humanity, new institutions like the United Nations, and new adjudicative bodies like the International Court of Justice and eventually the International Criminal Court, all designed to promote a just rule of law and all furthering liberal democratic principles."[32]

Referring to the four authoritative sources of modern international law, including customary international law, that are listed in article 38(1) of the Statute of the International Court of Justice,[33] Justice Abella sets out "two requirements for a norm of customary international law to be recognized as such: general but not necessarily universal practice, and *opinio juris*, namely the belief that such practice amounts to a legal obligation."[34] A practice that has crystallized into a norm of customary international law has equal force against all members of the international community.[35] She notes that the widely accepted automatic judicial incorporation into domestic law of customary international law that is not inconsistent with statute law can be traced to Blackstone's 1769 *Commentaries on the Laws of England: Book the Fourth*.[36]

Justice Abella observes, "as a result of the doctrine of adoption, norms of customary international law — those that satisfy the twin requirements of general practice and *opinio juris* — are fully integrated into, and form part of, Canadian domestic common law, absent conflicting law.[37]…Legislatures are of course free to change or override them, but like all common law, no legislative action is required to give them effect.[38]…To suggest otherwise by requiring legislative

---

32   *Nevsun, supra* note 1 at para 75, citing Philippe Sands, *East West Street: On the Origins of "Genocide" and "Crimes Against Humanity"* (Toronto: Penguin Random House, 2016) at 361–64; Lloyd Axworthy, *Navigating A New World: Canada's Global Future* (Toronto: Knopf, 2003) at 200–01.

33   *Statute of the International Court of Justice*, Can TS 1945 No 7 (entered into force 24 October 1945) (citing the description of article 38 as the "litmus test for the sources of international law" in Brunnée & Toope, "A Hesitant Embrace", *supra* note 30 at 11).

34   *Nevsun, supra* note 1 at paras 77–78, citing *Report of the International Law Commission*, 73rd Sess, Supp No 10, UN Doc A/73/10 (2018) at 124; *North Sea Continental Shelf*, [1969] ICJ Report 3 at 71; *Kazemi Estate v Islamic Republic of Iran*, 2014 SCC 62 (CanLII), [2014] 3 SCR 176 at para 38 [*Kazemi*]; Harold Hongju Koh, "Twenty-First Century International Lawmaking" (2013) 101 Geo LJ 725 at 738; Jean-Marie Henckaerts, "Study on customary international humanitarian law: A contribution to the understanding and respect for the rule of law in armed conflict" (2005) 87 Intl Rev Red Cross 175 at 178; Antonio Cassese, *International Law*, 2nd ed (Oxford: Oxford University Press, 2005) at 157.

35   *Nevsun, supra* note 1 at para 82, citing James L Brierly, *The Law of Nations: An Introduction to the International Law of Peace*, 6th ed (Oxford: Oxford University Press, 1963) at 59, cited in John H Currie, Craig Forcese & Valerie Oosterveld, *International Law: Doctrine, Practice, and Theory*, 2nd ed (Toronto: Irwin Law, 2014) at 116; Bruno Simma & Philip Alston, "The Sources of Human Rights Law: Custom, Jus Cogens, and General Principles" (1988) 12 Aust YBIL 82 at 104; *The Paquete Habana*, 175 US 677 (1900) at 686; Jutta Brunnée & Stephen J Toope, "International Law and the Practice of Legality: Stability and Change" (2018) 49 VUWLR 429 at 443. *Jus cogens*, or peremptory norms, are a subset of customary international law, recognized by the whole international community and from which no derogation is allowed (see discussion at para 83).

36   *Nevsun, supra* note 1 at paras 87–88, citing Gibran van Ert, *Using International Law in Canadian Courts*, 2nd ed (Toronto: Irwin Law, 2008) at 184–208; Pierre-Hugues Verdier & Mila Versteeg, "International Law in National Legal Systems: An Empirical Investigation" (2015) 109 AJIL 514 at 528. *Blackstone's Commentaries on the Laws of England*, online: *Yale Law School, Lillian Goldman Law Library* <https://avalon.law.yale.edu/subject_menus/blackstone.asp>.

37   *Nevsun, supra* note 1 at para 94, citing Oonagh E Fitzgerald, "Implementation of International Humanitarian and Related International Law in Canada" in Fitzgerald, *Globalized Rule of Law, supra* note 30, 625 at 630.

38   *Nevsun, supra* note 1 at para 94, citing Hugh M Kindred, "The Use and Abuse of International Legal Sources by Canadian Courts: Searching for a Principled Approach" in Fitzgerald, *Globalized Rule of Law, supra* note 30, 5 at 8.

endorsement, upends a 250 year old legal truism and would put Canada out of step with most countries."[39]

Asserting that international law had expanded from its "Grotian origins" limited to relations between states, the majority rejects Nevsun's argument that as a corporation it is immune from the application of customary international law norms that form part of the common law.[40] While some norms only relate to interstate relations and do not apply to corporations, "others prohibit conduct regardless of whether the perpetrator is a state," Justice Abella writes.[41] She notes how human rights have altered international law: "The past 70 years have seen a proliferation of human rights law that transformed international law and made the individual an integral part of this legal domain, reflected in the creation of a complex network of conventions and normative instruments intended to protect human rights and ensure compliance with those rights."[42]

She relies heavily on analysis by Harold Hongju Koh in "busting" the myth of corporate immunity to international law: "The commonsense fact remains that if states and individuals can be held liable under international law, then so too should corporations, for the simple reason that both states and individuals *act through* corporations. Given that reality, what legal sense would it make to let states and individuals immunize themselves from liability for gross violations through the mere artifice of corporate formation?"[43]

She concludes that "it is not 'plain and obvious' that corporations today enjoy a blanket exclusion under customary international law from direct liability for violations of 'obligatory, definable, and universal norms of international law,' or indirect liability for their involvement in what Professor Clapham calls 'complicity offenses.'"[44]

Justice Abella notes that the trial judge would have to determine if the norms were of a "strictly interstate character" and, if so, determine whether the common law should evolve to impose liability on the corporation.[45] With regard to "the breaches of customary international law, or *jus cogens*" alleged in the litigation, she finds that there are no Canadian laws that "conflict with their adoption as part of our common law" — indeed, she highlights numerous federal policies in favour of transnational corporate responsibility — and concludes that "the customary international law norms raised by the Eritrean workers form part of the Canadian common law and potentially apply to Nevsun."[46]

She asserts that the common law is capable of developing appropriate remedies for breaches of adopted customary international law norms "to keep the law aligned with the evolution of

---

39   *Nevsun*, *supra* note 1 at para 94, citing Verdier & Versteeg, *supra* note 36 at 528.

40   *Nevsun*, *supra* note 1 at paras 104–07.

41   *Ibid* at para 105, citing William S Dodge, "Corporate Liability Under Customary International Law" (2012) 43 Geo J Intl L 1045 at 1046; Harold Hongju Koh, "Separating Myth from Reality about Corporate Responsibility Litigation" (2004) 7:2 J Intl Econ L 263 at 265–67 [Koh, "Separating Myth from Reality"]; Andrew Clapham, *Human Rights Obligations of Non-State Actors* (Oxford: Oxford University Press, 2006) at 58.

42   *Nevsun*, *supra* note 1 at para 107.

43   *Ibid* at para 112, citing Koh, "Separating Myth from Reality", *supra* note 41 at 265 [emphasis in original].

44   *Nevsun*, *supra* note 1 at para 113, citing Koh, "Separating Myth from Reality", *supra* note 41 at 265, 267; citing Andrew Clapham, "On Complicity" in Marc Henzelin & Robert Roth, eds, *Le Droit Pénal à l'Épreuve de l'Internationalisation* (Brussels: Bruylant, 2002) 241 at 241.

45   *Nevsun*, *supra* note 1 at para 113.

46   *Ibid* at paras 114–16.

society."[47] She refers to Canada's obligation as a state party to the International Covenant on Civil and Political Rights[48] "to ensure an effective remedy to victims of violations of those rights" and the United Nations Human Rights Committee guidance that enjoyment of these rights can be effectively ensured by the judiciary in various interpretative ways.[49] With regard to the general principle that where there is a right there must be a remedy, the majority distinguishes the circumstances in the *Kazemi* case,[50] in that the remedy for torture committed by the state of Iran in breach of the *jus cogens* prohibition was barred by the State Immunity Act.[51] The majority finds that no such bar prevented Canadian courts from developing a civil remedy against a corporation that violated customary international law that was adopted into Canadian law.[52]

To Nevsun's argument that the harms could be addressed under recognized torts already pleaded by the Eritrean workers, Justice Abella asserts that the character of the alleged violations of customary international law were of a more public and heinous nature that shocked "the conscience of humanity" than ordinary domestic torts and needed to be acknowledged by the court to do justice and grant relief.[53] Leaving to the trial judge the question of how these novel claims should proceed, Justice Abella suggests there are different ways that a domestic court might deal with civil claims against a corporation. Based on adopted customary international law, for example, a court might recognize new nominate torts or, more directly, simply provide a remedy for the breach of customary international law. She indicates a preference for the latter, to avoid diluting or negating the doctrine of adoption and to permit "different and stronger responses" than might apply in typical tort claims, "given the public nature and importance of the violated rights involved, the gravity of their breach, the impact on the domestic and global rights objectives, and the need to deter subsequent breaches."[54]

The dissenting judges write two opinions. In the first,[55] there is agreement that the foreign act of state doctrine does not apply to the case, but disagreement on the notion that customary international law can be used to shape new civil remedies. In the other dissenting opinion,[56] there is disagreement on both these points. In the first dissenting opinion, Justice Russell Brown and Justice Malcolm Rowe argue that "the majority's reasons either depend on customary international law norms that do not exist or depend on affording to the doctrine of adoption a role it does not have."[57] They argue that the court cannot "change the doctrine of adoption

---

47   *Ibid* at paras 117–18.

48   *International Covenant on Civil and Political Rights*, 16 December 1966 (entered into force 23 March 1976).

49   *Nevsun, supra* note 1 at para 119, citing *General Comment No 31: The Nature of the General Legal Obligation Imposed on States Parties to the Covenant*, UNHRC, 80th Sess, UN Doc CCPR/C/21/Rev.1/Add.13 (2004).

50   *Kazemi, supra* note 34.

51   *Nevsun, supra* note 1 at paras 120–22, referring to the *State Immunity Act*, RSC 1985, c S-18 [*State Immunity Act*].

52   *Nevsun, supra* note 1 at para 122.

53   *Ibid* at paras 123–26, citing M Cherif Bassiouni, "International Crimes: *Jus Cogens* and *Obligatio Erga Omnes*" (1996) 59 L & Contemp Probs 63 at 69; Craig Scott, "Translating Torture into Transnational Tort: Conceptual Divides in the Debate on Corporate Accountability for Human Rights Harms" in Craig Scott, ed, *Torture as Tort: Comparative Perspectives on the Development of Transnational Human Rights Litigation* (Oxford: Hart, 2001) 45 at 62, n 4; Sandra Raponi, "Grounding a Cause of Action for Torture in Transnational Law" in *ibid*, 373; Graham Virgo, "Characterisation, Choice of Law, and Human Rights" in *ibid*, 325.

54   *Nevsun, supra* note 1 at paras 127–29, citing Gib van Ert, "What Is Reception Law?" in Fitzgerald, *Globalized Rule of Law, supra* note 30, 85 at 89.

55   Brown and Rowe JJ (dissenting in part).

56   Moldaver and Côté JJ (dissenting).

57   *Nevsun, supra* note 1 at para 224.

so that it provides a civil liability rule for breaches of prohibitions at customary international law."[58] They criticize the majority ruling for usurping the proper role of legislators, inviting chaotic pleadings, leaving generalist judges to determine what is and is not a rule of customary international law, and creating instability by giving too much authority to legal experts.[59]

In the second dissenting opinion, Justice Suzanne Côté, writing for herself, and Justice Michael J. Moldaver assert that while the law does evolve, "The widespread, representative and consistent state practice and *opinio juris* required to establish a customary rule do not presently exist to support the proposition that international human rights norms have horizontal application between individuals and corporations."[60] Justice Côté considers that, under the act of state doctrine, "a court should not entertain a claim, even one between private parties, if a central issue is whether a foreign state has violated its obligations under international law."[61] She cites the majority decision in *Kazemi* for the conclusion that "creating a universal civil jurisdiction allowing torture claims against foreign officials to be pursued in Canada 'would have a potentially considerable impact on Canada's international relations,' and that such decisions are not to be made by the courts."[62] She would extend this concern to "the case of litigation between private parties founded upon allegations that a foreign state has violated public international law."[63]

Justice Côté continues, "If Canadian courts claimed the power to pass judgment on violations of public international law by states, that could well have unforeseeable and grave impacts on the conduct of Canada's international relations, expose Canadian companies to litigation abroad, endanger Canadian nationals abroad and undermine Canada's reputation as an attractive place for international trade and investment. Sensitive diplomatic matters which do not raise domestic public law questions should be kept out of the hands of the courts."[64]

This proposed extension of an international law rule designed to protect diplomatic relations between sovereign states (and enacted into domestic law by the State Immunity Act) to make immune from scrutiny by domestic courts a Canadian transnational corporation that may have acted in complicity with a foreign state in breaching international human rights law would be an alarming development. Even states do not enjoy immunity when engaged in commercial activities,[65] so it would seem inappropriate that a transnational corporation whose raison d'etre is to engage in commercial activity should have immunity. One might ask what kind of global corporate citizen such a rule might engender, if the corporation were allowed to conspire with and profit from corrupt and despotic governments around the world without ever having to face justice. It would be more like Cannibal Boy let loose in a blood-soaked "human rights zone" than Christopher Nicholls's "woke" capitalist operating in a competitive environment and internalizing any negative externalities of its operations. One must further ask what kind

---

58   *Ibid.*

59   *Ibid* at paras 261–65. They were particularly incensed that Harold Koh's article carried such weight in the majority judgment.

60   *Ibid* at paras 269, citing James Crawford, *Brownlie's Principles of Public International Law*, 9th ed (Oxford: Oxford University Press, 2019) at 102, 607.

61   *Nevsun, supra* note 1 at para 286.

62   *Ibid* at para 297, *Kazemi, supra* note 34 at para 107.

63   *Ibid.*

64   *Nevsun, supra* note 1 at para 300; see also paras 301–05.

65   *State Immunity Act, supra* note 51, s 5 ("Commercial activity: A foreign state is not immune from the jurisdiction of a court in any proceedings that relate to any commercial activity of the foreign state").

of judicial system this would leave Canada with, where domestic courts — even the SCC itself — could not adjudicate on the most egregious transnational conduct of Canadian corporations if a foreign government was in some way implicated in the wrongdoing.

Toward Transnational Justice

This likely was a difficult decision for the SCC, as it was being asked to find a route to justice for the foreign victims of transnational harms caused by a Canadian company. Justice Abella went back to first principles — the birth of the UN system, with its enshrining of human rights — to ground her decision. She writes with a certainty about the contours of human rights that may be jarring to economic lawyers who are more inclined to see certainty in international trade and investment treaties and domestic corporate law. The dissenting judges decline to follow the majority because of their concerns about international law. Justices Brown and Rowe view customary international law as uncertain; they fear that generalist judges are not equipped to deal with it, and will be challenged to assess assertions of *opinio juris*. Justices Moldaver and Côté seem to view both international law and international diplomacy as the preserve of sovereign states and would relegate to domestic courts only a minor and subservient role, a view that may be difficult to reconcile with Canada's long constitutional history of judicial review. The dissenting judges also seem to be trying to close the barndoor on SCC adjudication of questions of international law, long after that horse has escaped. The SCC has been unavoidably deciding questions of international law for some time,[66] and has gained an international reputation for bringing clarity to important international law questions that need to be decided by domestic courts.[67]

Justice Abella has made simple what, for the last few decades, others seem to have tried to make confused. By going back to first principles, she asks why we have an international system of law and governance and how we can make sense of it in the age of globalization. The idea of going back to first principles is not new. It was evident in the approach of the Draft Norms in invoking the multitude of international humanitarian, human rights, labour and environmental commitments states have made as the foundation for corporate obligations to comply.

More recently, in a 2015 report, Alfred-Maurice de Zayas, the UN independent expert on the promotion of a democratic and equitable international order, invoked first principles to assess the compatibility of the international investment regime against states' commitments under the Charter of the United Nations, specifically articles 1, 2, 55 and 56.[68] He observed that, contrary to article 103 of the Charter, which stipulates that "obligations under the present Charter shall prevail," the "private justice" being meted out by arbitral panels routinely privileged states' economic commitments while ignoring their fundamental human rights, health, labour and environmental obligations.[69] His report asserted that "emerging customary international law of human rights," including "human rights provisions in international agreements, including

---

66   To name a few notable decisions, see *Reference re Secession of Quebec*, [1998] 2 SCR 217; *R v Hape*, [2007] 2 SCR 292; *Canada (Justice) v Khadr*, [2008] 2 SCR 125; *Kazemi*, *supra* note 34.

67   For example, *R v Miller*, [2017] UKSC 5, citing *Reference re Secession*, *supra* note 66.

68   *Report of the Independent Expert on the promotion of a democratic and equitable international order, Alfred-Maurice de Zayas*, UNHRC, UN Doc A/HRC/30/44 14 (2015), n 4 at 1, Summary, citing *Charter of the United Nations*, 26 June 1945, Can TS 1945 No 7, arts 1, 2, 55, 56.

69   *Report of the Independent Expert*, *supra* note 68 at 9–15.

International Labour Organization and World Health Organization (WHO) conventions, constitute an internationally binding legal regime with *erga omnes* implications."[70]

For transnational justice to make sense in this complicated and conflicted world, it needs to be grounded in first principles, in the foundations of the globalized rule of law as prescribed by the Draft Norms, de Zayas and the majority of the SCC in *Nevsun*. De Zayas writes: "An international order of sovereign and equal States under the *Charter of the United Nations*, committed to the rule of law, transparency and accountability must not be undermined by private attempts to replace it with an international order ruled by transnational enterprises lacking democratic legitimacy."[71]

From its opening words, the Charter of the United Nations is replete with language that could guide sovereign nations to cooperate to solve economic, social, cultural or humanitarian issues and ensure that all persons and corporations respect and adhere to those obligations insofar as they are relevant to them. While the Charter did not refer to the environment, it has become increasingly obvious that none of the above issues can be addressed adequately without considering and caring for the natural environment, as the effects of anthropogenic degradation of the natural environment are understood to be among today's most serious global security threats.[72] Despite its many imperfections as an instrument of global law and governance, the commitment of all peoples of all nations to collaborate on building a better world for all, as expressed in the Charter, resonates through the decades. The Sustainable Development Goals[73] provide a vibrant example of how fundamental principles can be renewed in international solidarity and made relevant to a changing world. By reaffirming fundamental principles and the importance of international rule of law, Canadian courts may be on the threshold of clarifying the legal status of the global corporate citizen and setting us on the path toward transnational justice.

---

70 *Ibid* ("Conflicting agreements or arbitral awards are incompatible with international *ordre public*, and may be considered contrary to provisions of the Vienna Convention on the Law of Treaties and invalid as *contra bonos mores*" at 1–2, Summary).

71 *Ibid* at 5.

72 See e.g. Intergovernmental Panel on Climate Change, *Global Warming of 1.5°C Special Report*, online: <www.ipcc.ch/sr15/>; United Nations Environment Programme, "Children on precipice of existential threat from lack of climate action", online: <www.unenvironment.org/news-and-stories/story/children-precipice-existential-threat-lack-climate-action>; Helen Clark et al, "A future for the world's children? A WHO-UNICEF-*Lancet* Commission" (2020) 395:10224 Lancet Commissions 605, online: <www.thelancet.com/journals/lancet/article/PIIS0140-6736(19)32540-1/fulltext>; Nathan Alexander Sears, "Existential Security: Towards a Security Framework for the Survival of Humanity" (2020) 11:2 Global Policy: Next Generation 255.

73 UN General Assembly, *Transforming our world: the 2030 Agenda for Sustainable Development*, UNGAOR, 70th Sess, UN Doc A/RES/70/1 (2015).

CONTRIBUTORS

Anita Indira Anand is professor of law and the J. R. Kimber Chair in Investor Protection and Corporate Governance at the University of Toronto Faculty of Law. Anita served as associate dean of the law school from 2007 to 2009, and as the academic director of the Centre for the Legal Profession and its program on Ethics in Law and Business. She was a senior fellow and member of the governing board at Massey College and is cross-appointed to the Rotman School of Management and the School of Public Policy and Governance, in which she served as the director of policy and research at the Capital Markets Institute. Her main research areas relate to the regulation of capital markets, with a specific focus on corporate governance, enforcement, capital-raising techniques and systemic risk.

In 2015, Anita was appointed by Ontario's Minister of Finance to the Expert Committee to Consider Financial Advisory and Financial Planning Policy Alternatives. She has conducted research for the Five-Year Review Committee, the Wise Person's Committee, the Task Force to Modernize Securities Legislation in Canada and the Commission of Inquiry into the Investigation of the Bombing of Air India Flight 182. She was the inaugural chair of the Ontario Securities Commission's Investor Advisory Panel (2010–2012) and the president of the Canadian Law and Economics Association (2009–2011). During the 2009-2010 academic year, Anita was a visiting scholar at the Bank of Canada and a Herbert Smith Visitor at the University of Cambridge. In 2005-2006, she was a Canada-US Fulbright Scholar and Visiting Olin Scholar in Law and Economics at Yale Law School. In 2012, she was appointed to the Bertha Wilson Honour Society by the Schulich School of Law for service to the legal profession. She has received research grants from the Social Sciences and Humanities Research Council of Canada, the Law Foundation of Ontario, the Connaught Foundation and others.

Enrique Boone Barrera is a CIGI fellow, focusing on international investment law and corporate governance. Enrique conducted his postdoctoral research at CIGI, examining the effects of investor-state arbitration on developing countries. As part of this project, he helped organize three regional workshops with public officials from Southeast Asia, Latin America and Africa. In addition, he has published his research in academic journals, books and blogs. Enrique has participated in multiple conferences, workshops and consultations with public officials regarding international economic law. His broad research interests include international economic law, property rights and governance, comparative law, and law and development.

During his doctoral studies, Enrique was a teaching fellow at McGill University's Faculty of Law and a research assistant on several projects regarding trade law and democracy, comparative law and legal education. His dissertation focused on how the allocation of property rights affects the exercise of political rights, and the relation between citizens and different government levels. Enrique holds a bachelor of laws from the Tecnológico de Monterrey, an LL.M. from Queen's University and a D.C.L. from McGill University.

Daniela Chimisso dos Santos has practised law in the extractive industries (oil, gas and mining) for 20 years. She has extensive national and international experience, including in Sub-Saharan Africa, South America and Asia. Daniela is principal at Invenient Solutions Consulting and a member of the board of directors of Transparency International Canada (TI). She is also the Canadian representative on a task force of the International Chamber of Commerce Commission on Arbitration and Alternative Dispute Resolution that addresses issues of corruption in international arbitration.

Daniela's recent projects include acting as national researcher for TI on a global project on mining for sustainability, as well as authoring original TI research entitled "The Perception of Corruption in the Extractives Sector in Western Canada." Daniela has lectured at several law faculties, including at Western University, the University of Toronto and Osgoode Hall Professional Development. Her research interests include institutional change, multinational enterprises and development, business and human rights, and corruption and extractive resources. Daniela graduated from the University of Rome, Italy, in international relations. She holds an LL.B. from Osgoode Hall Law School, an LL.M. in natural resources, energy and environmental law from the University of Calgary, and an S.J.D. from the Faculty of Law, University of Toronto.

Charles-Emmanuel Côté is a CIGI senior fellow, full professor and former vice dean for Academic Affairs and Continuing Education in the Faculty of Law at Laval University. He teaches courses on public international law, international economic law, constitutional law and World Trade Organization law. He is director of the Summer School on International

Investment Law and is co-director of the Centre for International and Transnational Law at Laval University.

Charles-Emmanuel holds a doctorate in civil law from McGill University. He has several professional memberships, including to the Canadian Council on International Law, the International Law Association and the Society of International Economic Law. He has been a guest professor, notably at Paris II Panthéon-Assas University, and has been an institutional and constitutional policy adviser to the Government of Quebec.

Oonagh E. Fitzgerald has had an extensive and varied career as a senior executive in the federal public service, providing strategic leadership in legal policy, advisory and litigation services in international law, national security, public law, human rights and governance at the following departments: Justice Canada, Human Resources Development Canada, National Defence and the Canadian Forces, and the Privy Council Office. She has served as president or director on several not-for-profit boards.

From April 2014 to February 2020, Oonagh established, led and completed the work of the International Law Research Program at the Centre for International Governance Innovation, delivering policy-relevant research and capacity building on pressing issues of international economic, environmental, intellectual property, Indigenous peoples' and human rights law.

Oonagh has taught in university programs of law, business and international affairs, and has mentored many graduate students and post-doctoral fellows. She has written, edited and co-edited several books, essay series, articles, policy briefs and commentaries, and presented as a keynote speaker and panellist at numerous national and international conferences and workshops on diverse international law topics.

Strongly committed to leading policy-relevant research to create a more equitable and sustainable world, Oonagh holds a B.F.A. (Hons.) from York University, an LL.B. from Osgoode Hall Law School, an LL.M. from the University of Ottawa, an S.J.D. (Doctor of Juridical Science) from the University of Toronto and an M.B.A. from Queen's University.

Edward Iacobucci is dean and James M. Tory Professor of Law at the University of Toronto Faculty of Law. He was appointed to the faculty in 1998, and as dean in 2015. He has been a visiting professor at Columbia University, the University of Chicago Law School, New York University Law School, Tsinghua University and the National University of Singapore. His teaching and research interests include corporate law and governance, securities law, corporate finance, competition policy, and law and economics more generally.

Richard Janda teaches extracontractual obligations, business associations, administrative process and environmental law. A former clerk to Justices Le Dain and Cory of the Supreme Court of Canada, he was also director of the Centre for the Study of Regulated Industries at McGill University. He is currently leading the Myko project (www.myko.org), which explores how to connect people to the environmental footprint of their choices in real time. He has written, among other things, on corporate social responsibility, digital law and theories of justice.

Rebecca Johnson is professor of law and the associate director of the Indigenous Law Research Unit at the University of Victoria Faculty of Law. A former clerk to Justice L'Heureux-Dubé of the Supreme Court of Canada, her research often turns to the place of story in the legal imagination. She currently teaches Business Associations, Legal Theory, Inuit Law and Film, and Indigenous Law: Research, Methods and Practices. She is also part of "Testify: A Project of the Indigenous Laws + the Arts Collective" and is a co-curator of two blogs focusing on innovations in legal education: *Project Pedagogy* and the Truth and Reconciliation-inspired blog *ReconciliationSyllabus*.

Cally Jordan is a former CIGI senior fellow and a full-time faculty member at Melbourne Law School (Australia). She began her academic career at the Faculty of Law, McGill University. She teaches and researches in the areas of corporate governance and financial regulation, from an international and comparative perspective. Most recently, she has held visiting positions at Georgetown's Centre for Transnational Legal Studies in London (United Kingdom) and Harris Manchester College, University of Oxford, as well as Duke Law School, the Max Planck Institute (Hamburg), the London School of Economics and the British Institute for International and Comparative Law. She was the inaugural P.R.I.M.E. Finance (Lord Woolf) Fellow at the Netherlands Institute for Advanced Study (Wassenaar).

Over a period of 20 years, Cally advised the World Bank on corporate governance and commercial, financial and corporate law. She is a senior research fellow at the C. D. Howe Institute and author of *International Capital Markets: Law and Institutions* (Oxford University Press, 2014), now going into its second edition. She will be teaching a course in international capital markets at Yale Law School in the fall of 2021. Cally has degrees in both civil law and common law from McGill University. She has practised in Canada, New York, California and Hong Kong, in particular, with the US law firm Cleary, Gottlieb.

Bonnie Leonard is a graduate of the University of Victoria Faculty of Law. She has worked as legal counsel in the community, been chief of the Kamloops Indian Band, and worked for 15 years with the Shuswap Nation Tribal Council, first as director of Aboriginal rights and title, and then as tribal director, using her years of legal and political experience to advise the Council of Chiefs on contract administration, strategic planning, policy development and implementation. She is currently legal adviser for the National Chiefs Office of the Assembly of First Nations in Ottawa.

Darcy Lindberg is an assistant professor at the University of Alberta Faculty of Law, where he teaches courses on Indigenous law, Indigenous peoples and the law, and Indigenous relationships to the environment. He is mixed-rooted Plains Cree, with his relations coming from Samson Cree Nation in Alberta and the Battleford area in Saskatchewan. His research focuses on the constitutional and legal theory of Plains Cree peoples in relation to lands, waters and animals. Darcy was called to the British Columbia and Yukon Bars in 2012, and practised law primarily in the Yukon Territory.

Jason MacLean is an assistant professor in the Faculty of Law at the University of New Brunswick, and an adjunct professor in the School of Environment and Sustainability at the University of Saskatchewan. His research focuses on transdisciplinary approaches to climate change and sustainability law and policy across multiple scales of governance. He holds a BCL and LL.B. from McGill University and a Ph.D. in law from the University of Alberta. Before entering academia, he clerked for Madam Justice Marie Deschamps at the Supreme Court of

Canada. He also practised international commercial arbitration at Shearman & Sterling LLP in New York and Paris, and corporate and constitutional law litigation at Osler, Hoskin & Harcourt LLP in Toronto.

Keith MacMaster is a Ph.D. candidate at the Schulich School of Law and lecturer at the Rowe School of Business, Dalhousie University. He primarily concentrates on legal issues in environmental finance and the need for new sustainable investment and insurance products. Keith's research focuses on two areas. The first aims at improving responsible investing and creating new sustainable financial products. At the heart of this research lie theories of materiality and the availability of climate finance data. The second research area seeks to ensure that the financial and liability mechanisms created for deep-seabed mining hold parties liable for any environmental damage that may occur. Keith graduated with an M.B.A. from the Ivey Business School at Western University and subsequently led the green strategies team, including leading the real estate and carbon neutral strategies for one of Canada's largest banks.

Lucas Mathieu is a graduate of Sciences Po Paris and McGill University Faculty of Law. He is currently a student at l'École du Barreau and plans to article at an international law firm. He will also clerk with H.E. Judge Abraham in 2020-2021 as part of the Judicial Fellows Programme of the International Court of Justice in the Hague. Lucas is interested in public and private international law, corporate social responsibility, and the interplay between the law and new technologies.

Christopher C. Nicholls holds the W. Geoff Beattie Chair in Corporate Law and is director of Business Law at Western University, as well as co-director of Western's interdisciplinary Centre for Financial Innovation and Risk Management. In 2013, he was named a Western University Faculty Scholar, and in 2016 received a Canada-US Fulbright Scholar award. He has been a visiting professor of law at Harvard Law School, a Herbert Smith Visitor at the University of Cambridge, a visiting scholar at the University of Melbourne, a visiting research scholar at the University of Tokyo and the Falconbridge Visiting Professor of Commercial Law at Osgoode Hall Law School. He has also been a visiting professor at the law faculties of the University of Toronto and Queen's University. He has acted as a consultant to private law firms, government and regulatory agencies and as an expert witness. A frequent speaker on corporate law topics in judicial education programs organized by the National Judicial Institute, he has also lectured to academic and professional audiences in Australia, Canada, Japan, South America, the United Kingdom and the United States.

Before beginning his academic career, Chris practised corporate and securities law with major law firms in Toronto and in Hamilton, Bermuda, and is currently chair of the board of directors of the Mutual Fund Dealers Association of Canada. An author or co-author of six books and numerous academic articles, his work has been cited by Canadian securities commissions and many Canadian courts, including the Supreme Court of Canada.

Hugo Perezcano Díaz was the deputy director of International Economic Law at CIGI and previously a senior fellow. Prior to joining CIGI, he was an attorney and international trade consultant in private practice. Hugo worked for the Mexican government's Ministry of Economy for nearly 20 years, serving as head of the trade remedy authority, and formerly as general counsel for international trade negotiations. He was lead counsel for Mexico in investor-state dispute settlement cases under the North American Free Trade Agreement (NAFTA) and other international investment agreements, as well as in dispute settlement cases between states conducted under trade agreements that include NAFTA and the World Trade Organization agreement.

Ksenia Polonskaya is a former CIGI fellow. She holds a Ph.D. from Queen's University, an LL.M. from the University of Toronto and an LL.B. from Kuban State University (Russia). She is a contributor to *Investment Claims* (Oxford University Press) and was previously an associate editor at the *University of Toronto Faculty of Law Review*. Her papers have appeared in Cambridge University Press publications, the *Melbourne Journal of International Law*, *The Law & Practice of International Courts and Tribunals* and the *Leiden Journal of International Law*.

Malcolm Rogge is a research fellow of the Corporate Responsibility Initiative at the Harvard Kennedy School of Government. For more than 20 years, Malcolm has practised at the intersection of human rights and business — as a legal scholar, lawyer, activist and documentary filmmaker. His international award-winning documentary film *Under Rich Earth* (2008), about a mining conflict in Ecuador, is held by more than 50 university and college libraries worldwide and is used in courses such as Property Rights, Social Justice, and the Environment (University of Arizona) and International Investment Law and Arbitration (National University of Singapore). *Under Rich Earth* was adopted as evidence and cited extensively by the international investment tribunal in the groundbreaking (and controversial) 2016 *Copper Mesa Mining Corp v Ecuador* decision (PCA 2012-2). Malcolm holds an S.J.D. from Harvard Law School and is a member of the Global Business and Human Rights Scholars Association. He is a barrister and solicitor of the Bar of Ontario.

Douglas Sarro is a doctoral candidate at the University of Toronto Faculty of Law and an adjunct professor at Osgoode Hall Law School. Before pursuing an academic career, he clerked for the chief justice of Ontario, practised corporate law at Sullivan & Cromwell LLP in New York, and served as a senior adviser at the Ontario Securities Commission. He holds an Honours B.A. from the University of Toronto and a J.D. from Osgoode Hall Law School, where he graduated as gold medallist. He is admitted to practise law in Ontario and New York, and holds the chartered financial analyst designation.

Sara Seck is a former CIGI senior fellow and an associate professor and associate dean of research at the Schulich School of Law and the Marine & Environmental Law Institute at Dalhousie University. She has published more than 40 articles and book chapters on business and human rights, public and private international law, and environmental and climate justice, often with a focus on extractive industries.

Sara is co-editor of *Global Environmental Change and Innovation in International Law* (Cambridge University Press, 2017); co-editor (with Penelope Simons) of a 2019 special issue of the *Canadian Journal of Women and the Law* on resource extraction and the human rights of women and girls; and co-editor of the forthcoming *Cambridge Handbook on Environmental Justice and Sustainable Development*. She is a founding member of the editorial board of the *Business and Human Rights Journal* and currently serves as its book review editor. She serves as a director of the Global Network on the Study of Human Rights and the Environment, and was previously a member of the International Law Association's Study Group on Business &

Human Rights. Prior to joining the Schulich School of Law in 2017, Sara was a member of the Faculty of Law at Western University for a period of 10 years. In 2015, she received an award from the International Union for the Conservation of Nature's Academy of Environmental Law for her groundbreaking research contributions on sustainable mining and environmental justice.

Penelope Simons is an associate professor in the Common Law Section of the Faculty of Law at the University of Ottawa. Her research focuses on business and human rights and, in particular, on the human rights implications of domestic and transnational extractive sector activity; state responsibility for corporate complicity in human rights violations; the regulation of transnational corporations; gender and resource extraction; and the intersections between transnational corporate activity, human rights and international economic law. She is the co-author, with Audrey Macklin, of *The Governance Gap: Extractive Industries, Human Rights, and the Home State Advantage* (Routledge, 2014). She also co-authored, with Tony VanDuzer and Graham Mayeda, *Integrating Sustainable Development into International Investment Agreements: A Guide for Developing Country Negotiators* (Commonwealth Secretariat, 2013).

Penelope is a member of the Human Rights Research and Education Centre, the Interdisciplinary Research Group on the Territories of Extractivism and the Center for Environmental Law and Global Sustainability, all at the University of Ottawa, as well as the Social Sciences and Humanities Research Council-funded Canadian Partnership on Strengthening Justice for International Crimes. In 2018, Penelope was awarded the Walter S. Tarnopolsky Award, recognizing her as "an individual who has made a significant contribution to human rights."

Chris Tollefson is professor of law at the University of Victoria. His research interests include environmental law and policy, natural resource management, climate law, regulatory and governance theory, and experiential learning. The third edition of his environmental law casebook (co-authored with Meinhard Doelle) was published by Thomson Reuters in 2019. His teaching and scholarship are closely informed by his work as a public interest litigator, including as counsel of record on various energy, pipeline and climate-related cases. He also represents Indigenous and public sector clients in a range of litigation, law reform and consultation settings. He is a former president of Ecojustice, founding executive director of the Pacific Centre for Environmental Law and Litigation, and principal of the firm Tollefson Law.

J. Anthony VanDuzer is a professor and the Hyman Soloway Chair in Business and Trade Law in the Common Law Section of the Faculty of Law at the University of Ottawa, as well as an adjunct research professor at Carleton University's Norman Paterson School of International Affairs. He has also taught at the Queen's University Bader International Studies Centre in England, the Westfälische Wilhelms-Universität in Germany and the University of Waikato in New Zealand. Tony has written widely on investment, trade in services and corporate law. With Patrick Leblond, the CN-Paul M. Tellier Chair on Business and Public Policy at the University of Ottawa, he has just completed editing *Promoting and Managing International Investment: Towards an Integrated Policy Approach* (Routledge, 2020). Together with University of Ottawa colleagues Penelope Simons and Graham Mayeda, he wrote *Integrating Sustainable Development into International Investment Agreements: A Guide for Developing Country Negotiators* (Commonwealth Secretariat, 2013). Tony has also provided advice and technical assistance on services and investment issues to governments in Canada as well as in transition and developing economies around the world, including El Salvador, Ukraine, Thailand, Russia, Bangladesh, Pakistan, the African Union and the countries of the Caribbean.

Edward J. Waitzer is a former CIGI senior fellow. He was chair of Stikeman Elliott LLP from 1999 to 2006, and remains a senior partner whose practice focuses on complex business transactions. He also advises on a range of public policy and governance matters. Edward is a professor and the Jarislowsky Dimma Mooney Chair in Corporate Governance and director of the Hennick Centre for Business and Law at Osgoode Hall Law School and the Schulich School of Business at York University. Edward served from 1993 to 1996 as chair of the Ontario Securities Commission and was formerly the vice president of the Toronto Stock Exchange. He has written and spoken extensively on a variety of legal and public policy issues, and serves or has served as director of a number of corporations, foundations, community organizations, editorial boards and advisory groups.

ACKNOWLEDGEMENTS

This book has the bittersweet honour of being the last output from CIGI's International Law Research Program (ILRP). I wish to acknowledge how grateful I am to CIGI and the Province of Ontario for supporting international law research over the six vibrant years of the ILRP's existence, with all its wonderful outcomes: the publication of a wealth of books, papers, online essays, commentaries and videos on important current issues of international law; doctoral theses and post-doctoral scholarships completed; and the building of a Canadian community of international lawyers connected with the world.

The patience, understanding and flexibility of the contributing authors and the CIGI Publications team, working in difficult and uncertain circumstances, are gratefully acknowledged for enabling this important project to reach fruition. I would like to acknowledge in particular Stephanie Drung's excellent and enthusiastic project management on this book and many other CIGI projects, Nicole Langlois's brilliant and empathetic editing, Abhilasha Dewan's imaginative cover design, Melodie Wakefield's elegant layout, Carol Bonnett's sage editorial guidance, Susan Bubak's careful final editing, Spencer Tripp's stewardship of the project and Rohinton Medhora's insight in permitting the project to proceed to completion as CIGI made momentous strategic shifts.

Many sparkling lights contributed to the ILRP through a dazzling array of scholarships and fellowships, books, conferences, workshops, essays, videos and social media buzz. As we disperse and move on to new priorities, we know that the constellation of relationships, research networks and ideas that we ignited and forged will continue, expanding ever outward.